Understanding Information and Computation

For Jimmy, Pat and Don.
Special thanks to Keith and Ian.
You are all dearly missed.

Nature's grand book which stands continually open to our gaze, is written in the language of mathematics. Its characters are triangles, circles and other geometrical figures, without which it is humanly impossible to understand a single word of it; without these, one is wandering around in a dark labyrinth.

Galileo Galilei, 1623

Understanding Information and Computation

From Einstein to Web Science

PHILIP TETLOW

Routledge
Taylor & Francis Group

LONDON AND NEW YORK

First published 2012 by Gower Publishing

2 Park Square, Milton Park, Abingdon, Oxon OX14 4RN
711 Third Avenue, New York, NY 10017, USA

Routledge is an imprint of the Taylor & Francis Group, an informa business

First issued in paperback 2016

Gower Applied Business Research
Our programme provides leaders, practitioners, scholars and researchers with thought provoking, cutting edge books that combine conceptual insights, interdisciplinary rigour and practical relevance in key areas of business and management.

British Library Cataloguing in Publication Data
Tetlow, Philip.
  Understanding information and computation : from Einstein
  to Web science.
  1. World Wide Web. 2. Mathematics--History. 3. Physics--
  History. 4. Information theory. 5. Information retrieval.
  I. Title
  004.6'78-dc23

ISBN 978-1-4094-4039-0 (hbk)
ISBN 978-1-138-27506-5 (pbk)

Library of Congress Cataloging-in-Publication Data
Tetlow, Philip.
  Understanding information and computation : from Einstein to Web science /
  by Philip Tetlow.
    p. cm.
  Includes bibliographical references and index.
  ISBN 978-1-4094-4039-0 (hardback)
  1. Computational complexity. 2. Machine theory. 3. World Wide
  Web. I. Title.
  QA267.7.T47 2011
  003'.54--dc23

                                                                    2011052792

Contents

List of Figures

List of Tables

About the Author

Philip Tetlow is an Executive IT Architect in IBM's UK Business Analytics and Optimisation practice. He holds the world's first PhD in Web Science and was the author of the award-winning book *The Web's Awake* in 2007. He is a Chartered Engineer, a Fellow of the Institute of Engineering and Technology and a one-time member of the World Wide Web Consortium, having actively helped with the take-up of the Semantic Web.

Acknowledgements

First I must credit the unquestionably insightful work of Professor Stuart Kauffman and particularly thank him for the encouragement and inspiration with which he has followed my more recent work. I must next credit Professors Roger Penrose, Seth Lloyd, David Deutch, Lee Smolin, Ian Stewart, Robert Laughlin and Brian Green, all physicists and mathematicians of one kind or another. I deeply admire their work and their particular aptitude for lateral thinking. Large parts of this book are based on the insights they have brought to the world. I must also pay tribute to Google's Dominic Widdows, for if it were not for his brilliant book *Geometry and Meaning*, this book would still be three-quarters complete. Next I must thank Dr John Tait, Dr Chris Bowerman and Professor 'Keith' van Rijsbergen, for it is they who have taken time out to bring me back down to earth when the temptation was to linger amongst the clouds. Profound thanks are also a due to my long-suffering friends and colleagues Richard Hopkins, Kevin Jenkins, Brad Jones, Ian Nussey, Rick Robinson, Ian Charters, Mark Salthouse, Ian Devo, Karen Smith, Dav Bisessar, Tommy Giovannelli and D.J. McCloskey of IBM, Professors Wendy Hall and Nigel Shadbolt, Professor Yorick Wilks, Craig Gannon, Chris Brown, Alistair Miles, Tom Croucher, L.J. Rich, Dr David Hazelton, Bill Joynes and Graham Klyne, for they chose to stick around and suffer 'the speech' way past the point where reasonable individuals would have made their excuses and left. Next I must thank the various reviewers who tirelessly worked to polish and shine my final drafts. They include Alastair McCullough, Angus Cameron, Jim Zalles, Jonathan Moshinsky, Tess Moffett, Peter Lancett, Sukhvinder Phalora and Roman Podolczuk. Finally and deliberately I save the greatest debt of gratitude until last. It is with true humility that I must thank two inseparable brothers. They are my uncle, Dr Stanley Tetlow, and my dear father Dr Alan Tetlow. They have passed on more to me than I could ever pass on to others.

Foreword

By Yorick Wilks

The next time you crave to tweet that all-consuming idea or poke that newest of acquaintances, spare a thought for what you are about to do. The snippets of information you choose to send might be exactly the same as those used in a letter to a friend perhaps thirty years ago, but today things are quite different. Then your words would almost certainly have been received only by those you wrote to and would have turned into nothing more than cherished memories, even though good paper can last four hundred years, as computer people sometimes forget! But today those words have the potential to reach vast numbers of people and could easily remain in their original form and accessible to anyone well beyond your natural life span. Some people understand this and use it to good effect, but most do not. Andy Warhol's world of fifteen minutes of fame for all is very close to where we are today, yet still we have little idea what that means for us as individuals, communities or society as a whole.

This issue is not just about the changing ways in which we communicate. It is more about our hunger for information and our increasing ability to get it, to process and to share it. It is also about how recent creations, like the World Wide Web, have changed our way of life and how we apply such information constantly in that life. These changes have done so much for those privileged enough to have access to its supporting technologies – and that now means everyone with a high-spec mobile phone – but has the nature of information itself changed as a result? Indeed, have we ever understood information well enough even to ask this question, and should we care?

Information is absolutely central to everything we do and understand, and so, yes, we should care and care deeply. Science has tried many times and under many descriptions to get at the fundamental nature of information, yet still we only have a fragmented picture as that slippery word 'information' shifts from computing to linguistics to quantum physics and so on ... . But this is not a matter for pessimism, just because there is no single view of what information is. We now understand that some of the most advanced fields of science rely heavily on the notion of information for their existence and that the tools they have developed to advance scientific thinking can be turned back on information itself, and I am thinking here of quantum information and the possibility that researches at the very smallest level of entities in physics may reveal a great deal about the nature of information. Think how Einstein's speculations about time in physics came to tell us so much about time itself in his theory of relativity. Some of the algorithms in use when we search the Web were first intended to explain the innards of the atom. All this suggests that we have to be brave and radical when thinking about information and not look only in the obvious places.

Enter Phil Tetlow. I was introduced to Phil some time ago through a mutual friend who had believed we might have something in common, and he was right. Since then our paths have crossed many times and we have shared many interesting discussions. This is what academics like me expect to happen when we meet new people, but Phil is not an academic and does not want to be one. He works for a large technology company and makes his living as a consultant. More precisely he is an IT Architect who designs and implements some of the largest and most complex information systems we have today. In essence he lives inside the field itself and is motivated quite differently from those who do pure research. What drives him is not the desire to find results in support of an idea, but rather the search for ideas and reasons behind the day-to-day occurrences he sees in large-scale systems. This often leads him to think in ways that would make most academics nervous. He is not so much interested in meticulous proof, but rather in new ways to unlock the doors in front of him. This is more an engineering perspective than that of a scientist and it has led him to be bold and outspoken. He spots a problem, speaks to those he knows to be experts about such things and then shares his thoughts with those around him in the hope that more ideas will be sparked off. This is the case here with his second book. In its writing I know he has tried out these ideas on world experts; and in many of these areas he is himself an expert. Those who initially created the Web and who are its guardians today are included on that list, but it does not stop there. He has gone on to seek out senior physicists and mathematicians and this has taken him well out of his comfort zone. Speak to him directly and he will be the first to tell you that he is neither a physicist nor a mathematician, and he will openly admit that what you are about to read could ultimately fail rigorous challenge in both areas, but that's not the point. What Phil has recognised, and recognised rightly, is that things are changing at great speed. If new ideas are not forthcoming now, we may well lose control of the Web. If his thinking is correct, then this may well have been a predictable conclusion all along. What you will find in these pages, therefore, is a courageous attempt to reshape the way we look at information and computing, a huge effort to take a look at it all from a fresh perspective. It is creative, novel and in many ways captures the thoughts that his contemporaries share, but have not had the time or conviction to write down. I respect him very much for that and I like this book for the same reason, and am eager to see it widely read.

Yorick Wilks
Professor of Artificial Intelligence (Emeritus) at the University of Sheffield, Senior Research Fellow at the Oxford Internet Institute, Senior Scientist at the Florida Institute for Human and Machine Cognition and British Computer Society Lovelace Medal winner 2010

Foreword

By L.J. Rich

'That's Napoleon's Clock on stage behind you,' they said, as I contemplated how on earth I was going to talk to a gathered audience of two hundred thought-leaders and business pioneers at IBM's 'Smarter Analytics' sustainability summit in London, June 2010. This was a tough crowd, easily as tough as some of the less savoury venues I'd performed at in one of my past lives as a gigging piano player.

I stood in the annexe of the Royal Palace the summit was being held at and hoped Phil was right. When I'd met him a few months earlier, I told him my idea for the keynote speech. I wanted to talk about the history of communication, statistically analyse the Eurovision Song Contest and play fake Bach to the gathered business dignitaries.

His eyebrows danced a little in the way that they do, and I imagined his brain as an elegant but eccentric machine, whirring and clicking – a sound not dissimilar to Bletchley Park's World War II code-breaking machines. Of course Phil loved the premise; it's in his mischievous nature to put a musical cat amongst the business pigeons and watch the resultant pecking and/or scratching. Of course, words like 'ecology, economy and society' sounded much more like elements of a keynote speech than my proposals, yet Phil could see that using a liberal arts view as a starting point would show that everything is connected to how we use, receive and translate information.

Take the Eurovision Song Contest – most people would agree it's as much about politics and geography as it is about music. But computer-generated authentic and emotional-sounding 'Bach' music, although obscure, was an extremely effective way of introducing the power of analytics and the issue of ethics – it demonstrated how we can be fooled by information – or enriched by it.

As it happened, the talk went down a storm – the fake Bach was a real hit, and the seemingly impossible task of trying something as obscure as music analysis to issues that big companies have to deal with on a global basis was indeed accomplished with aplomb and admiration. I was relieved when I took my bow and tried not to look too pleased with myself as I sauntered off stage. And I was euphoric! I had made an impact on influential and powerful people by grasping and shaping the eccentric and obscure, crystallizing those thoughts, and connecting them to real life in the hope that others could see my world. Of course, this was the sort of thing Phil has been doing for years – so it's no wonder we became friends.

At first, and, okay, at second and third glance, Phil Tetlow is easily as complex and as simple as some of the concepts he attempts to unravel in this book. His wry smile, infectious enthusiasm and improbable Yorkshire/Geordie brogue sit at odds with an undeniably planet-sized brain. His ideas and thoughts, like all the best ones, seem (to an amateur like me) to be finely but precariously balanced on that well-documented sword-edge of genius. Here, I thought, was someone who wasn't afraid of speaking his mind, even if not everyone could receive on his frequency.

Fast forward to summer 2011 – and, during one of our many lengthy and gloriously surreal conversations Phil asked me to give him my take on the Web, and integrate it into a foreword to his next book. I like to imagine the way I felt may compare somewhat to the feeling I'd get if Bach popped back from the eighteenth century and asked me to write him a concerto – I felt dis-concerted. Why (I asked) did he want me – a non-Web-science person – writing one of the two forewords to this, a highly specialised and Web-sciency book?

Phil would say that my credentials are sound: I was an early adopter, Webwise, having taken to email in 1993. Later, I had immersed myself in the social media scene during the 'Birth of Twitter'. I've also spent time as a TV producer for BBC Click, one of the globe's most widely distributed technology programmes, and was largely responsible for the growth behind its Twitter account, which had 1.85 million followers at the time of writing.

Phil also proclaimed that I'm 'relevant'. When asked to elaborate, he gruffly commented on my ability to spot next-generation trends and memes ahead of the curve – 'gravitational wells' as he called them. Hang on, I said, the Web has gravity? Turns out Phil's written another book all about that. At the time, I remember thinking 'Ah, of course he has,' as if anything else was preposterous.

A few weeks later, I felt ready to tell Phil how I saw the Web. Now, fully prepared for the eyebrow thing, I made sure he was sitting down and holding a pint of beer to steady himself. I took a breath and shared with him my viewpoint: the Web – as a mirror. A huge and flecked antique of a thing, scratched in places, shiny or even magnified in others. Its huge and uneven gaze held up to the offline society, a strange reflection of at-once darkest and purest moments in humanity. A reflection of the banal and the extraordinary. The minutiae of our everyday lives and lunches, searchable in the same breath as global crises and countless taxonomies. Vast swathes of information gathering momentum, our online avatars enriched by interactions with other mirrored people. I told him I thought the Web isn't good or bad, it just is. Like People, Music, the Sky, the Universe!

You can imagine where the eyebrows were at this point. And now the beer glass was empty. But I could see Phil's brain was full – there he was, processing my grand and excitable unscientific extrapolation with a few more internal clicks and whirrs, filtering and sifting the information to present a clear and relevant result like a good natured organic search engine. It's all information after all, I would imagine him saying, as zeros flipped over to ones and back again with pleasing wooden clunks. There's a place for that information, I just need to find where it fits, he would say, trying to find and hold the shape of the Web for us all to see. I like to think that Web science, or 'What Phil Does', is an attempt to chronicle and present these shapes to a wider society, so that we have a hope of understanding more about the Web, and perhaps even about ourselves.

So, to the book. For those intending to at least read the first few chapters, a friendly caveat: anyone who's flicked through the pages and felt a little uneasy at the generous sprinkling of 'science words' should relax. Read the whole paragraph through, and you'll absorb more than the words on the page – to my mind, a rich landscape of theoretical thought experiments appear – rather like those odd 'magic eye' pictures that don't make sense unless you're looking at them correctly.

Although the book touches upon gravitation, dark matter, quantum mechanics and geometry, it's the story of those areas, not the science. Strange?

Certainly. But to me, it does make some kind of sense. The unconventional re-purposing of words from the fields of physics and mathematics to attempt to tell the story of Web science sounds like a perfect way for Phil to crystallize those eccentric thoughts and connect them to our own way of seeing the world. Those of us who don't have the Tetlow CPU installed can at least access some of the files on our slightly obsolete but still functioning wetware.

So, make some tea, and prepare to explore the deep brain workings of someone who truly makes the Web work. Allow your mind to wander as it contemplates the eccentric insights contained within. These wild-eyed proto-visions of Web science in its infancy could yet lead to new theories and advancement in a field that is still being defined. Or this book could also be the utterly incomprehensible, yet fabulous, ramblings of a genius.

Indeed, quantum theory would dictate it is, er, both (at least until you read it). Either way, it's an unconventional and entertaining book that 'reads you back' – and, I think, a welcome and refreshing take on a subject that seems destined to be explored in great detail as we crash on through this century. We humans have created something unique in the Web, which is already used for extraordinary things. The book gives us a chance to look at this creation from another perspective. And if our imagination is up to the task, we could unlock even more of the incredible potential that the Web holds.

So, it merely remains for me to encourage you, dear reader, to go! Go forth into the unexplored, good luck and click wisely. Any further clunking and whirring you may hear will be your own.

L.J. Rich, London, September 2011
Manager, Perfect Pitch Productions Ltd.

Preface

I start where the last man left off.

Thomas A. Edison

When I started to write this book I singularly wanted to write about the World Wide Web. I really did. The Web is a safe zone for me and I knew that much still needed to be said about this fascinating sociotechnical system. Nevertheless the path of my investigations refused to run straight. The more deeply I read and the more I studied, the more I realised that the things I was interested in simply covered a much broader spectrum. Like a taut piece of elastic, the more I tried to pull the subject matter back towards a Web focus, the more resistance I felt. In the end I gave up and followed the path of least resistance.

In truth I was, and still am, interested in only one thing, and surprisingly that's not the Web at all. Rather I have an innate fascination for 'information' and all that it entails. Information is easily the most underestimated and poorly understood of things, for it plays an absolutely central role in everything we do and perceive. In many ways it literally is our world. Yet although it has been treasured and traded since the very dawn of our consciousness, only recently has science begun to realise its true worth. Because of such things I advise you to proceed with care as you read. I say this not to add dramatic effect, but merely to point out the nature of some of the material to come. Whilst working on this book I had known for some time just how poorly understood information is and also knew that many valuable insights lay outside the areas where most would normally look. Although much can be gleaned from fields such as information technology and computer science, in many ways they only scratch the surface of information's essence. To get truly close one must look further afield and probe in areas such as developmental biology, theoretical physics and advanced mathematics. This causes a significant problem, as such fields use and abuse their own definitions of information in inward-looking ways, rarely peering over the edge of their respective 'boxes' to share the best bits of their insight. At best this implies a lack of communal understanding and at worst it serves to underline that we simply do not have a sensible grasp on the subject matter yet.

In 2007 I was lucky enough to have my first book published. In *The Web's Awake* I made some rather far-reaching and provocative claims about the Web and the information held within it. For months after the book's launch I worried. I worried about being slated by the critics, about being ridiculed by the academics and about not getting the message across. In the end none of that came to pass, but that year of waiting and worrying taught me a lot, primarily showing that I had been overly nervous in writing the book. With hindsight I wish I had been bolder and this book is, in part, an attempt to address that. This time around I have tried to connect a number of ideas that might appear extreme at first sight and I hope you will accept the risk associated with this approach. Whenever and wherever within my reach I have tried hard to qualify the associations made and the conclusions reached, but in some cases there is simply no direct evidence available today to support the ideas presented. To some, I fully understand that this will be unsettling, but the aim of this book is very much to challenge convention. It is hence a book almost entirely about theory, framed by someone with many years' experience of large-scale IT architectures.

Although we might be intimately familiar with the information around us on a daily basis, that actually holds us back in many ways. Each morning we might rise and look in the mirror at the familiar features of our face. We might leave our homes through familiar doorways and walk along familiar paths to work, school or wherever. And all of this is obviously assisted by the presentation of information to us and our ability to absorb and understand it. Disappointingly though, such experience adds little to our understanding of what information actually is. Rather, such data-loaded interactions merely relate to the conveyance of individual information fragments, each linked into the complex mesh of knowledge and understanding that helps keep us in step with our own particular interpretation of reality – the onward march of our everyday life stories. We rarely stop to think about the nature of the information itself. But this we can indeed do, by reaching out to various abstract schemes of description, as Michael Schneider so eloquently describes:

> Looking closely at nature, the first insight we obtain is that, behind the apparent proliferation of natural objects, there is a far lesser number of apparently fixed types. We see, for example, that through every generation cats are cats and are programmed for catlike behaviour. In the same way, every rose has the unique characteristics of a rose and every oak leaf is definitely an oak leaf. No two specimens of these are ever exactly the same, but each one is clearly the product of its formative

type. If it were not so, if animals and plants simply inherited their progenitors' characteristics, the order of nature would soon dissolve into an infinite variety of creatures, undifferentiated by species and kinship.

This observation, of one type with innumerable products, gives rise to the old philosophical problem of the One and the Many. The problem is that, whereas the Many are visible and tangible and can be examined at leisure, the One is never seen or sensed, and its very existence is only inferred through the evident effect it has upon its products, the Many. Yet paradoxically, the One is more truly real than the Many in the visible world of nature all is flux. Everything is either being born or dying or moving between the two processes. Nothing ever achieves the goal of perfection or the state of equilibrium that would allow it to be described in essence. The phenomenon of nature said Plato, was always 'becoming,' never actually 'are.' Our five senses tell us that they are real, but the intellect judges differently, reasoning that the One, which is constant, creative, and ever the same, is more entitled to be called real than its ever-fluctuating products.[18]

In my personal search to fathom information's truths I have taken in some rather interesting and eclectic material. At first I was drawn to the well-established worlds of data processing and classical computer science. Then, in more recent times, I have drifted in and out of the Web world, spending time assisting with organisations like IBM and the W3C.[1] All of this has proved hugely rewarding, but, alas, none of it ultimately answered my innermost questions on information. Hence I gradually turned to the natural sciences for assistance and started to focus on how the very universe itself goes about the business of information processing.

Once one realises that the universe is nothing more than the biggest computer in existence – taking in information in the form of matter and transforming it over time – it soon becomes clear that it has to be the ultimate source of information's definition. Because of this I have tried hard to look across the full spectrum of natural information processing systems for answers. I have studied the way in which atoms interact and just how the weird world of the subatomic contributes; I have investigated how biological systems evolve, and have, in due course, become fascinated by how information can be considered in terms of Einstein's ideas on relativity, gravity and light. I have

---

1   World Wide Web Consortium.

even stopped off to contemplate just what insights entities like black holes, strings and superstrings might add, and, not surprisingly, the value-add has been significant. Indeed this is so much so that the works of physicists such as Stephen Hawking, Michael Green and Lee Smolin have changed my whole perspective on information's definition. Today I no longer think of information in terms of cold, abstract concepts. Today, for me at least, information is vibrant and alive in a very real sense. Now I actually have a problem making the distinction between physics and computing as a direct result of them both depending on information for their very existence. In the simplest of terms, physics is computing and computing is physics. What is important is that information is the bridge that links them both and in such regard its definition can, in many ways, be physicalised too.

Speak to any truly hard-core information engineers and they will talk about information as having dimensions and scale, levels and abstractions, viewpoints and perspectives. To them information is real, as real as you might be to me. It has form and subtlety, movement and strength, grace and poise – almost an energy and mass of its own. But most importantly of all, and without the need to reach out to analogy for explanation, it might even be intimately linked to the physical laws of the universe. Just as the atoms in our bodies are glued to our planet's surface by gravitational attraction, similar attractors also appear to influence information at large scales. The question is now not so much if such laws are relevant, but rather if they might be served better in terms of information and computation than the various equational variants served up by science thus far. Perhaps the universe is not physical at all? Perhaps it is just all just information? Perhaps movies like *The Matrix* might have been right all along and we are just living out our lives in one huge and magnificent dream, a moving hologram of some grander being's creation, shining in from the edge of the universe? Fiction surely? Fantasy certainly? Actually no, there is some very strong evidence to suggest that information is absolutely central to the universe's being.

Some things we know for certain already. We know, for instance, that quantum mechanics provides an extremely strong theoretic model on which to build our understandings of computation and information. The algorithm at the heart of Google's phenomenal success and unbelievable speed, for example, owes much more to the world of subatomic physics than might be expected. Furthermore there are some computations that just cannot be done efficiently without the leap of faith needed to allow randomisation as a key ingredient – the quintessential differentiating property that makes quantum mechanics systems stand out from their atomic-level cousins. We also know that to derive meaning from information we need an appreciation of those who are to use it and the uses to which it will be put. Thus not only is there a need to understand the information in flow itself, but we must also be sympathetic to the observation point of the user or consumer. Two individuals might interpret the same piece of information in totally different ways simply because of their own immediate contexts. This makes certain aspects of information relative, in much the same way that Einstein described our universe in the early years of the twentieth century. What is more intriguing, though, is that certain aspects of information are also invariant, making their presentation identical to all those who choose to investigate them. Intuitively this appears at odds with Einstein's ideas, but in fact it is totally consistent.

Such insights may appear radical to the point of being unbelievable, but that in itself is important. Our understandings of information need a good shake up. Over the past half-century we have made unbelievable advances in computing, but still we have not really moved forward in the way we think about the very stuff over which we compute. Progress was made, however, by Claude Shannon in his seminal work *A Mathematical Theory of Communication*[17] in 1948. This introduced information theory as a branch of applied mathematics and engineering and concentrated on the quantification of information. Shannon's information theory was developed to find fundamental limits on the compression and reliability of communicated data and since its publication it has been broadened to find applications in other areas such as statistical inference, networks other than communication networks as in neurobiology, the evolution and function of molecular codes, model selection in ecology, thermal physics, quantum computing, plagiarism detection and other forms of data analysis. The insights of Shannon and those who would follow have indeed proved pivotal, but there is an important point to remember here in that although information theory, as currently formulated, describes how to handle information – how to process or compute with it – it provides little in the way of a descriptive framework by which to understand its fundamental nature. Shannon never told us what information is. His work was only concerned with how much of it can be moved along a channel like a copper wire. The 'meaning' of the information concerned, or its semantics, was left out of his account[25].

There are others who have added valuable pieces to the jigsaw nonetheless, and in many cases they have not seen Shannon-like fame for their sizable contribution. Keith van Rijsbergen, for instance, has done some superb work on information retrieval and David Deutsch, Seth Lloyd and others have simply blazed a trail when it comes to understanding how information ties to fundamental physical models of the universe. But again, the picture is still not complete. Mathematicians like Andrei Kolmogorov have added further pieces by suggesting that the information in any given symbol string can be equated to the shortest program that can produce it in a 'universal computer'[25], but still the puzzle has bits missing. Some pieces may be within sight now but still the whole has not yet been made from its parts. Hence the need for a book like this. For right or wrong it attempts to piece together a whole picture, and, even if wrong, it still outlines the very strong need for others to attempt to do it better.

By the very nature of the material covered, this book is highly theoretical and academic. That said, I think it is important to mention that I am by no means an academic in the truest sense of the word. Rather I choose to make my living as a consultant, hopefully practising what I preach. I think that's important. I like to keep my sleeves rolled up and my hands dirty. But this pragmatic streak does have its setbacks. For instance, my preferred writing style is much less formal than that favoured by academics and I can see why such a style might be considered shallow by those who seek precision. Furthermore those who just want the basics may also be disappointed, as the engineer in me dearly wants to explain everything down to the last nut and bolt. I know this is a conflict, but I hope it is one you will allow. If I have done this right, I should have both enlightened and entertained by the time you have read the last chapter. Large parts of this book also cover some very deep physics and rather complex mathematical concepts by necessity, so I must also point out that I am neither physicist nor mathematician by training or practice. Rather I am an IT Architect who has spent most of his career working on very large IT systems, typically with very large data content. Even so I hope I have brought together physics, mathematics and information theory in an accurate and valuable way.

Because of the complex nature of the material and ideas covered, you may also notice some repetition. When I have read texts of similar length, depth and complexity I have been acutely worried that the detail would drag me away from the main themes involved. For that reason I reiterate several points at times. The intention behind this is solely to signpost the way clearly.

There is one big question that I must address before we can move on to the main content of the book; why concentrate on Einstein and Web Science in the subtitle? The answer is actually obvious. As you might expect with any reference to Einstein in a title, this text will, at least in part, discuss fundamental physics and explicitly look to Einstein's work on relativity. But rather than this discussion being based on observations and ideas centred on the physical world, as in Einstein's original works, we will focus on the semi-synthetic domain of the World Wide Web instead. This is surprisingly easy repositioning, as the Web is a hugely complex and highly connected dynamic information space, much like the physical world that Einstein pondered over so intently. There is a historical twist too, as when Sir Tim Berners-Lee was in the process of inventing the Web, he worked at the CERN[2] labs in Geneva, first in 1980 as a software consultant and then from 1984 to 1991 as part of a fellowship programme in the data acquisition and control group there. CERN is where the world's finest particle physicists congregate to do their best work on the most fundamental laws of the universe. It is also the place where the world's largest particle accelerator can be found, and it is this device that accelerates atoms to close to the speed of light only to smash them to smithereens through vicious and wilful acts of collision. The physicists do this not for fun but to investigate the tiny fragments of reality that such collisions spew out, and it is through their work that we are able to search for proof of some of the most abstract and wonderful ideas humankind has ever had. This prompts talk of laws, properties and particles with weird names and even stranger behaviours. To the physicists such particles spin, vibrate, attract and repel as if they have a life of their own, but to us they simply sound like imaginative thinking straight from the pages of a *Star Trek* script. But then that's the point. These scientists quite literally are on the edge of science fiction. They are the ones who point the way to our future. They are the select few who stand at the absolute limit of human understanding, and Tim Berners-Lee was right amongst them when he invented the system that would eventually become the World Wide Web.

During his time at CERN Berners-Lee was simply immersed in physics. He almost bathed in it. He would assist with ongoing experiments by hunting down various bits of information and collating them for use by his colleagues. He would sit at coffee tables and talk about weird and wonderful topics like string theory and standard models of this and that. So, for him, the world of cutting-edge science was very much part of his everyday life. A more important part of his life was concerned with applying the computers of the day to the task of modelling scientific ideas, and as a consequence he became frustrated with the way that the various electronic documents at CERN were scattered

---

2 The name CERN derives from the name of the international council (Counseil Européen la Recherche Nucléaire) which originally started the facility. The council no longer exists, and 'Nuclear' no longer describes the physics done there, so, while the name CERN has stuck, it is not regarded as an acronym.[19]

across the systems in use. This prompted him to think of ways in which this morass of information might be better structured and it was through this work that his genius was helped by those immediately around him. He already knew, for instance, that standard types of index, like the one toward the back of this book, are particularly ineffective when referencing information scattered across numerous disparate locations, but it was the quantum physicists who most probably reminded him that two things can be intimately connected regardless of the 'distance' between them. The physicists referred to this as quantum entanglement, and merely saw it an exquisite side effect of quantum mechanics. Berners-Lee saw it as something much more tangible and applied the concept to great practical effect.

As far back as the early 1980s he mused:

> *Suppose all information stored on computers everywhere were linked. Suppose I could program my computer to create a space in which everything could be linked to everything else.*[19]

And later that decade he finally crystallised his thoughts in formal proposal to CERN for what would eventually become the World Wide Web. In this he wrote:

> *An intriguing possibility given the large hypertext database with typed links, is that it allows some degree of automatic analysis ... Imagine making a large three-dimensional model, with people represented by little spheres, and strings between people who have something in common at work.*

> *Now imagine picking up the structure and shaking it, until you make sense of the tangle: perhaps you see tightly knit groups in one some places, and in some places weak areas of communication spanned by only a few people. Perhaps a linked information will allow us to see the real structure of the organisation in which we work.*

Forget about the Web's eventual birth and the great brush fire of technological take-up that would follow. These two paragraphs are perhaps Berners-Lee's greatest contribution to science and to all of human history. Replace 'three dimensions' with 'any number of dimensions' and 'people' with 'subatomic particles', 'atoms', 'planets' or even 'entire galaxies' and another comparable model emerges. Replace the 'organisation in which we work' with 'the reality within which we all exist' and we get a far grander aspiration than the one ultimately realised in the World Wide Web. What we have actually done is summarise the mission statement of all of physics. We have defined the basic criteria for modelling the entire universe.

Perhaps this is telling us something? Perhaps the Web has more than passed the test as a model for all huge, highly connected information spaces? Perhaps the universe too is just one such mind-blowingly large information space? So, just as Berners-Lee might have been influenced by physics for his inspiration in the Web's design, might the physicists now also look to the World Wide Web as a model to help explain some of the more fundamental characteristics of the universe? The ties certainly appear strong and little research has yet been undertaken to either prove or disprove the proposition. Hence the book before you, and the fascinating set of possibilities it contains. It is not about the World Wide Web per se, but rather something far greater and grander. It also, hopefully, represents a story structured in such a way that will lead on without too steep a climb. Chapter 1 first tries to construct a contemporary view of the Web and explain how it might be analogous to some of the oldest and most stable theories in all of science. Next, in Chapter 2, we examine the problems of choosing a descriptive framework and go on to choose geometry as the language with which we will try to explain the ideas to follow. Chapter 3 then steps in to welcome the science that will accompany these ideas and leans on a historical perspective to assist with the process of introduction. Chapter 4 explains several weaknesses of classical geometry, again from a historical perspective. This gives way to Chapters 5 and 6, which construct a contemporary geometric framework better suited to our needs. Chapter 7 continues by specifically bringing physics centre stage and Chapter 8 stays with this theme by extending the geometric patterns first introduced in Chapters 5 and 6. Chapter 9 then underpins the discussion by explaining why such extensions might well be relevant in informational or computational systems of high scale and complexity. This next directs us into a brief run of chapters that look at reformulations of modern physics with a decidedly informational and computational flavour. That gives Chapters 12 and 13 their purpose. Chapter 14 again introduces more ideas based on physics, and Chapter 15 attempts to bring everything together into a single model. Chapter 16 duly tries to provide evidence in support and, lastly, Chapter 17 adds conclusions and final commentary.

Philip Tetlow, 19 September 2011

Introduction

If you want to build a ship, don't drum up the men to gather wood, divide the work, and give orders. Instead, teach them to yearn for the vast and endless sea.

Antoine de Saint-Exupery

One balmy summer's night, when the sky is clear and the smell of freshly cut grass hangs heavy in the warm still air, take time out, find a calm open space and gaze up at the stars. What do you see? As you take in the vista of shimmering dots that glisten in the blackness of space, surely you see beauty? Surely you see the majesty of the universe before you? If you do, then you are not alone. Ever since man could look up at the stars, others have marvelled at such beauty and some have even dared to question why it should be so. From such curiosity came the very essence of science itself.

The attention of physics is entirely focused on the universe and all it contains, as it tries to understand the very most fundamental workings of all we perceive as real. But physics is not an island. It is not self-sufficient when it comes to the tools needed to explain what it seeks to describe. In particular, physics carries a high reliance on mathematics and uses it as the predominant language through which it chooses to speak. So tight is this relationship that we can consider mathematics to be the bedrock on which physics is placed, the very foundation from which our deepest understandings of the universe are built. But there are still deeper foundations. Mathematics itself is based on the concept of individuality and the ability to group such individualities together into more useful concepts. From this the familiar concepts of numbers, arithmetic, geometry and algebra are created and today we put them to work with a high degree of success.

For most who care to consider such matters, that's it, dig down to the very base of mathematics and the roots go no further. Once it is understood where the basic building blocks come from, there is nothing below. But what if there was something below, something holding up numbers, all other mathematical concepts and all the various fields of science above that too? If that were the case then surely that something must be the real stuff from which the universe is made? Surely that something must represent the very signature of everything itself?

In recent times the ideas behind information and computation have seen their profile rise and with the advent of technologies like the Internet and the World Wide Web it's not hard to see why. Yet most still see information technology and its near relation computer science as resting on top of physics and mathematics. We even have fundamental models of computation that clearly line up with fundamental physical models such as quantum mechanics. But what if we chose, for some rebellious reason, to turn the whole model on its head? What if we chose to suggest that physics and mathematics were founded on the notions of computation and information; numbers, arithmetic, algebra, quantum mechanics ... everything?

Most contemporary scientists would wince at the proposition of mathematics not being fundamental, but there are a growing few who would not. Ask your everyday scientist where information and computing should sit in the stack of scientific disciplines and they will most likely respond with confusion. Perhaps above sociology and economics, they might suggest, going on to say that entities like the Web are clearly propped up by such things. But there are those who think differently. To them the universe is just one gigantic computer system feeding on its own information and changing in ways we choose to consider as the reality around us.

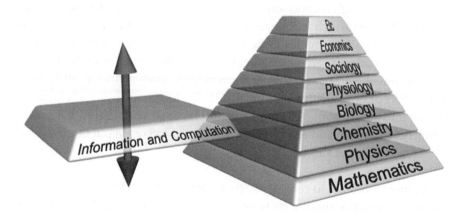

Figure 1.1   Where in science should information and computation sit?

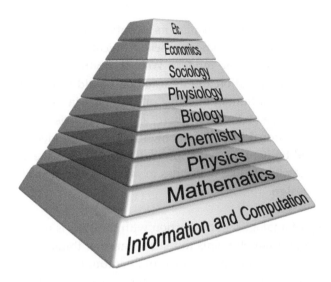

Figure 1.2   Information and computation as the bedrock of all other sciences

The World Wide Web is a truly remarkable innovation. For large sections of this planet's population it now touches our lives through a veritable explosion of change. Some influences are obvious, like the personal knowledge gained from basic Web browsing, but many are not so apparent. For instance we now see extreme cases far removed from the interactions we might traditionally consider as normal within our global society's fabric. These predominantly relate to the vast collection of autonomous Web software now chattering away in the background of our existence. Many refer to the components of this intertwined mesh as collaborating Web services, but this is really a generalisation that has become quickly outmoded. What is profoundly relevant, however, is that the world around these components has changed in recent times and a tipping point has been reached beyond which can be found an automated and intelligent environment hitherto beyond mankind's reach.

Why should this be so? The answer cannot so much be found with the software itself, or not at least if we are happy to consider such software one instance at a time. Rather it comes from the increasingly complex mesh of software-upon-software, computation-upon-computation and information-upon-information into which each individual component is now being placed. From this diverse mixture of connectivity an emergent property may now be starting to rise. This is the swarm intelligence of the Web; the common interpretation of its emergence is predominantly technical. But the Web is not wholly technical. The intention behind its inception may well have been so, but today it has evolved into a complex sociotechnical machine that is radically different. To characterise the modern Web as anything other than a global fusion of society, computation and information would be to do it an injustice. It is simply the largest human information construct in history. Furthermore the emphasis must be on 'machine' here, as evidence exists in support of the Web as a computational device in its own right, independent of the skeletal support donated by its underlying Internet. This changes the game for Web-based software as it acts like molecules in an overall system of much richer, more natural, design.

This string of analogies in connection with the Web is used for deliberate reason, as current research points to the relevance of thinking taken from the physical sciences. In particular the areas of quantum mechanics and relativity stand out as holding particular promise. This implies a number of unfamiliar consequences for those who wish to understand the next generation of the Web-like systems. It also offers great promise for those who work in the classical sciences. Not only is the Web the largest synthetic system humankind has every created, but it also provides the largest sample set of data in existence, outside the informational mass of the very universe itself. If this could be, or more likely when it is, analysed across its full breadth and depth, the chances are high that new types of complex geometries, patterns and trends will be found. The search will then be on to investigate if fundamental laws are at play in their formation and how these might relate to other fundamental laws already known.

It is already established fact, for instance, that the quantum model of computation has greatly strengthened our very understanding of what computation is. So it is plausible to suggest that thinking from physics' other great school of thought – that of the relativists – might also contribute in a similarly profound way. In fact, both physics and computing have already embraced the essence of relativity as a general underlying principle in many of their most fundamental models, the physicists commonly referring to it as 'background-independence'[14] and computer scientists favouring the term 'context-free'.[15] What Albert Einstein taught us was that at larger scales the differences between observable phenomena are not intrinsic to the phenomena but are due entirely to the necessity of describing the phenomena from the viewpoint of the observer.[6] Furthermore in the 1960s a different explanation of relativity was proposed, positing that the differences between unified phenomena were contingent, but not because of the viewpoint of a particular observer. Instead physicists made what seems to be an elementary observation: a given phenomenon can appear different because it may have a symmetry that is not respected by all the features of the context(s) to which it applies – an idea that gave rise to gauge theory in quantum physics. This only helps to suggest that if quantum mechanics presents a fundamental model of the universe[48] which should in turn, one day, be unified with other fundamental models of the universe, such as relativity, then perhaps the most fundamental models of computation are yet to come.

Those who subscribe to the quantum school of computation also freely align with the idea that the laws of quantum mechanics are responsible for the emergence of detail and structure in the universe.[21] They further openly consider the history of the universe to be one ongoing quantum computation[21] expressed via a language which consists of the laws of physics and their chemical and biological consequences. The laws of general relativity additionally state that at higher orders of scale, the complexity and connectivity of the physical fabric of the universe must be seen as curved and not straight, physical – space itself being considered as simply a warped[1] field through its most fundamental definition. Indeed the geometry of space is almost the same as a gravitational field.[2] All of this points to an alternative way of looking at reality, a way that relies on distinctly different geometries to the straight line variants with which we are generally familiar. In many ways too, mainstream theories of computation also need a refresh of perspective and history tells us not to be worried too much about such matters. Geometry suffered its own crisis long before computing. In 1817 one of the most eminent mathematicians of the day, Carl Friedrich Gauss, became convinced that the fifth of Euclid's[2] axioms[3] was independent of the other four and not self-evident, so he began to study the consequences of dropping it. However, even Gauss was too fearful of the reactions of the rest of the mathematical community to publish this result. Eight years later János Bolyai published his independent work on the study of geometry without Euclid's fifth axiom and generated a storm of controversy which lasted many years. His work was considered to be in obvious breach of the real-world geometry that the mathematics sought to model and thus an

---

1   This does not mean that there is some other fixed geometry that characterises space – that space is like a sphere or a saddle instead of a plane or straight line. The point is that the geometry of space can be anything at all, because it evolves in time.
2   Euclid, also known as Euclid of Alexandria, was a Greek mathematician, often referred to as the 'Father of Geometry'.
3   If a line segment intersects two straight lines forming two interior angles on the same side that sum to less than two right angles, then the two lines, if extended indefinitely, meet on that side on which the angles sum to less than two right angles.

unnecessary and fanciful exercise. Nonetheless, the new generalised geometry, of which Euclidean geometry is now understood to be a special case, gathered a following and led to many new ideas and results. In 1915, Einstein's General Theory of Relativity suggested that the geometry of our universe[4] is indeed non-Euclidean and was supported by much experimental evidence. The non-Euclidean geometry of our universe must now be taken into account in both the calculations of theoretical physics and those of a taxi's global positioning system.[16][99][100][101] This drives the point that what is naturally instinctive is not always right.

More on the Web and a Brief History

Might the Web provide a way to the change of perspective sought in computation? In order to start to answer this question we must first further clarify what the Web is not. It is not, for instance, the Internet, although it is dependent upon it. The two are sometimes perceived as synonymous, but they are not.[2] For this reason any use of the colloquialisms like 'the Net' in reference to the Web can only serve to confuse and hence should be frowned upon. The Internet is a communications network, a global framework of wires, routing devices and computers on which the Web rests, and to think of the Web just in terms of electronics and silicon would be wrong. Other terms like 'Information Super Highway' may also be easily misconstrued as characterising the Web but don't really quite get there. They do not convey the truly global, interconnected nature of its vast information bank, instead perhaps conjuring up unnecessarily images, heavily dependent on microprocessors and tin.

The Web is not as youthful as one might first think either. Computing pioneer Vannevar Bush outlined the Web's core idea, hyperlinked pages, back in 1945, making it a veritable old man of a concept on the timescale of modern computing. The word 'hypertext' was also originally coined by Ted Nelson in 1963, and can be first found in print in a college newspaper article about a lecture he gave called 'Computers, Creativity, and the Nature of the Written Word' in January, 1965. That year Nelson also tried to implement a version of Bush's original vision, but had little success connecting digital bits on a useful scale. His efforts were hence known only to an isolated group of disciples. Few

---

4   Considerations of the shape of the universe can be split into two parts; the local geometry relates especially to the curvature of the observable universe, while the global geometry relates especially to the topology of the universe as a whole—which may or may not be within our ability to measure.

of the hackers writing code for the emerging Web in the 1990s knew about Nelson or his hyperlinked dream machine, but it is nonetheless appropriate to give credit where credit is due. From such beginnings, the origins of the Web as we would begin recognise it today eventually materialised in 1980, when Tim Berners-Lee and Robert Cailliau built a system called ENQUIRE – referring to *Enquire Within upon Everything*, a book Berners-Lee recalled from his youth. While it was rather different from the Web we see today, it contained many of the same core ideas.

It was not until March 1989, however, that Berners-Lee wrote *Information Management: A Proposal*, while working at CERN, which referenced ENQUIRE and described a more elaborate information management system. He published a formal proposal for what would become the actual World Wide Web on 12 November 1990 and started implementation the very next day by writing the first Web page. During the Christmas holiday of that year, Berners-Lee built all the tools necessary for a working Web in the form of the first Web browser, which was a Web editor as well, and the first Web server. In August 1991, he posted a short summary of the World Wide Web project on the alt.hypertext newsgroup. This date also marked the debut of the Web as a publicly available service on the Internet. In April 1993, CERN finally announced that the World Wide Web would be free to anyone, with no fees due – and the rest, as they say, is history. The Web quickly gained critical mass with the 1993 release of the graphical Mosaic web browser by the National Centre for Supercomputing Applications which was developed by Marc Andreessen and Eric Bina. This again was a seminal event as prior to the release of Mosaic, the Web was text-based and its popularity was less than older protocols in use over the Internet . Mosaic's graphical user interface swept all that aside and allowed the Web to become by far and away the most popular protocol in use.

In more recent times it has become indisputable that the Web is having an increasingly profound impact on the way that we, as individuals and social groups, go about our everyday lives. But regardless we should not forget that it is only one integral part in humanity's ever-growing ability to create and process information. Putting the Web into this wider context, an impressive picture is painted, as the much credited 'didyouknow' presentation at www.shifthappens.com helps to explain:

- There are over 2.7 billion searches performed on Google each month.

- The number of text messages sent and received every day exceeds the population of the planet.

- More than 3,000 new books are published every single day.

- It is estimated that 1.5 exabytes (1.5 × 1,018) of unique new information were generated in 2007. That's estimated to be more than in the previous 5,000 years.

- Predictions are that by 2013 a supercomputer will be built that exceeds the computation capability of the human brain.

- Predictions are that by 2049 a $1,000 computer will exceed the computational capabilities of the human race.

Such statistics are indeed impressive, but pointing out an exponential growth in information and our appetite to consume it is simply not enough. To appreciate the full picture, the great sea-change under way in our population's demographic must also be understood. In the 400 years from 1500 to 1900, the human population of this planet increased at an average rate of just fewer than 3 million people per year. However, in the 100 years from 1900 to 2000, the average yearly increase grew to 44 million – nearly a 15-fold increase. So by such reckoning some calculations state that there are now more people alive today than all the humans who have ever lived since the dawn of civilisation. A profound conclusion if true, but it is only one of a number of related profound conclusions, if further conjectures are to be believed:

- 99 per cent of all the scientists who have ever lived are alive today.

- 99 per cent of all the geniuses who have ever lived are alive today. Likewise, 99 per cent of all the idiots who ever lived ... are alive today.

- More information is contained in one daily edition of the *New York Times* than was openly available in the entire seventeenth century.

- More new information is now publicly published every day than an army of 10,000 people could absorb. In fact, 10,000 people couldn't even catalogue it all.

- The acceleration of the acceleration in population growth is accelerating. Merely two decades from now there will be seven billion people living on this planet, a staggering figure in anyone's books.

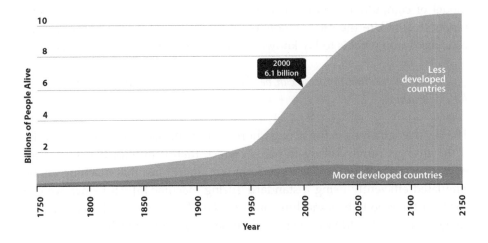

Figure 1.3   Global population growth

In fact, to borrow a quote from the Web site providing most of the statistics above, 'shift' truly is happening. Humankind is experiencing change as never seen before and the rate of that change is accelerating at a heart-thumping pace. Couple this with the staggering rate at which the information we are producing is also accelerating and a clear conclusion must be reached. The Industrial Revolution of the eighteenth to the nineteenth century may well have seen major changes in agriculture, manufacturing, transport and so on, and a had a lasting effect on most aspects of our culture and society, but the changes we are experiencing today are of a magnitude far greater. This outlines the revolution of our time, and perhaps the greatest revolution that mankind will ever see. This is the Information Revolution and few yet understand its real significance.

New Ways in Which the Web Might Compute

In the late 1960s and early 1970s it seemed as though the Turing machine[5] model of computation was at least as powerful as any other model of computation, in the sense that a problem which could also be solved efficiently in the same model of computation could also be solved efficiently in a Turing machine model to simulate the other model of computation. This observation can be condensed into what is today known as the strong Church-Turing thesis:[6]

> *Any algorithmic process can be simulated efficiently using a Turing Machine.*

The key strengthening in the strong Church-Turing thesis is the word efficiently. If the strong Church–Turing thesis is correct, then it implies that no matter what type of machine we use to perform our algorithms, that machine can be simulated efficiently using a standard Turing machine.[6] And since we can consider the Web to be a machine of sorts, the Church-Turing thesis similarly suggests that it should be open to simulation via a Turing machine.

The first major challenge to the strong Church-Turing thesis arose in the mid 1970s when Robert Solovay and Volker Strassen showed that it is possible to test whether an integer is prime or composite using a randomised algorithm. That is, the Solovay Stressen test for primality[6] used randomness as an essential part of the algorithm. The algorithm did not determine whether a given integer was prime or composite with certainty. Instead the algorithm could determine that a number was probably prime or else composite with certainty. This was of especial significance at the time as no deterministic test for primality was then known. Thus it seemed as though computers with access to a random generator would be able to efficiently perform computational tasks with no efficient solution on a conventional determinist Turing machine. This discovery inspired a search for other randomised algorithms which has paid off handsomely.[6]

Randomised algorithms pose a challenge to the strong Church-Turing thesis, suggesting there are efficiently solvable problems which cannot be

---

5   A Turing machine is a theoretical device that manipulates symbols contained on a strip of tape. Despite its simplicity, a Turing machine can be adapted to simulate the logic of any computer algorithm, and is particularly useful in explaining the functions of a CPU inside a computer. The 'Turing' machine was described by Alan Turing in 1937. Turing machines are not intended as a practical computing technology, but rather as a thought experiment representing a computing machine. They help computer scientists understand the limits of mechanical computation.
6   The property associated with numbers only divisible by themselves and 1.

efficiently solved on a deterministic Turing machine. This challenge appears to be easily resolved by a single modification to the thesis:[6]

> *Any Algorithmic process can be simulated efficiently using a probabilistic Turing Machine.*

This is a supremely profound adjustment as it suggests that not all computation is discrete, that it is not 'black and white'. It further implies that Alan Turing's vision of computation is incomplete and begs the question as to if any further single model of computation is better or more 'complete'.

Motivated by this question the physicist David Deutsch asked whether the fundamental laws of physics could be used to devise a model of computation stronger that that embodied in the strong Church–Turing thesis. Because the laws of physics, and ultimately the universe, are quantum mechanical, Deutsch was naturally led to consider computational devices based upon the principles of quantum mechanics. These devises, quantum analogues of the machines defined 49 years earlier by Turing, led ultimately to the modern conception of the quantum computer.

So a simple and immediate question is presented: if the Web can be considered as being an computational entity, what type of computer is it – classical, in a truly Church-Turing sense, quantum in a more contemporary sense, a mix of the two or something completely different? Trying to answer this question will be very important to us as our story unfolds.

Throughout most, if not all, of our recent digital history we have worked hard to engineer software to drive our computational devices towards a specific purpose or set of purposes. In doing so many useful programming languages have appeared and been applied with great success. Through such creativity we have literally tried to climb inside the machine and convince it to do our bidding, pushing it in minute yet explicit increments towards a destiny of our own choosing. 'Our code shall fit inside the box and the box shall do precisely as we ask', has been the IT industry's mantra to date. However, with the complexity and scale of the Web today we are presented with the opportunity to construct systems in a radically different way. It is now possible to 'glue' together 'software', creating it on the fly from a variety of locations and technologies. Indeed the Web is now allowing us to also question the very nature of software itself. For example, it is a common misconception that computer systems are built from two types of component: hardware and software. That is actually not true. There is one further type of component that is invariably left off the list – us. Without humans to create and run such systems they most certainly have no purpose. So, more correctly, computational systems – as we commonly understand them today – need three ingredients to survive. Hardware, software and the 'wetware' that constitutes the thought processes inside our heads to create, run and maintain such systems.

The powers of wetware are consistently underplayed in IT circles, but let's not forget that wetware is the only self-supporting element in the equation we have just described. Ever since intelligent beings have lived on our planet they have grouped together to create higher orders of computational capability. They have literally self-constructed their own computational systems. Take bees as a perfect example. There are over 20,000 known species of bee alive on Earth today, so they must be considered as a highly successful form of life. Yet each bee has little intelligence and thus little right to claim credit for such success. So where does this success come from? The answer comes from the swarm, the collective presence essential to every individual bee's survival. The swarm takes the bee's meagre intellect and adds it to the capabilities of all its brothers and sisters. It stitches together something far greater than the sum of its parts and allows a grander intelligence to emerge. And this capability is common across all forms of wetware, not just bees. Some species exploit it more than others and we humans are not impervious or immune to its attraction. We choose to live and congregate in cities, for instance, and such cities can be thought of as being computational and intelligent in many ways. Likewise a liking for swarm behaviour is showing through on the Web, through sites like Facebook, Bebo and many other online communities. So, just as a swarm of bees can be considered to have emergent intelligence, the coming together of minds on the Web must also be considered as having the same, or similar, emergent potential. Add to that the potential of the significant computational power of the software and hardware we bring with us to the Web and an emergent intelligence the likes of which we have never seen before is created.

Newton's Bucket

In 1689 Sir Isaac Newton conducted an experiment with a bucket containing water. The experiment is quite simple and can be tried by almost anyone. All you need to do is half fill a bucket with water and suspend it from a fixed point with a rope or some similarly flexible cord. Rotate the bucket, twisting the rope until it is reasonably tight. Next hold the bucket steady and let the water settle. At this point let the bucket go and watch what happens.

Immediately the bucket starts to rotate due to the tension in the twisted rope, but, at first the water inside does not follow this motion, remaining fairly stationary and flat on its surface. Slowly, however, the water begins to rotate with the bucket and as it does so its surface becomes concave, as indeed Newton's himself described:[20]

> ... the surface of the water will at first be flat, as before the bucket began to move; but after that, the bucket by gradually communicating its motion to the water, will make it begin to revolve, and recede little by little from the centre, and ascend up the sides of the bucket, forming itself into a concave figure (as I have experienced), and the swifter the motion becomes, the higher will the water rise, till at last, performing its revolutions in the same time with the vessel, it becomes relatively at rest in it.

Before too long the spin of the bucket slows as the rope loses its original tension and begins to twist in the opposite direction due to momentum.[7] The water is now spinning faster than the bucket and its surface remains concave.

This is an experiment that is easy to visualise and is one that we have all probably done at play at some time in our lives. As the bucket spins, the water rises up the sides of the bucket. Big deal, that's obvious, right? Well ... perhaps not. Newton was someone who never accepted the obvious and, on this occasion, he wanted to push further than accepting everyday observation. As always Newton wanted to understand the underlying principles involved and he used this experiment to ask a very fundamental question – what does spin itself mean?

It certainly doesn't mean spinning relative to the bucket, as might instinctively be thought. After the bucket is released and starts spinning, the water stays flat for a time, hence demonstrating that the two are not completely bound to one another. Eventually, however, friction builds up between the water and the sides of the bucket and this causes the two to start to move together until they ultimately become comparable in their motion. As part of this process the water's surface becomes concave as centrifugal force compels the water to move out from the centre of the rotation. After the bucket stops

---

7   In classical mechanics, momentum is the product of the mass and velocity of an object.

and the water goes on spinning relative to the bucket, its surface maintains its concave shape until the energy in the system dies down and friction can no longer counteract the levelling influence of gravity. Thus the shape of the water's surface is not determined by the spin of the water relative to the bucket.

Newton then went on to push the experiment further, theorising that it might be undertaken in a completely empty space. This time he considered a different variant in which two rocks are tied together with a rope at a point in deep space, far from interference from any gravitational field. To run the experiment he imagined the rope being rotated about its centre, thereby becoming taut as the rocks pull outwards.

In this version of the experiment a particular problem is deliberately introduced, in that in such a vast empty space there is nothing obvious against which to measure the rotation. This posed the basic question, that if we can't measure rotation, how can it exist at all? From this, Newton deduced that, regardless of the huge void, there had to be some means of comparison within reach, and that something had to be space itself. This was a major theoretical breakthrough and provided his strongest argument in support of the idea of absolute space – the container in which everything exists and against which all things can be compared.

Having made this jump Newton returned to his bucket experiment and proposed that spin can only ever be considered as a property with respect to an absolute space, the universal container which we implicitly consider as our everyday interpretation of the world around us. When the water is not rotating with respect to absolute space then its surface is flat but when it spins with respect to absolute space its surface is concave. Thus he somewhat reluctantly wrote in his *Principia*:[8]

> *I do not define time, space, place, and motion, as they are well known to all. Absolute space by its own nature, without reference to anything external, always remains similar and unmovable.*

For Newton, the boundaries of absolute space were necessary to make sense of the universe even at local levels, but he was uncomfortable with the fact that the human mind could never grasp the true meaning of these through any of our

---

8   *Philosophiæ Naturalis Principia Mathematica*, Latin for 'Mathematical Principles of Natural Philosophy', often called the *Principia*, is a work in three books by Sir Isaac Newton, first published 5 July 1687.

natural senses. We just had to accept the existence of absolute space without being able to touch, smell, touch or hear it. It was beyond our experience, yet was intrinsic to everything we experience, a paradox that has challenged science ever since the second it entered Newton's mind.

Other scientists, like Leibniz,[9] did not believe in absolute space, however. He argued that space only provided a means of encoding the relation of one object to another. It made no sense to claim that the universe was rotating or moving through space. He supported his argument with philosophical reasoning, but faced with Newton's bucket, he had no answer. He hence felt compelled to declare:

> *I grant there is a difference between absolute true motion of a body and a mere relative change of its situation with respect to another body.*

For nearly two centuries Newton's case for absolute space did not see much contest, but after Einstein introduced the special theory of relativity in June 1905 the concept of absolute space was no longer seen as tenable. Through his deep insights into the structure of space and time, Einstein was able to cast aside Newton's ideas of a fixed space in which the universe plays out its life. But there was a trade-off involved. Even though special relativity does not rely on the constant nature of absolute space, it still has its absolutes. Absolute spacetime is a feature of special relativity which, contrary to popular belief, does not claim that everything is relative. Although velocities, distances, and time intervals are relative, the theory still sits on a theorised platform of absolute space-time. In special relativity observers moving at constant velocities relative to each other would not agree on the velocity of a bucket moving through space, nor would they agree about the time that has elapsed during any bucket experiment, but they would all agree on whether the bucket was accelerating or not.[20]

Einstein further expanded on his ideas of relativity in 1915, with his more famous theory of general relativity. Through this he incorporated acceleration and gravity, but even before the theory's publication he claimed that Newton's interpretation of the bucket experiment was partially incorrect. He did so in a letter which he wrote to Ernst Mach[10] in 1913 in which he agreed with Mach's

---

9 Gottfried Wilhelm Leibniz was a German mathematician and philosopher.
10 Ernst was an Austrian physicist and philosopher, remembered for his contributions to physics such as the Mach number and the study of shock waves. As a philosopher of science, he was a major influence on logical positivism and through his criticism of Newton, a forerunner of Einstein's relativity.

view that Newton's bucket could be seen as spinning relative to the planets around it. Einstein even included 'Mach's principle' into general relativity. The theory is based on the equivalence of gravity and acceleration, something which has been checked experimentally today to a high degree of accuracy. Hence, the behaviour of Newton's spinning bucket is, as Mach claimed, determined by the gravitational forces of all the matter in the universe. But this this leaves a problem remaining, as Einstein conceded and in that general relativity cannot explain the behaviours expected in Newton's two-rock version of the experiment. This is because the vast emptiness which Newton suggested surrounding his two rocks and rope can be seen as a universe in which no matter exists and hence little or no[11] gravity is present. This leads all observers to agree when the rock system is spinning through acceleration.

In 1918, however, Joseph Lense and Hans Thirring[12] obtained approximate solutions for the equations of general relativity for rotating bodies. Their results show that a massive rotating body drags space-time round with it. This is now called 'frame dragging' or the 'Lense–Thirring effect'. In 1966 Dieter Brill and Jeffrey Cohen showed that frame dragging should occur in a hollow sphere and in 1985 further progress by H. Pfister and K. Braun showed that sufficient centrifugal forces would be induced at the centre of the hollow massive sphere to cause water to form a concave surface in a bucket which is not rotating with respect to the distant stars.

Frame dragging has recently been verified experimentally. This involved using the rotating Earth as the massive body and putting a satellite into orbit with a gyroscope which kept it pointing in a fixed direction. Although the Earth has only a tiny frame dragging effect it was possible to detect the extremely small deviation of the gyroscope which it caused. A report of the experiment can be found on the NASA website.[93]

Berners-Lee's Box

So why this digression into physics again when we are supposed to be discussing information and computing? Some, like Isaac Newton, argue strongly that the universe must be finite and complete, whereas others, like Einstein, place less emphasis on such absolutes. Even so, all still rely on the need for some form

---

11 It is possible to argue that there will be gravity produced by the mass of the rock system, but this is negligible and will not produce the necessary forces to make the rope become taut.
12 Josef Lense and Hans Thirring were Austrian physicists.

of fixed context or background to make their ideas work. Newton reached out and proposed constraining raw space, while Einstein extending this proposition to incorporate the changing vista of space-time. Furthermore, the broader scientific community appears not to be in dispute about what is using this background context. At its most basic level that thing is 'information' and its use within any background context we have commonly come to known as 'computation'. Hence the link and a reminder of the proposition that physics is simply computing and computing is simply physics.

All physical systems contain information by their very constitution. Atoms have a certain number of parts and occupy certain points in space-time at a given point in the universe's history. This is all information and as it changes over time to create the very fingerprint of reality itself. In addition, our most fundamental understandings of reality, the nuts and bolts at the base of quantum mechanics itself, suggest that all the matter can be seen as being entangled regardless of any notion of space. Everything is simply capable of informational connectedness regardless of its position in the universe and the ongoing dance of everything around it.

Now, take a step back for a moment and think of the World Wide Web instead. Here too can be found an informational space which some would see as finite. Others, on the other hand, would prefer to lean towards a definition more closely aligned with infinity. Also each blob of information contained within the Web possesses the innate capability to link to all others, as if entangled without regard for the differences or similarities between it and everything else. To some, in fact, the model of the Web is deeply analogous to physical models of the universe and, for them at least, many strong parallels exist. What is particularly useful about the Web, though, is that as a model it has undoubtedly gained great acceptance and credibility through direct interaction and use, indeed more so, one could argue, than all of science's interactions with the natural world to date. This raises a huge potential in that if the Web can indeed be considered as being analogous to the universe, then might we not use it as a platform for experimentation to try and confirm or extend our understandings of reality itself? Could Tim Berners-Lee's child be considered as the equivalent of Newton's absolute space or Einstein's absolute space-time? Only time will tell, but herein can be found a beginner guide to try and find out.

2

Dot-to-Dots Point the Way

I have not proved that the universe is, in fact, a digital computer and that it's capable of performing universal computation, but it's plausible that it is.

Seth Lloyd

What is information in the first place, or data for that matter? Are the two really different or are they just two interpretations of the same thing?

Intuitively when we talk about data we reach out and think of collections of numbers and characters, strung together in a way that makes them useful. Words, sentences, dates and so on, all spring to mind as good examples, but to classify them as data would be quite wrong. Each is actually more akin to information.

On its own data is meaningless. The number 19061966 is worthless in isolation, for instance, merely representing a sequence of digits. Add some structure to it in the form of a couple of well-placed hyphens or slashes and its starts to make more sense, becoming easily recognisable as a date of some kind. But it is only when context is set and we are told that this is actually someone's date of birth that the true value of the information contained is released. We can push this further and even suggest that individual numbers and characters involved are not really data either. To quote Brian Green's marvellous book, *The Fabric of the Cosmos*, one can 'think of the English alphabet. It provides an order for 26 letters – it provides relations such as a is next to b, d, is six letters before j, x is three letters after u, and so on. But without the letters the alphabet has no meaning,' no information content as it were, no 'super-letter, independent existence.' Instead the alphabet comes into being with the letters whose lexicographic relations it supplies. The converse is obviously also true of the characters held within, for without their individual relationships within the alphabet the meaning they carry would be, for all intents and purposes, valueless. Information needs to be interpreted in relation to something else for any worth can be established. It needs a reference point to hang from and without that all that can be found is data. In such a way, take the example of a line drawn in the sand. Without some further explanation of its purpose it carries little relevance. Likewise points drawn on the blank canvas of space are also data-like. To those who have studied astronomy they might easily be interpreted as some named constellation, but for the non-astronomer to make such a judgement call must they must first consult a wealth of reference material.

This all points to a simple yet powerful relationship between data and information:

$$Information \;=\; Data \;+\; Structure \;+\; Context$$

Conjecture 1   Information's magic formula

Hold onto this equation as it is important. It is written across almost everything we see and do in our world. Sometimes its appearance is obvious and sometimes it is shaded by many veils of subtlety, but nevertheless it is always there. Through it, all events and everything associated with then them hang together. Without it, chaos would reign. Here it may be formulated in a simple and concise way, but this is just one of many variants that have been put to work on many complex problems. As one particularly powerful example of its application, take the work of Christiane Nüsslein-Volhard and Eric Wieshaus, who have used it to study the embryonic development of the fruit fly.[22] Their work has emphatically demonstrated that intracellular genetic processes provide a self-contained mechanism for making sense of the various elements needed to provide intrinsically informative systems. In their case, descriptive and positional proteins provide the data and structural elements of the equation, while the surrounding chemical concentrations of such proteins provide the appropriate developmental context for the right cells to form in the right place at the right time. This inbuilt choreographed cascade of combining complexity results in the system we refer to as metabolism.

Geometry, Space and Relationalism

Think back to your childhood and remember those wet weekends waiting for the rain to stop and your friends to call. It was during episodes like this that many of us were introduced to the type of puzzle commonly known as a 'dot-to-dot'. The concept is simple. Take a blank sheet of paper and sprinkle it with a collection of apparently random small dots. Next pair each dot with a unique number starting at one and incrementing all the way up to the last visible dot on the page. The trick to solving such puzzles is to join the dots in rising numerical order using a straight line between each. By doing so the outline of a picture should be revealed. Bunny rabbits, butterflies and perhaps cartoon elephants are all the kind of pictorial surprise one might expect from such puzzles, but the potential for expressions is, of course, almost limitless.

Apart from being great fun there is a serious side to the inner workings of a dot-to-dot. As we all know, the dots on the page are rarely, if ever, placed randomly, and the order in which they are numbered is also no mistake. Both placement and order have a specific task to do, being aimed solely at guiding the individual around the page in order to decode the picture trapped within. But dots, numbers and lines are not the only important ingredients in a dot-to-dot puzzle. Intuitively one might also suggest that the paper on which the puzzle is laid out must also play a vital role, as indeed it does. It provides the means by which the puzzle is contained. Lay a typical-sized dot-to-do down on a flat surface, and it protrudes upwards by a small amount – the thickness of the paper to be exact. So the uppermost surface of the paper limits the region within which the puzzle can be acted upon in the direction facing away from the table. Likewise, the page's sides do the same across the other two available dimensions in space.

This may appear obvious, but it actually raises a couple of interesting dilemmas. What, for example, if the piece of paper on which the puzzle was drawn were of infinite length, width or depth? What effect might that have on the information contained in the puzzle? Think about it long enough and it should become clear that the effect could be quite dramatic, for under such circumstances how could anyone determine how far a point was into the page in any direction? For that matter, how could anyone determine if it was indeed a piece of paper on which the puzzle was drawn? These questions, and others like them, highlight an important property brought about by the edges of the paper, and, in particular, the points in space at which they meet. This is because they provide the markers, or reference points, against which the world outside the puzzle can be compared and contrasted. Not only do they give us a means by which the contents of the puzzle can be contained, measured and hence described, but they also provide a means by which everything else in the outside world can be referenced in relation to such things.

In technical terms the dots of the puzzle, and indeed the vast number of miniscule points that make up the paper's surface, can all be seen as coordinates, locations in space that can be identified by one form of description system or another. In the case of our puzzle, its system only comprises a single number for each consecutive dot that needs a line to be drawn to and from it, but equally, more complex description systems could be used that contain more numbers, characters or symbols denoting as many aspects of the dot's location as necessary. Maps traditionally use two values to describe their points, for instance, and these are respectively referred to as a coordinate's latitude and longitude. Some maps even use a third element as part of their description system, adding height above sea level to project their information out into the third dimension. By collecting such points and lumping them together with their various descriptive data schemes, maps and dot-to-dot puzzles are hence often both referred to as being coordinate systems. Such systems are also often referred to as geometries in their own right or even frames of reference. All of these terms will be used frequently later, but for our immediate purposes, the best name for such a scheme is the one that appears in the equation above, as they provide the context in which information's magic formula unfolds.

Puzzles like dot-to-dot are indeed a form of geometry, which is a branch of mathematics concerned with questions of dimension: the size, shape, and relative position of things or concepts. In essence it's all about describing space, and geometry is one of the oldest branches of mathematics. Initially a body of practical knowledge concerning lengths, areas and volumes in the third century BC, geometry was put into the most basic of its forms by the Greek philosopher Euclid, who set the standard for many centuries to come by laying down a simple set of mathematical rules through which his understanding of geometry could be conveyed. This was Euclid's legacy and his name still embodies the type of geometry we are mostly taught in school. The introduction of the naming convention we now formally understand as coordinates by René Descartes[1] in the seventeenth century also had a profound impact on geometry. That and the development of rudimentary algebra at the same time marked a new era for spatial mathematics, as geometric concepts, such as plane curves, could now be represented analytically as equations using symbols and characters denoting

---

1   René Descartes was a French philosopher, mathematician and physicist.

interchangeable values. This played a key role in the emergence of another branch of mathematics we now know as calculus, in the seventeenth century.

Since the nineteenth century discovery of geometries that do not need to be bound by Euclid's rules (geometries we now refer to unsurprisingly as being non-Euclidean), our ideas on space have undergone a radical transformation. For instance, contemporary geometry now trades in concepts such as manifolds; regions that are considerably more abstract than the familiar three-dimensional space of our world as Euclid saw it. To those unfamiliar with it, non-Euclidean geometry can seem weird in the extreme, but it really involves nothing more complicated than adding more descriptive data to the dot-to-dot puzzle we have just described. Thus the spaces it describes can theoretically stretch out into an infinite number of dimensions in a mind boggling number of ways. Even so, the roots of geometry are firmly planted in frameworks for capturing and communicating the spatial aspects of our own familiar three-dimensional world and the way that all things in it relate to each other over the distances involved. This is what makes geometry more accessible than other parts of mathematics. Our brains and bodies are literally hard-wired to accommodate it. For instance we have precisely the right number of eyes to allow our minds to function in three dimensions. They effortlessly provide a rough estimation of distance, and thereby assess which objects around us are close or far away. Furthermore because this can be done in real time, they are essential with movement, both towards and away from things of interest and danger. So, by implication, geometry is also an essential part of our survival kit.

Puzzles: Points, Lines and Other Interesting Stuff

Consult the *Oxford English Dictionary* for the definition of 'structure' and you will find the following:

> *noun 1. the arrangement of and relations between the parts of something complex. 2. a building or other object constructed from several parts. 3. the quality of being well organised.*

Definitions two and three are, of course, relevant to the overall meaning of the word 'structure', but it is the first definition that is of the most value when considered in the context of information. As the dictionary states, structure is all about how one thing relates to another; how things are linked as part of a greater thing, be that an idea, an equation or something more tangible like the bones in the human body. But, as mentioned earlier, the concept of how things are linked is worthless without a context in which to frame it and data that can anchor a link at both ends. Think of it like a bridge over a river. Without solid ground on either side, the bridge could never be supported, and without the river itself, the bride would have no meaningful purpose. Likewise, without the bridge, it would not be possible to reach either bank from the other. Tie river, bridge and banks together, however, and we essentially return to the concept of a coordinate system.

Consider again the concept of a dot-to-dot puzzle, but this time think of a completed version, with all points linked together using straight lines. Focus on the image of the completed puzzle in your mind's eye for one moment and consider how the image it contains has been brought into existence – for structure plays several important roles. The straight lines between each of the consecutive points provide one type of structure, describing how one point links to the next. But that's not all, because they also act as a stand-in mechanism through which the counting order of the dots can be derived, by following one straight line after another. Furthermore, collectively the lines act as a perimeter, marking out the limits of the image hidden within the puzzle. Not only do they convey the image's overall shape, but they also specify the region where the inside of the shape ends and the outside of the puzzle begins. They essentially differentiate the answer to the puzzle from the puzzle itself. This is a subtle, yet important point, as structure not only provided a means to associate two differing things together, but also provides a means for differentiating between two things that might not necessarily be considered separate.

So the lines and dots in our puzzle play a critical role, but in many cases on their own they are not enough to convey all the information present in a particular idea or system. This is because there is an element deliberately missing in dot-to-dot puzzles and to show what this is all we need to do is ask exactly where on the puzzle' paper each dot to be connected lies.

The answer to this question is simple if the puzzle is drawn on a piece of paper with right-angular corners and straight edges, and to show why all we need is a ruler of some sort and a steady hand with which to make measurements. Just take the ruler and hold it at a perfect right angle to any edge, then measure the distance in from that edge to a dot. Next do the same from a perpendicular edge and a method of location through the intersection of the ruler's placements is provided. Assuming that the width and height of the paper on which the puzzle is drawn are comparable with that of the ruler that now gives us all the details needed to locate all the dots in the puzzle, doesn't it? Well, actually no, but we are nearly there.

As should be obvious, all right-angled quadrilaterals – or the typical shape of a page on which we might expect a dot-to-dot puzzle – have four sides. That is to say the sides comprise a pair of parallel sides and a second pair perpendicular to them. Given a point at random anywhere inside such a quadrilateral on a flat plane, the chances are that it will not be the same distance from any combination of these sides. This raises a problem, as how might we know from which sides any measurement was made to get the point's location? To solve this conundrum, one of the horizontal and vertical edges involved in such measurements must be traced back to the corner at which they meet. Once found, this becomes significant. In fact it holds such significance that it has been given a special name – the 'origin'. It not only provides a means of identifying the important sides in any measurement, but it also gives a starting point from which measurements can be made and calibrated. This makes it the starting point for referencing any point around it and hence the last element needed for us to use geometry practically. In fact, in many ways, the toolkit we have just described and geometry are one and the same thing and with the inclusion of an origin, this toolkit brings together all the elements in information's magic equation. Not surprisingly this toolkit also has a name, being commonly referred to as a 'coordinate system' and its value stretches far beyond the constraints of mere rectangles, pages, dots and straight lines.

Name any point on a flat surface as an origin and it is possible to locate any other point on the same surface relative to it, no matter how far away it is or in what direction. Furthermore, draw any two perpendicular lines out from an origin and more mathematical capabilities are produced. Such lines are collectively known as 'axis' and independently they hold the names 'abscissa', or 'x' axis in layman's terms, and 'ordinate', or 'y' axis, again in regular parlance. Measurements from each are hence usually recognised as x and y values of a particular location. Not surprisingly, the locations pointed to by such pairs of offset are referred to as 'coordinates'. These are often specified in the format $P(x,y)$, where P is the coordinate, or point in space being described, and x and y are obviously abscissa and ordinate offsets, as can be seen in the example below.

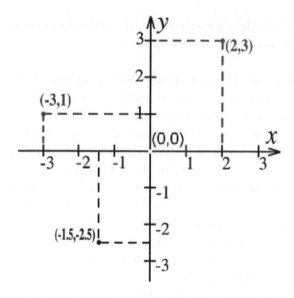

Figure 2.1   A two-dimensional coordinate system

Naturally this scheme is not restricted to two dimensions. By adding one more line, perpendicular to the first two, coordinates in three-dimensional space can be specified, and theoretically an infinite number of dimensions can be added thereafter – although we would clearly not be able to visualise these higher dimension in the same manner as those of the familiar three-dimensional physical world around us. What's more, by allowing individual points to be referenced through a series of coordinate values, namely x, y ... z and so on, not only is a system produced for outlining location across a number of dimensions, but a formulaic method for relating one property to another is created. This raises geometry from the lowly level of the purely positional, bringing it through the world of algebra and out and into the domains of information and computation.

Because René Descartes was the first to apply algebra to geometry, it is sometimes known as Cartesian geometry, as well as obviously being referred to as analytic geometry. It springs from the idea that any point in two-dimensional space can be represented by two numbers, any point in three-dimensional space by three, and so on. And because lines, circles, spheres and other figures can be thought of as collections of points in space that satisfy certain equations, they can be explored via equations and formulae rather than as simple collections of coordinates, or 'graphs' to use their more formal name. As a further brief history, the Greek mathematician Menaechmus solved problems and proved theorems by using a method that had a strong resemblance to the use of coordinates and it has sometimes been said that he was the first user of analytic geometry. Apollonius of Perga, in *On Determinate Section*, dealt with problems in a manner that might also be called an analytic geometry of one dimension, with his question on finding points on a line that are in a ratio to others. Apollonius in the *Conics* further developed a method so similar to analytic geometry that his work is sometimes thought to have anticipated the work of more contemporary academics by some 1,800 years. His application of reference lines like diameters and tangents is essentially no different to our modern use of a coordinate frame, where the distances measured along a diameter from the point of tangency represent the abscissas, and the segments parallel to the tangent and intercepted between the axis and the curve represent the ordinates. He further developed relations between the abscissas and corresponding ordinates that are equivalent to rhetorical equations of curves. However, although Apollonius came close to developing analytic geometry, he did not manage to do so, ultimately missing out some key details. The eleventh-century Persian mathematician Omar Khayyám also saw a strong relationship between geometry and algebra, and was moving in the right direction when he helped to close the gap between numerical and geometric algebra with his geometric solution of the general cubic equations, but again his work was overshadowed by Descartes some 500 years later.

Functions, Geometry, Computation and Information

In its simplest form the mathematical concept of a function expresses dependence between two quantities, one of which is given – the independent variable, argument of the function, or its 'input' – and the other produced – the dependent variable, value of the function, or 'output'. A function therefore associates a single output to each input element drawn from a fixed set of elements, such as the numbers found in the set of all real numbers[2] ($\mathbb{R}$).

There are many ways to realise a function, for example by a formula, equation or a geometric plot as outlined above. But these are not the only means by which a function can be brought into existence. It is just as valid to think

2   In mathematics, the real numbers may be described informally as numbers with an infinite decimal representation, such as 2.4871773339 ... The real numbers include the rational numbers, such as 42 and –23/129, and the irrational numbers, such as π and the square root of 2.

of a function by way of any algorithm that computes it or by any complete description of its properties. Sometimes a function can even be described through its relationship to other functions, which hence opens up its context through in infinity of possible links, each following another and fanning out in all possible directions. Some refer to this as functional composition, in that if z is a function of y and y is a function of x, then z is a function of x and we may describe this type of relationship informally by saying that the composite function is obtained by using the output of the first function as the input of the second. This feature distinguishes functions from other mathematical constructs, such as numbers or other symbols of representation, such as characters in the alphabet of a natural language like English or Chinese. It thereby provides the theory of functions with its powerful structure. Indeed, so powerful is this notion of function-to-function structure that it gives us one of the very foundations of modern mathematics and is integral to our very notion of computation itself.

Because a function can be thought of as a mathematical formula, a geometric plot and a computational algorithm that might realise both, a significant point can now been made. When thinking of computing as a functional activity, it becomes completely interchangeable with the ideas of certain types of both mathematical function and geometric plot. In fact this is so important that we should really highlight it further by way of a simple equivalence:

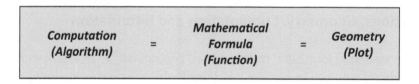

Conjecture 2   The equivalence between computational algorithm, mathematical function and geometry

Although definitions of computation are dealt with in much greater depth in later chapters, it is important to get this out in the open now. In fact, let's make a rather large leap of faith and serve up another two variants to stand alongside it for now:

Information	=	*Formula*	=	*Geometry*

Conjecture 3 The equivalence between information, mathematical function and geometry

Information	=	*Computation (Algorithm)*

Conjecture 4 The equivalence between information and computation

All of these conjectures are obtuse and demand much more explanation, but all that will come in time. All that matters for now is that there are two very strong proposals on the table, in that information and computation can been seen as being equivalent, at least in some regard, and both can be described via of mathematical function, algorithm or geometry. Of these three descriptive approaches we are going to choose geometry as our primary vehicle from this point on, but it is important to note that either of the others could equally be used for our purposes.

If Geeks Could Draw

So, geometry it is. But what type of geometry might typically be used amongst the community who chose to study and work with information and computation? Will simple Cartesian plots do, or perhaps just coordinate-free scribbles on some arbitrary plane, like a sheet of paper?

As might be expected, the answer is not so clear cut. Computer scientists and information engineers use a number of graphical techniques to describe and convey their ideas and designs. In some cases there is indeed a need to tie specific concepts to a point within some form of coordinate framework, but such rigidity is still rare. More common examples use a reduced form of geometry known as topology. This is the branch of mathematics which studies the properties of a space that are preserved under continuous deformations, and when the discipline was first properly established it was known as *geometria situs*, Latin for 'geometry of place' and *analysis situs*, Latin for 'analysis of place.'

Topology grew out of geometry, but unlike geometry, is not concerned with measurement properties like the distance between points. Instead, topology focuses on the study of properties that describe how a space is assembled, properties like connectedness and orientability. Topology searches for solutions to problems relating to the geometry of position in the truest sense of the word. It is a large branch of mathematics that includes many subfields. The most basic and traditional division within topology is point-set topology, which establishes the foundational aspects of topology and investigates such concepts as compactness and connectedness.

Examples of topologies include flowcharts and state diagrams, and most share a few things in common. Firstly representation in two dimensions is the norm. This is basically for historic reasons. The first engineers to work with modern-day digital computers had no screens with which to work, as in those days punched-card readers and teletype machines provided the only means with which to interact with the computer systems under their control. Hence they resorted to pencil and paper to draw their schematics and create their designs. The second commonality relates to how concepts are represented within such schematics and specifically how they are linked. As might be guessed there are many different types of schematic used by those interested

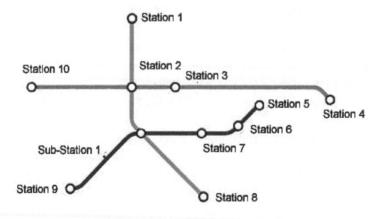

Figure 2.2   A simple topology

in information and computing and many different drawing conventions within each type. Boxes, circles, triangles and so on are all used in various forms, but the symbols themselves are of less important than the underlying geometric ideas in use. That is, each symbol of interest used can be thought of as a single reference 'point' within the schematic containing it. Thus, in the simplest of terms, each can be likened to a point on a piece of paper. Relationships between elements are consequently normally shown as a line between two points. Sometimes such relationships are curved for ease of navigation or effect, but most often straight lines are used. Furthermore, because the order in which elements are presented is important in such diagrams, the lines between elements are generally given an arrow head to show the order in which the schematic should be read – just like the numbering system in the dot-to-dot puzzles we considered earlier. In such cases the schematic in question is given the special name of a 'directed graph', and in circumstances where order is not of importance the first term is of course dropped.

Take all the hype out of graphs like these and they are not too distant from our humble dot-to-dot puzzle. They simply show how one point in a system is linked to another and, optionally, in what order. It is this simplicity that is their greatest strength. Like the puzzle, both the individual lines and points involved convey specific information while their totality can convey something

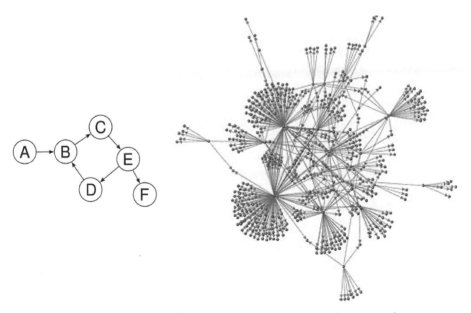

**Figure 2.3(a) and 2.3(b)   Simple and more complex examples
of connected graphs**

far richer. Essentially both dot-to-dot puzzles and graphs are the same in that they hold a solution when complete. Just like a mathematical function, they act as a bridge between an answer and its various subcomponents, their act of completion corresponding to the equals sign in any complete mathematical formula.

Given that the most common form of a graph consists of straight lines drawn between points on a flat plane, such graphs are often thought of as a subset of Euclidian geometry and correspond to the mathematical system laid out in his seminal book *Elements*. This is the earliest known text which systematically discusses geometry and has been one of the most influential books in all of human history, as much for its method as for its mathematical content. The *Elements* begins with plane geometry which is still taught in schools today. It then goes on to discuss the solid geometry of three dimensions, although Euclidean geometry has been successfully extended to any finite number of dimensions. Much of the *Elements* states results of what is now called number theory, proved using geometrical methods.[23]

For over 2,000 years, the adjective 'Euclidean', in relation to geometry, was unnecessary as no other form of geometry had been conceived. Euclid's principles seemed so intuitively obvious that any theorem proved from them was deemed true in an absolute sense. Today, however, we have many other self-consistent non-Euclidean geometries, the first having been discovered in the early nineteenth century. Indeed one consequence of this is that we no longer take it for granted that Euclidean geometry is best for describing physical space. Because of this, one implication of Einstein's theory of general relativity tells us that Euclidean geometry only provides a good approximate description of physical space when the local gravitational field is not too strong.[23] This will prove to be essential to us later, but for now we shall use Euclid's geometry purely to show its inherent weaknesses and especially its weaknesses when used to describe information and computation.

Euclid and the Distance between Two Points

Before going any further it is worth mentioning one very important fact about Euclid's geometry. When any two points are plotted and a straight line is drawn between them, the length of that straight line will always be calculable by a simple formula whose solution will always be finite and measurable.

This length is given by:

$$\text{Distance} = \sqrt{((x_1 - x_2)^2 + (y_1 - y_2)^2)}$$

This is Pythagoras's famous equation and we shall hear more about him and his equation later. But for now, just marvel at its elegance. Its formulation may appear intuitive if not obvious, and some might think it could be applied to every type of line when we need to know its length. But this is not true. A straight line is only one type of line from the vast collection of all possible curves – it being a curve with no curvature – and every single other type of curve's length cannot be measured using Pythagoras's equation. Even so, as long as any line, straight or not, does not go on forever, the idea of measuring its length is still valid. Lines that go on forever, however, present an obvious problem and indeed we now know of some types of line that can be infinitely long, yet still superficially take up very little 'distance'. One such example of a line with infinite length is the Kotch curve. This is comprised of an ever repeating pattern known as a fractal, which is generated by a simple replacement rule. This states that at each step, the middle third of each line segment involved must be replaced with two sides of a right triangle having sides of length equal to the replaced segment. To illustrate, two iterations of this rule on a single line segment give us:

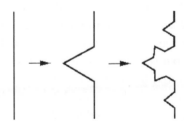

Figure 2.4   The generation of a Koch curve

To generate a true Koch curve, the rule is applied indefinitely over a donor straight line, thereby producing ever increasing levels of intricacy and length in the pattern produced. This type of iterative extension to length needs radically different mathematical attention to calculate its length, but it is still possible with some care. Thus if the length of the initial line segment is l, the length L_k of the Koch curve at the n_{th} iteration of its extension rule can be calculated as:

$$L_k = \left(\frac{3}{4}\right)^n l$$

All of this may appear to have little to do with information and computation but, in fact, its connection is both strong and profound. In essence it dictates that the amount of information contained between any two points in a Euclidean space is limited and that tells us a lot about the ways in which we normally think about information and computation today; that is so long as we use Euclidean graphs as the mean by which we choose to describe both as we do here. Extend this idea slightly and it is also possible to see that each step in a computation or each element in a collection of information can be given a size using some unit scheme or rule[3] and that that size can be calculated by methods like Pythagoras' theorem. It also means that Euclidean graphs with lines of the same length are a distinct possibility. Call such a length a standard unit and such graphs becomes truly important, as they correspond to one of the most fundamental interpretations of computation known to us, by way of a model know as a Turing Machine. Not surprisingly we shall be hearing much more of such machines and alike in the chapters to come.

Projective Geometry Points the Way to a More Open Mind – What is Straight?

One of the first things we learn when we start to study geometry is that a point is a zero dimensional thing, in so much as it can be seen as having position within a particular 'space', but no immediate size along any of that space's dimensions. And if we consider an infinite set of such points, lying side by side, it is quite possible to form a line. As we have already discussed, over 2,000 years ago Euclid told us that if this line lies 'evenly' between its end points, it can be considered as being 'straight.' From this we can immediately notice two things; firstly that such a straight line is defined in terms of its constituent parts, and secondly that the value of any straightness is not defined at all. So, what is 'straight'? Intuitively we might suggest that it is 'evenly', but if Euclid were to have been asked 'what is 'evenly'?' he would most probably have returned by simply stating that it is 'straight'. This would provide us no idea whatsoever as to what straightness is unless we had experienced before we ever thought of such things in geometric terms. In the field of projective geometry, however, it is possible to come at the problem in a different way. In this interpretation of geometry there are three types of most basic ingredient in space, namely the point, the straight line and the plane, of which the latter has the property of 'flatness' – a quality intimately connected with the 'straightness' possessed by a line. Each of these axioms is considered as being of equal weight with the others

---

3   Often referred to as a 'metric'.

as, for instance, a line can be considered as being constructed of an infinite number of points and similarly a point can be considered as being constructed from an infinite number of line intersects passing through it. Straightness and its cousin, flatness, are not normally defined. They are qualities which it is assumed we have already intuitively experienced and understood. And strangely this, which in reality is the most difficult of all matters, normally causes the onlooker the least trouble. For we all 'know' deeply and intuitively what straightness is, and whether a thing is straight or crooked.[26]

During the last century and a half of study, almost all geometry has been seen to be intimately connected with the idea of transformation, which itself is akin to the idea of computation. In modern topology for instance, many sophisticated and very powerful transformations are studied. But if we were to turn to the text books and ask what distinguishes a projective transformation from all others, for instance, text after text would point out that projective transformation are singularly 'algebraic.' And since this little word seems to be a virtually indistinguishable from projective geometry, it is right that we should examine it in more detail.[26]

What do we mean when we say a transformation is 'algebraic?' It simply means that it is something that can be expressed by an algebraic equation. So what does it mean to be algebraic? Let's consider a simple equation and by so doing ask, for example, what the x and y s found in Cartesian, or two-dimensional Euclidean geometry, are. They are certainly not numbers as they normally carry no fixed quantity. But we can say that they are quantity-less elements or 'variables', which nonetheless act according to all the laws of number. So when we say that projective transformations are algebraic, we are in fact specifying that their underlying geometry is one which works according to the laws of number. If we are also looking for reasons to support our belief that projective geometry is specially significant at this point we could hark back to the ancient Pythagorean doctrine that the secret of number is the secret of all things, and that the universe rings with the cosmic music which at all times sounds forth as the nature of number.[26]

But it will perhaps be more useful for us to recall a little more elementary algebra. Remember that if we think about a simple equation with two variables, say x and y, their relationship can be expressed via a simple Cartesian graph. Hence two such simple graphs, as seen in Figures 2.5(a) and 2.5(b), can be thought of with their relevant equations. As they are considered it should be obvious that the first has a unique quality which sets it immediately apart from

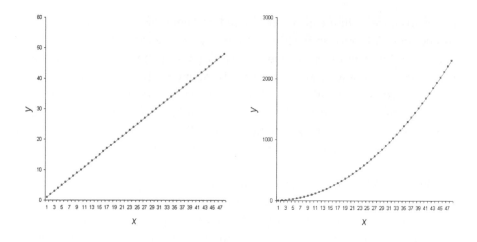

Figures 2.5(a) and 2.5(b)   The Cartesian graphs for $y = x$ and $y = x^2$

the other, in so much as it is straight whereas the other is curved. Furthermore, when the relevant equations are examined to see where the difference lies, it can be seen that the curved graph hold at least one variable bearing an index – the little number in the air above the variable x. In the straight line graph, no such index is present. Actually that's not strictly true. In reality every variable carries an index, but where that index is *1* mathematical convention chooses not to list it. Thus indexes of power *1* are generally silent in most forms of algebraic articulation.

Now we can spell out a general rule: whenever the indices of all an equation's variables are equal then, and only then, will a graph produce a straight line. Given this it is possible to see straightness in a rather different light. This allows us to move towards a substantive definition which may perhaps be even more fundamental than the concept of straightness itself. We can begin to see straightness as that quality that is associated with 'oneness'.[26]

By oneness it is also relevant to read 'equivalence' and ultimately 'symmetry', and such things have particular relevance when considering geometry and computation within any mathematical framework. So, if, for example, we were to consider the possible range of values open for use as indices in straight line equations, the answer is obviously infinite, given that it is possible to think of limits ranging from negative infinity through to positive infinity. It also therefore follows that an infinite number of straight line plots are possible. But here's the thing. If we were to consider the number of equations possible where indices are not equivalent, not only are there an infinite number of opportunities for graphing, but in fact the magnitude of such an infinity must be larger than that where indices equivalence is in place. Furthermore the size of this infinity is not just a little bit bigger, but is significantly bigger. This might appear a mind-bending proposition, as to most the idea of 'infinity' is simply associated with the single largest number there is. But unfortunately infinity does not work like that under the covers. Contemporary mathematics has a number of rabbit holes down which an inquisitive mind can disappear and infinity is one of those. Since the work of Georg Cantor[4] in the second half of the nineteenth century, mathematics has had to come to terms with the idea that there is not just one legitimate definition of infinity, but that there are indeed an infinite number of such legitimate definitions.

Definitions of infinity aside, a very important point has just been made in that there are many more geometric cases where indices are not equivalent than where they are. Hence it is both algebraically and geometrically valid to state that straight lines are a special case rather than the norm. In simple terms that means that curves are much more prevalent in any mathematical space of possibilities and by such a token all fundamental model of transformation and thus computation must be biased towards curvature. In essence, 'curves reign' in the world of computation. This might seem like a tenuous link, but it will be a major thread in the story to follow. If one thinks of the idea of computation as being nothing more than the process of changing input into output, then it immediately becomes clear that it is simply an elaboration on the theme of transformation. Consider next that such transformation can be described both in algebraic and geometric terms and place computing firmly the realms of mathematics. Consider also that information is a very close relative of computation and the same treatment can also be applied. Finally consider that geometry has an inbuilt propensity to favour curved representations over straight and a tension is immediately identified. This is because historically we have been spoonfed Euclid's teachings which have falsely left us with a taste for straightness over curvature. Hence we still try to draw out our ideas with as many straight as we can, even though contemporary mathematics tells us that there might be better ways. In simple terms we have become blinkered and even today many, if not most, graphical interpretations of information and

---

4   Georg Cantor was a mathematician, best known as the inventor of set theory, which has become a fundamental theory in mathematics. Cantor established the importance of one-to-one correspondence between sets, defined infinite and well-ordered sets, and proved that the real numbers are 'more numerous' than the natural numbers. In fact, Cantor's theorem implies the existence of an 'infinity of infinities'.

computing still reach out to the aesthetic simplicity of that which is straight. This is indeed a shame for if we let our imaginations run free and are brave enough to embrace other forms of geometry, then some truly remarkable possibilities start to open up.

Geodesic Relevance

Let your mind's eye focus and think of a box. Not just any type of box, though: think of something like a shoe box or a match box perhaps; the sort that is open to the air across one surface once the lid is lifted. Next think on some small insect, such as a spider, positioned at one of the corners on the upper most lip. Finally pose the spider a problem: if it wanted to follow the shortest route from its current location to the opposite corner in the bottom of the box, what would that path look like? Instinctively you might think that the spider should travel immediately downwards, following the edge of the box made by the nearest two sides, then make a quick dash along a perfectly straight diagonal across the floor of the box – as in Figure 2.6(a). On this occasion, however, instinct is misleading and should the spider follow this route it will travel a certain distance unnecessarily.

A slick technique to solving this brainteaser is to open up the box and lay it flat, as in Figure 2.6(b). Once this is done the actual quickest path becomes overwhelmingly clear and it can be seen that a smart spider would choose to take a route that travels across two of the faces of the box in a rather unexpected

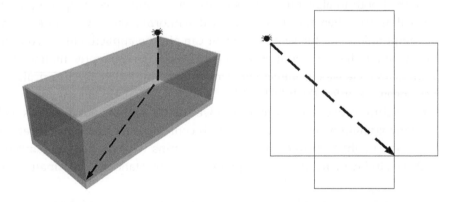

Figures 2.6(a) and 2.6(b)   The spider's routes across the surface of the box

way. This is because the surface across which the spider is being asked to travel isn't flat and this presents a particularly relevant example of a problem that faces us when we think of computation through the use of geometry.

As stressed already, history has formed convention so as to lean us in the direction of using points and straight lines. Project this into the third dimension and we can bring in the concept of flatness. But to push the point once more, such regularities are rare in the set of all possible geometries. Furthermore it is somewhat limiting just to confine such rareness to that which is being described in geometric terms. The very frameworks or 'spaces' within which such geometric descriptions can take place can also be curved rather than 'straight' and the easiest way to think about this is to visualise another problem. Imagine drawing an equilateral triangle on a flat piece of paper and then inspecting all three internal angles. As with all equilateral triangles on a flat plane, each will measure precisely 60°. Now ask yourself if it might at all be possible for these angles to ever be anything else. Again instinct should suggest that this is impossible, but yet again instinct will be proved wrong. Instead of drawing such a triangle on a flat sheet of paper, if we did the same on perfect sphere, the interior angles of the shape would not be 60°, but would rather be a mind-boggling 90°, as can be seen in Figure 2.7b.

The point to this illustration should hopefully be clear, for it elegantly shows how geometry can trip up the unsuspecting. Take a familiar concept like a common-or-garden triangle and view it through a slightly different geometric lens and some quite astonishing things can happen. In just the same way, both information and computing can appear quite different when inspected in different ways. But then that's the whole point behind the serious analysis of any subject. Science is about picking different vantage points and peering in

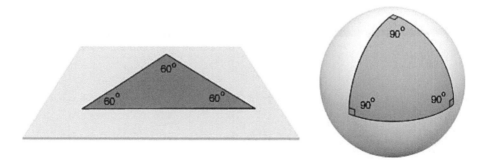

Figures 2.7(a) and 2.7(b)   The interior angles when drawn on a flat plane and a perfect sphere

as deeply as possible. First inspiration allows us to find a new perspective, then investigation probes the new insight that perspective brings, and finally conformation hopefully follows as others clamber to the same view point and compare notes. It is this process that allows us to reach out into the unknown and see beyond the non-obvious. It is this that makes science so valuable to us and it is this that makes science so much fun.

3

Hitler, Turing and Quantum Mechanics

I believe that at the end of the century the use of words and general educated opinion will have altered so much that one will be able to speak of machines thinking without expecting to be contradicted.

Alan Turing

Now that we have trusted in geometry as the language we will use to discuss and describe both information and computation, we need consider the best of modern models that use and apply it. In particular we first need to focus on an understanding of computing and we need to understand how and why this has been updated in recent times.

The history of computing actually goes as far back as it is possible to go; back to the very dawn of the universe itself in fact. This is for good reason as the universe is both the largest and oldest computing device in existence. It takes in information, in the form of matter and space and changes it as it chases the arrow of time. Mankind's own efforts at computing are minuscule by comparison, but it is possible to trace back to the point when cavemen started to roll pebbles around as an aid to understanding the world around them. By doing this they may have perhaps been trying to achieve something computationally very simple, like coming to terms with the number of man-eating predators they had managed to avoid that day. But such pebble-rolling still involved a big leap in abstract thinking and was a significant milestone in our evolution. Number systems came a little later, with herders in the Middle East being understood to have formalised numeric vocabularies so as to account for the livestock they owned. Yet later such number systems were mechanised through the emerging disciplines of philosophy and mathematics, with the Persians commonly being recognised as producing the first man-made computing device in the form of the abacus. From there we have to jump forward many centuries and almost arrive at modern times before we encounter further practical improvements. Mathematicians such as lattice multiplication introduced by Arab mathematicians certainly contributed along the way but it was not until 1822, when Charles Babbage[1] proposed the use of his difference engine in a paper to the Royal Astronomical Society that things really started to move apace. Even so, it wasn't until the mid twentieth century that the real revolution started and the modern digital computer was born.

The Legacy of Two World Wars

The pace at which science and technology advanced in the twentieth century was truly staggering. At its start, horse-drawn transportation was the norm, as was gaslight and hand-pumped water supplies in the cities. Electricity was a luxury for the privileged few, and remote communication was still dominated by the use of pen and paper. Nevertheless an increasing swiftness of change was being felt. The Industrial Revolution had made settlements across the globe swell with an influx of those eager to make their fortune and with them came economic prosperity on a scale unseen before. This struck at the very heart of human nature, driving both individuals and governments to be more defensive, ambitious and ultimately aggressive. Eventually it all boiled over and wars engulfed many nations ensued. The First World War is credited with having taken 15,000,000 lives, but even that was not enough to quell the ever increasing tension. As the industrial powerhouse of Europe began to creak under its success a great depression decended and Adolph Hitler saw his chance to rise to power in Germany. The conflict he would trigger spread across the globe like a plague and its consequences would be written down as one of mankind's worst mistakes.

In the midst of all this turmoil a bright young student was starting to make his mark on the world. Born in Maida Vale, London in 1912, Alan Turing showed a natural inclination toward mathematics and science as a child and was solving advanced problems by the age of 15 without having even studied elementary calculus. This eventually led him to the door of King's College, Cambridge where he graduated with a distinguished degree and in 1935 was elected as a Fellow at King's College on the strength of a dissertation on the central limit theorem.

---

1   Charles Babbage was an English mathematician, philosopher, inventor, and mechanical engineer who originated the concept of a programmable computer.

Midway through 1936 he submitted a momentous paper entitled 'On Computable Numbers, with an Application to the Entscheidungs problem'. This reformulated Kurt Gödel's[2] 1931 results on the limits of proof and computation, replacing Gödel's universal arithmetic-based formal language with what are now referred to as Turing machines – formal and simple devices for undertaking computing.

By 'computing' it's important to understand what Turing was referring to at the time. Rather than thinking of the type of digital marvels we see as humdrum today, Turing thought of computation as a far more human endeavour. In his day computers were typically individuals employed as actuaries and the act of computing referred to dull, repetitive tasks such folk undertook as part of their daily routine. Turing, however, chose to generalise the concept of such mundane work and henceforth proved that his 'machines' were capable of performing most conceivable mathematical problems so long as they could be represented in some form of algorithm. In fact, for many years to come, Turing and most others believed that his machines could compute all algorithms. In effect Turing asked himself, what he did when he computed a result. In doing so he noted that he wrote symbols on a piece of paper, modified the symbols according to a precise set of rules, wrote new symbols down as a function of that stage of the calculation and carried on until, if all went well, he had the answer he wanted. By understanding this Turing abstracted these procedures into a machine comprising a number of internal states given by symbols. In addition it has an infinitely long 'tape' divided into sections onto which one symbol or no symbol can be drawn, and a 'head' which can read the systems from the tape and hence determine the machine's state at any given point. The reading head reads the symbol at a specific starting point on the tape, which tells it to remain in position or move one step to the left or the right, and also tells it whether to write a new symbol on the tape at the current location, depending upon the symbol it reads and the internal state. The process repeats and through this Turing showed that this device could perform most 'effectively computable' computations. Indeed we now loosely define 'effectively computable' to mean computable on a Turing machine.[25]

Turing machines are to this day a central object of study in theory of computation and, Turing went on to prove that there was no solution to the Entscheidungs problem by first showing that the halting problem for Turing machines is undecidable. That is, it is not possible to decide, in general, algorithmically whether a given Turing machine will ever finish its work on

---

2   Kurt Gödel was an Austrian logician, mathematician and philosopher.

a given problem. While his proof was published subsequent to similar work by Alonzo Church,[3] Turing's thoughts are considered more relevant. His proof was also novel in its explanation of a 'Universal (Turing) Machine', which is a Turing machine with the property of being able to read the description of any other Turing machine and carry out what that other Turing machine would have done. It is not at all obvious that such a machine, a machine capable of performing any definite method, could exist. Intuitively we might think that more complex tasks would need more complex machines. In fact they do not and it is sufficient to have a specific limited degree of complexity involved. More laborious tasks only need to have more storage capacity and more time to compute.

Today it is almost impossible to read Turing's 1936 work without thinking of a Turing machine as a computer program, and the Universal Turing Machine as the computer on which different programs can be run.[4] We are now so familiar with the idea of the computer as a fixed piece of hardware, requiring only fresh software to make it do entirely different things, that it is hard to imagine the world without it. But Turing's genius is that he imagined the Universal Turing Machine 10 years before it could be implemented using electronics.

Now we can use modern-day computers to simulate the working of a Turing machine, and use the screen as a window on what in 1936 was only possible in Turing's imagination. This is no accident – the whole point is that the computer embodies the principle of a Universal Turing machine, which can simulate any Turing machine. It was also essential to Turing's 1936 work that a Turing machine could be thought of as data to be read and manipulated by another Turing machine. This is the principle of the modifiable stored program on which almost all electronic computers now depend.

Turing during World War Two and Beyond

Of course World War Two was a truly terrible period, and a defining moment in mankind's history, but not all of its effects were bad. In particular it prompted two things of immediate technological benefit insofar as governments poured more

---

3   Alonzo Church was an American mathematician and logician who made major contributions to mathematical logic and the foundations of theoretical computer science. He is best known for the lambda calculus, Church–Turing thesis, Frege–Church ontology, and the Church–Rosser theorem.

4   If it seems puzzling that a Universal Turing Machine is itself only a particular kind of Turing machine, remember that a computer can be emulated as a program on another computer.

money than ever before into research and development and, more importantly, it concentrated the minds of the some of the world's most brilliant thinkers. Into this boiling caldron of inspiration and activity jumped Alan Turing and it was no coincidence that on 4 September 1939, the day after the UK declared war on Germany, Turing reported to Bletchley Park, the wartime station of Government Code and Cipher School (GCCS) and became deeply involved with breaking German ciphers. First he started building on cryptanalysis work carried out in Poland by Marian Rejewski, Jerzy Różycki and Henryk Zygalski, before the war, and then contributed several insights into breaking both the Enigma machine – an electro-mechanical rotor device used for encryption by the Nazis – and the Lorenz SZ 40/42 cipher. Swept along by the war effort, within weeks Turing had designed an electromechanical machine which could help break Enigma codes faster than ever before. Indeed Professor Jack Good, a cryptanalyst working at the time with Turing at Bletchley Park, later said: 'Turing's most important contribution, I think, was of part of the design of the bombe, the cryptanalytic machine. He had the idea that you could use, in effect, a theorem in logic which sounds to the untrained ear rather absurd; namely that from a contradiction, you can deduce everything.'

In December 1940, Turing worked out a way to crack the naval Enigma indicator system, which was more mathematically complex than the systems used by the other enemy services. In July 1942 he also devised a technique for use against the Lorenz cipher used in the Germans' new Geheimschreiber machine, or 'secret writer', which was one of those codenamed 'Fish'. He also introduced the Fish team to Tommy Flowers who, under the guidance of Max Newman, went on to build the Colossus computer, the world's first programmable digital electronic computer. A frequent misconception, however, is that Turing was a key figure in the design of Colossus; this was not the case, but he was most certainly the driving force behind its architectural blueprint and the ultimate success of the myriad of digital electronic computers that would follow.

In 1945, Turing was awarded the OBE[5] for his wartime services, but his work remained a secret for many years. A biography published by the Royal Society shortly after his death recorded: 'Three remarkable papers written just before the war, on three diverse mathematical subjects, show the quality of the work that might have been produced if he had settled down to work on some big problem at that critical time.'

---

5   Order of the British Empire.

Add a Twist of Quantum Mechanics

Turing's blueprint for a universal computer remained unchallenged for over 30 years until advances in the area of computational complexity began to question the limits of his model. The first publication on computational complexity appeared in 1956, but this Russian work took a long time before it was recognised in the broader academic community of the West. Because of this it was not really until 1967 that the field gained real traction.

At its heart computational complexity holds the problem of algorithmic efficiency, which questions how economically a set of instructions can be computed. What was noticed in the late 1960s and early 1970s was that it seemed as though the classically discrete Turing model of computation was at least as powerful and efficient as any other model of computation. That was in the sense that a problem which could be solved efficiently in some model of computation could also be solved efficiently in the Turing model by using a Turing machine to simulate the other model. This observation was codified into a strengthened version of the famous Church–Turing thesis – a summary of the work simultaneously done by Alonzo Church, Stephen Kleene and J.B. Rosser between 1934 and 1936:

> Any algorithmic process can be simulated efficiently using a Turing machine.

The key strengthening in the strong Church–Turing thesis is critically the word 'efficiently', as if the strong Church–Turing thesis is correct, then it implies that no matter what type of machine we use to compute an algorithm, that machine can be simulated efficiently using a standard Turing machine. This is an important strengthening as it implies that for the purposes of analysing whether a given computational task can be accomplished efficiently, we may be restricted to the analysis of the Turing machine model of computation.

Regardless, despite its clear abilities, a major challenge to the strong Church–Turing thesis arose in the mid 1970s when Robert Solovay and Volker Strassen showed that it is possible to test whether an integer is prime[6] or composite using a randomised algorithm. That is, the Solovay–Strassen test for primality [27][6] used randomness as an essential part of the test. Thus it seemed as though computers with access to a random number generator would

---

6   In mathematics, a prime number (or a prime) is a natural number which has exactly two distinct natural number divisors: 1 and itself.

be able to perform computational tasks efficiently with no efficient solution on a conventional deterministic Turing machine.

Randomised algorithms pose a challenge to the strong Church–Turing model of efficient computation, suggesting that there are efficiently solvable problems which, nevertheless, cannot be efficiently solved on a deterministic Turing machine. This challenge appears to be easily resolved by a simple modification to the strong Church–Turing thesis as follows:

> *Any algorithmic process can be simulated efficiently using a probabilistic Turing machine.*

This ad hoc modification has the potential to threaten the stability of the thesis. Might it not turn out at some later date that yet another model of computation allows the efficient solution to problems that are not efficiently soluble with Turing's model of computation? So, might there be a way to find a single model of computation which is guaranteed to be able to simulate efficiently any other model of computation? Motivated by this question and the concept of fundamentalism in computational models, in 1985 David Deutsch[7] asked whether the laws of physics could be used to derive an even stronger version of the Church–Turing thesis. Deutsch looked to fundamental physical theory to provide a foundation for the Church–Turing thesis that would be as secure as the status of that physical theory. In particular Deutsch attempted to define a computational device that would be capable of simulating any arbitrary physical system. Because the laws of physics are ultimately quantum mechanical,[8] Deutsch was naturally attracted to consider computing devices based upon the principles of quantum mechanics.

A quantum computer is a device for computation that makes direct use of quantum mechanical phenomena, such as superposition and entanglement, to perform operations on data. The basic premise of quantum computation is that quantum properties can be used to represent data and perform operations on it. Although quantum computing is still very much in its infancy, experiments have been carried out in which quantum computational operations have been executed on a very small number of 'qubits', or quantum binary digits. Both practical and theoretical research continues with interest and many ongoing initiatives support quantum computing research to develop quantum

---

7   At the time of going to print David Elieser Deutsch is a physicist at the University of Oxford.
8   That is to say that currently our most axiomatic understandings of the universe are quantum mechanical.

computers for both civilian and national security uses and if large-scale quantum computers can be built, they will be able to solve certain problems much faster than any of our current classical computers.

This move from Turing's vision of computation and that offered by Deutsch is an important one, for it moves the focus away from abstract mathematical theory and firmly places physical models centre stage. Moreover it merges the foundations on which our fundamentals understandings of the real world are based with those of computing in its very purest sense. This is a shocking revelation as computing can be far from 'real' in its many incarnations. Computer graphics have brought us some rather imaginary examples for instance. Today computer-generated films characters like Shrek from Dreamworks Studios are a stalwart of Western popular culture, but would we readily expect to see Shrek walking down the street towards you, Donkey in tow? Of course not, but nevertheless the very stuff from which Shrek and the ground on which he may be walking in this apparition can be explained from the same basic standpoint. In a very bona fide ways Shrek's world and ours result from the act of nothing more than computation and both appear to depend on the most fundamental laws of physics. Most stop in sheer disbelief at this idea, but this is by no means the end of the mind-bending involved.

The history of quantum mechanics essentially began with the 1838 discovery of cathode rays by Michael Faraday, the 1859 statement of the black body radiation problem by Gustav Kirchhoff, the 1877 suggestion by Ludwig Boltsmann that the energy states of a physical system could be discrete and the 1900 quantum hypothesis by Max Planck – that any energy is radiated and absorbed in quantities divisible by discrete 'energy elements'. Although Planck insisted that his idea was simply an aspect of the absorption and radiation of energy and had nothing to do with the physical reality of the energy itself, in 1905 Albert Einstein suggested that light itself consists of individual bundles of energy, which later, in 1926, came to be called photons. From Einstein's simple postulation came an outbreak of debating, theorising and testing which ultimately matured into the entire field of quantum physics.

The Great Conflict in Physics

Quantum mechanics is not the whole picture, however. The modern world of physics is founded on the two tested and demonstrably sound theories of general relativity and quantum mechanics; theories which appear to contradict one another in the deepest of ways. The defining propositions of both Einstein's theory and quantum theory are indisputably supported by rigorous and repeated empirical evidence. Nonetheless, while they do not directly contradict each other theoretically, at least with regard to their major claims, to this day science has proved oblivious to every attempt to link them in a joined-up manner. Furthermore, Einstein himself was well known for discarding some of the claims of quantum mechanics. While clearly creative in this field, he did not accept many of the more philosophical consequences of quantum mechanics, like the lack of deterministic causality and the proposition that a single subatomic particle can occupy numerous areas of space instantaneously. He also was the first to notice some of the apparently exotic consequences of quantum entanglement and use them to formulate the Einstein–Podolsky–Rosen, in the hope of showing that quantum mechanics had unacceptable implications. Regardless of many noble attempts to reconcile the differences between quantum mechanics and general relativity, a divide still exists. There are quantum theories which incorporate special relativity – for example quantum electrodynamics which is currently the most accurately tested of all physical theories – and these lie at the very centre of modern particle physics. But they still do not provide a clear route to a single coherent theory.

Such complications aside, an important point is raised at this stage. Physics is a field which majors on the dynamic transformation of the universe and all that it contains, but it specifically chooses to ground itself through the various 'elements' involved in such dynamics, and absolutely states that such elements must be 'real' in order to take part. The field of computation is identical in all regards apart from one, in that it does not predicate its outputs on the need for anything real to be involved. Thus it is possible to reformulate all of physics into an entirely computational framework, but it is not possible to offer the reverse opportunity. This is simple to see when we consider that it is easy for a computer to model something physical while it is impossible for a computer program to interact with the physical world without the aid of some physical hardware to do so. Computation is hence a descriptive superset of physics and is more encompassing. Physics is part of computation and not the other way round.

Now, if physics can be understood as a computational model and, as already stated, the most encompassing underlying model of computation can be seen as being based on one of the two most fundamental models in physics, what about the fit between physics' other fundamental model and computation? What about the value of Einstein's great gift? Could the idea of general relativity hold significance for computer science? This is a central question addressed underlying the remainder of this book.

4

A Different Perspective on Numbers, Straight Lines and Other Such Mathematical Curiosities

I realise that in this undertaking I place myself in a certain opposition to views widely held concerning the mathematical infinite and to opinions frequently defended on the nature of numbers.

Georg Cantor

Now that we have laid down some basics and started to think about how we might begin to look at information and computation in a different way, there is unfortunately still a need to digress and investigate a couple of commonplace misconceptions in the field of mathematics. Given that many consider computing to have firm roots in mathematics it is only right to pay these attention, given that one of our ultimate goals is to challenge this very premise head on.

Historians have found pictorial evidence dating back long before the earliest written records that indicates some knowledge of elementary mathematics and of time measurement based on the movement of the stars. As an example, palaeontologists have discovered ochre rocks in a cave in South Africa which are about 70,000 years old and are adorned with scratched geometric patterns. Further prehistoric artefacts discovered in Africa and France have been dated as between 35,000 and 20,000 years old and they too suggest early attempts to quantify time.[31] There is even evidence that women devised counting to keep track of their menstrual cycles – 28 to 30 scratches on bone or stone, followed by a distinctive marker.[31] The Ishango bone, found near the headwaters of the Nile River, in the northeastern Congo, may be as much as 20,000 years old. One common interpretation of its purpose is that is the earliest known record of attempts to sequence the prime numbers in the manner of ancient Egyptian multiplication. It is also known that pre-dynastic Egyptians of the fifth millennium BC pictorially represented geometric spatial designs. Likewise, it has been claimed that megalithic monuments in England and Scotland, dating from the third millennium BC, incorporate geometric ideas such as circles, ellipses, and Pythagorean triples in their design.[31]

The earliest known mathematics in ancient India dates from 3000–2600 BC and belongs to the Harappan civilisation of North India and Pakistan. They developed a system of uniform weights and measures that used the decimal system, a surprisingly advanced brick technology which utilised ratios, streets laid out in perfect right angles, and a number of geometrical shapes and designs, including cuboids, barrels, cones, cylinders, and drawings of concentric and intersecting circles and triangles. Mathematical instruments included an accurate decimal ruler with small and precise subdivisions, a shell instrument that served as a compass to measure angles on plane surfaces or in horizon in multiples of 40–360 degrees, a shell instrument used to measure 8–12 whole sections of the horizon and sky, and an instrument for measuring the positions of stars for navigational purposes. The Indus script has not yet been deciphered, hence very little is known about the written forms of Harappan mathematics. Nonetheless, archaeological evidence has led some to suspect that this civilisation used a base eight numeral system and had a value of π, the ratio of the length of the circumference of the circle to its diameter.[31]

The earliest extant Chinese mathematics dates from the Shang Dynasty at around 1600–1046 BC and consists of numbers scratched on a tortoise shell. These numbers were represented by means of a decimal notation. In this case the number 123 is written, from top to bottom, as the symbol for 1 followed by the symbol for 100, then the symbol for 2 followed by the symbol for 10, then the symbol for 3. This was the most advanced number system in the world at the time and allowed calculations to be carried out on the 'suan pan' or Chinese abacus. The date of the invention of the suan pan is not certain, but the earliest record dates from AD 190, in Xu Yue's *Supplementary Notes on the Art of Figures*. [31]

Given such ancient roots, the idea of mathematics and all it contains appears so familiar to us all today. But history has a habit of playing tricks and science is littered with examples where incorrect or incomplete prior art has diverted the search for truth substantially. The work of Isaac Newton is a case in point. Even though his laws of motion led to significant advances in the late seventeenth centaury, it took over two hundred years for science to realise that they don't work at astronomic scales. It is true that several further advances in science and mathematics would be needed before Einstein overtook Newton's genius, but the fact that few sought to challenge Newton's insight obviously retarded progress in physics. Indeed, complexity of the mathematics involved aside, it is still Newton's ideas that are quoted before Einstein's in the normal run of education, even though the more modern work subsumes all prior breakthroughs. The same is also true of mathematics and to prove the point we shall start with something fundamental and pick on the concept of numbers.

Make a clenched fist with either hand and place it firmly in your field of view. Now slowly start to spread your fingers back out in order, one by one. As you do, count the number of extended fingers as they unfold: one, two, three and so on. The system used here, which we commonly refer to as counting, should be familiar to all given that it is one of the schemes taught to children around the world as part of their elementary education. From this falls out a familiar type of number, and the one that most would recognise if asked for a starter description of numbers on the spot. These are counting, or 'natural' numbers, often referred to as $\mathbb{N}$ in mathematical circles, and they can be seen to stretch from one to infinity thus:

1,2,3,4,5 ... ... ∞

The next type of number scheme is that of the 'whole' numbers, which are comprises natural numbers together with zero:

0, 1, 2, 3, 4, 5, 6, ... ∞

Then come the 'integers', again often referred to by mathematicians using the letter $\mathbb{Z}$, and these involve the natural numbers, zero and the negatives of the naturals:

$-\infty$ ... ... , −6, −5, −4, −3, −2, −1, 0, 1, 2, 3, 4, 5, 6, ... ∞

Following on come the 'rational', or fractional, numbers whose mathematical symbol is $\mathbb{Q}$. These are technically regarded as ratios or *divisions* of integers. Or, in other words, a fraction is formed by dividing one integer by another integer.

Observe that each new type of number contains the previous type within it. The wholes are just the naturals with zero thrown in, the integers are just the wholes with the negatives thrown in and the fractions are just the integers with all their divisions thrown in; remember that we can turn any integer into a fraction by putting it over the number one – a fact that will become extremely important to us later.[32]

Once fractions have been introduced they lead on to another major classification of numbers – those that can't be written as fractions. Remember that some fractions can be written as decimals of finite length, like 0.5, 0.76 and so on. A further collection can be written as a recurring decimal that trails off forever and the faction 1/3 – formed decimally as 0.3333 ... – can be seen as a perfect illustration of this. There are, however, some numbers that cannot be written so cleanly and not surprisingly there are referred to as the 'irrationals'. Examples include the square root of two and the constant π. That is to say 3.14159 ... ... in decimal, from geometry. The rationals and the irrationals are two totally separate number types; there is no overlap.[32]

Putting these two major classifications together gives us the 'real' numbers, represented by the mathematical symbol $\mathbb{R}$, but this is still not the end of the story. There are some numbers that do not compute naturally. For instance there is a mathematical rule which states that if we multiply any negative number by another negative, the answer produced always comes out as positive value. This, of course, includes the special group of multiplications, known as squares, in which a negative might be multiplied by itself to produce a positive number. This creates a problem for mathematicians as it leaves a hole in the landscape of all possible numbers by missing out the possibility for negative numbers having square roots. So how, for example, might it be possible to calculate the square root of minus one ($\sqrt{-1}$), if minus one squared (-1^2) is positive 1?

Mathematics got around this problem by inventing a new number around the time of the Reformation. At that time nobody believed that any 'real world' use would be found for this new number other than easing the computations involved in solving certain equations. Because of this it was viewed as being a pretend number invented for convenience sake. This new member of the number family was named 'i', after 'imaginary', because 'everybody knew' that i wasn't 'real'. Thus calculations purely involving this type of number are still referred to as being imaginary ($\mathbb{Z}$) and the imaginary (i) itself is defined as:

$$i = \sqrt{-1}$$

Therefore:

$$i^2 = \left(\sqrt{-1}\right)^2 = -1$$

But this may lead falsely to the conclusion that:

$$i^2 = \left(\sqrt{-1}\right)^2 = \left(\sqrt{-1^2}\right) = \sqrt{1} = 1$$

Nevertheless this isn't logical. There are already two numbers that square to 1; namely –1 and +1. And i already squares to –1. So it's not reasonable to suggest that i should also square to 1. This points out an important detail in that when dealing with imaginary numbers we gain something, in the ability to deal with negatives inside square roots, but also lose something in that some of the flexibility and convenient rules we used to have when dealing with square roots are changed. In particular, we must always deal with the imaginary part of any equation first.

Thus:

$$\sqrt{-9} = \sqrt{9 \times (-1)} = \sqrt{9} \times \sqrt{-1} = \sqrt{9} \times i = 3i$$

Now that imaginary numbers are out of the way, fortunately our classification of numbers is nearly complete, but there is still one final common place type of number that needs to be considered. These are called 'complex' numbers and their definition is not that far removed from that of the imaginary number i. Quite simply, complex numbers are an extension of the real numbers obtained by adjoining an imaginary unit. The set of all complex numbers is usually denoted by $\mathbb{C}$ in mathematical terms and are very often written in the form:

$$a + ib$$

where a and b are real ($\mathbb{R}$) numbers, and i is the imaginary unit as explained earlier. The real number a is called the real part of a complex number, and the number b the imaginary part. For example, $3 + 2i$ is a complex number, with real part 3 and imaginary part 2.

Further number types do exist, such as Algebraic numbers, transcendental numbers, quaternions, octonions, sedenions, Cayley-Dickson construction and split-complex numbers, but these are mostly confined to higher mathematics an need not trouble us for the purpose of our story.

When Greed Gets in the Way

Now that our quick tour of numbers is complete, we should spend some time thinking about what numbers actually are. Their use is so commonplace in our modern-day world that we often forget what they are actually about and what creates them. We almost trade them as objects through their familiarity alone: 'four' is just four, we think. It stands on its own without any further explanation needed. But this is wrong and to trivialise numbers in such a way is a mistake. Numbers are not isolated objects, as indeed the very term 'object' itself is often trivialised and misinterpreted. Numbers are actually the outcome of an act of creation, not something that just 'exist' in a vacuum. They are the output of some act of doing, some form of computation. Just as a chair may be an object that is the created from the labours of a carpenter, so all numbers are the output of some mathematical equation's work. To get to four, for instance, we have to perhaps understand what precedes it in the series of integers. We have to understand and justify its order in this standing by the act of counting from zero upwards. In such a way the number four becomes synonymous with that very act of counting with limits applied. This makes the number that very act of limited accounting. And indeed it is only by thinking of numbers in terms of the act that creates them that a true definition can be found. Furthermore there is some relevant word play involved here. The terms 'act' and 'computation' are perfectly interchangeable in such a definition, so numbers, all numbers, are merely computed quantities. In such a sense, so are all objects as they are merely the product of taking in a collection of raw materials and changing them into some composite new thing.

> All numbers are the output of some computation and are thus synonymous with that computation

Conjecture 5   Numbers and Computation are Synonymous

Now let's return to the history books again and not forget why numbers came to prominence in the first place. Numbers obviously relate to the notion of quantity in some way – the amount of something that might be relevant to a particular problem or circumstance. The question is – how? To answer this, two particular verbs come to mind in that numbers *account* for or *measure* something in relation to something else. They tell us how big something is in accordance with a known *scale*. So hold that thought, think about the word 'scale' and literally conjure it up in imagination.

Look up 'scale' in the dictionary and a definition like the following will soon be found:

> Scale: *Often, scales. a balance or any of various other instruments or devices for weighing: We gave the parents a baby scale. The butcher placed the meat on the scales.*

This gives more insight into the history of mathematics, and indeed the whole of science, than might at first be apparent, for it provides a motive behind centuries of investment in the field of numbers. The term 'scale' obviously has a literal meaning as an instrument for the purpose of measurement and its first and primary use will have been as a means to engage in fair trade. In short, numbers and their associated scales have provided, and still provide, a means by which possession can be gauged and commercial exchange can be regulated. In turn this makes explicit the relationship between numbers and the concepts of wealth and standing. So, in general, the more someone is perceived to own or possess, the greater the wealth and standing associated and the greater the importance of numbers in their life. This uncovers another hidden and important twist. Possession, wealth and trade are all economic constructs, heavily biased towards the promotion of growth or expansion. They all have mathematical underpinnings in that all concentrate on the mathematical operation of addition, the process of putting things together to make a greater whole. Multiplication is similar too in that it can be viewed as simply a faster way of achieving the same ends as addition. Hence, for purely historical and cultural reasons, it could be argued that mathematics and all its number systems may itself be prejudiced towards computations that achieve cumulative effect. However, if we choose to take a broader view, this is surely not the case. Numbers can just as equally be seen to function in an opposing manner. If a merchant of old were seen to own a vast pile of gold coins he could just as well use numbers as a means of identifying how his fortune were composed, breaking it down into smaller piles of coins of whatever denomination. In such a way, mathematics and the numbers it reigns over can act both as glue and knife, able to stick things together and split then apart.

Furthermore, if we were to look at the number systems themselves there is some logic in arguing that mathematics is itself biased against the historical and cultural preferences outlined above. As we have already seen, there is a natural order to the way in which the various number systems are arranged. Like the shells of a Russian doll, naturals fit within integers, which fit with in rationals, irrationals and so on. The further into the order we go, the more dependency there is on being able to specify smaller and more complex units of representation. Naturals and integers may appears as 'whole' units in their own right, but after that there is an absolute reliance on being able to split such wholes down in to ever more exquisite detail so as to allow classification to take place. Reach the point where the rational number scheme is introduced and 'wholeness' simply loses its value. What's more, as one number system sits within the other it must be possible to represent lower-order schemes in terms of higher-order mathematics. Thus rationals can be described in exactly the same way as irrationals, and if their fractional element runs out within a few decimal places it is possible to think of a number running out to infinity, simply by adding an infinite tail of zeros. So it is the way with integers and rationals, in that all whole numbers can simply be thought of as a fraction whose lowest denominator is one and an infinite number of zeros following after the decimal point.

This brings us on to the main point about numbers. Already it has been explained that it is better to think about numbers as functions or, better still, computations involving fractions, but it is better still if we give such computations a general classification. So here it is:

> All numbers, can be thought of as computations for use in splitting

Reinterpretation 1   On the definition and use of numbers

We shall see the value of such an assertion in later chapters, but for now the vital point to take away is that the idea of splitting is critical to mathematics and that that naturally follows through into understandings of information and computing. In fact all forms of logic are built upon it in one way or another.

Not All Edges Are Straight

Never underestimate the power of what has gone before: although it is generally considered that the Greeks inherited their early mathematics from the Babylonians and the Egyptians, the legacy they eventually passed on is considerable. Historians traditionally place the beginning of Greek mathematics to the age of Thales of Miletus, at around 624–548 BC. Little is known about his life and work, so little in fact that his day of birth and death are estimated from the eclipse of 585 BC, which occurred while he was probably in his prime. Despite this it is generally agreed that Thales was the first of the seven wise men of Greece. The Theorem of Thales, which states that an angle inscribed in a semicircle is a right angle, may have been learned by Thales while in Babylon but tradition has it that he provided a demonstration of the theorem. It is for this reason that Thales is often hailed as the father of the deductive organisation of mathematics and as the first true mathematician. Thales is also thought to be the earliest known man in history to whom specific mathematical discoveries have been attributed. Although it is not known whether or not Thales was the one who introduced into mathematics the logical structure that is so ubiquitous today, it is known that within 200 years of Thales the Greeks had introduced logical structure and the idea of proof into mathematics.[33]

Another important figure in the development of Greek mathematics is Pythagoras of Samos (*c.*580–500 BC). Like Thales, Pythagoras also travelled to Egypt and Babylon, but settled in Croton, Magna Graecia. Pythagoras established an order called the Pythagoreans, which held knowledge and property in common and hence all of the discoveries by individual Pythagoreans were attributed to the order. In antiquity it was customary to give all credit to the master, so Pythagoras himself was given credit for the discoveries made by his order. Aristotle for one refused to attribute anything specifically to Pythagoras as an individual and only discussed the work of the Pythagoreans as a group. One of the most important characteristics of the Pythagorean order was that it maintained that the pursuit of philosophical and mathematical studies was a moral basis for the conduct of life. Indeed, the words 'philosophy' (love of wisdom) and 'mathematics' (that which is learned) are said to have been coined by Pythagoras. From this love of knowledge came many achievements, not least of which were most of the material in the first two books of Euclid's *Elements* – the most successful and influential textbook ever written.[33]

Euclid, also known as Euclid of Alexandria, lived during the Hellenistic period and is the historical figure often referred to as the Father of Geometry.

He is most commonly believed to have been a Greek mathematician, active in Alexandria during the reign of Ptolemy I between 323 BC and 283 BC. Little is known about Euclid and some now claim that there is no conclusive evidence either of his authoring the *Elements* or even of his having existed. Nonetheless even if he is partially or entirely fictitious, Euclid is a very important figure in the history of mathematics and science.[34]

Euclid's *Elements* is believed to have been written around 300 BC and is a mathematical and geometric discourse consisting of 13 books. It is still considered a masterpiece in the application of logic to mathematics. In historical context, it has proven enormously influential in many areas of science. Scientists like Nicolaus Copernicus,[1] Johannes Kepler,[2] Galileo Galilei,[3] and Sir Isaac Newton[4] were all patently influenced by the *Elements*, and applied their knowledge of it to their work. Indeed, so influential is the work that mathematicians and philosophers like as Bertrand Russell,[5] Alfred North Whitehead[6] and Benedict de Spinoza[7] have all attempted to create their own foundational 'Elements' for application in their respective disciplines, by adopting the axiomatised deductive structures that Euclid's work first introduced.[34]

The success of the *Elements* is due primarily to its logical presentation of most of the mathematical knowledge available in Euclid's day. Much of the

---

1   Nicolaus Copernicus was a Renaissance astronomer and the first person to formulate a comprehensive heliocentric cosmology, which displaced the Earth from the centre of the universe.
2   Johannes Kepler was a German mathematician, astronomer and astrologer, and key figure in the seventeenth-century scientific revolution. He is best known for his eponymous laws of planetary motion, codified by later astronomers, based on his works *Astronomia Nova*, *Harmonices Mundi*, and *Epitome of Copernican Astronomy*. They also provided one of the foundations for Isaac Newton's theory of universal gravitation.
3   Galileo was an Italian physicist, mathematician, astronomer and philosopher who played a major role in the Scientific Revolution. His achievements include improvements to the telescope and consequent astronomical observations, and support for Copernicanism. Galileo has been called the 'father of modern observational astronomy,' the 'father of modern physics,' the 'father of science' and 'the Father of Modern Science.'
4   Sir Isaac Newton was an English physicist, mathematician, astronomer, natural philosopher, alchemist, and theologian who is considered by many scholars and members of the general public to be one of the most influential people in human history. His 1687 publication of the *Philosophiæ Naturalis Principia Mathematica* (usually called the *Principia*) is considered to be among the most influential books in the history of science, laying the groundwork for most of classical mechanics.
5   Bertrand Russell was a British philosopher, logician, mathematician, historian, socialist, pacifist, and social critic.
6   Alfred North Whitehead was an English mathematician who became a philosopher. He wrote on algebra, logic, foundations of mathematics, philosophy of science, physics, metaphysics, and education.
7   Benedict de Spinoza was a Dutch philosopher of Portuguese Jewish origin.

material is not original to him, although many of the proofs are his. All the same, Euclid's systematic development of his subject, from a small set of fundamental principles to deeply important results, and the consistency of his approach throughout, encouraged its use as a textbook for about 2,000 years. The *Elements* still influences modern geometry books today. What's more, its logical self-evident approach and rigorous proofs remains the cornerstone of mathematics. But this can be seen as much of a disadvantage as it is an advantage, given that his rigor can sometimes blinker even the brightest of students and leave them less open to accepting the much wider spectrum of geometries now available in modern mathematics.

Although the *Elements* is primarily a geometric work, it also includes results that today would be classified as number theory, and thus it has bearing on contemporary algebra. A construction used in any of Euclid's proofs required a proof that it is actually possible. This avoids the problems the Pythagoreans had with irrationals, since their misleading proofs usually required a statement such as 'Find the greatest common measure of ...'.

Volume one of the *Elements* begins with 23 definitions, such as point, line and surface, and then goes on to specify five postulates and five 'common notions ', all of which are today called axioms. These are the foundation of all that follows as his legacy:

- Postulates:

  - A straight line segment can be drawn by joining any two points.
  - A straight line segment can be extended indefinitely in a straight line.
  - Given a straight line segment, a circle can be drawn using the segment as radius and one end-point as centre.
  - All right angles are equal.
  - If two lines are drawn which intersect a third in such a way that the sum of the inner angles on one side is less than two right angles, then the two lines inevitably must intersect each other on that side if extended far enough.

- Common notions:

  - Things which equal the same thing are equal to one another (Euclidean property of equality).

- If equals are added to equals, then the sums are equal (addition property of equality).
- If equals are subtracted from equals, then the remainders are equal (subtraction property of equality).
- Things which coincide with one another are equal to one another (reflexive property of equality).
- The whole is greater than the part.

Now here comes the crunch: these basic principles reflect the interest of Euclid, along with his contemporary Greek and Hellenistic mathematicians, in constructive geometry. The first three postulates basically describe the constructions anyone can carry out with a compass and an unmarked straight edge – a marked ruler being forbidden in Euclid construction.[34] This may seem an innocent enough declaration, and indeed, in isolation, it is, but when the overall effect of its influence is considered down the ages, its impact becomes quite profound. To understand this, we have to pay attention to the term 'straight edge' and further understand that this dictates a fundamental reliance on straightness for Euclid's form of geometry to work. It is also interesting that the *Elements* makes no attempt to deny its dependence on the tools available to philosophers of the time. This is obviously why the compass and the straight edge receive such emphasis: in that period they could be trusted implicitly and on such grounds those who derived new thinking from their use could have confidence in the validity of their reasoning and ideas. But that's not where the emphasis on straightness stops. Just as the certainty inherent to the straight edge and compass was imparted to the *Elements,* so was this certainty passed on to those who referenced the *Elements* as a trusted text. This sent waves of intellectual enslavement out into the future all the way to our present day. This causes obvious problems for it is very well to say that all good advances in human knowledge are based on the certainties of what has gone before, but it should be remembered that greater truths may lie just out of reach and demand letting go of all that we know as 'truth'. This is particularly true in the sciences, where incremental advances are most often seen as the most solid. Thus, given the profile of, and confidence in, Euclid's work over the ages, it should come as no surprise that most advances have been made in areas closely aligned to 'straightness'. Think of systems that change over time for instance. In these 'dynamic' systems we can most often, and quite legitimately, change 'straightness' to read 'linearity' and this provides a predominant reason why the study of linear systems has historically seen great attention and gained some very well-known successes.

Not surprisingly too, look up 'linear' in the dictionary and you will find:

- adjective

1.   *of, consisting of, or using lines: linear design.*

2.   *pertaining to or represented by lines: linear dimensions.*

3.   *extended or arranged in a line: a linear series.*

4.   *involving measurement in one dimension only; pertaining to length: linear measure.*

5.   *of or pertaining to the characteristics of a work of art in which forms and rhythms are defined chiefly in terms of line.*

6.   *having the form of or resembling a line: linear nebulae.*

7.   *Mathematics.*

  i.   *consisting of, involving, or describable by terms of the first degree.*
  ii. *having the same effect on a sum as on each of the summands: a linear operation.*

8.   *Electronics. delivering an output that is directly proportional to the input: a linear circuit; a linear amplifier.*

9.   *threadlike; narrow and elongated: a linear leaf.*

Origin:

1635–45; belonging to lines

There is an obvious reliance on the notion of lines here, but there is also a hidden dependency. If we know where a line starts – where its point of origin is – and the direction in which it is heading, we can predict any desired point along its course. In short, lines are predictable and by such a token so are most of the problem areas studied by science up to all but the most recent of times. Isaac Newton's famous equations of motion are linear, for instance, in that we can use them to predict any given future state of a system in motion so long as we know enough information about its current condition. Famously herein can be seen not only one of the greatest advances in science, but also one of its greatest retardants, for through its success was also granted greater faith in the 'truth and value of straightness'.

Because of this strength of faith it might seem strange to ask why anyone should want to diminish its value. But this is an important challenge and one that results in an elegantly simple answer, as we have already seen. Remember that not all lines are straight and that not all systems are predictable or linear in straightforward ways. If it were not for history's cosy relationship with the *Elements* and its adoration of the straight line, then it is quite plausible that even greater discoveries would have been made by Newton and his contemporaries down the ages. With hindsight, Euclid is equally as likely to have held back science as to have accelerated it.

How Infinity helped to Overthrow Euclid

Georg Cantor was a German mathematician, born in Russia in the mid eighteenth century. He is best known as the creator of set theory, which later became one of the foundations of modern mathematics. Cantor established the importance of one-to-one correspondence between sets, defined infinite and well-ordered sets, and proved that the real numbers are 'more numerous' than the natural numbers. All of these are important contributions to mathematics but it is his insight into infinity and the fact that there may well be an 'infinity of infinities'[35] that should be of particular interest to us.

Through his work Cantor started a revolution he never intended or wanted simply by posing himself a straightforward question – how big is infinity? Although his eventual answer proved an incredible feat of imagination, others had also chosen to play with this brainteaser before. Galileo Galilei, the Italian physicist, mathematician, astronomer and philosopher had earlier thought about circles and realised that they are simply shapes with an infinite number of infinitesimally small, straight sides. This creates an illogical paradox, as Galileo understood, as if we draw a bigger circle outside the one just drawn, split it into an infinite number of straight sides, then draw lines out from the centre of both, the divergence of these lines means that there are gaps in the infinite division of the outer circle. This then means that more lines are needed to radiate out from the central point in order to create infinite division in the outer circle. But of course this is impossible, as an infinite number of divisor lines already exist. This perplexed Galileo to the point that he gave up on the problem, declaring it impossible to understand the infinite.

Cantor broke through Galileo's obstinacy by considering a smooth curve of motion, made of an infinite number of infinitesimally small straight lines. In this, each line represents an instant in which nothing moves. Like frames of film, if we run one after another we get motion. The whole thing relies on infinity, but it works and Cantor knew that. But he also knew that the very notions of the infinitesimal and the infinite are not really valid in this context. No matter how far we divide the curve it is always valid to consider further partitioning. The reverse is the same when it comes to infinity, in that it is equally as valid to consider the concept of onwardly adding infinity to infinity, no matter how large each infinity is in turn. So, or in Cantor's mind at least, there could never be any meaning to anything being either the 'smallest' or the 'largest' thing possible. For Cantor there was a range of infinities that stretched on an infinite number of times.

Of particular relevance, Cantor's reasoning can be thought of in terms of magnification and can also be used to question the validity of a straight line's definition. Suppose we have a perfectly straight line of infinite length. We create it and let it stand on its own. Now let's zoom out, courtesy of one of Cantor's higher-level infinities. At this point only one of two possible observations are of interest geometrically; either our original infinite line is part of a longer infinite line, or it represents merely one section of an infinitely larger curve, as the workings of Cantor's theory might possibly suggest. This again is logically paradoxical as there is a need to trade the individual definitions and scales of the infinities involved for any real detail of the proposition to make sense. This is, of course, impossible, so there is only one sensible conclusion to draw in that it is as equally valid to consider a straight line to be as curved as it is straight!

This might seem ludicrous, until one learns that there are always two possible types of curvature at play in any one given situation. The first is referred to as *intrinsic* curvature, or that curvature that is possessed by the immediate *thing* under consideration, while the second is referred to as *extrinsic* curvature, which relates to the curvature of the space or plane in which the immediate *thing* is being considered. Extrinsic curvature is hence more significant than intrinsic curvature, as its presence overpowers, or subsumes, any intrinsic curvature in a domain or region over which it spreads, no matter how many dimensions[8] are involved.

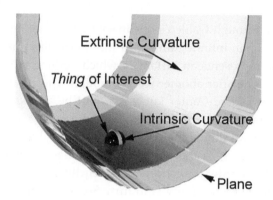

Figure 4.1   Intrinsic and extrinsic curvature in a plane and its contents

This may appear a million miles from anything to do with information and computing, but it's not. Advances in mathematics and science, especially during the last century, have started to lift the lid on certain types of systems that are anything but 'straight', and geometry is often the preferred means of discussing and describing such new types of 'non-linear' system. Furthermore, wherever the term 'system' comes into play, we can be sure that it relates to some kind of computation. All systems, no matter what their type, also contain information of one form or another and, in the end, it all simply falls down to how precious we are about your own individual interpretation of both. All that can truly be said, however, is that:

> There is no compelling reason to favour straightness over curvature when considering a generic geometric framework (for the purpose of understanding computation and information)

Reinterpretation 2   On the use of lines over curves in any definition of computation and information

---

8   May also be read as 'degrees of freedom'.

5

Twists, Turns and Nature's Preference for Curves

Far from showing that human beings are 'nothing but machines', it confirms our insistence that we are essentially subjective creatures living through our own mental constructions of reality.

Margaret Boden

Now we need to return to geometry again and how it might be used as a language for describing information and computation. In doing so, it is important for us to remember that not all forms of computation are restricted to the synthetic domains of electronic machines like those born from Turing's ideas. The natural world computes as well and this becomes overly apparent when one thinks of computation purely in terms of symmetry and change. As a tree grows, a kind of computation is taking place as the seed transforms itself into a sapling and then on into a fully matured system of branches, leaves and roots. So too a mountain computes. It may be laid down by millennia of dying crustaceans at the bottom of some ancient ocean, or be thrown up as if overnight by some gigantic volcanic eruption, but still, at some point in the past, its form will have been somewhat different to that of today. What's more, at some arbitrary date in the future it is almost entirely certain that it will be different yet again. No matter how small or discreet, some form of change will have taken place and computing will have been done.

When trying to make comparisons between the types of 'natural' [9] computation found in the physical world and more synthetic variants such as those found in systems like the World Wide Web, one fact must be remembered, in that by definition, real-world computing manifests itself through physical presence and the observable change[1] of that presence over time. Thus the blooming of a flower, the weathering of a rock face and the collision of two subatomic particles all hold up as equal examples of computation in the raw.

---

1   The term 'change' can also be seen as meaning 'pattern'.

To appreciate the lack of distinction it is necessary to cut to the very core of computing and examine the underpinning fundamentals that transcend all of its possible variants. Such a reductionist viewpoint relies heavily on underlying mathematical formality and for such reason the fundamental patterns on which computing itself is built are also intrinsically formal and, by implication, inherently simple. Simple, that is, in a mathematical sense.[2]

The concept of sets is central to systems theory,[3] of which computation is a significant part. Set theory is the mathematical study of collections. It encompasses the everyday idea of collecting objects or ideas together to consider them in unison and includes thinking to help describe the various elements and collective relationships involved. Accordingly it is, along with logic, one of the many cornerstones of mathematics. This is again important to us, as all mathematics can in the broadest sense be viewed in terms of sets as well – a set being seen as a collection of things which can be thought of as a single object.[10] Furthermore, from a computational perspective, four main themes of categorisation overlay basic set theory. These can be seen as concerning:

Table 5.1   A summary of computational categorisation themes

	Categorisation	Computational Properties Derived
1	The identifiable objects* and concepts that any computation is interested in	• Identity • Addressability
2	The associations, constraints and/or transformations between those objects and concepts	• Association • Transformation • Connectivity
3	The methods of grouping both objects and concepts together	• Aggregation • Abstraction • Encapsulation
4	The types of the objects, concepts, associations and groups used.	• Typing

* Here the term 'object' is used in a loose sense.

---

2   Requires a small amount of information to describe.[21]
3   Systems theory,[88] in its broadest sense, is the interdisciplinary study of organisation within the context of a definitive system. It covers a wide range of fields, including mainstream digital computing.

Key to the idea of sets in computing is the property of 'discreteness' across both membership and set definition. That is unambiguous differentiation across all aspects, attributes and components involved in the grouping characteristics of a given system, with regard to both static spatial qualities and temporal transformations.

Paul Benacerraf's [102] work in this area has proved seminal as he introduced the concept of mathematical structuralism in the 1960s. Through this, Benacerraf addressed the view in mathematics which treats mathematical statements at face value, so committing mathematical formulae to a realm of eternally abstract objects and concepts with no direct connection to the real world. Benacerraf further posed a dilemma, questioning how we can actually come to know such objects or concepts if no causal relation with the observer is in place. In other words how can mathematical concepts, or abstract notions of computing, be of any value if they have no direct effect in the real world? Benacerraf further questioned why multiple set theories exist that allow the reduction of elementary number theory into sets, so raising the problem of which set theory is true.

The answer to Benacerraf's concerns led to structuralism becoming a viable philosophical school of thought within mathematics. This is through the belief that the essence of mathematical concepts or variables lies in their relationships with the wider structure of their mathematical context as a whole. This rhetoric then runs on into the area of computational theory, providing a firm basis on which to explain the same concepts in a wider 'systems' context. Structures are hence exemplified in abstract systems in terms of the relations that hold true for that system.

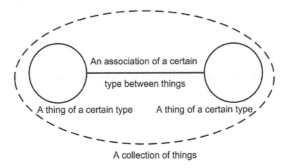

Figure 5.1   The basic triple model[4]

---

4   In mathematics, a triple is an *n*-tuple with *n* being 3. A triple is a sequence of three elements. It is not a set of three elements, as the ordering of the elements matters, and an element can be

At its most mathematically simple, structuralism can be seen to generate graph structures commonly referred to as 'triples'. These can be considered as depicting the smallest sequence of constituents required to form a line or 'arc' within a conceptual graph – that sequence being the encapsulation of a single predicating relationship between a *subject* and *object* node – a start and end point in simple terms. It is important to note that on their own such patterns do not contain enough content to adequately address the entire range of differentiation needed across graph axioms,[5] however. This is because at least two arcs and two nodes are needed to demonstrate differentiation across both arc and node types and hence outline the full vocabulary of axiomatic Lagrangian[6] interaction patterns possible. This is also a concept needed to form the most basic 'true/false' construct in Boolean logic and the fundamental unit of distinction in the physical world – a concept often referred to as 'symmetry breaking'.[40][2]

Symmetry is a regularly used term, often interpreted to mean 'balance' or perhaps 'harmony', or sometimes even 'beauty'. Mathematics and physics carry an inbuilt appreciation for the same qualities in symmetry, but also use a more stringent definition, stating that 'something has symmetry if one or more of its properties remain unchanged when some other property is changed'.[7][40] A group of 10 identical objects possesses symmetry; line them up and it's impossible to know if any or all of them have switched position in the line. But if the line were composed of five objects that had one shape, followed by five that had another, some of the symmetry is broken by observable variation. Swapping numbers five and six, for instance, would produce an obvious change.

To help visualise this idea, graphs similar to Feynman diagrams found in quantum mechanics [2] can be used as a means of expressing the patterns involved. Such graphs are typically used to show how particular or possible aspects of a system interrelate or change, capturing relationships or transitions between a system's individual elements or states in a graphical form. Several variations of such diagrams exist. In one variant the steady state of a system

---

present more than once in the same triple.

5   Individual arcs and nodes.

6   A Lagrangian $\mathcal{L}[\varphi_i]$ of system undergoing continuous change or activity is a function that summarises the dynamics of the system. It can also be considered as a description of the interaction between fundamental 'elements/constituents' at a particular level of abstraction.

7   An equally good definition also states that a symmetry is an operation that doesn't change how something behaves relative to the outside world. For example, one can rotate a ball and it does not necessarily change as it is still a sphere.[2]

can be drawn as an arc between two points or nodes, often drawn as circles if at all. Alternative representations can choose to use the reverse convention, using nodes to represent steady states or constituent parts and arcs to represent transitions or relationships between them. Arcs can thereby represent a 'step' in the characteristic(s) of the underlying system or problem space being studied. In their sparsest forms, like Feynman's schematics, such diagrams describe the interaction between two facets of a system as a quantified outline of their interaction.

A graph drawing should not be confused with the graph itself, the abstract, non-graphical structure which it represents. What matters is which vertices are connected to which others by how many arcs and not the exact layout – although thinking we will encounter in later chapters does rely on layout precision. In practice it is often difficult to decide if two drawings are isomorphic and hence represent the same graph. Depending on the problem domain some layouts may be better suited and easier to understand than others.

As explained earlier, graphs using just arcs between nodes imply that the relationships involved are commutative.[8] Graphs containing arrows instead of lines imply directionality or relational order. At the start of any such arrow, the point at which a system last became stable is hence represented, and at its tip is the point at which the system ultimately changes condition. Such change can also be understood as a break in the underlying system's symmetry. Graphs can hence be seen as being generically isomorphic in their capability to describe structural and transformational characteristics of a system or problem space.

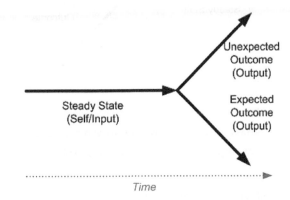

Figure 5.2   A state-based directed graph showing spontaneous bifurcation: an example of the 'Y'-shaped pattern

---

8   In mathematics, an operation that is independent of the order of the objects concerned.

Systems undergoing spontaneous [2] or self-generated change, or symmetry breaking, as through bifurcation,[9] can therefore be described using a graph of the type shown in Figure 5.2 with transformation into all possible states – often considered to be 'true/false' or 'expected/unexpected' outcomes, as depicted by Boolean logic – being shown as two further outbound arrows. Such spontaneous systems are sometimes referred to as being *exergonic*[10] in nature and in graph representations of their behaviour, the steady state duration of any arrow is of little concern.

Induced bifurcation, again sometimes referred to as being *endergonic*,[11] needs one further arc to represent the external causal source of change – as shown in Figure 5.3. This can be considered as an extension to 'Y'-shaped pattern in Figure 5.2, thereby creating a more encompassing model which is capable of describing both spontaneous and induced symmetry breaking via the inclusion of the optional actuating leg. Basic aggregations models, such as sequences, clusters, hierarchies, ontologies and so on, can hence be created by linking multiple 'X'-shaped patterns together.

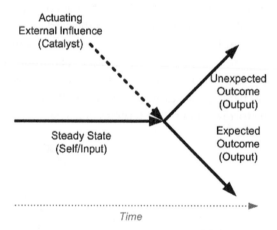

Figure 5.3   A state-based directed graph showing induced bifurcation: an example of the 'X'-shaped pattern

---

9   Common in chaotically emergent systems.[5][13][14][15]
10   Exergonic typically means 'releasing energy in the form of work'. By thermodynamic standards, work, a form of energy, is defined as moving from the system to its surroundings. Thus, an exergonic process, as contrasted with an endergonic process, is one that releases energy from the system, of which it is a part, to the surroundings.
11   Endergonic means 'absorbing energy in the form of work'. Endergonic reactions are not spontaneous.

Bifurcation

Bifurcation is a term normally used to describe forking or splitting structures, but further special cases can also be considered. In particular it is acceptable for one or both of the resultant branches produced to be effectively null.[12] In such circumstances ' X '-shaped patterns can also be seen to cover the concept of qualitative change or deviation, which includes the concept of halting.

This is a big step for us as we have just introduced a geometric method by which both splitting and change can be described. By doing so we can now tie together the reasoning behind the last chapter and this, as we should now have made it clear, shows that mathematics and computation are intimately linked and that the notion of splitting is fundamental to both. Thinking about splitting and its relevance, especially in computing, thus allows a number of new perspectives to open up and a new range of descriptive practices to be used.

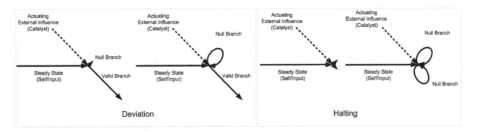

Deviation   Halting

Figures 5.4(a), (b), (c) and (d)   Qualitative change in terms of bifurcation, showing nullification of outbound branches via both nonexistence, 5.4 (a), and cyclic arcing[13]

Switching and Non-Determinism

None of the above should surprise those familiar with basic computer architecture, as the ' X ' and ' Y ' patterns described above merely present graph-based schematics for actuated switching. The important point, however, is that these patterns are relevant across all systems theory and at a number of levels. They might just as well have been introduced on the premise of real-world

---

12 A logically valid branch that will either halt without further effect or be cyclical without further effect.
13 Note that in the case of cyclic arcing the arcs involved inherently contain self-symmetry and are hence 'unobservable' in a computation and informational sense. This renders them null as no computational transformation is presented.

behaviours like a single species of animal splitting in two or the formation of a black hole in some far-off galaxy, let alone the division of mere numbers. This is a blunt, yet overwhelmingly powerful observation as a relay is nothing more than a special type of switch that opens and closes under control of another circuit. It is also therefore one of the most important components in modern day computers and in just about all systems of notable complexity. Regardless, there are some less than obvious observations here and these are crucial. Bifurcation is not only a defining characteristic of deterministic switching systems, but is it also a common trait amongst certain types of non-deterministic, 'chaotic' or complex system. Furthermore, it is closely associated with concept of emergence in such systems, a concept that underpins mainstream thinking on such matters as evolution and ultimately the existence of life.

Computational Curvature

For aggregation, and hence abstraction, to take place in systems, relationships[14] need to form between the constituent parts involved. This rests on all the elements involved in a relationship being part of a wider collection or composition of at least two, not necessarily materially distinct, things that differ in at least one way, be that via static characteristic or state.[15] Furthermore aggregates only come in two basic types: mathematical sets and sequences. In sets the order of constituent elements is unimportant, whilst order is paramount in sequences. Sets are therefore the most encompassing type of collection, as sequences can also be viewed as a special type of set – a 'well ordered' set to be mathematically precise.

It is essential to connect the notion of aggregation with that of the relationships[16] between the various elements involved. This is because only through the process of aggregation can complexity be cultivated, relying principally on the compounded effect of underpinning relationships as its feedstock.

Mathematically sequences are ordered aggregates based on a particular and continual type of progression. Such progressions are often complex, and under rare, but not statistically implausible, circumstances systems incorporating

---

14 Graph arcs.
15 That is, at least one symmetry is broken between both nodes (elements) at either end of an arc (relationship).
16 Interaction also being considered as a form of relationship.

such types of complexity can spontaneously form in self-organising ways. Thus, given the right conditions, credible macro-level processes of evolution can take hold.

Significant portions of both the natural and digital world rely heavily on the notion of sequential association. Time is sequential, for example, with each consecutive second following its predecessor in a well-understood fashion. In a similar manner traffic lights change, apples fall to earth and the threads of a computer program hang together. Furthermore, take a well-defined sequence of operations and the concept frequently referred to as an algorithm is formed.

When thinking of the syntax of any arbitrary 'string' of information, convention suggests the use of a straight line directed graph, like the one below, for visualisation purposes. Unfortunately, however, this depiction is somewhat deceptive, as sequences need not always follow a 'straight' course.

Sequence Element A   Sequence Element B   Sequence Element C   Sequence Element D   etc

Figure 5.5   A 'conventional' representation of a sequence using a directed graph

For a sequence to form there are principally two requirements: firstly that one or more elements must be present and, secondly, that these elements are arranged in some particular order. This may appear straightforward, but there are strong dependencies on symmetry involved. For example, symmetry breaking must be present to force noticeable boundaries within a sequence, promote discreteness and allow ordering to take place. Add the capability to switch between different ordering schemes, through the notion of bifurcation, for example, and the potential to compose extremely complex and elaborate systems of rules, processes and information is formed.

This essential notion of inter-elemental symmetry breaking is often overlooked, but it is nevertheless always present. The arrowheads in the direct graph above provide markers to indicate the points at which symmetry breaks, for instance, as well as denoting directionality. But these are merely graphical shorthand added for convenience. Such breakpoints can be represented using countless other methods and manifest themselves in the real world in innumerable ways across a myriad of observable properties. Physical shape, weight, texture, colour, electrical potential and so on are all the result of aggregated patterns of symmetry breaking and without such help no evidence of progressive change would ever be apparent and two neighbouring elements in any given sequence might as well be considered as one continual same – they would simply be unobservable[17] in their own right. Simple sequences therefore provide examples of a consistent rule of symmetry breaking imposed uniformly across a set of more than one element.

This one dimensional linearity of change further provides a path between extreme simplicity and extreme complexity, as each successive element in a sequence must be absolutely as expected across at least one universal feature. This thereby creates at least one symmetry[18] of the whole through the many smaller asymmetries of its parts and this regularity of asymmetries is central to the concept of abstraction and hierarchy, affording the ability to categorise complexity at ever higher levels. Sequences hence depict regularly divergent themes, chains of expected asymmetric progression leading to higher orders of organisation, no matter how complex they might be.

Returning to the axiomatic 'X' and 'Y' patterns characteristic of symmetry breaking introduced earlier. This time, to simplify representation we can remove the arrow heads and create a scenario where external influences are not needed to bring about change; that is to say the basic Y pattern. To further simplify the point of interest here we can insist that all cases of change are as expected. By doing so, two of the arcs in an 'X'-shaped graph become redundant – namely those needed for actuation and unexpected outcomes. In this way the boundary between subsequent elements in a sequence can be shown as one arc veering away from the other along a tangential path. This produces a much less artificial model of differentiation than simply using arrow heads, with the angle of the tangent between the two arcs marking change borders and hence outlining the break in symmetry present.

Using this graphing technique produces a characteristic 'kink' or 'bend' between neighbouring arcs. And when more arcs are added, this pattern ultimately forces the sequence's structure to 'bend' around a curved path. Such

---

17 Observability relates to a property of the system state that can be determined by some sequence of physical operations. For example, these operations might involve submitting the system to various electromagnetic fields and eventually reading a value off some gauge. In systems governed by classical mechanics, any experimentally observable value can be shown to be given by a real-valued function on the set of all possible system states.

18 Constant property.

curvature therefore makes it equally relevant to think of sequences as being curved rather than straight.

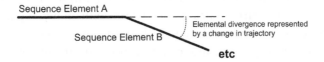

Figure 5.6   A conceptual graph of element-to-element change in a sequence, producing a characteristic 'kink' or 'bend'

This now allows a number of similarities of form to be studied. Classical Newtonian [2] viewpoints on science and engineering might well favour the straight lines of Euclidean geometry, but the natural world also has inbuilt preference for the curvature built in to more generalised views of geometry, primarily out of a need to reduce energy consumption. Galaxies spiral, seeds and petals mostly cluster in accordance with spiral placement patterns and the helical structures of RNA and DNA curve for similar reasons. All are examples of rounded sequential progression based on minimal energy coefficients.

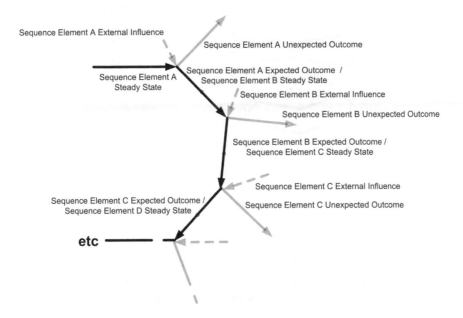

Figure 5.7   A two-dimensional directed graph showing a sequence of equally sized elements. Note: arrow heads are added merely for the purpose of familiarity of convention

In collections where progression not only dictates the ordering of elements within a group, but also the size of those elements, highly regular spiralling structures can be produced and, unsurprisingly, due to their geometric simplicity, such schemes occur frequently in the natural world. The fact that they are also fractal further has a direct link with many higher orders of complex phenomena. In particular one such arrangement, known as a Fibonacci sequence, appears to play an interesting, if not crucial, role in the way that certain parts of the physical world hang together.

But why this emphasis on curvature in nature, and what has this got to do with the information or computing? The point is merely to demonstrate that sequential structures are just as prolific in natural systems as they are in those made by man, and that the notion of curved geometries derived through sequential arrangement may actually be preferential, if not more fundamentally encompassing, than straight line alternatives in certain contexts[19] – a concept

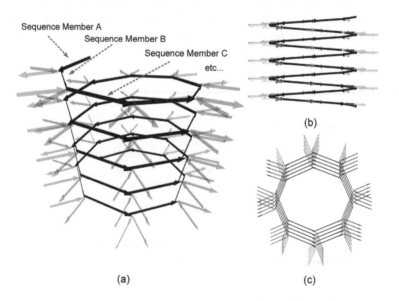

Figures 5.8(a), 5.8(b) and 5.8(c)   A three-dimensional graph showing a sequence off linearly diverging elements. Note: arrow heads are added merely for the purpose of familiarity of convention

19 Frames of reference where the underpinning environment is itself curved. Examples include space-time curvature in general relativity.

recognised through Bernhard Riemann's[20] work on geodesic[21] geometry in the 1850's, for example.

It is a well-known fact that the majority of the Web, for instance, is constructed from long intertwined hyperlinked chains of information and process. In addition, studies have recently shown that the Web possesses a fractal structure from many different perspectives. The common conceptualisation of its maelstrom of pathways, however, is one in which traditional Euclidean geometry is applied.

An alternative model is presented here, one intended to specifically cater for multidimensional information spaces which incorporate strangely loopy[22][2] undulating[23] manifolds similar to those found in fitness landscapes[24] and the concept of coevolution. Such manifolds are also considered as being the outcome of the complex compounding of a finite vocabulary of Lagrangian 'X' patterns at a number of levels. These concepts provide the foundation for such ideas as Web Life[25] and advocate a metaheuristic viewpoint whereby the Web can be seen as being analogous to a bag of loosely entangled springs[26] of information and transformation – a conceptualisation not dissimilar to that favoured by scientists researching into protein folding.

---

20 Georg Friedrich Bernhard was an influential German mathematician who made lasting contributions to analysis and differential geometry, some of them enabling the later development of general relativity.
21 In mathematics, a geodesic is a generalisation of the notion of a 'straight line' to 'curved spaces'. In presence of a metric, geodesics are defined to be (locally) the shortest path between points on the space.
22 A strange loop arises when, by moving up or down through a hierarchical system, one finds oneself back where one started. Strange loops may involve self-reference and paradox.
23 'Undulating' is used as a loose term here to convey the concept of information spaces that are not constant across all dimensions. In such spaces the landscapes described are not flat. Instead a more preferential analogy is to call to mind the surface of the ocean, that being incredibly dynamic, with great waves and small ripples in it.[2]
24 Sometimes also referred to as 'knowledge landscapes'.
25 The Web Life concept considers the Web not as a connected network of computers, as in common interpretations of the Internet, but rather as a sociotechnical machine capable of fusing together individuals and organisations into larger coordinated groups. It argues that unlike the technologies that have come before it, the Web is different in that its phenomenal growth and complexity are starting to outstrip our capability to control it directly, making it impossible for us to grasp its completeness in one go. A set of emergent characteristics and behaviours are now starting to appear, it suggests, that we have not programmed individually. These are apparently starting to increase in number and strength.
26 A quantum view of such 'springs' might well be seen as spinning fundamental particles.

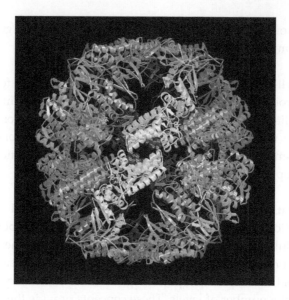

Figure 5.9   A conceptualisation of the Web by way of a protein analogy[27]

This idea is not as radical as it might first appear. In fact modern physiology appears to be warming to such ideas. It is well understood, for example, that curves provide some of the most economic structural geometries possible. Furthermore, it has long been established that constructing such curves out of anything that has discrete value must involve broken symmetry across all the units involved. Therefore, given nature's propensity for economy, an in-built preference for bundled coils of information and computation should be clear. That's why most low-level biological material comes curled up for example. The helix axis of DNA *in vivo*[28] is usually curved as a point in case. This is a necessary condition, as the stretched length of the human genome is about one metre and needs to be 'packaged' in order to fit into the nucleus of a cell.

---

27 Originally taken from http://www.biochem.mpg.de/xray/projects/hubome/thermosome.html. From 6 September 2007 this image is no longer available at that URL.

28 *In vivo* (Latin for (with)in the living). *In vivo* is used to indicate the presence of a whole/living organism, as distinct to a partial or dead organism, or a computer model.

6

Curves of Curves

*Everyone knows what a curve is, until he has studied enough mathematics
to become confused through the countless number of possible exceptions.*

Felix Klein

So the first leap has been made and we have now laid out the start of a proposition advocating a shift in position for information and computation. This shift is more of a side-step than a radical repositioning, but its subtleties are nonetheless important.

Now that we have started down a road that favours curves and not Euclidean straightness, it would be wrong to restrict such descriptive capability merely to the concept of generalised sequences. What we need to do next is look at how each element in any given sequence can be thought of in terms of straight lines, curves or both, and in doing so there is a need to re-examine what a sequence actually is in the first place.

The strictest definition of a sequence demands that it be composed of at least one or more elements, as we have already seen. From this it is perfectly legitimate to think of any or all items within a given sequence as being a sequence in its own right. In such a way the number three can be thought of as being the third prime number in the ordered sequence of all prime numbers starting at zero, for example – one being the second prime, zero the first and so on. Furthermore the number three can independently be thought of as a sequence comprising itself and no other number. This gives it its own identity, making it stand out. On its own the number three carries its own fully contained meaning and definition. It simply 'is' the number three, or rather any or all computations that produce it, and so shall it be forever more.

For our immediate purposes, we can divide the notion of sequences into two types: those with one and only one element and those with more. Such a division causes a problem, however, as it highlights a flaw in the reasoning outlined in the last chapter. Back then the overall idea was only to interpret sequences with more than one member as having curvature, with each individual member still being considered a straight line, as supported by established graph theory. This is also similar to the ideas going all the way back to Georg Cantor's day in the late nineteenth century. Cantor was a mathematician who eventually descended into insanity as a consequence of his work, but through his ideas on infinity he also became interested in the idea of curves. Consequently he developed a deep frustration with the reasoning of previous philosophers, such as Galileo, who had been content to work with definitions of a curve's *smoothness* which were reliant on collections of internal straight lines as part of the curve's geometric makeup. Admittedly such smoothness could be made up of an infinite number of infinitesimally small straight lines, and it was through such a realisation that Cantor began to question the very nature of infinity itself and his true legacy was formed. Today, Cantor's work continues to inspire some of the world's best mathematical minds, but the inherently ungraspable beauty of his work unfortunately led to his ultimate isolation, hysteria and undignified death in an asylum.

Discussing Cantor again may seem like a strange digression but it points to the next step change in thinking we need. Instead of thinking about curvature in terms of straight line units, it is also plausible to think of each unit being a curve in itself. This still leaves us open to Cantor's old self-reflexive problem, however, which questions what type of units constitute these lower-level curved units in the first place. But this is counterproductive for our purposes, so instead we shall introduce the notion of a 'pure' curve, perfect that is in all its curvature and indivisible in every respect other than through its understanding as a complete whole. In such a way the curved base units we need are just curves and are not open to further reduction or interrogation. This is, of course, an oversimplification but for our purposes it will serve well enough as a bridge to more important ideas. By making such a substitution it is now not only possible to think of sequences as having curved paths as a result of their cumulative composition, but also in terms of every element that makes up that composition. Simply put, we can now start to think of sequences as paths of curves within curves. Take this to its extreme and we could legitimately conceive of a model where each element in the sequence is curved to the point where it is completely looped back on itself, and by using this form of representation each sequential element could form a full twist in a coil that runs from one end of the sequence to the other, as per Figure 6.1. This diagram is presented in a three dimensional form to help emphasise the 'loopiness' of the concept involved, but it is important to note that dimensionality is of little consequence to the point being made at this point. For such reasons it is equally valid to think of the loopiness involved being spread out over one to an infinite number of dimensions. This may seem an alien concept to those unfamiliar with higher-dimensional mathematics, but it's worth just trusting in it for now, as it is not only plausible to think of dimensions beyond familiar degrees of freedom, like depth, height, width and even time, but it's absolutely essential in many fields of modern science.

At first sight the image in Figure 6.1 might seem a fanciful exaggeration purely for visual effect. But it is not, for this ability to loop back or 'spin' on itself is key to the picture of information and computation that is to follow. For now though we shall say nothing more about this idea, as we need to dig deeper into theoretical physics before its real importance and implications can become truly clear. All that matters for now is that we accept that sequences can be though as being coil-like as well as straight and leave it at that.

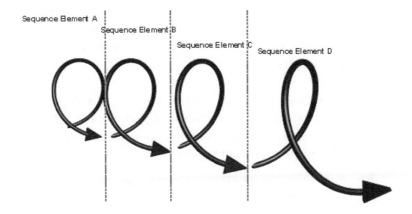

**Figure 6.1   An example of a sequence make out of looping elements.
Note: arrow heads are added merely for the purpose of familiarity of
convention**

A Fresh Look at the X and Y Patterns

In the previous chapter you will recall that we introduced the concept of the 'Y'- and, more encompassing, 'X'-shaped patterns to cover the concept of symmetry breaking and its place in the notion of sequence, and this includes various related concepts such as branching or forking and convergence. This collection, loosely summed up is very powerful as it provides a range of patterns that cover the full spectrum of 'change' types within any given system. Thus, in common parlance, the ' X '-shaped pattern provides the base from which a geometric language to describe change can be formed.

Announcing such a language poses a number of questions, not least of which relates to the composition and content of its vocabulary. On its own a singular geometric pattern for describing change is not enough. To fully articulate the descriptive potential involved, a way must be found to understand all possible configurations, or outcomes, of the pattern as a result of its use. This can be done by first thinking of all the geometric configurations available for describing each of the legs in the pattern, which is easy given that there are only two possible variants for each leg. One relates to the leg being 'observable' from a given computational perspective and the other obviously relates to the opposite, in that such a leg is transparent or 'unobservable' from a given point of view. Unfortunately it will take the entire next chapter to explain the importance of observability in this context, so again unfortunately, you must take such things on faith for now and accept that the notation we will use employs 'straight' lines to represent those legs that are observable and 'curved' lines to represent those that are not.

As there are four legs in the ' X '-shaped pattern, all with one possible observable configuration and one non-observable configuration, that gives us 16, or two to the power four,[1] possible configurations per pattern instance. In other words, our language consists of 16 words.

Figure 6.2   The overlaid vocabulary of the ' X '-shaped pattern

---

1   2^4

The figure above shows all 16 variants of the ' X ' pattern laid out on top of each other. For clarity this diagram is again presented in three dimensions with the non-observable configurations of each leg highlighted in the lighter of the two shades shown. Logically this configuration can be thought of as comprising four zones, arranged in two domains of two, these being positioned side by side with one zone on top of the other in each domain. Within each of the four zones can be found one leg of the ' X ' pattern – observable leg variants being shown as a diagonal line and unobservable variants being shown as a hollow circle, as in Figure 6.3(a) below.

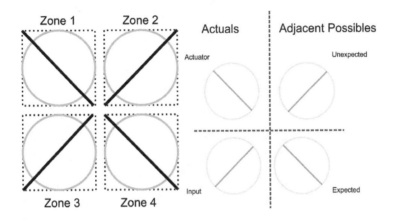

Figures 6.3(a) and 6.3(b)   The overlaid vocabulary of the ' X '-shaped pattern, now split into zones and drawn in two dimensions. Figure 6.3(a) purely defines the zones while Figure 6.3(b) adds further explanation to each zone

To understand these diagrams it is important to realise that they read from left to right. On the left-hand side the Actuals domain (comprising zones 1 and 3) can be seen and this represents what we might think of as the last known stable state of a system. An example of such a state might be the last computed element in any given algorithm (the bottom left quadrant of the diagram or the 'input' leg) and an external trigger that might potentially cause it to change (the top right quadrant of the diagram or the 'actuator' leg). On the right-hand side can be seen the Adjacent Possibles domain (comprising zones 2 and 4) which represents the next potential state or condition of a system. An example here might be the next possible state of a given computation, both expected (bottom right quadrant or 'expected' leg) and not (top right-hand quadrant or 'unexpected' leg').

Take away the overlay and each individual configuration of the pattern can be enumerated as seen below, with each individual configuration now being assigned a unique identifying number.

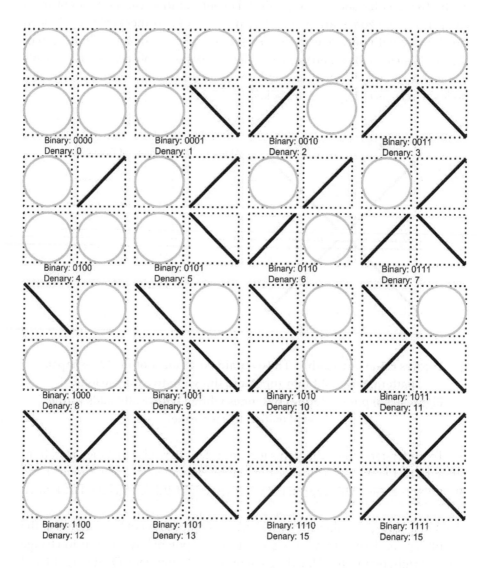

Figure 6.4   The individual configurations of the ' X '-shaped pattern

It is now not only possible to represent each geometric permutation of observable and non-observable leg variants within the ' X ' pattern, but it is also possible to assign a numeric value or 'name' to each. This is done by reading each of the configurations' zones in reverse order and assigning a '1' to it in every case where a diagonal line, or observable leg, is found, and a '0' where a circle, or non-observable leg, is found. This provides a simple and effective means of naming each configuration, as by no accident this scheme also corresponds to the binary numbering system. Hence by simple conversion between bases, the equivalent denary numbers can also be produced. Obviously denary numbers are merely used for familiarity, but any other numbering system or naming scheme could have been used as long as the uniqueness of each permutation is guaranteed. Through such enumeration, the full vocabulary of the ' X '-shaped pattern is given.

Now the Show Really Begins

The act of enumerating the ' X '-shaped pattern might look trivial but over the past few pages we have actually covered a lot of ground. A number of new concepts have been introduced and all without any real attempt to explain why they are needed or why they are important. We have seen that sequences of information and computation can be thought of as being curved and that in some cases this curvature can be further thought of as producing *loopy* or *spin-like* qualities. We have dissected such curves and proposed that even at the lowest component level they can also be thought of as having curvature, loopiness or spin. In fact, without making too much of a leap of faith, we started to think of sequences of both information and computation as being strings of spinning 'stuff'. We have further looked at how such 'stuff' might take part in change processes that are independent of any specific level of detail or abstraction. This has been done by introducing two forms of abstract pattern, namely the ' X '- and ' Y '-shaped patterns, and through these we have seen that networks of conditional change can be constructed. Last, but by no means least, we have introduced a language comprising 16 geometric 'words' or patterns to describe such networks at their most basic level. So, in essence, we have outlined a means for describing both computational and informational structure in systems regardless of their type of context.

To some this would be an impressive feet but, there is a very strong need not to be complacent. This is because we have to remember that the foundations of our language lie in the geometry of a sequence and rely upon that geometry as the only means for description. Consequently the language we have created can do a fine job of articulating the structure an algorithm or information sequence but can do nothing to describe the 'stuff' from which that structure is made. This is a potentially damaging proposition as, if we think back to our original equation in Chapter 2, structure provides only one of the parts in information's magic formula, yet it has taken a great deal of effort to explain it thus far. So will it take just as much to explain the others elements involved? Thankfully the short answer is no as structure can be seen as underpinning the other elements involved. Explaining why this is so is not as simple as one might like, however, as it involves a journey well outside the bounds of classical computer science and information theory. In fact it is not so much a journey as a real boys' own adventure leading us to challenge some of the most fundamental understandings in science today. It will question several fundamental models we currently hold dear as a means to describe our universe and ultimately seek to point a way forward that both transcends and combines these models into a single perspective, a perspective that describes the universe and everything in it as being informational entities that change over time. This is a computation model, a model that acknowledges the fact that the universe *is*, without apology, the greatest computer that ever has and ever will be created within the bounds of all reasonable and meaningful perception. This obviously raises the stakes considerably, but by purely considering the universe as an abstract computer we need not trouble ourselves with a large proportion of the baggage that comes with the science created to describe the universe up to this point. We need not consider, for instance, many of the emergent properties that form as a consequence the universe's everyday computation. Temperature is a fine case in point. It is an observable output of the universe and, as far as we know today, can be experienced at every known point in the universe. Although we have insights and methods with which to observe and predict it, what it is and indeed the very idea of how it folds into higher-level understandings of the universe are of little consequence to us. What we do need to worry, and worry intensely, about is the very structure of the universe itself. This takes us away from the safety of contemporary, popular understandings of computation and lands use firmly in the field of theoretical physics.

7

To Process or Not?

All science is either physics or stamp collecting.

Lord Kelvin

Let's lighten things up for a few moments ... .

In some corner of a bland, ambiguous open-plan office somewhere in the world today there is a high likelihood that the following scenario will play out. The office's token computer technician will raise his head from his coffee-stained keyboard and stare in the direction of the large cupboard-like object in the corner of the room. This is Mecca for our technician, the very spring from which geek-like status rises. Somewhere in the back of his subconscious a survival mechanism has kicked in and he has realised that it has been over an hour since he satisfied his craving for caffeine. He rises slowly and heads towards the office's coffee machine for the third time that morning.

Others in the office also appreciate the significance of this strategically placed appliance. Fortunately for them, however, they are not so reliant on the dark, strong liquid that spews out from within. For them it represents something else, it is the place where socialising takes place, it is the place where relationships are formed, it is the place where *real* business is done. It marks the absolute centre of the office.

As our technician reaches the machine he is struck by a new sign only just posted on the notice board beside. In big bold letters it announces the arrival of a new blend of coffee. 'Rich Roast, fresh from the plantations of deepest Brazil', it screams. 'That's for me!' he mumbles under his breath, and without a second's hesitation his hand shoots forward to press the appropriate button on the machine's well-fingered front panel. Just before skin touches plastic and the machine is prompted into its grinding and boiling routine, our technician stops, mortified, unable to proceed any further. His eyes have just scanned the small print at the bottom of the advertisement. The words read, 'Our company is environment friendly. Before you sample the delights of this wondrous blend, why not consider donating $1 to help neutralise the carbon footprint created while bringing it to you? Please place your contribution in the box provided below.' Not only is the technician now unable to order his coffee, but he has been engulfed by a wave of confusion that will ultimately ruin his day.

This overly cruel caricature might sound extreme but it serves as a good introduction to important misconception about information. To our technician the choice of the new coffee is initially straight forward. It satisfies his immediate need and is a good choice based on a small number of reasonably established facts and preferences. The term 'rich' in the advertisement equates to strong coffee in his mind and the fact that it is new to his range of his experiences immediately raises his excitement levels. Basically he likes strong coffee and he likes being excited, so everything adds up to a positive experience with very low risk involved. It's a sure bet, he is going to try it. But, although he is a coffee devotee, he is also a caring individual and is deeply concerned about the welfare of the planet. He has spent many hours reading about what is believed to be the root cause of global warming and exactly how its effects will touch each and every one of our lives in years to come. His head literally carries a dossier of facts, opinions and feelings all related to the subject and all are currently at war with his body's need to drink more coffee. He is confused. He simply cannot get over his dilemma.

This is a simple if somewhat overblown illustration of a problem that can debilitate us all. On one hand we have a small, well-defined and well-understood collection of information which we can easily interpret and control and on the other a vast, poorly defined collection of information competing against it. At face value, weighing up one against the other should not cause much of a problem. After all they are both just collections of information, right? Well yes, but as you probably get the idea by now – the problem is not quite as simple as that.

It's All Relative

Let's continue with a brief experiment. Look around you and find a reasonably small yet weighty object. A bunch of keys will do. Next find a location that is still and free from disturbance – perhaps one corner of your living room or office. Now raise the object above your head with one hand and prepare to catch it with the other. Let it go as soon as you feel comfortable and watch it fall to earth. Now here comes a question: as your object fell, at what speed do you think it hit your palm?

Those familiar with Newton's laws of motion should be smiling right now as they know full well that we have established equations for predicting such things. For them, if the duration of free fall were one second, it would be reasonably easily to calculate the speed at which object and palm met: approximately 4.5 metres per second in this case. But to what degree of certainty can we be sure of this answer?

In making this calculation an implicit assumption has been made, one which states that you, or someone relatively close to you, has observed the object's flight. But what if that individual was not positioned in your immediate vicinity and was watching from some distant vantage point like the surface of Mars perhaps? If this were the case then would it not also be correct to add the speed at which the Earth travels through our solar system in the direction of the falling object relative to Mars? Move the observer out further still, to a distant galaxy perhaps, and would it not then also be relevant to add the speed at which our own galaxy travels through the known cosmos? How about a position beyond the known cosmos, or … ? As you can no doubt see, a theme is developing which makes clear the role of location in the act of observation. Galileo, the Italian physicist, mathematician, astronomer and philosopher, had a name for this concept, referring to the link between the locations of the observer and of that being observed as a 'frame of reference'. In point of fact this notion is so powerful and important that Albert Einstein picked up on it many years later, using it as the basis for his model of special relativity. Through such a perspective it is just as valid to think of a bunch of keys travelling at four times the speed of sound as it is at 4.5 metres per second, so long as the position of the observer can be justified in relation to the motion of the keys.

This brings us on to an interesting point about the Einstein's great work. The common understanding is that he radically changed ideas on the way the universe hangs together, teaching us that at larger scales, space and time become inexorably linked and by being so do some very strange things to the very fabric from which our reality is created. Certainly the former of these statements is true. Einstein did indeed have a profound and lasting effect on our understandings, but it is not necessarily true to say that he fundamentally described the way the universe actually works, even to the smallest degree. More truthfully he explained how the universe is observable to us as individuals and therefore how our senses may perceive our surroundings as being real.

By doing so he emphasised the role of the observer and thus described 'physical' reality in a very human terms. The universe might, in fact, work in fundamentally very different ways, but Einstein's real gift was to point out that mankind is only equipped to interpret and justify it in a restricted number of ways, be they ultimately right or wrong. That is not to belittle Einstein's truly seminal insight, but it is to deliberately highlight our limitations with regard to understanding the ultimate context in which we are all placed. Einstein paid us a great compliment, in fact, by holding mankind central to a particular and provable interpretation of the universe. In one single step he made the study of physics at high scales inextricably anthropomorphic. But then so is science at all but the most abstract extremes.

Placing humankind at the centre of science might seem like an overly obvious thing to do, as how could anyone possibly attempt to understand the world around them if they were not able to see it directly in some humanly possible way? This is indeed a very deep and philosophical question that has held the attention of many a serious scientist throughout history. And until the recent theoretical and technological advances of the last century it truly remained a conundrum too far. Today, however, we have apparatus that can probe well beyond the limits of the human senses. We have atomic force microscopes with demonstrated resolutions of fractions of a nanometre – more than 1,000 times better than the optical diffraction limit. Through such equipment we can literally interact with things just above the atomic scale. Furthermore we now have methods of crossing the atomic-subatomic barrier and inspecting the innermost core of atoms themselves. Huge, complex and vastly expensive machines, like the particle accelerator at the centre of the Large Hadron Collider (LHC) on Franco-Swiss border, are proving successful in stripping apart hydrogen nuclei, for example. This is done through the simple brute force of smashing such nuclei together at close to the speed of light and monitoring the ensuing debris flung out from the collision. But even this extreme may not represent the absolute pinnacle of our ability to survey our surroundings. We have branches of mathematics that can extrapolate beyond even the most extreme empirical data available. Mathematical techniques such a gauge theory can literally take us to places where human inspection might never be possible, thereby helping to predict phenomena which we can only hint at through less ethereal methods. Mathematics can help predict the very vastness of the cosmos itself right down to the very essence from which each and every subatomic particle is made. In a very real sense it is the black magic in the contemporary scientist's toolkit.

Whilst in the throes of reinterpreting of Einstein's work, let's not stop with just one reinterpretation, and further examine his contribution to science in general. For instance, many might consider Einstein to be a great physicist, perhaps even the greatest physicist that has ever lived. But might it not also be correct to consider him as a great computer scientist as well? No, hold your laughter for a few seconds more and consider this proposition with an open mind. Einstein most probably never came into contact with anything like the machines we commonly refer to as 'computers' today, but he most certainly possessed a great insight into the theories of computation. This is because he was unquestionably an enlightened modeller with a wonderful awareness of how transformation or change, and thus computation, creates the world around us. But for us to appreciate this fully we must first go further with our understanding of what computing is all about.

Some rules first. Discard any preconceptions. Forget about mainframes, PCs, touch-sensitive tablets, laptops, silicon chips and network cables. Don't think about COBOL, C or Java. Instead think of the unrefined idea of computation and go right back to basics. The very most straightforward model of computation is one that breaks down into two parts, namely data and the actions used to process it. We shall come to the concept of information and how it differs from data later, but for now let's just focus in on this strange notion of 'process'.

Figure 7.1(a), shows probably the first diagram a student with any interest in computing ever sees. It's real beginners' stuff. It outlines how some form of input – raw data in our case – can be presented to some form of *unit* for the purpose of deriving some form of desired output from it. The model's elegance is stunning as it gets over the very essence of what computing is in one small, exquisite step. But therein can be found a problem, as it is actually too powerful. It is so powerful in fact that it carries the unfortunate ability to mislead in all but the most highly developed understandings of computing. So for now we shall discard it and only return once some mainstream definitions of computation have been covered. Figure 7.1(b) is much better for us immediately, as it highlights a big weakness in contemporary thinking about computing and provides a way through to a much clearer appreciation.

The important point to concentrate on in both the Figure 7.1(a) and 7.1(b) is that there are different types of arrow straddling both boxes, in that they relate to inputs and outputs. For most common understandings, if computation is to be seen to be done, both need to be present and, more importantly, both must be

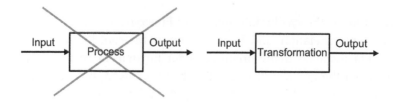

Figures 7.1(a) and 7.1(b)   The incorrect and correct interpretation of computation (classical version)

different in at least one noticeable way. That is why the term 'transformation' is far more relevant to common-or-garden definitions of computing than 'process'. 'Transformation' insists on change being present, whereas 'process' simply implies action without the need for change. For example, we could multiply the number one by itself a million time and unless we were to explicitly count the number of times such the operation were undertaken there would be no noticeable evidence of any work being done. A lot of effort may well have been expended, but the difference obtained by iterating around the task would be unnoticeable and, for all intents and purposes, no meaningful computation will have taken place. The computation is null in other words and may as well be empty.

$$Input \neq Output$$

Thus a practical understanding of computing suggests that there is a need for noticeable difference between that which is consumed by and that which is produced from any functional unit trying to describe itself as 'computer'. This can be simplified through the formula given above, but it is worth pausing at this point, as a play on words has been deliberately introduced and certain terms have been avoided for good reason. A better definition might be to state that a computation has no real value if one cannot observe a difference between that which an input originally provides and that which the computation ultimately creates. There, it's been said. The important word is out in the open. The one word that is essential to a truly insightful understanding of computation. That word is 'observation' and in the physical world, or at least at the scales at which we can interact with it, for something to be 'observable', noticeable computation must be present in the observation process. Even the act of viewing a stationary object involves change, as light rays hit the retina of the onlooker's eyes having bounced off the item under inspection. In truth, significant parts for physics and computation are both about the very same thing, that being the observation of change from the perspective of recognised vantage points. In a very real sense they are one and the same thing.

Einstein's Epitaph

From a very human perspective the act of observation is intimately bound with the idea of light. Einstein was enthralled by this idea and all it entails. Indeed he probably understood its place in science better than any other physicist to this day. If one were to study his theories on relativity, for instance, even at a cursory level it is clear that light plays a central role. Being a significant constant it is so central that it might be more accurate to describe his ideas as headlining light's role in making the universe evident, rather than describing how the universe actually 'is'. In such a way the concept of relativity, in Einstein's eyes at least, becomes inextricably linked with that of observability and so implies that change of some kind has to present in relation to that being observed. In other words, even when not immediately apparent, anything under inspection, or something directly interacting with it and the observer, must be undergoing transformation for observation, and hence relativity, to be legitimate at all. Again the term 'transformation' is essential to this viewpoint, and therefore so is computation. By being so it therefore emphasises the link between Einstein's thinking and concepts central to classical definitions of computing. If we think of a ray of light travelling through space, for example, it is relatively easy to see it as the input to a simple computation. As it bounces off or passes through an object or substance a change takes place and the ray changes its role from that of input to that of output by way of a change in its trajectory, wavelength or velocity perhaps. That said, now focus back on our chosen definition of 'transformation', as in Figure 7.1(b), but this time consider it in terms of light. If you recall, we initially berated the term 'process' in favour of 'transformation'. This was on the grounds that observable change must be present for any computation to be noticeable and therefore 'valid', thereby fitting nicely with everyday understandings of how light behaves around us. But there is a less than obvious yet important flaw with this model, especially when describing computation in terms of everyday observability.

Unfortunately there is no gradual way in which to introduce this flaw. It just has to be stated cleanly in the best possible terms:

There is absolute no need for all forms of computation to be relevant to the notion of observability as commonly understood through human experience.

This may seem like a crazy proposition, but it is nevertheless a reality and one which adds an extremely important twist to any generalised understanding of computing.

Symmetrical Computation

Under most common circumstances computation can indeed be thought of in terms of human experience. A computation ingests something in the form of data, then squirts out some different data by return. That's the way that work is done. Even so there are a number of special cases where this is not the case and yet computing, indeed lots of computing, can still be seen to have taken place. Just because input is present and work is done does not necessarily imply that change must be manifest in any resulting output.

We have already seen this in the case of one multiplied by itself, but now take the mathematical equation $x=y^2$; that is to say x equals y multiplied by itself. As in all formulae of this type, y can be seen as the input to the equation, x the output and the '$=$' sign the actual act of computation involved in the equation. Under most conditions x will not equal y^2 once the calculation has taken place, but there are at least two not so special cases where this is will always be the true. These relate to values of y equal to not only one but also zero. Set y to either of these values and we could repeat the calculation until the end of time, as long as the powers involved are natural numbers ($\mathbb{N}$), and no noticeable difference would be seen between what goes in and what comes out. The only exception is that zero to the power zero always yields one, but that represents an extremely special case. So, if truth be told, it would be possible to dedicate the entire computational might of the universe to this task for the rest of eternity and still it would yield no apparent or observable effect. The fundamental laws of mathematics would simply prevent change from being seen in any output, yet still vast amounts of work would have been done involving huge amounts of energy.

Examples like these highlight a particular set of computational transforms. These occupy a special place in both the way the physical world is materialised and the overall manner in which we perceive the synthetic variants of computation familiar to us today. These are symmetrical transformations – computations that can be applied to an object or idea without any apparent alteration being encountered by an arbitrary and independent observer. Turn a uniform rubber ball about its centre, rotate a uniform cube through 90^0, flip a flat piece of clean paper over, even change the order of the two letter 'm's in the word 'symmetry' itself and so long as the viewpoint of anyone looking on does not change and their senses are masked while the change takes place, nothing will be noticeably different. The symmetry of that being observed will stay the same and the frame of reference between that being observed and those doing the observation remains undisturbed.

Try this for yourself; it's easy and will not take up much time. In doing so you should realise the startlingly simplicity of the concept. It is something we all learn to recognise at an early age and to most it soon becomes familiar to the point of instant acceptance. Some may have actually pondered on it at length and reached a point of deep appreciation. Symmetry is often interpreted to mean 'balance' or perhaps 'harmony', or sometimes even 'beauty'. A mathematician or physicist sees the same attributes in symmetry, but defines the idea this way: 'something has symmetry if one or more of its properties remain unchanged when some other property is changed'.[12] A group of ten identical objects possesses symmetry. Line them up and it's impossible to know if any or all of them have switched position in the line. But if the line were composed of five objects that had one shape followed by five that had another, some of the symmetry is broken by observable variation. Swapping objects five and six, for instance, would produce an obvious change.

This again brings us to question what symmetry actually is. As mentioned, a symmetry is a transformation that preserves an object's structure. But as we have seen many times now, we could quite legitimately change the term 'transformation' to 'computation' and the definition would remain the same. In such a way it is essential to understand that symmetry is an act of doing rather than a 'thing'. It is more the rules we apply to a thing rather than the thing itself. It is the dish and not the recipe.[30]

The Three Key Words in the Definition of Symmetry

There are three key words in the definition of symmetry, these being *transformation, structure* and *preserve* and it is worth considering all three in turn:

Transformation: Think of an object and consider all the various things we might do to it. In principle we could bend it, turn it through some angle, squash it, stretch it, paint it, heat it and so on. But within the context of symmetry the choice of actions available is restricted by the second of our key terms.

Structure: The obvious idea of an object's structure consists of the mathematical features that are considered significant and relevant to its form. For example an object might have sides or faces and these might well be curved or straight, possess certain measurements such as length, depth and so on.

Preserve: The structure of any transformed object must match that of the original. If an object had five faces originally, so it must have the same after a symmetrical transformation has been applied, and so on.

This brings us back to think about our earlier definition of computation in which the term 'transformation' won over that of 'process', but this time around the victory can be seen as being deeply flawed: by insisting that change is present, the term 'transformation' can only be used to successfully describe computations that are asymmetrical. 'Process', on the other hand, is not so choosey, allowing a broader range of outcomes and being tolerant of both asymmetric and the symmetric variants. Hence it is actually 'process' that should win out over 'transformation' and it is this term that we shall carry forward in later discussions to cover the fully spectrum of computational characteristics.

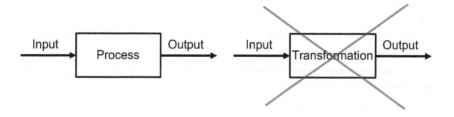

Figures 7.2(a) and 7.2(b)   The incorrect and correct interpretation of computation (contemporary and more accurate version)

Invisibility, Nothingness, Negation and Halting

By accepting the validity of 'process' over 'transformation', a startling conclusion can be reached in that there are certain types of computation will and always remain hidden. And this begs the question as to just how common such computations might be? Instinct suggests they should be rare, but in fact this need not necessarily be the case. To demonstrate this let's return to the simple equation in the previous section. This can be generalised to the form $x=y^n$, where n represents a power to which y can be raised. Again this has interesting nuances when one and zero are considered as inputs and in such cases almost all real number values of n will again not see a noticeable difference between input and output. Great fun perhaps, but what's the real point here? It's really quite simple, since one and zero are by far one of the most important numbers in all modern computing – representing the various bit values spread across every single digital computer in the world today. Furthermore, under certain circumstances, one can be seen as being interchangeable with the Boolean variable 'TRUE' and zero with 'FALSE', hence playing an important role in the formality of 'standard' logic. This is indeed important, as it implies that all self-supporting computations of a self-reflexive nature will show no discernible evidence of their existence, in terms of their output, when in a continuously TRUE state or FALSE state. They are entirely symmetrical, in other words, and hence present as unobservable entities from all points outside their internal composition. For all intents and purposes they are invisible to the outside world and might as well be considered as being null. That's not to say that the inputs and outputs involved themselves disappear, but that the distinction between them is meaningless for most practical purposes. To go through this by way of an example, take a process, any process, that consumes a Boolean TRUE value then multiplies it by itself an arbitrary number of times. For our example we'll stick to, say, three multiplications then output the result:

$$TRUE^3 = TRUE * TRUE * TRUE = TRUE$$

As can be seen, input and output remain the same. Furthermore it is possible to increase the complexity of this algorithm and make its output dependent on some internal variable. Even under such condition the computation would still remain invisible until a spontaneous change in that internal variable produces a causal effect on the output and thus breaks the symmetry of its parent.

There is, of course, a time element that has not been explicitly mentioned here, and to consider this let's assume that the above example involves the input being raised to an infinite power. Obviously this would imply an infinite number of iterations which, in turn, would take an infinitely long period to compute. In Turing terms the algorithm would simply be without end and would not 'halt'. Because of this the computation may actually become noticeable to the observer, purely on the grounds of its reluctance to break its symmetry. But that is not real symmetry breaking on the part of the computation, it is simply a consequence of things changing in the environment around it and the respective asymmetries involved. For this also to work, the observer involved must be present at the point when the computation starts and have some measurable means to know that time is passing – position of one of the observable asymmetries in the surrounding environment, in other words.

Now to the immediate point: if we consider a model of computing that is devoid of time and which is solely dependent on its definition in terms of demonstrable transformation of the informational content it serves, the halting problem obviously disappears, and even in models where time is an important consideration, if the internal workings of such computations are not made visible to an external observer, if they remain in perfect symmetry, that is, there is no way to discern that computation is actually under way nor is there any way to measure the work being done. Again the work content is invisible, and we could quite legitimately surmise that the 'machine' undertaking the computation was broken. Furthermore there is symmetry to the very idea of halting itself and this begs us to ask how we might know if a computation has actually been completed if time were not a factor in its execution?

To provide some form of answer, perhaps think of a light on the front of a black box which is supposedly doing some computing. Without knowing if this light relates to the box's input, output or ongoing computational state, there would simply be no way of knowing if the box's work were still under way. The only way of knowing would be if the condition of either the black box or its light changed once all work was finished. This might sound obvious, but there is an additional complication. Suppose the computation had finished and the box were actually doing nothing, for nothing in itself possesses symmetry. Technically speaking, 'nothing', – that is the empty set in mathematical terms – has exactly one symmetry, which comes from the unique function produced from the empty set on itself. So if, in this example, 'nothingness' shared the same outward signs as the supposed computing going on in the box, and it were represented by the same light being switched on, then we'd be no better off.

This is a deliberately tortuous illustration but it serves to bring out a very important point in that the lack of anything being present, be that information or computation, is also symmetrical and is hence invisible to the outside observer unless disturbed by intervention. Put in overly analogous terms, we can only ever know if anything is in front of us unless we prod it! Light[1] normally does that for us in the real world, but take that free gift away and symmetry can play some really funny tricks. Just like a blind man in a dark quiet room, 'nothing' will not make itself known unless something bumps into it. More specifically, symmetry will only reveal its hiding place through actuation of some kind. The 'X'-shaped pattern once again reminds us of this truth.

The Work of Computing

There is one final point to be made before we can move on. We are now starting to talk about a model of computing where terms like 'work' and 'energy' are not out of place. By doing so it should be mentioned that such a model, for our purposes, is purely abstract and independent of any physical realisation. Because of this we need not restrict ourselves to thinking in terms of examples where actual *energy* is involved. Such examples might include a laptop's presentation of a document, a human using a pencil and paper, or even the very universe itself manipulating every single subatomic particle in existence. All need real energy to take place, but our model only needs the *idea* of energy to work and that is important as it allows us to take some blatant liberties. All physical systems dissipate energy of one form or another as a result of doing work. The pistons in a steam engine, for instance, give off heat and noise purely as a result of their motion. This is extraneous to the primary work task at hand but nevertheless commonly generates a means by which that task can be identified. In our model, however, we assume absolute perfection with regard to 'energy' use and assume that no such secondary leakages will ever take place. Furthermore this assumption is extended to cover all information conversion and associated computations. This gives a theoretical model with perfect energy and information conservation across all relevant measures, a condition that the physicists might choose to refer to has having zero entropy. This fights against the expectations of the famous second law of thermodynamics, which sees entropy as a measure of the unavailability of a system's energy to do work. Entropy is a frequent by-product of isolated or 'closed' physical processes and regularly serves to get in the way of theoretical modelling. It is often a measure of the randomness of 'molecules' in a system and is central to the fundamental

---

1   Also sound, touch and so on.

thermodynamic relation which deals with physical processes and whether they occur spontaneously. Contemporary science thus implies that an increase in entropy is a direct consequence of spontaneous or self-actuated change – self-generated computation in other words – but it is as yet unclear if this consequence needs to be carried forward when dealing with computational models in a singularly abstract sense. For such reasons we shall choose to sidestep it here. Besides it is clear that in certain types of 'open' system, such as those typically associated with modern technological advances like the Web, for instance, negative entropy actually prevails and order is brought forth from disorder. This is because such domains offer higher potential for the take-up of any side effects produced by ongoing change. They simply soak up entropy and use it for positive effect, thereby inverting its potentially destructive impact. The rise of Apple's *iTunes* website is a prime example. Some might surprisingly have seen an increase in the Internet's capability to transfer vast and diverse volumes of data as a bad thing, but not Steve Jobs[2] and his colleagues at Apple. The Internet was originally designed for military purposes in the late 1950s when there was a need for a network design that could withstand the extremes of nuclear attack. At that time the Internet's implied use was highly specific and most certainly not focused on the mass sale of popular music. Jobs and his team saw different facts and serendipitously reapplied the technology to reinvent the music industry. Could anyone have originally predicted the death of vinyl[3] as a result of a need to survive in the face a nuclear war? Certainly not. It was well beyond the gift of even our most creative thinkers at the time. It was an adjacent possible waiting to happen as a direct and unpredictable consequence of positive feedback in the high-tech industry.

Thermodynamic complications aside, symmetry's computational transparency provides a real bonus for us and clears up a problem hinted at in Chapter 5. When the '*X*'-shaped pattern was introduced back then it was delivered off the back of bifurcation in a way that implied it was universal across all types of system. Even so, at first sight, there is a property of bifurcation that might not appear to follow through into all possible variants of the '*X*'-shaped pattern. Bifurcation absolutely demands *two* outputs past the point of split, whereas this may not appear clear with our '*X*'-shaped pattern. In many ways it can be seen as a forking process, whereas the '*X*' pattern tries to be more encompassing and takes in types of change that only require one noticeable output. To make this more evident think of the following two examples: firstly,

---

2   Steven Paul Jobs was an American business magnate and inventor.
3   Pressed vinyl was the primary material used to store recorded music prior to the invention of CDs and the mass distribution of media digitally over the Internet.

if we were to heat a flat dish of oil uniformly from below, at a certain critical temperature its surface's uniformity would break and the onset of a complex pattern of convection cells would be seen. These are typically hexagonal, with a few pentagons thrown in, and all much the same size – a phenomenon referred to as Rayleigh-Bénard convection. So the overall symmetry of the oil's surface breaks down and is replaced by the symmetries of the emergent hexagonal patterns and the *calm* oil in between. One symmetry is replaced by two. Think also about a wooden ruler held over the edge of a desk and against which increasing pressure is applied on its overhang. At some point the downward force might be so great that it will snap the ruler in two. Here again symmetry is broken as the wholeness of the ruler is shattered and replaced by the two symmetries of the broken halves now present. But, from one perspective at least, we do not have two rulers as a result of the breakage. Instead only one broken ruler is left with, at best, two broken pieces. The system has not split in two. It has simply changed in the direction of the breakage. A better example relates to the counting of numbers. Count from 1 to 2 and a symmetry is broken, in that 1 is no longer 1 and we have moved on to 2. This process has not resulted in two numbers being produced but just a chance from one to the other, so one number's symmetry has been replaced with that of the other.

So was the 'X'-shaped pattern introduced under a false premise, and if not how might it be altered to bring it back into line with the universal bifurcation model? The answer lies in the number of observable outputs present. Look at a singular change, like that of the our counting example in the light of both symmetrical and asymmetrical perspectives, and it is possible to reformulate into a two-legged forking pattern similar to that of bifurcation. Only having one noticeable output does not necessarily imply that change can only ever have one and only one output. It is also perfectly valid for such phenomena to have more than one output, of which only one has a mandatory obligation to be asymmetrical, and hence noticeable, from the point of view of the observer. As symmetrical outputs would be invisible, they would be null with regard to all measurable relevancies, but would be relevant from all computational perspectives

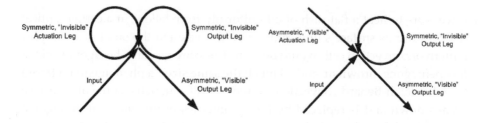

Figure 7.3(a) and 7.3(b)   A variant of the 'X'-shaped pattern showing two output legs, only one of which is observable

The Figures above show such a configuration, with Figure 7.3(a) showing a self-actuating pattern and 7.3(b) showing an externally actuated variant. Again the important point to note is that only the asymmetric legs of the pattern are obvious, yet all four legs are relevant from a purely computational perspective.

8

Information and Computation as a Field

What we see strongly suggests that the magnetic field is indeed helical.
If it is so, then this tells us a lot about the role magnetic fields might
play in molecular clouds and star formation. It would be a major piece of
evidence in trying to solve this mystery of how stars form.

Timothy Robishaw

We have now talked about some tricky stuff. We have considered geometry, numbers, patterns, symmetry and much more. We have even stopped off to think about how certain forms of computation, and perhaps information, might actually be invisible yet still be perfectly valid. All of this might seem truly radical if not mind-bending, but hold onto your hat for there is still more mind bending to come. This is not at all to sensationalise any of the topics or ideas covered up to this point, but is because we are trying to seek out something that is radical in itself and that demands some significant changes of perspective.

If we were to look at all the possible configurations of the 'X'-shaped pattern, as originally outlined in Figure 5.3 in Chapter 5, and its various configurations, as outlined in Chapter 6, one configuration stands out in particular as being peculiar. This is the first of the configurations or X_0 for short – if we are to follow the naming convention created earlier.

In this configuration nothing much appears to be happening, or at least be visible to the observer, as all legs possess perfect symmetry. Indeed it might appear entirely uninteresting, given that it presents a picture where nothing *appears* to be going on at all. But that's the point. Because it possesses no asymmetry it is particularly relevant. Think about this 'nothingness' from the point of view of pure computation and an interesting perspective appears. Rather than nothing happening, there is in fact an abundance of opportunity for processing to be taking place.

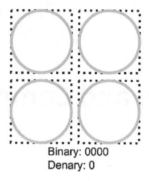

Binary: 0000
Denary: 0

Figure 8.1 X_0 **as originally shown in Figure 6.4**

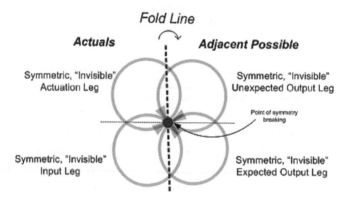

Figure 8.2 X_0 **outlined in more detail**

Take a step back for one moment and think about each of the legs purely in terms of process as defined in the previous chapter. In doing so, remember that two types of computation can exist – symmetrical and asymmetrical – and that the symmetric variant is not always apparent via external observation. Do this and X_0 suddenly bursts into an explosion of potentials within which symmetrical computation can take place, its four symmetrical legs happily coexisting together. Within it can be found a perfectly symmetrical *input*, seamlessly undergoing actuation by another perfectly symmetric leg and producing two perfectly symmetrical *outputs*, one entirely as expected and the other showing an alternative and equally symmetrical path. This might appear impossible, as from the point of view of the observer it suggests 'something' coming forth out of 'nothing' and 'nothing' coming forth from 'something'. But, as we now know, 'nothing' is a perfectly legitimate form of 'something' in computational terms, and hence the scenario works.

There are more twists hidden in the pattern, however, as closer inspection reveals yet more symmetry. If we were to split the pattern in two, for instance, and think of the left-hand legs – here referred to as 'Actual' legs – as its inputs, and the right-hand legs – here referred to as 'Adjacent Possible' legs – as its outputs, as illustrated previously in Figure 8.2, then a further line of symmetry can be shown running down the middle. This allows us to think of *folding* the pattern in two along this line, so that the outputs from this configuration can feed back as inputs again in a recursive manner. This combines the Actual and Adjacent possibles into a simpler pattern, as shown in Figure 8.3 below, and lets us remove the idea of pre- and post-symmetries from the schematic. It also allows us to concentrate on the underlying problem space purely in terms of symmetric self-sustainability and then to go further to focus on the point at which the symmetries involved can indeed eventually break. In short, the bottom half of the figure eight-like schematic produced by folding relates to a capability that naturally encourages a state of things 'as they are', while the top half can be seen as discouraging this perpetuation by constantly waiting for its chance to destroy any status quo.

It is, of course, possible to reduce this 'figure of eight' still further by invoking the symmetry between the two remaining legs of the pattern and folding again, but this is a step too far as it takes away the point of the pattern itself in that it is designed to illustrate the interplay of one or more elements in the act of information or computation representation.

As we will be referring to this eight-shape-like variant of the 'X'-shaped pattern frequently we shall give it a specific name and call it $_8X_0$ for convenience.

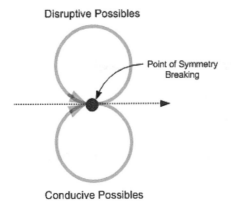

Disruptive Possibles

Point of Symmetry Breaking

Conducive Possibles

Figure 8.3   The reduced figure of eight representation of X_0

If we now consider both 'loops' of $_8X_0$ as being opposite to the other, there is further non-obvious detail that needs to be added concerning the point of intersection between both. This location is shown as a large dark dot in Figures 8.2, 8.3, 8.4, 8.10, 8.11, 8.12 and 8.13 and is obviously the only point in the configuration where symmetry can break – as it is the only point where interaction can take place and noticeable change can occur. It thereby also represents the singular point at which it the pattern can change into any of the other fifteen possible configurations open to the 'X'-shaped pattern. Given also that $_8X_0$ can be seen as being generically descriptive over both information and computation – in that we have proposed that computation has a time dimension and information has not – it is quite legitimate to think of this pattern moving through some relevantly higher dimension such as time, as illustrated by the thin and dotted dark horizontal arrow in Figure 8.3. The easiest way to think of this is to see $_8X_0$ as if it were rolling 'forward' like the wheels of some old fashioned mangle,[1] and through such motion it should hopefully be clear that some form of trajectory must be involved as the two *loops* involved roll out their existence. Showing such a trajectory as a straight line again raises a familiar problem, though, as we have been deliberately trying to avoid straight-line geometry. For this reason we should therefore ask if it may not be better to draw such a higher-dimensional path as an arc if not a complete circle. Furthermore should there not be one such path but two, the first relating to the route of any expected symmetry breakage and the second representing the path of any other alternative outcome? This then leads Figure 8.3 to be redrawn as shown below:

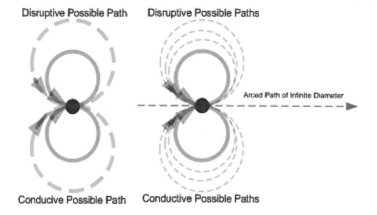

Figures 8.4(a) and 8.4(b)   **Alternative versions of** $_8X_0$ **(in two dimensions)**

1   Please see http://en.wikipedia.org/wiki/Mangle_(machine) for further information.

Bringing Spirals Back into the Picture

By representing the higher dimensional paths of $_8X_0$ using curves, yet another problem is unfortunately highlighted. Given that all the legs involved are self-reflexive, should not all their potential higher-dimensional paths also be the same? If this were indeed the case then the variant of $_8X_0$ shown in Figure 8.4(b) would result, which hints at the possibility of there being an unlimited number of curved, self-reflexive paths, across any number of higher dimensions. Furthermore, take this to its logical extreme and such paths can be seen as having a range of diameter ranging from the infinitesimal to the infinite as more and more dimensions are added. Even if we think of $_8X_0$ as having only one higher-dimensional path then that must 'extend' within such a higher-dimensional space by default as the two loops of the pattern roll forward.

This is an extremely important realisation, as it leads to a set of strange yet wonderful paradoxes. Take any $_8X_0$ instance with a particularly short higher-dimensional path – that is to say where its loops have tiny diameters – and in geometric terms it can be thought of as being a point entity. Patterns with longer paths obviously fall into a category where they may be thought of as being multiply elliptical,[2] one ellipse for each loop in the pattern. Yet take such path-lengths to their extreme and there is at least one special case where

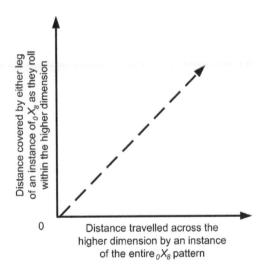

Figure 8.5   The path of $_8X_0$ through its higher dimension

---

2   In that a circle is only a special kind of ellipse.

loop diameters are infinite and so their geometry can be thought of as being 'straight' around the point at which symmetry can break. That is because the curvature of a circle with infinite diameter is flat about any given point on that diameter. This is both strange and wonderful and demonstrates that $_sX_0$ can be viewed as being faithful to point, curved and straight line geometries all at the same time.

Such strangeness is not such a significant leap, once thought about carefully. If you remember, when the concept of computational curvature was first introduced back in Chapter 5, we mentioned that the angle of deviation between two elements in a sequence need not be constant and therefore must relate to some function which itself is part of the makeup of the sequence. This not only opens up the possibility of the curvatures involved being perfectly circular, but also opens up the possibility for other similar types of geometry to be equally valid. One such variant is that of spiralling trajectories. What's more, such spirals might actually be more attractive from a computational perspective, as the type of function needed to produce them is exceptionally simple and thus extremely computationally efficient.

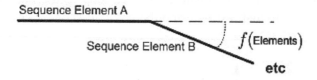

Figure 8.6   A conceptual graph of element-to-element change in a sequence, producing a characteristic 'kink' or 'bend' as a result of a function rather than a constant angle of deviation

A spiral is typically a planar curve that is flat like the groove on a record. Spirals may therefore be described most easily using polar coordinates,[3] where the radius r is a continuous function of angle θ that preserves any ordering of the

---

3   In mathematics, the polar coordinate system is a two-dimensional coordinate system in which each point on a plane is determined by an angle and a distance. The polar coordinate system is especially useful in situations where the relationship between two points is most easily expressed in terms of angles and distance; in the more familiar Cartesian or rectangular coordinate system, such a relationship can only be found through trigonometric formulation.

elements present.[4] A circle should hence be regarded as a degenerate version of a spiral, the function not being strictly monotonic.[28]

Some of the more important types of spiral include:

- the Archimedean spiral, where $r = a + b\theta$

- the Cornu spiral or clothoid

- Fermat's spiral, where $r = \theta1/2$

- the hyperbolic spiral, where $r = a/\theta$

- the lituus, where: $r = \theta-1/2$

- the logarithmic spiral, where $r = ab\theta$; approximations of this are common in nature

- the Fibonacci spiral and golden spiral, which are special cases of the logarithmic spiral

- the Spiral of Theodorus, which is an approximation of the Archimedean spiral composed of contiguous right triangles[28]

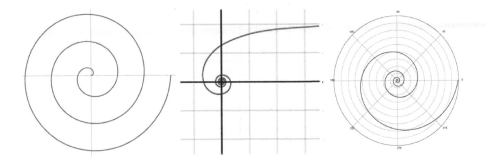

Figures 8.7(a), 8.7(b) and 8.7(c)   Examples of two-dimensional spirals, namely an Archimedean spiral, a hyperbolic spiral and a logarithmic spiral

---

4   This is often referred to as a monotonic function.

Enter the Helix

Spirals and helixes are two geometries that are easily confused, but which nevertheless represent two quite different types of object. Unlike spirals, helixes need an extra third dimension in which to form. For instance, track a spiral as it is drawn over time and a helical path will be followed in space-time. Time, or any real world dimension for that matter, need not necessarily be the extra dimension added, so long as an extra dimension is indeed present. And this point will become increasingly important as our story unfolds. Needless to say the helix's geometry will also play a crucial role, and because of this we should emphasise this critical point about its added dimension by starting to think in complex terms; complex, that is, as in complex planes in geometry.

In mathematics, the complex plane is a geometric representation of geometric systems involving the use of complex numbers[5] ($\mathbb{C}$) and is established by gluing the real axis to a perpendicular imaginary axis. Hence the complex plane can be thought of as a modified Cartesian plane, with the real part of a complex number being represented by a displacement along the x-axis and the imaginary part by a displacement along the y-axis.[29]

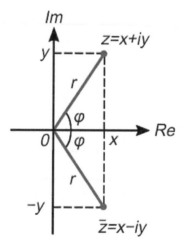

Figure 8.8   **An illustration of the complex plane. The imaginary numbers run up and down on the vertical coordinate axis**

---

5   That is involving $\sqrt{-1}$.

As we first noted in Chapter 4, complex numbers are those numbers whose squared value is a real number not greater than zero and can therefore be thought of a multiples of $\sqrt{-1}$ – often referred to as either i or j. Thus, if y is a real number ($\mathbb{R}$), then $i.y$ is an imaginary number, because:

$$(i \times y)^2 = i^2 \times y^2 = -y^2 \leq 0$$

Complex numbers were first conceived by the Italian mathematician Girolamo Cardano,[6] who called them 'fictitious' during his attempts to find solutions to certain types of equations known as cubics. The solution of a general cubic equation may require intermediate calculations containing the square roots of negative numbers, even when the final solutions are real numbers, and the introduction of complex number provided a way around this. This ultimately led to the fundamental theorem of algebra, which shows that with complex numbers it is always possible to find solutions to a specific subset of a more generalised set of formulae known as polynomial equations.

The point here is nothing more than to show that it is perfectly legitimate to add a new property or dimension to any problem-solving activity. That is so long as it assists in revealing hitherto unseen details of that problem and ultimately adds to the value of both the solution and its workings. If you prefer, think of such additions as being like a small knife used to open up the various casings of a tightly fitting Russian doll. Without such a tool it would be impossible to look inside such a fascinating object and all the shaking in the world will do little to uncover its inner workings. All that will result is a frustratingly obvious rattle which tells of more detail within, all tantalisingly out of reach of the enquirer.

In such a way, let us freely experiment by adding yet another dimension to $_8X_0$ and consider it as if the paths in Figure 8.4 were being 'pulled out' into helixes of increasing diameter along that dimension. For now let's not worry about what this new dimension might represent and just be safe in the knowledge that we can justify it properly at some later point. It may well relate to some mathematically complex property and this might indeed contribute towards a full description of $_8X_0$'s full description, but the real thing to understand is that we are now moving from two- to three-dimensional representation.

---

6   Gerolamo Cardano was an Italian Renaissance mathematician, physician, astrologer and gambler.

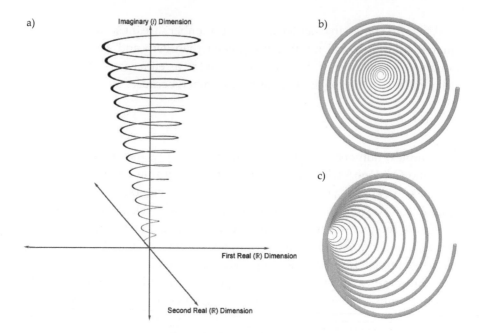

Figures 8.9(a), 8.9(b) and 8.9(c)   A spiral drawn out over an imaginary plane to produce a cone-shaped helix. The figures show the same helix from different points of observation

Adding this new dimension gives significantly more freedom to the way in which we can think about spiral configurations and consequently the idea of sequences of self-similar information and computation. In particular it allows us the ability to think in terms of multidimensional 'spaces' covered, or contained, by such sequences. Again, however, it is important to stress that such spaces are not 'real' in any true sense that we might be able to compare to worldly objects such as a brick or a chair. Even so, as three dimensions are being used, in this case at least, it is still possible to think of $_8X_0$'s pattern as being cone-shaped overall within three such dimensions of relevance.

$_8X_0$ in Three Dimensions

Given that we have established that a sequence of computation or information can be thought of as a conic,[7] or cone-shaped, region in three-dimensional space, such a model can be applied to all 16 ' X '-shaped pattern configurations

---

7   Having the form of, resembling, or pertaining to, a cone.

introduced in Chapter 5. To do this let's again concentrate on $_8X_0$ first as this is the easiest of the configurations to consider, given that it basically consists of two spiralling cones tied together about their point of potential symmetry breaking. This is shown in the diagram below.

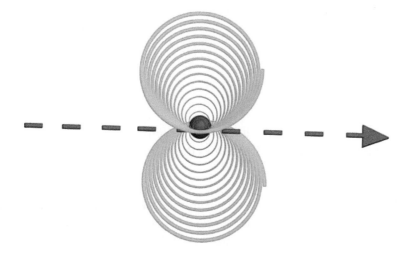

Figure 8.10 $_8X_0$ **in three dimensions**

Looking at this representation it should be clear that it is made up of two cones, placed together, as in Figure 8.11(a), with their sharp ends positioned about the point of symmetry breaking. This indeed could be true, but interestingly this is not the only configuration in which two conical spirals can be placed to achieve the same effect. Look at Figure 8.11(b) and you will see two cones lining up about the same point so that their blunt ends face in exactly opposite directions. This too produces exactly the same effect as seen in Figure 8.11(a) from certain vantage points. Indeed the same effect can be seen from exactly the same vantage point, as the overall pattern conjures up an elegant trick of the mind.

The latter of these two patterns happens to be extremely significant in the world of physics, as will be explained in Chapter 12. In fact it is so significant that a number of important theories hang off it and it has been given the name of the scientist who first demonstrated their relevance.

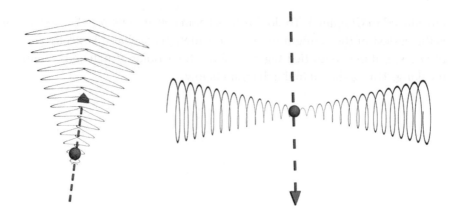

Figures 8.11(a) and 8.11(b)   Equally valid configurations of $_8X_0$ in three dimensions. Figure 8.11(b) shows the Minkowski Configurations

Hermann Minkowski was a nineteenth-century German mathematician of Jewish and Polish descent, who created and developed the geometry of numbers and who used geometrical methods to solve difficult problems in number theory, mathematical physics and the theory of relativity.[36] In particular Minkowski showed the relevance of double-coned configurations, similar to that presented in Figure 8.11(b), in special relativity and by so doing greatly assisted Einstein in his work on general relativity. For this reason we shall henceforth refer to this arrangement of cones as a Minkowski configuration.

Introducing the Idea of Fields

Adding an extra dimension to the 'X'-shaped pattern adds real value as it allows both computation and information to be thought of in terms of 'volume' rather than just simply flat 'area' as has been traditional in graphing theory. This also adds greater 'reality' in the sense that we can now relate to the pattern, at least in an analogous sense, in terms of our own worldly experience, where the three dimensions of height, breadth and depth play a critical role in defining the expanse around us. Indeed by considering information and computation over three dimensions this even draws to mind some very powerful similarities to phenomena common to our real-world experience. Both information and computation are very ethereal things. Just like the field associated with, say, a powerful magnet, we can't touch either of them directly, but we can relate to the spaces they occupy though indirect evidence. Aids such as compasses and iron filings might provide the means by which such evidence is collected in the case of a magnetic field, but other techniques come to mind that we could use to identify information and computation in the synthetic worlds that interests us.

In detailing such techniques it must be remembered that each leg involved in the ' X '-shaped pattern merely represents the end point of two sequences of either information or computation that collide and the start point for two more that converge. This consequently means that the pattern itself can be considered as providing a 'container' in which four such sequences can be captured through their causal interaction. The contents of this container can further be considered as a singular whole by simply abstracting up a level and realising that such an entity can only hold a fixed range contents in line with every possible permutation of symmetrical and asymmetric legs allowed in its underlying pattern. In this way each container can be given a type according to a particular ' X '-shaped pattern permutation. What's more, such aggregations can themselves be considered as units in higher level aggregate patterns. Or, in other words, they can be seen as combining with other such aggregations in three or more dimensions in an ever increasing ladder of abstraction – the higher dimensional implications of which will become important in later chapters.

This is where the Minkowski configuration starts to help us and we shall specifically consider its usefulness by considering how two $_{8}X_{0}$ patterns might interact. If we do so, the following configuration can be seen:

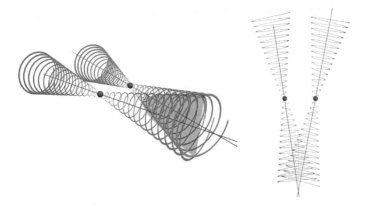

Figure 8.12(a) and 8.12(b)   Two views of the interaction between two Minkowski configurations

The important feature to note here is the pattern created on the plane where the two front cones intersect. This is a parabolic interference pattern as shown below in grey:

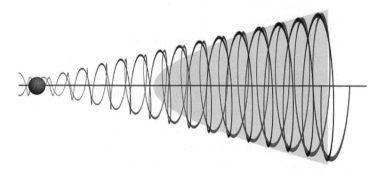

Figure 8.13   The parabolic interference pattern produced by the intersection of two cones of separate Minkowski configurations

Parabolas are one of a family of shapes known as conic sections and we shall next move on to investigate why such shapes should be of significance to information and computing.

9

Why Are Conic Sections Important?

Poetry is as precise a thing as geometry.

Gustave Flaubert

In mathematics, a conic section, or just 'conic', is a curve obtained by intersecting a cone, or more precisely, a circular conical surface, with a plane. A conic section is therefore a restriction of a quadric[1] surface to the plane. Conic sections, in all their various forms, were named and studied as long ago as 200 BC, when Apollonius of Perga undertook a systematic study of their properties.[39]

In all, there are three types of conics named the ellipse, the hyperbola and parabola. The circle can be considered as a fourth type, as it was by Apollonius of Tyana[2], or as a kind of ellipse, thereby making it inclusive to the three original forms. The circle and the ellipse arise when the intersection of cone and plane is a closed curve. The circle is obtained when the cutting plane is parallel to the plane of the generating circle of the cone. If the cutting plane is parallel to exactly one generating line of the cone, then the conic is unbounded and is called a parabola. In the remaining case, the conic formed is hyperbolic. In this case the plane will intersect both halves, or nappes, of the cone, producing two separate unbounded curves, though often one is ignored.[39]

The conic section is a key concept in abstract mathematics, but it is also seen with considerable regularity in the material world, with many practical applications in engineering, physics, and other fields. Furthermore the conic section may well hold the key to addressing an apparent weakness in the 'X'-shaped pattern. Before that can be considered, however, we must first

---

1 'quadric', or quadric surface, is any n-dimensional hypersurface.
2 Apollonius was a Greek Neopythagorean philosopher from the town of Tyana in the Roman province of Cappadocia in Asia Minor. Little is certainly known about him. Being a first-century orator and philosopher around the time of Christ, he was compared to Jesus of Nazareth by Christians in the fourth century and by various popular writers in modern times.

understand that there are two types of possible behaviour in computational systems, those being linear and non-linear.

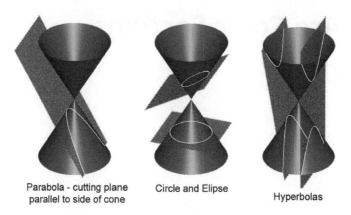

Parabola - cutting plane   Circle and Elipse
parallel to side of cone
                                                      Hyperbolas

Figures 9.1(a), 9.1(b) and 9.1(c)   The various types of conic section

Linear Systems

Look up linearity in the dictionary and the following definition will be found:

linear

—adjective

1.   *of, consisting of, or using lines: linear design.*

2.   *pertaining to or represented by lines: linear dimensions.*

3.   *extended or arranged in a line: a linear series.*

4.   *involving measurement in one dimension only; pertaining to length: linear measure.*

5.   *of or pertaining to the characteristics of a work of art in which forms and rhythms are defined chiefly in terms of line.*

6.   *having the form of or resembling a line: linear nebulae.*

7. *Mathematics.*

    a. *consisting of, involving, or describable by terms of the first degree.*

    b. *having the same effect on a sum as on each of the summands: a linear operation.*

8. *Electronics. Delivering an output that is directly proportional to the input: a linear circuit; a linear amplifier.*

9. *threadlike; narrow and elongated: a linear leaf.*

Linearity is often seen as property synonymous with predictability, just as in the way that we can predict the next point on a straight line with relative ease so long as we know the path of all previous points. And in many ways that is very true, but it is not the entire picture. In the purest mathematical sense linearity is about much more than a straight line graph. In the jargon, it means additive and homogeneous, and these abstruse terms can be illustrated best by using a set of simple diagrams. In reading these, assume that a system produces output y for an input x:

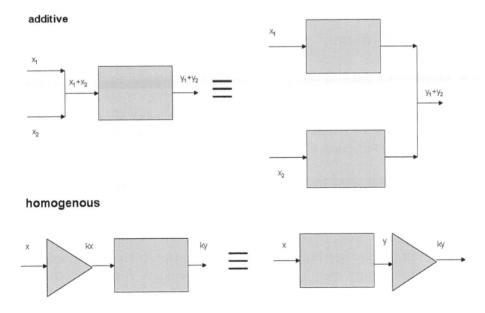

Figure 9.2 Diagrammatic descriptions of linearity

Literally this means that any linear system produces the same output for two added inputs,[3] or for an input multiplied by a constant, whether those operations are carried out before or after the signals pass through the system. [37] This is a property often referred to as superposition and in algebraic notation it is written:

$$f(x + y) = f(x) + f(y)$$

$$f(k \times x) = k \times f(x)$$

If a system is linear, it is amenable to analysis by linear algebra, which is a vast mathematical structure of immense power. Methods of linear algebra include algebraic geometry, matrices, vector spaces and transforms (such as Fourier).[37]

There is no equivalent non-linear algebra, and non-linear systems have in general to be treated on an ad hoc basis.

In the real world, apart from the electromagnetic properties of a vacuum, truly linear behaviour is virtually unknown. Fortunately, however, many systems are effectively linear over a restricted range of variables.[38]

Non-linear Systems

In mathematics, a non-linear system is one which is obviously not linear, that is, a system which does not have any superposition property, or whose output is not proportional to its input. Less technically, a non-linear system is any problem where the resultant output variables cannot be written as a linear combination of independent inputs.[38]

Non-linearity is the most abundant classification of system found in the natural world and supports a number of characteristics analogous to structures found in computation. Aggregation, classification and logic of sorts can all be found in certain types of non-linear systems, but it is important to stress that the term 'analogous' here brings with it specific variants of such characteristics. Linear systems carry such traits too, but they are much 'cleaner' in terms of conventional thinking like that found in traditional computer science. In such a sense the ideas of computation and information are, of course, ubiquitous

---

3   Often interpreted as a 'signal'.

across all of systems theory – the interdisciplinary field of science and the study of the nature of complex systems in nature, society and science – which by definition covers both linear and non-linear variants.

Given the proposed universal nature of computation and information there is an immediate cross-check for the 'X'-shaped pattern, as we should question if it too can be found in to be applicable to both linear and non-linear systems.

In the case of linear variants, the answer is unequivocal, in that the pattern provides the foundational framework on which switching and causal interaction are built. So in simple terms, this means that inputs are allowed to flow in and that two[4] resultant paths are allowed to flow out under regulation as outputs. It's a straightforward structure made up of paths fanning out from a causal point as a direct result of all relevant and accumulated inputs – superposition is preserved, but only in special cases where inputs and outputs are additive or homogeneously equivalent. This need not necessarily always be the case, so the pattern also covers non-linear variants as well and this leads to an interesting observation in that in complex non-linear systems 'X'-shaped-like behaviour can be seen at a number of different levels of abstraction. Whilst at the most fundamental level the 'X'-shaped pattern can be seen as the basis by which all axioms break symmetry and thus aggregate or change, it can also be seen as the mechanism by which aggregates themselves aggregate or change, one example of which is the process or bifurcation.

Back to Bifurcation

Many computational systems depend on parameters – inputs that may not be directly associated with the inbound data under transformation, but which nonetheless have a direct bearing on any transformation undertaken. Normally the gradual variation of a parameter in such systems corresponds to the gradual change in the outputs produced. However, there are certain circumstances where the number of outputs changes abruptly and the structure of the computation undertaken varies significantly when a parameter passes through some critical range even slightly – for example, the onset of convection and turbulence when the flow parameters are changed in dynamic fluid systems. This type of phenomenon is known as bifurcation and it is the hallmark of

---

4   Remember that one or both of these paths may be unobservable to the observer.

qualitative change in the nature of a dynamic system, a partial differential equation or a delay differential equation.

Many naturally occurring phenomena that are based around cyclical or apparently random transformations[5] can be explained through bifurcation, and, in particular, the theory of generalised thermodynamics elaborates greatly on the concepts involved. Of specific interest is the work of Ilya Prigogine[6] and his colleague Paul Glansdorff[7] who studied the stability of far-from-equilibrium systems. That is to say, systems that have undergone sufficient activity from a point of known stability as a result of their inputs – heat energy in the case of thermodynamics – to make their current state, or future states, distinct. As a result of their work the Glansdorff–Prigogine criterion was formed which states that far-from-equilibrium systems may become unstable as they are driven further from balance and that there may arise a 'crisis' or bifurcation point at which the system prefers to leave the steady state, evolving instead into some other stable state:

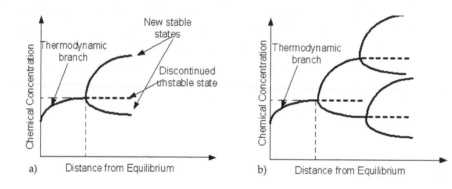

Figure 9.3(a) and 9.3(b)   Systems far from equilibrium can split into two stable states, as in (a). As the distance from equilibrium is increased even further, more and more stable states become possible, as in (b) (dashed lines indicate unstable states)

---

5   One example of phase doubling is the Belousov–Zhabotinski reaction discovered in the 1950s. This is a chemical reaction that results in a cyclical colour change in the resultant solution.
6   Ilya, Viscount Prigogine, was a Russian-born naturalised Belgian physical chemist and Nobel Laureate noted for his work on dissipative structures, complex systems, and irreversibility.
7   Paul Glansdorff, a French physicist noted for playing a major role in the development of the theory of dissipative structures with Belgian chemist Ilya Prigogine, the first presentation of which was jointly published in 1971.

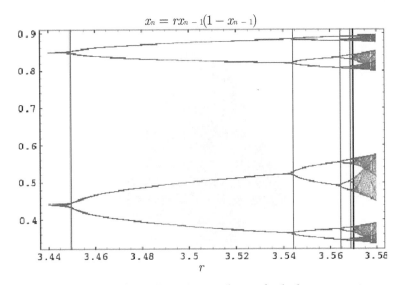

$$x_n = rx_{n-1}(1 - x_{n-1})$$

Figure 9.4   Bifurcation as a mathematical phenomenon

Bifurcation and its resultant pattern, commonly known as 'period doubling' fit well with the notion of binary logic and the 'X'-shaped pattern, although, at first sight, there may not appear an exact fit.

As the name itself suggests, bifurcation relates to two phenomena arising from a single split source, with the resultant legs of the associated plot curving away from the point where symmetry has broken. This is not unlike the behaviour we might expect from a linear system, only this time the causal structure is due to multiple, and often unforeseen, combinatory factors. Furthermore the macro-graph structure of a bifurcating system is similar to that of its less complex and lower level linear cousins, in that a single asymmetric input can be seen prior to the point of symmetry breaking which is then followed by the obligatory two outputs – both being asymmetric in almost all bifurcation cases.

But this is may not be the end of the relationship between the 'X'-shaped pattern and non-linear systems. Look closely at the curving, folk-shaped patterns produced when period doubling in bifurcation occurs – as those seen in Figures 9.3 and 9.4 – and observe that they appear surprisingly conic in form. Consider also that any given cone can have an infinite number of conic sections as it is sliced in various ways. In the case of hyperbolic cross-sections, this can be roughly illustrated as shown in Figure 9.5, and each cross-section can be

Figure 9.5   A cone split into hyperbolic conic sections

thought of mathematically as (half) a hyperbola according to the following equation:

$$\frac{x^2}{a^2} - \frac{y^2}{b^2} = 1 \text{ or } \frac{y^2}{b^2} - \frac{x^2}{a^2} = 1$$

This is a somewhat restricted case, however, as different types of cross-section can be produced depending on how any given cone is sliced as we have already discussed. By changing the intersection angle and location of cross-section it is possible to create a circle, ellipse, parabola or hyperbola; or in the special case where the plane of intersection that touches the tip of the cone,[8] a point or line can be produced, as shown by the dotted lighter coloured lines in Figure 9.6. Furthermore, such special cases are so well known and important in mathematics that there is a special name for the lines involved and they are called 'asymptotes'. In this context asymptotes can hence be seen as straight lines approached by a given curve as one of the variables in the equation of the curve tends towards infinity.

---

8   Its vertex.

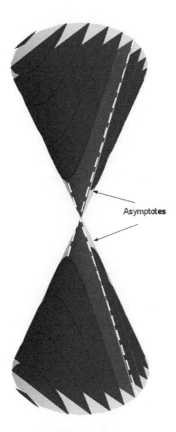

Figure 9.6   Intersecting straight lines produced by way of conic section

By using conic sections and their associated asymptotes, cones provide a general model within which the splitting, or bifurcation, patterns of both linear and non-linear systems can be represented; asymptotes providing the familiar diverging straight lines associated with linear systems and more curved conics covering the patterns produced by non-linear schemes.

In mathematical terms a conic section can be generalised according to the following formula:

$$a \times x^2 + b \times x \times y + c \times y^2 + d \times x + e \times y + f = 0$$

where a, b, c, d, ..and f are coefficients[9] and x and y are variables. This may be fascinating from the perspective of pure mathematics, but its relevance to information and computation needs some explanation, however. To highlight such importance it firstly must be appreciated that conics do not necessarily need a flat intersecting surface with a cone to be produced. Take two cones, or double cones as in Figure 8.12(a) in Chapter 8, and allow them to overlap or intersect and a conic section will be produced. This, of course, implies that the interaction or two cones can be seen a mechanism for producing conic patterns. This is particularly important for the 'X'-shaped pattern as, if symmetrical information and computation can be represented by such twin cones, this leads to a remarkable conjecture:

> Conic Sections correspond to the interference pattern produced when two symmetrical computations or information sequences of high enough scale interact or overlap

Conjecture 6   Conic sections are computational or information interference patterns

To put this in planer terms, if it is possible to consider information and computation as being analogous to the idea of a field, conic patters might provide evidence of field interference and perhaps further assist with the identification of hitherto unidentified systems or collections of information at high scales.

To qualify this assertion further, think about the way that radar works. Up to this point we have used examples where we have deliberately had two known sources of symmetrical information or computation and these have been brought together so as to deliberately examine the patterns produced by their interaction or overlap. But what if we only had one such source at hand, yet strongly suspected the existence of more? Rather than looking for such additional entities directly, might it not make more sense to look at the interference patterns of the first as it's interacts with its immediate environment? Just as with radar it might be possible to use such a seed pattern to seek out other non-obvious informational or computational entities within the locale.

---

9   A constant multiplicative factor of a certain object. For example, in the expression $9x^2$, the coefficient of x^2 is 9.

Note, however, that when referring to such sources as being 'at hand', there is no deliberate inference that the distance involved is as understood in terms of the real world dimensions of space. Rather, 'closeness' is more likely to be akin to ideas based on 'similarity' or 'meaning'. Note also that it is important to reinforce the role that scale plays here, as there is a need for large quantities of either information or computation, or both, to be present before suitable Minkowski cones can form and the patterns we are discussing here can manifest as a direct consequence of their inter-relationships.

Fractals, Power Laws and Conic Relevance

As you might expect, we are leading up to something. Recent studies have shown conic-like patterns to be important and prevalent in the biggest semi-synthetic[10] information system known to man. The World Wide Web is known to be discernibly irregular in its formation at just about every level and across every characteristic. For instance, the original language at its core, the hypertext mark-up language HTML, is a 'non-sequential', non-linear technology that glues together Web resources to form a corpus of utterly unplanned global organisation. In short it is complexly 'messy'. Unlike traditional text where the distance between the start and the end of a statement or sentence is finite and measurable, the introduction of a hypertext link renders the measurement of distance, and hence directly attained understanding, almost useless. Follow the inserted hyperlink and it could theoretically lead off on an infinitely long trail to amass the entire collective knowledge of humankind before it eventually winds its way back to where it left off. This is poles apart from the Euclidian view of the world that powered the advances of the Industrial Revolution. It is both fascinating and compelling, therefore, that the next technical revolution, the Information Revolution, powered by the Web, has gone back to nature for its inspiration. No longer are we facing a mechanical world of straight lines and the predictable outcomes of close quarter's cause-effect. Instead a non-linear world of complex patterns and holistic perspectives lies ahead. What is also interesting is that the Web is not alone in its classification as a complex 'messy' system. The universe is full of such examples. Galaxies are messy, weather systems are messy and coast lines are messy. In fact nature loves messiness and the more complex a system gets, in general, the more the level of this 'intertwined jumble' of messiness increases. But that is not to say that there is no regularity to such messiness: quite the contrary. Step away and regularity

---

10   In that the Web is a sociotechnical system built from hardware, software and wetware, wetware being the billions of humans who interact with it and build it on a daily basis.

rapidly starts to appear, often in terms of repeatable and self-reflexive fractal structure and power law relationships.

Fractals come straight from the sweet spot at the centre of complexity, being 'repetitions of the same general patterns, even the same details, at both ascending and descending scales'.[10] They tell us that the universe and all that it contains is made up of folded realities within self-similar worlds, and today modern science is quickly realising the important role that fractals play in a number of critical areas in science.

The term 'fractal' was invented by Benoit Mandelbrot, an IBM researcher, to describe the new geometry of shapes that form in the wake of dynamic systems. Fractal patterns are all around us, above us, within us, everywhere. Trees are fractals, with their repeated pattern of large and small branches, with similar details found even in the smallest twigs. Even a single leaf shows fractal repetitions of the whole tree in both its shape and the branching in its veins. Examine a cauliflower and you find fractal geometry at its best, with florets arranged at self-similar scales. For a total fractal experience, peel the leaves from an artichoke. Photographs taken through electron microscopes and far-ranging telescopes reveal that images from vastly different scales evoke a feeling of similarity and recognition. A spiral nebula that measures hundreds

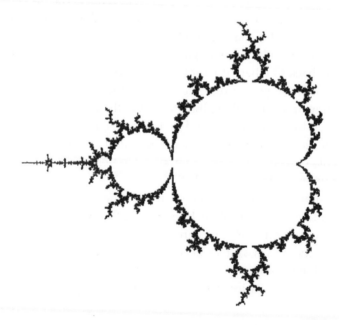

Figure 9.7   The Mandelbrot set as an example of a fractal geometry

of light-years across looks remarkably similar to something that measures a thousandth of a centimetre, say the eye of a firefly. One can be seen as the fractal resonance of the other, the resonance of the microcosm to the macrocosm. The patterns in the weather, the turbulence in the winds, the rhythm pounded out by an African drummer, the rituals performed by queens and shamans and celebrants of the New Year, the courtship habits of peacocks and prairie dogs, the landscapes of nature and the inscapes of dreams, all embody fractal phenomena.

These examples point to the universality of the fractal as a central organising principle of our most complex systems, and that includes the Web. Wherever we look in our world the complex systems of nature and time seem to preserve the look of details at finer and finer scales. Fractals show a holistic hidden order behind things, a harmony in which everything affects everything else, and, above all, an endless variety of interwoven patterns. Fractal geometry allows bounded curves of infinite length, and closed surfaces with infinite area. It even allows curves with positive volume and arbitrarily large groups of shapes with exactly the same boundary. This is exactly how our lungs manage to maximise their surface area. Indeed most natural objects are composed of many types of entangled fractals woven into each other, each with parts which have different fractal dimensions. For example, the bronchial tubes in the human lung have one fractal dimension for the first seven layers of branching, then there is a divergence of geometry and a different fractal dimension appears as used in the finer grades of airway.[10] Indeed John Archibald Wheeler, a friend of Albert Einstein and a protégé of Niels Bohr, the famous quantum physicist, was once quoted as saying that 'no one will be considered scientifically literate tomorrow who is not familiar with fractals'.[10]

The world we live in is not naturally smooth-edged in the round; it has been fashioned with rough edges. Smooth surfaces are the exception in nature. And yet science have thus far chosen to favour a geometry that only describes such 'roughness' rarely, if ever. This stems from our much-loved Euclidean geometry and mostly concentrates on ideal shapes such as spheres, circles, cubes and squares. Of course these shapes do appear in the real world, but they are mostly man-made and not born of nature.[10] Nature prefers to deal with non-uniform shapes and irregular edges. Take the human form, for example; there is certainly symmetry about it, but it is, and has always been, indescribable in terms of Euclidian geometry. It is quite simply not a uniform shape. In plain English, fractal geometry is the geometry of the irregular, the geometry of nature, and, in general, fractals are characterised by infinite detail, infinite length and the absence of smoothness or derivative.

But let us also not forget that fractals are not restricted to the purely natural world. They quite happily inhabit synthetic problem spaces as well. Invisible assemblies as truly intangible as traffic, a democracy or a computer program all have the capability to embody fractal characteristics. Just as in the natural world, simple base patterns form the foundation for all the computer systems in existence today, with many such patterns sharing exactly the same characteristics as those fundamental to many naturally occurring complex phenomena.

Fractals relate to the Web in many wonderful and important ways. For instance they provide a framework for patterned repetition on the Web, but not just any old kind of repetition. Fractals allow repetition to unfold across an infinite number of dimensions and scales, thereby creating hierarchies of structure for free. Web pages within websites, websites within communities, communities with cultures and economies and so on, all these complex organisations are provided through the ubiquitous support of fractals. But there is more to fractal Web structures than just pure hierarchy support. For instance there is strong evidence to suggest that notions of knowledge and hierarchy are closely linked. Knowledge can be expressed in terms of mental hierarchies that behave very much like rules that are in competition, so that experience causes useful rules to grow stronger and unhelpful rules to grow weaker. Furthermore, plausible new rules are generated from a combination of old rules. In support of such thinking, psychologists like Richard Nisbett and Keith Holyoak and the philosopher Paul Thagard have produced experimental evidence to suggest that these principles could account for a wide assortment of 'Aha!' type insights, ranging from Sir Isaac Newton's experience with the falling apple to such everyday abilities as understanding an analogy.[40] In particular they argue that these principles ought to cause the spontaneous emergence of default hierarchies as the basic organisational structure of human knowledge – as indeed they appear to do. We use weak general rules with stronger exceptions to make predictions about how things should be assigned into categories: 'If it's streamlined and has fins and lives in the water, then it's a fish', but 'if it also breathes and is big, then it's a whale'. We use the same structure to make predictions about how things should be done: It's always 'i' before 'e' except after 'c'', but if it's a word like 'neighbour', 'weight' or 'weird', then its 'e' before 'i'. So we use the same structure again to make predictions about causality: 'If you whistle to a dog, then it may come to you', but 'If the dog is growling and raising its hackles, then it probably won't.'

The theory says that these default-hierarchy models ought to emerge whenever the principles are implemented and thereby promotes the notion of the Web as a cogitating entity. This may not be in any conscious sense as we would traditionally recognise the concept of mind, but rather as a mechanism capable of storing and assimilating information nonetheless.

Fractals are also closely associated with power laws, often also referred to as log-log[11] laws because of the relationships between the properties being linked. Such laws are a special kind of mathematical relationship between two quantities. If one quantity is the frequency of an event, the relationship is a power law distribution if the frequencies decrease very slowly as the size of the event increases. For instance, an Earthquake twice as large is four times as rare. If this pattern holds for Earthquakes of all sizes, then the distribution is said to 'scale'. Power laws also describe other kinds of relationships, such as the metabolic rate of a species and its body mass – commonly referred to as Kleiber's law – and the size of a city and the number of patents it produces. What this relationship means is that there is no typical size in the conventional sense. Power laws are found throughout the natural and man-made worlds and are an active study of scientific research.

Mapping the Web in its entirety is an almost impossible task, akin to mapping a gargantuan maze. If it were possible to rise above such a maze, in a helicopter say, the task of mapping would be easy, however, as we would simply draw the layout seen below. But there is no such means by which the Web can be observed. This is because its virtual existence does not directly correspond to anything we can understand in a material sense. So we are restricted to entering the maze and keeping track of where it leads.

What a strange contrivance we have made for ourselves. We have built the Web, but we cannot easily tell exactly what it is that we have built. Thus we must investigate its form as though we were blind, feeling out its contours little by little. In 1999 Réka Albert, Hawoong Jeong and Albert László Barabási of the University of Notre Dame in Indiana did exactly that, by sending a robot[12] into

---

11 The term 'log' is short for mathematical logarithm.
12 A robot in this sense is common parlance on the Web for a software program that is a software agent. A robot interacts with other network services intended for people as if it were a real person. One typical use of bots is to gather information.

the maze of the Web and directing it to map out its virtual pathways. The robot was a computer program which was instructed to enter a Website and follow all its hyperlinks. These took the robot to an assortment of other websites, at each of which it would repeat the same process. On each outing the robot kept a record of the number of outgoing hyperlinks it encountered from each page. To conduct this search for all several billion or so of the pages on the Web would have been far too much for the robot to accomplish. Instead, the researchers told their program simply to stay within the bounds of their university's many web pages. This alone comprised a fine sample of some 325,729 HTML documents, interconnected by nearly 1.5 million hypertext links, and the researchers hoped that it would be sufficiently large and representative to act as a model of the Web as a whole.

As a result of this study, Albert and her fellow workers found that the probability distributions of both incoming and outgoing links in the graph their studies produced were dependent on power laws. Most pages had few links; a few had many, and each time that the number of links was doubled, the number of pages with that many links decreased by a constant factor. The result is not obvious. Although we might intuitively expect fewer pages with many links than just a few, a power law is by no means the only relationship consistent with this. In fact we might have expected the most plausible relationship to fit a statistically 'normal' bell curve, with most pages possessing an average of perhaps three or four links. But the power law relationship says that there is no such preference – no scale to the connectivity of the network. A power law is scale-free.

$$y = ax^k$$

A power law relationship between two scalar quantities x and y is such that the relationship can be written as above, where a – the constant of proportionality – and k – the exponent of the power law – are constants.

Power laws can be seen as a straight line on a log-log graph since, by taking logarithms of both sides, the above equation is equal to that shown below:

$$\log(y) = k\log(x) + \log(a)$$

Such power laws tell us that the Web is a special kind of small world network, one in which small average path lengths between two randomly selected nodes, coupled with a high degree of node clustering, combine to give a compelling criterion for connectivity: as the number of nodes in the network grows, the average path length increases very slowly.[13] Essentially it is relatively easy to get from one point in the network to another, no matter how large the network is.

The researchers at Notre Dame found also that a graph constructed to have the same power law distribution of connectivity as they had observed for their section of the Web does indeed show such characteristics.

So the Web is a small world and one in which its organisation is very specifically characterised by a power law or scale-free connectivity. Albert and her colleagues estimate that if the entire Web has the same structure as the Notre Dame University domain, then any two of its Web pages are separated by just an average of just nineteen links. This is a somewhat larger span than in the six degrees common in certain types of social networks, but it is still a remarkably small number all the same. This means that anyone can get from one extreme of the Web to another in fewer steps than it take a normal man to run a hundred yards! From hand-care to hacking, Homer Simpson to homeopathy, it's all just around the corner on the Web.

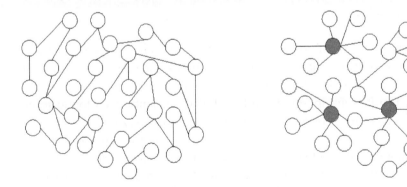

Figures 9.8(a) and 9.8(b)   Examples of a Random and Scale-Free Graphs

13 To be more mathematically precise, the characteristic path length is proportional to the logarithm of the number of nodes.

In fact power laws seem to be a recurring pattern on the Web. Lada Adamic at the Xerox Research Centre has uncovered this kind of probability distribution in the number of pages per Website, for instance. Furthermore, in 1998 she and her collaborators discovered that users who surf the Web also obey power law statistics. Surfing is the common alternative to using search engines such as Google directly. You find a Website that looks as though it might contain the information you want and then follow its hyperlinks to other pages until either you find what you are looking for or you conclude that it is not out there at all.

Most users will happily surf not just from one page to another but from site to site. But Adamic and her colleagues considered only the surfing pathways that surfers take within single sites. They were interested in how 'deep' people go – how many clicks they follow, on average, before quitting the site. By looking at various data sets – the behaviour of over 23,000 users registered with the service provider AOL, and visitors to the Xerox Website, for example – they found that the probability distribution function of the number of clicks on a site obeyed a power law, or something very close to it.[71]

But what does a scale-free network actually look like? In a random graph most nodes have roughly the same number of connections and the structure looks relatively uniform throughout – as exemplified in the graph shown in Figure 9.8(a). In a scale-free network, however, most nodes have only one or two links, yet a small but significant proportion are highly connected – as illustrated in Figure 9.8(b). Thus the structure is very uneven, almost 'lumpy', seemingly dense or pinched in some places but sparse in others. It is these highly linked nodes that provide the shortcuts, the backbones that make the Web such a small world.

One particular type of power law common on the Web is known as Zipf's Law in honour of its inventor, the American linguist George Zipf. When first stated it was intended to show that the relative frequency of a word is inversely proportional to its rank in any given text, but it has since been found to be prolific across a number of phenomena outside linguistics. Zipf got more and more enthusiastic about such types of distribution and he later discovered similar relations in other subjects, such as in the distribution of inhabitants valid in different countries. More recently Zipf's Law has been shown to have strong relevance in large-scale informational systems, such as the Web, for instance illustrating how the popularity distribution of websites works. Accordingly

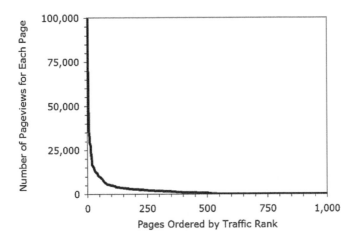

Figure 9.9   An example power law distribution and its hyperbolic shape

the 100th most popular website in the world gets approximately 1/100th of the traffic of the most popular site, and the 2,000,000th most popular website would see 1/2,000,000th of the most popular website's traffic, leading to a curve that looks like this:

Now on to the truly remarkable thing: plot the kind of power law relationship, as found on the Web, and a certain type of geometry can be seen. Zipf's Law produces a hyperbolic curve, so again a highly conic theme plays through. This unfortunately often results in confusion by making it open to consideration as a member of a much wider family of hyperbolic distributions, and these should not be confused with the specific type of hyperbolic distribution to be introduced later in Chapter 16. This confusion arises because that distribution relies on its logarithmic function to move away from its native 'bell-shape' structure and gain hyperbolic conic status. Even so, promote Zipf's Law through the same logarithmic function and it still produces a plot that can be considered as being conic – in that a straight line can be seen as an asymptote.

Zipf believed in the validity of his law so strongly that he justified the annexation of Austria by Germany by stating that his law would fit better! After Zipf's first investigations his relation has been found in many subjects areas, from the distribution of students in English universities to the number of articles handling different topics in a scientific magazine and, more recently, the occurrence of non-coding junk sections DNA. All obey Zipf's Law.

Figure 9.8 An example power law distribution and its hyperbolic shape.

10

The Gifts that Newton Gave, Turing Opened and Which No One Has Really Appreciated Yet

If we knew what we were doing, it would not be called research, would it?
Albert Einstein

Between 1685 and 1686 Sir Isaac Newton composed his famous *Principia Mathematica*, one of the most well-known and influential scientific texts of all time. In it he immortalised his laws of motion, ideas that would have a profound effect on humanity from that point forward. Indeed, so insightful were his ideas that they remained unchallenged for over three hundred years. Not until the arrival of Einstein and the unveiling of his work on relativity did anyone manage to improve on them, and even then the advances made only really come into their own when vast scales are considered. At small scales, Newton's laws still stand strong, faithfully telling us how objects will move and the physical properties involved will interlock.

Newton's laws form the basis for classical mechanics, directly relating the forces acting on a body to the motion of that body. In the simplest of forms they can be expressed as:

First Law:

Every object in a state of uniform motion tends to remain in that state of motion unless an external force is applied to it.

This is essentially Galileo's concept of inertia, and hence is often termed simply the 'Law of Inertia'.[41] In particular, the first law specifies that an object at rest remains at rest and an object in motion will remain in motion unless acted on by an unbalanced force.

Second Law:

The relationship between an object's mass m, its acceleration a, and the applied force F is $F = ma$. Acceleration and force are vectors and hence have directional properties and in this law the direction of the force vector is the same as the direction of the acceleration vector.

This is the most powerful of Newton's three laws as it allows quantitative calculations of how velocities change when forces are applied. Notice that according to Newton, a force causes only a change in velocity – commonly referred to as an acceleration – it does not maintain the velocity as had earlier been thought by the Greek philosopher Aristotle.[41]

This is sometimes summarised by saying that under Newton, $F = m \times a$, but under Aristotle $F = m \times v$, where v is the velocity. Thus, according to Aristotle there is only a velocity if there is a force, but according to Newton an object with a certain velocity maintains that velocity unless a force acts on it to cause acceleration – a change in the velocity. Interestingly, Aristotle's view seems to be more in accord with common sense, but that is because of a failure to appreciate the role played by frictional forces. Once all forces acting in a given situation are taken into account it is the dynamics of Newton,[1] not of Aristotle, that are found to be in accord with the observations.[41]

Third Law:

For every action there is an equal and opposite reaction.

This law is exemplified by what happens if you step off a boat and onto the bank of a lake: as you move in the direction of the shore the boat tends to move in the opposite direction, thereby creating a perilous situation if not careful.[41]

From these laws, several equations of uniformly accelerated linear motion, or linear dynamics as it is often called, can be derived. In their classical form these can be seen as:[2]

---

1   And also Galileo.
2   Please note that for the purposes of presentation, all multiplication signs ('$\times$') have been removed from the equations listed, as is convention. Hence, for example, the term 'at' can be read as '$a \times t$'.

$$v = u + at$$

By substituting (1) into (2), we can get (3), (4) and (5)

$$s = \frac{1}{2}(u + v)t$$

where

$$s = ut + \frac{1}{2}at^2$$

s = the distance between initial and final positions (displacement) (sometimes denoted R or x)

$$v^2 = u^2 + 2as$$

u = the initial velocity (speed in a given direction)

v = the final velocity

a = the constant acceleration

$$vt = \frac{1}{2}at^2$$

t = the time taken to move from the initial state to the final state[42]

More precisely these laws can be stated by thinking of a body as being between two instants in time: one 'initial' point and one 'current'. If a (acceleration) is constant, a differential ($a\partial t$), may be integrated over an interval from zero to Δt [3] Δt ($\Delta t = t - ti$), to obtain a linear relationship for velocity. Integration of the velocity yields a quadratic relationship for position at the end of the interval. Don't worry too much about the '∂' and 'Δ' too much at this stage, as they will be fully explained shortly.

$$v = v_i + a\Delta t$$

where:

$$s = s_i + v_i \Delta t + \frac{1}{2}a(\Delta t)^2$$

v_i is the body's initial velocity

s_i is the body's initial position

And its current state is described by:

$$s = s_i + \frac{1}{2}(v + v_i)\Delta t$$

v, the velocity at the end of the interval

s, the position at the end of the interval (displacement)

$$v^2 = v_i^2 + 2a(s - s_i)$$

Δt, the time interval between the initial and current states

a, the constant acceleration, or in the case of bodies moving under the influence of gravity, g.

Newton's work on motion is beyond doubt an act to surpass the contribution of most geniuses, but it still has its limitations. In particular we now know that his laws break down when at least one of the key properties involved increases in size. When large distances (s) are involved, for instance, the predictions produced by Newton's equations start to veer away from

3   Where $\Delta t = t - t_i$.

actuality and need correction. Even so they do provide an invaluable platform from which many deep understandings can and have been formed. Normally such understandings are quoted in relation to the physics of the natural, but, with a little lateral thinking they can be seen to be as being deeply insightful from a purely computational perspective as well.

Differentiation: Computation in All but Name

Recall that computation is all about change. This is especially important for equations like those associated with Newton's laws of motion, as change is quite literally central to their composition and credibility.

Take the equations in total and look at the variables involved. They are distance (s), speed or velocity, (v), acceleration (a) and time (t) and an interesting computational relationship can be found. Velocity, for example, can be shown as a change of distance in relation to a change in time, or, in other words, the rate of change of distance over time. Now engage in a slight act of lateral thinking, replace the critical verb in that last sentence and we might as well be referring to velocity in terms of computation, that is, velocity is the rate at which distance computes[4] over time. At first reading, such as a statement might appear to be mind-bending thought, but that is only because our lives have subconsciously conditioned us to think of speed in terms of human experience rather than as a purely abstract concept. For us, speed naturally evokes many associations. The wind rushing through our hair as we cycle down a country lane, the thrill of the fair ride as we spin out of control, all have immensely emotional tie-ins that want to distract us from the underlying reality. But in actuality, velocity is just another example of computation at work.

The importance of the computation involved does not stop with velocity in the field of linear dynamics. As the give-away name suggests, the entire field is focused on change. Hence, acceleration also has a computational relationship with velocity in that it can be shown to be its rate of change over time. So acceleration is both the rate at which velocity computes and the rate at which the rate at which distance computes. This is not a mistake in the wording, it is merely a description of one computational relationship built upon another. In fact, so important is the rate at which change is manifest that mathematics has formulated a whole branch to deal with it. This is the branch of differential calculus. Regardless of the name it is important to labour the point that has

---

4   Note that the concept of time is implicit in the term 'rate'.

just been made. Differential calculus could, for instance, be rephrased as the study of 'the rate at which computation is done'. That would be incorrect, however, as 'doing' implies that time must be involved in the 'act', as is our normal understanding of computing. 'Rate', here, however, only refers to the intensity of chance present in any given property, relative to some other known property and in such regard it is a truly abstract notion. Such a relation could quite plausibly involve the rate of change of any given thing with regard to peas, chickens, submarines or whatever anyone wants. There simply is no requirement to introduce time into the equations involved in their purest of abstract forms. Only when time is explicitly involved do we get anywhere close to our commonplace understandings of computing.

Differential calculus is the study of how the outputs from functions change when their inputs vary. The primary object of study in differential calculus is the derivative which, for a chosen input value, describes the behaviour of a function near that input value. Furthermore, for a real-valued function of a single real variable, the derivative at a point equals the slope of the tangent line to the graph of the function at that point. In general, the derivative of a function at a point determines the best linear approximation to the function at that point.[42]

The process of finding a derivative is called differentiation. The fundamental theorem of calculus states that differentiation is the reverse process to integration, another obviously related branch of mathematics.[42]

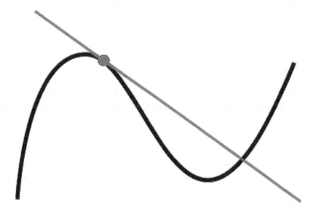

Figure 10.1   The graph of a function, drawn in black, and a tangent line
to that function, drawn in grey. The slope of the tangent line equals the
derivative of the function at the marked point[42]

As already indicated, differentiation has applications in all quantitative disciplines. In physics, for example, the derivative of the displacement of a moving body with respect to time is the velocity of the body, and the derivative of velocity with respect to time is acceleration. Newton's second law of motion states that the derivative of the momentum of a body equals the force applied to the body. The reaction rate of a chemical reaction is a derivative. In operations research, derivatives determine the most efficient ways to transport materials and design factories. By applying game theory,[5] differentiation can provide best strategies for competing corporations.

As an example, suppose that x and y are real numbers and that y is a function of x – that is, y can be described by: $y = f(x)$. Also suppose that the function involved is linear, so it can be expressed over all possible values of y as a straight line plot.[6] In such cases the plot can be described algebraically as $y = f(x) = mx + c$, where m and c are real numbers depend on the exact path the plot. In such circumstances m is called the slope and is given by:

$$m = \frac{change \quad in \quad y}{change \quad in \quad x} = \frac{\Delta y}{\Delta x} \, 7$$

However, this only works for linear functions. Non-linear or non-straight line, functions do not have a well-defined slope. The derivative of a function at the point x is hence the best possible approximation to the idea of the slope of the function at the point x. It is usually denoted by $f'(x)$ or, more commonly by:

$$\frac{\delta y}{\delta x}$$

Together with the value of y, or the function itself, at point x, the derivative of the function determines the best linear approximation, or linearisation, of the function near the point x. This latter property is usually taken as the definition of the derivative.

---

5   Game theory is a branch of applied mathematics that is used in the social sciences, most notably in economics, as well as in biology (particularly evolutionary biology and ecology), engineering, political science, international relations, computer science and philosophy. Game theory attempts to mathematically capture behaviour in strategic situations, or games, in which an individual's success in making choices depends on the choices of others.
6   Usually using Cartesian geometry.
7   Where the symbol Δ (the uppercase form of the Greek letter delta) is an abbreviation for 'change in'.

A closely related notion is the differential of a function which relates to an infinitesimal change in its value about the proximity of any given input to the function. This reformulates the previous equation to:

$$m = \frac{computation \quad on \quad y}{computation \quad on \quad x} = \frac{\Delta y}{\Delta x}$$

and may hence be thought of as 'the output of a given computation taking y as its input, in relation to the output of a given computation taking x as its input'. This is a particularly important rephrasing, as large parts of both mathematics and science are based on the concept of the derivative and associated differentials. What's more, derivatives themselves can be integral parts of mathematical equations. These are, not surprisingly, known as differential equations. An ordinary differential equation is one that relates functions of one variable to their derivatives with respect to that variable. A partial differential equation is a differential equation that relates functions of more than one variable to their partial derivatives. Differential equations arise naturally in the physical sciences, in mathematical modelling, and within mathematics itself. For example, it is possible to return to Newton's second law, which describes the relationship between acceleration and position, and state it as the ordinary differential equation:

$$F(t) = m\frac{\delta^2 s}{\delta t^2}$$

Where:

m is mass

s is distance

t is time

Distance and Space as Synthetic Concepts

It's all very well to talk about the reframing derivatives and differentials in terms of computation, but doing so without an equivalent reframing of the concepts being differentiated adds little value. As individuals it's easy to think of the physical world in terms of change. Our entire life is caught up in the change of at least one property that pervades every aspect of the world around us. That is, of course, time, and its constant onward march is an essential ingredient in both the way our universe works and the manner in which we perceive it. Distance is also a constant factor for us. Whether an object is pressed up against us, or is a billion light years away, the very fact that we can refer to it by its location relative to our own means that distance, and the space that comes with it, is undeniably very real. And because it is real, or at least appears real to us, it can be measured. We have distance-specific scales and units, gauges which can be compared against any reasonable distance to classify it in terms of the rules and names defined within such measuring schemes. Thus we have systems designed for describing the proportions of the 'realness' that engulfs us, at least in terms of distance. But what if we wanted to describe systems that are not real in any physical sense and which may not be founded on such familiar concepts as distance and time? What if we wanted to describe a completely synthetic system made up of completely synthetic elements? How, for example, might we measure the characteristics of any given computer program or string of information?

This question was actually answered in Chapters 2 to 5, when we showed how geometry can be used as a language to describe both information and computation. Fortuitously geometry has to be measurable, as it is founded on the very idea of 'space'. This need not necessarily relate to the type of space we experience around us in the everyday world, but for any given case for geometry, for that geometry to exist it needs to be constrained within something capable of description in terms of spatial dimension. Not surprisingly one of the names we give to such dimensional containers is 'space'. By way of an example, a sheet of graph paper containing squares of equal size can be referred to as a Cartesian space and on it can be drawn any number of geometries for the purpose of description.

Continuing with Cartesian space we can once again think about a computation or string of information as comprising three linked elements which we could graph accordingly:

Figure 10.2   The directed graph of a three-element computation or sequence of information. Note that the arrow heads are merely added for convenience and are not necessarily needed

This representation may look straightforward enough, but it actually hides an issue. Taken as a whole it suggests three units of 'something' linked together one after another. As such, measurement might appear plain and no further discussion about scale need take place. However, this is not strictly true. All that such a diagram really tells us is that three 'somethings' are involved and are linked together. Although the lengths of the arcs used to represent them are the same, there is no explicit mention that the 'somethings' themselves are the same size. By way of an example, one might think of describing an elephant then a monkey and lastly an ant. Obviously the physical presence of an elephant is somewhat larger than that of a monkey or an ant, so the diagram could be misleading if we need to know anything about the size of the animals involved. It only specifies the three animals, or elements, and tells us precious else other than the order in which they are named and should perhaps be recalled.

It is possible, however, to think of graphing in terms which can represent the size of each element involved. Let's take another example and this time think of a library comprising three books. We can be more specific about the books and say, for instance, that the first book is the Bible, the second is Shakespeare's *Romeo and Juliet* and the last contains the lyrics to the Beatle's song 'Penny Lane'. Producing a graph that takes into account the size of the concepts being modelled is relatively easy in this case, as all the books involved are made up from the same elements, namely words and characters. Hence it is possible to draw each arc in the graph of the library to a scale which correlates to either the number of words or the number of characters contained in each book. That is so long as we make it explicit that a scale is being used which is relevant over all three elements.

An approximation of the resultant library graph can be seen in Figure 10.3 and as you might imagine, this now shows consecutive arcs proportionately decreasing in length. This is a big step forward, but there is one final problem to be overcome. In both the above cases all the arcs relate to something – some item or concept that needs more information other than its name to describe it. Yet, physical space does not need to be like that. If we were to think about cutting a line through the centre of the Earth from the North to the South poles, every single section of that line would be occupied by something.[8] In general terms, the atoms comprising the innards of our planet would act like the characters in our library example. Now, however, think of a similar line, between the surface of the Earth and, say, the surface of the Sun, and large parts of that line would be occupied by absolutely nothing at all, courtesy of the vacuum of space. This

8   At least to atomic scales.

**Figure 10.3   The directed graph of a three-element computation or
sequence of information, this time close to scale**

is a characteristic of space that has puzzled physicists for centuries, in that it can exist without anything existing within it. It therefore does not necessarily require any information to describe its internal content and we can simply characterise it via properties of its whole. For this reason it is perfectly valid to state that it is 149,597,870,000[9] metres from the Earth to the Sun and not have to worry about the number of atoms, or anything else, in between.

Intuitively the same is not true of computation and information. Take away the individual instructions from a given computer program and any capability to compute would be removed. Do the same with all the characters or symbols in a sequence of information and surely the ability to inform would be obliterated as well? This may appear correct, but the truth is actually quite the opposite!

Remember that in Chapter 7 it was explained that there are two types of computation and information, those being asymmetric and symmetric, of which only the asymmetric variant is observable. This then raises two very interesting possibilities in relation to the concept of space. The first questions whether space, any space, can truly ever exist in an empty state, for if we cannot directly observe any symmetric computation or information present, how can we draw the conclusion that it is not there? The usual answer to a question like this is to propose tests which can highlight any such existence through indirect means. This implies inspection of some connected property which is asymmetric and indeed such tests may well exist. In astronomy and cosmology, for example, *dark matter* is a hypothetical entity that is (as yet) undetectable by its emitted radiation, but whose presence can be inferred from gravitational effects on visible matter. Dark matter is proposed to explain the flat rotation curves of spiral galaxies and other evidence of 'missing mass' in the universe. According to present observations of structures larger than galaxies, as well as Big Bang cosmology, dark matter and dark energy account for the vast majority

---

9   Give or take 6 metres.

of the mass in the observable universe.[10] The observed phenomena which imply the presence of dark matter include the rotational speeds of galaxies, orbital velocities of galaxies in clusters, gravitational lensing[11] of background objects by galaxy clusters such as the Bullet Cluster, and the temperature distribution of hot gas in galaxies and clusters of galaxies. Dark matter also plays a central role in structure formation and galaxy evolution, and has measurable effects on the directional dependency of the cosmic microwave background. All these lines of evidence suggest that galaxies, clusters of galaxies and the universe as a whole contain far more matter than that which interacts with electromagnetic radiation.[44] In other words, large parts of the universe are simply invisible to us thus far.

The second interesting possibility relates to potential; that is the ability of any given space to hold content and specifically informational content. Thinking of a square two-dimensional sheet of graph paper evenly marked with millimetre squares from edge to edge, even if there is nothing drawn upon it other than the lines to mark the boundaries between squares, it still carries a huge potential to hold information. If we consider each square as a 'location' in which information can be stored by shading it in with some appropriate colour, then we can even measure the paper's storage potential by multiplying the number of squares along two adjacent edges with the number of shading colours available. In just the same way an 'empty' box can be seen has holding a potential in the form of its volume, and so too does the surface of a stage as a group of actors play out a story over a blissful evening's entertainment. All are, in fact, not just examples of potential storage containers, but are examples of active memory. They provide the ability to hold information and/ or computation in relation to any given number of measurable dimensions. In the case of our own tangible space, such dimensions are physically familiar to us, but there is nothing stopping the number or type of such dimensions from being limitless or any of them having to relate to the real world as we understand it. It is perfectly acceptable to think about the generalised concept of space, and hence memory, as having relevance across length, depth, breadth, time, colour, weight, spottiness, the number of Vulcan toe clippings present, the weight of yak hair shed in the spring by a Nepalese brook or whatever. Space as an abstract concept, and as seen as memory, is theoretically limitless in terms of both dimensions and scale.

---

10 A term taken directly from the referenced text, but the term 'asymmetric universe' is just as valid here.
11 A gravitational lens is formed when the light from a very distant, bright source (such as a quasar) is 'bent' around a massive object (such as a cluster of galaxies) between the source object and the observer.

> Space is active memory

Conjecture 7   Space as memory

There is one further stipulation to add, in that space memory must be 'active' for it to have any real value. If any of the squares in our graph paper were to be punched out by forcing a pencil through the page, they would lose their potential to hold content and hence become worthless. Each square must be both capable of both being referenced via the scales describing every one of the graph paper's spatial dimensions and its content must also be describable in terms of at least one other dimension. A single pencilled in square on the sheet can so be identified as valid and active if, and only if, we can determine the number of squares into the page along its length and breadth and we can distinguish its shading as being different from that of the paper on which it is drawn. Any similar shadings outside the graph paper – say on the surface on which it lies – cannot count as being valid or 'active', as they cannot be located in terms of the space of value to us.

Time as a Synthetic Concept

Time is slightly trickier to think about than space in terms of information and computation. To start with a number of common misconceptions normally get in the way. Most, for example, would consider the current state of the universe to be a direct consequence of the passage of time, almost as if time were one of, if not the, most fundamental driver in its creation. This may certainly be what we see directly, but as we have already seen, observation itself can be somewhat misleading. By considering time to be fundamental we are, in effect, saying that it is as pure a concept as you can ever get; that time is not made up of anything other than time and time is not created by anything other than, perhaps, the divine wishes of some higher being than us. A comforting proposition perhaps, but truth is only as good as the last great theory to match up against it through a list of well-founded observations. Time does not have the luxury of a very long list however. Certainly there are many things we know about time and our confidence in such things is justifiably high, but there are many things we have simply not even begun to fathom out yet. Time always appears to travel forwards, for instance – a phenomenon commonly known as the 'arrow' of time – yet physical processes at the subatomic level are believed to be either entirely or mostly time symmetric, meaning that the theoretical statements that describe them remain true if the direction of time is reversed. In spite of this, when we describe things at the macroscopic level it often appears that time is not symmetric, in that it has an obvious direction or flow. The arrow of time being any progression that exhibits such time-asymmetry. Conflicts like this shout out loud that there is something wrong, something incomplete or incorrect in either our current theories or the results of our experiments. Time, it seems, needs more time before it will give up its innermost secrets.

Given that most of our knowledge of time has been validated through many different types of experiment, it is reasonable to assume that it is not experimentation or analysis of experimental data that is at fault. That only leaves theory in doubt. Before revisiting such theories, however, there is a minor need to backtrack and frame time by way of a quick recap on space. The uniform space in which we can move without restriction in all three directions does not naturally come with its own metric. As such concepts like lengths and angles are meaningless unless they can be compared against a form of standard unit. When such a standard is applied we shift from a uniform sensory space to metric geometry. By abstracting further, Euclidean geometry is transformed into the familiar three-dimensional geometry of the Cartesian framework in which geometric shapes such as points, lines and so on are designated by real ($\mathbb{R}$) numerical coordinates, ordered sequences of numbers, equations and alike.[46]

For us in the material world, time is experienced in the form of changing sequential positions where mass points are located. The one dimensional quantity of all points in space through which such mass passes is referred to as a path line. The process of successive, point-by-point relations can hence be seen as the generation of a continuous line or curve through space and can be described algebraically in the form of $x = x(\theta)$, with a real ($\mathbb{R}$), continuous parameter $\theta \geq 0$ whereby the curve originates with a constant increase of θ ,from the point of origin $x = x(0)$. Since the selection of the parameter θ is specified only with the exception of one-to-one continuous transformations, we can speak of *topological time*, which designates only the sequence of points in time without the use of unit measuring aids. In other words, time can stand on its own with no other justification other than a direct relationship to space.

On the continuum of topological time a measuring system can be added by reference to any continual uniform physical movement, such as an accurate clock going about its normal business of tick-tocking. By such application, we get the necessary tools to describe, compare and calculate with time in terms of our everyday experiences. This has proved extraordinarily useful, if not essential, to the physical sciences, but there is no reason to stop with a measuring system based purely on any physical property such as the mechanical movements of a clock. Remember that such ticking is simply an example of a computation, as movement itself is simply a form of transformation. So it is perfectly legitimate to replace the clock with the concept of an abstract computing device so long as each of the actions it is allowed to perform is equally uniform in terms of its duration against some other property. From this idea it is also possible to consider space as a purely abstract concept by way of its binding with time or any abstract machine in its place. This leads to a conclusion in that so long as we allow ourselves the indulgence of conceptualising an abstract computer which goes about any task presented using work units of equal duration, abstract equivalences of both time and space can be formulated without too much effort. Likewise a similar reverse is true in that if we start with the concept of an abstract space accompanied by some suitable unit measuring system and work backwards, we get an abstract computing machine for free.

The existence of time also implies the absence of a particular symmetry in any such system in which it is involved, in that things in that system must visibly transform from moment to moment for us to even understand the notion of *moment to moment*. If there were perfect symmetry between how things are now and how things where then, if the change from moment to moment were of no more consequence than the change from a perfectly uniform rotating a cue ball, then time as we normally conceive it simply wouldn't exist.[21] It is this lack of symmetry, or rather presence of asymmetry, that is one of the fundamental cornerstones of any definition of computation. Even so this does not imply that time is indispensable in any such definition, it simply outlines that some form of regular symmetry breaking is essential for computation to be observable. So if, for example, we were to think of an imaginary universe in which time were absent, it would be perfectly legitimate to expect computation to still take place there so long as the time dimension were replaced by an equally regular characteristic through which computational change can be measured and represented. And note that the only stipulation on this dimension is one of asymmetric regularity. This is a qualitative, not necessarily quantitative, constraint on the dimension as each of its metric units may be arbitrarily big or small.

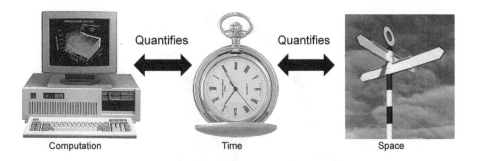

Figure 10.4   The relationship between computation, time and space

Time in Less than Conventional Terms

Now that dependencies between computation, time and space have been mapped out, it is possible to think again about time, but now in somewhat less than conventional terms. So let's propose a radical rethink. Let's propose that time is indeed a fundamental property but that it is not self-supporting, instead being an output of some act of computation. By doing so we shall throw away the idea that time 'just is', and question what drives it to come into existence in the first place.

To start with let's simplify things and think of the universe as a humble sausage machine like the one below. We could, of course, stay rather technical and again choose to talk in purely terms of computation and information, but there is an important point to be made here and sausage machines provide a nice and uncomplicated analogy to work things through.

In most texts, time, and indeed space for that matter, are seen as being separate from the sausage machine and exist independently of it. This implies that sausages will always exist with or without the need for the machine to produce them. In such a way there may ultimately only ever be a limited number of sausages available, but that's the price to pay for independence. Choosing to include the machine in time's makeup obviously produces a different scenario, in that so long as there are enough ingredients going in to the machine and power to drive it, there will always be an unlimited supply of fresh sausages coming out – assuming, that is, that it never breaks down. This, of course, begs the question as to where such an infinite supply of ingredients and power might come from. The answer to this is unclear, or so science tells us thus far, but one possible response states that time itself is recyclable and

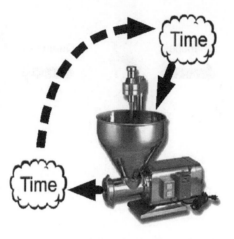

Figure 10.5   A universal time sausage machine

that once created its future is certain in that it will always eventually be fed back into the machine at some point to create more 'fresh' time. Both the idea of time's creation from an infinite stockpile of ingredients and its potential to be recycled therefore rest on one critical concept. This is that time is created by the sausage machine and has no immediate influence on its operation. It provides no power, impetus, tempo or direction to the machine, in other words, and without the machine, time would simply not exist. This adds an interesting complication to models of time, as in most common interpretations it is time and not some other entity that is seen as a driving force, dragging existence with it as it marches its way forward. In such a world-view time's role is interchanged with that of the sausage machine, itself spewing out the hallmarks of reality as it does whatever it does. This is all well and good, but the reverse situation is obviously equally plausible. Ask yourself what the universe might look like if no computation took place at all; if no galaxies span around its centre, if no planet moved around another, if no atom combined with any of its neighbours or if no subatomic particle buzzed about around its infinite possibilities of location. In such a world would time exist? It would be impossible to tell, for even the neurons in our brains brain would be frozen to the point of not being able to consider the problem itself. In a very real sense time would indeed not only have stopped, but it would also have ceased to have any meaning to everything and everyone caught up in the computational void. It would not exist by any known reference or relation unless it were made possible to step outside the void and observe it from a distance. That would, of course, be impossible, which makes the obliteration of time is made a very real possiblity if computation is not considered as an essential part of its makeup. In other words the sausage machine is in, no matter which way we choose to look at it!

This is not in disagreement with models of time we have had for some while. Two of these are dominant but are often seen as being incompatible. The tensed theory most resembles the popularly-held view of time, in that it requires there to be a present moment – the 'now' – and a distinction between events in the past, present, and future. Events in the past are hence considered to be real, as are events in the present, whereas events in the future will be real at some point. Notice that the 'now' moves. This apparent movement of the 'now' is an essential feature of the tensed theory of time.[47] However, theories such as the Wheeler–deWitt[12] equation suggest a universe in which all of time is laid out just as the three dimensions of space dimension are laid out, and that there is no moving 'now'. All times are equally real: as there is no special 'now', there is no distinction between past and future. This forms the tenseless theory of time in which the apparent flow of time is considered to be just an illusion of human perception due to the asymmetry of the time dimension. That is to say we can remember the past, but we cannot remember the future. This then gives the illusion of a flow of time with the unknown future becoming the fixed past.

Most physicists would favour the tenseless theory as the more accurate representation of time. It is also referred to as the 'block universe' because the relationship between space and time can be viewed as being laid out as an unchanging four-dimensional block.

Because of such a conflict the whole notion of reasoning about time starts to disintegrate, but it's worth pushing just a little further by supposing that our theoretical sausage machine really might exist and that time might indeed be one of, if not its only, output. This then leads us to ask as to where the machine itself might get its power from to create time. Cosmologists would have us believe that such 'energy' was made freely available when the universe was born, after the Big Bang some 13½ billion years ago. This satisfies their curiosity, but frustrates the hell out of the philosophers, who persist on trying to reason where the Big Bang itself got its energy from. To date no one truly knows for certain. All we can say for certain that that energy, matter, space

---

12 In theoretical physics, the Wheeler–deWitt equation is a functional differential equation. It is ill defined in the general case, but very important in theoretical physics, especially in quantum gravity.

and time are all intimately linked and that also means that computation and information have to be caught up in the mix somewhere.

Turing and Time

The sausage machine analogy can be enhanced to provide a more complete understanding of time within a computational framework. As explained in Chapter 3, a universal computer of the type originally outlined by Alan Turing needs a small, but specific number of components to work. One of these is a tape on which the symbols of the 'program' the machine is directed to compute are held. As the machine runs it moves the tape past a sensor one symbol at a time for consideration in much the same way that one sausage might be created after another in our hypothetical time machine.

Replacing the sausage machine with a Turing machine has particular implication, however. Just like our sausage machine, there is nothing stopping the tape from being a loop, rather than a strand of infinite length, thereby producing a never-ending stream of symbols over which the machine must compute. If the content of this loop were static, then we might expect the behaviour of the machine to also remain limited and predictable. Nevertheless, even under such restriction, predictability of any output produced is not assured, as pointed out by the work of those like Stephen Wolfram[13].[45] Today it is well understood, for example, that vastly complex results can be produced from apparently simple and innocuous sets of instructions.

Treating time as the tape in an abstract universal 'program' also carries a number of advantages. As explained in earlier chapters, it is possible to think of both information and computation as providing the foundations on which all other fields of science are laid. Through this the rules of mathematics must be created on the underlying rules of information and computation. Likewise, physics, and therefore our understandings of the material world, must be laid on the rules of mathematics, or else the hierarch of science would fall apart. This mandates that all physical phenomena must be based on sound mathematical, computational and informational principles, not least of which is the presence or lack of symmetry. Hence, if we assume time to indeed be an integral part of

---

13 Stephen Wolfram is a British physicist, software developer, mathematician, author and businessman, known for his work in theoretical particle physics, cosmology, cellular automata, computational complexity theory, computer algebra, the Mathematica software application, and the Wolfram Alpha computational knowledge engine.

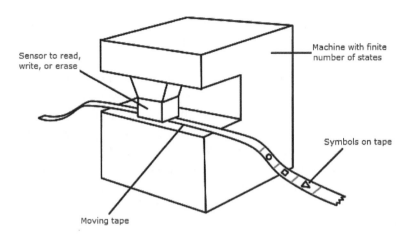

Sensor to read, write, or erase

Machine with finite number of states

Symbols on tape

Moving tape

Figure 10.6   An example Turing Machine

a universal computer, then that computer must be capable of computing the entire set of instructions open to it – the equivalent of being able to 'understand' every possible symbol that could ever be presented to its sensor. Some of these symbols might obviously be strung together in particular fundamental patterns and again the universal computer must be able to successfully deal with each, given we assume that there can never be the possibility of the computer breaking and our universe throwing an error.

Considering these computational patterns, they will obviously have their own characteristics and the universal computer must be general enough to cater for all valid types. This is where mathematics starts to point out some interesting insights by way of our knowledge of symmetry in mathematical terms. Some mathematical equations, the equivalent of computational patterns in this instance, are known to be symmetrical for example, but not all. We know, for instance, that $a + b = c$ is exactly the same as $b + a = c$. In the lingo this is referred to as 'communitivity' and is the ability to change the order of something within something else without changing the end result. Regardless of how it is dressed up, this is really symmetry at work. Now consider the equation $a - b = c$. This will never produce the same result as $b - a = c$. Subtraction is therefore said to be non-communitive and fundamentally asymmetric in nature. This not only restricts subtraction to computation in one direction, but imposes the same restriction on any machine trying to accomplish that computation. In other words, to be an all-encompassing device a universal computer's tape cannot travel back and forth at will. Just like time in the classical text books, the tape must have an arrow and be irreversible.

Strangely enough, though, thinking of time in terms of a universal computer's tape not only relieves time's burden for keeping time, but also lessens the need for us to rely on the notion of a tape at all. A particular objection to the idea of tensed time is related to a question which has puzzled philosophers for millennia. In other words, 'how fast does time flow?' If the 'now' moves then it must move with respect to some time reference and, as already mentioned, a universal computer could quite easily provide that reference. In such a case the machine can be considered as a clock outside the 'known universe' and would provide the standard by which the tape is run. In such respects the machine would be the master, or global, time keeper, with the tape its obedient slave. This localises any notion of time within the vicinity of the tape, a property that will prove essential to us later.

Localising time in such a way and freeing it from the pressure of having to provide the drum beat for all around it has one final and significant advantage. If we forget about the potential movement of the tape in relation to any sensor for a second, we can now consider the tape purely in terms of its capability to hold information. After all, what is the tape but purely a series of locations lined up one after another, each presumably occupied by a symbol of relevance to a particular computational task? But then what is space if not exactly the same thing but with the added luxury of three dimensions instead of just one? This leads to a remarkable conclusion in that, from at least one perspective, space and time can be considered as exactly the same thing: nothing more than different types of memory. This leads to a reformulation of our understanding of both space and time and again the use of a common computational model comes in useful in doing so. Time can hence be considered as local or 'internal' memory and more precisely defined as memory which is inherently bound up in with the internals of any given universal computer. Space can be seen as external memory, or memory which can be called upon as a consequence of a universal computer working over its local tape.

> Time is the active internal memory of a universal computer

Conjecture 8   Time and the idea of a universal computer

> Space is the active external memory of a universal computer

Conjecture 9   Space and the idea of a universal computer

More on a Universal Computational Framework

There is a certainly a fashionable trend in physics to treat the behaviour of the universe as if it were a vast, discrete computer. This sees the universe as described by information that is modified over time just like information is transformed in a conventional computer. It's no real big deal when considered at such a superficial level. So if the universe is a computer, then what, precisely, is it computing and what might its outputs be? Obviously at least one of its outputs it has to be the state of the universe as seen by the sum total of all the positions and velocities of all the particles within it. As Seth Lloyd[14] says in his book *Programming the Universe*,[48] 'What does the universe compute? It computes itself.' He goes on to say:

> The world is composed of elementary particles – electrons, photons, quarks – and each elementary piece of a physical system registers a chunk of information: one particle, one bit. When these pieces interact, they transform and process that information, bit by bit. Each collision between elementary particles acts as a simple logical operation.

It is quite literally as if we are stepping through a computer program, each step of the algorithm modifying the states of the computer variables and registers – its memory. As John Barrow[15] says, 'We now have an image of the universe as a great computer program, whose software consists of the laws of nature and which run on hardware composed of the elementary particles of nature', a viewpoint that falls in line with a number of theories now loosely defined under the heading digital physics. This is a highly controversial area of science that repulses some physicists. But for others it tempers their insecurities about what physical, tangible, reality is. In the absence of any suitable definition, all we have left are yes or no answers to our questions about the environment

---

14 Seth Lloyd is a professor of mechanical engineering at Massachusetts Institute of Technology. He refers to himself as a 'quantum mechanic'.

15 John David Barrow FRS (born 29 November 1952, London) is an English cosmologist, theoretical physicist and mathematician.

around us. Thus, all we really have left is information, and that information is all we have to define our real, tangible universe. As Ed Fredkin[16] once said, 'I've come to the conclusion that the most concrete thing in the world is information.'

Thinking of information as being fundamental causes problems nonetheless, as in such a view information should never get lost. This contradicts at least one well-established theory known as Landauer's[17] Principle. This explicitly states that in order for a computational process to be physically reversible, it must also be logically reversible, and implies that when information is lost in an irreversible circuit, it becomes entropy with an associated amount of energy dissipated as heat. Some see this as being a fundamental barrier to a completely computational view of the universe as it strongly correlates with the second law of thermodynamics – one of the most solid laws in the field of physics. Nevertheless this does not take into account any direct relationship between information and energy and excludes any notion of energy simply being an information isotope – information in one of many possible forms. We know this to be the case, however, from Einstein's famous law $e = mc^2$, which lays out the universe purely in terms of energy. And given that information is contained within the universe, it must be formed from energy was well ... but more about that later. For now it is sufficient to comment that Landauer's Principle has led to the infamous black hole information loss paradox in which physicists often talk about information rather than matter because information is thought to be more fundamental. So, let's also lay down a marker and make a grossly unqualified statement about the relationship between information and energy by saying:

$$\boxed{\text{Energy = Data}}$$

Conjecture 10   Energy and Data

This is without doubt the most profound statement in this entire book, but notice that there is no direct mention of information, only data. This might appear both alluring and frustrating at the same time, for it adds no real value at this point. Nevertheless, hang in there. It is impossible to explain this equation yet, as a lot more context setting needs to take place before the deep meaning

---

16 Edward Fredkin is an early pioneer of digital physics.
17 Rolf William Landauer was an IBM physicist who died in 1999.

contained can be explained properly. That we shall do in the next chapter. For now let's just be content with considering the types of data with which we are familiar and firstly think about letters or words on a printed page.

We may prefer to think of such data in abstract terms, as symbols contributing toward some raw concept or idea, but nevertheless it is impossible to escape from the physical presence bound up in the page. On the surface of any given page's paper must rest the ink used to form the relevant symbols. This must be made of some chemical compound or other with its specific combination of chemical elements binding together to make the ink's presence felt in the physical world. Each of the chemicals, in turn, has a fixed composition of protons, neutrons and electrons and so on. Dig down deep enough and you will soon penetrate the subatomic world where quantum mechanics rules. Probe this world as far as modern science will allow and, surprise, surprise, all that is left is energy in one form or another. Try a second example and think of the very contemplations whizzing around your mind at this precise moment in time. It's easy to see these as corresponding to abstract snippets of data free to bounce and play at the behest of your brain's higher functions. But here again it is impossible to escape from physical reality. Our brain's physiology ultimately boils down into nothing more than chemistry, and then on down into pure energy no matter how hard we try to pull away from the idea. Every thought we have ever had, every exquisite dream and every profound insight we have given the world, amount to nothing more than the entanglement of energy as it dances around our various skulls. Beauty is created from the act of interaction, not from that which is interacting. To many this might be a sobering though, but there is no way of getting away from it. No matter how much we might want to cling to the finer capabilities of the human condition, capabilities like creativity and emotion, energy, as the one and only base ingredient, is always there. This somewhat destroys any philanthropic views of data we might cherish and makes for a very cold and clinical universe and all that exists and happens within it.

The Halting Problem

Moving on, let's consider another problem. Let's imagine we have a computer program and we want to know if it will ever complete its given task or simply get stuck in an infinite loop of unobservable and purely symmetrical confusion. This act of completion is often referred to as 'halting' in computing circles and, if you think about it, just running the program on its own will never give us an answer for all cases. This is because even if the program does not stop after, say, a million years that would not prove that it will never stop. So there is no way to tell directly if a program will ever complete just by running it. With that in mind consider writing a second really intelligent program aimed at telling us if the first program will finish merely by examining its program code. Clever perhaps? Unfortunately not, as, for that cleverer program, there will always exist a cleverer program which it is unable to tell whether the clever program will complete or not. The problem hence just swallows itself and is said to be incomputable – a conundrum commonly referred to as Turing's Halting problem.

> *The proof of the halting problem is beautiful, and is worth presenting here.*

The first step requires us to imagine that we have managed to create our 'halting tester' – the first clever program in our example above – which can solve the halting problem for all computer programs. We will later show that this results in a contradiction, so this perfect halting tester could never actually exist. But for now let's refer to this tester as 'HaltTest' and specify that it takes two inputs:

1.   A program, P.

2.   An input, I, for the program P.

Let's also call the output from the tester '$Loop$' if the program P goes into an infinite loop when it is given I as input, and '$Halt$' if the program P runs to completion and stops.

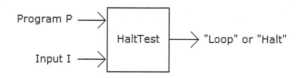

Figure 10.7   HalfTest with its two inputs

Next it is important to understand that a computer program can be expressed as a string of data. So it can be treated as input and we can insert the same program, P, to both inputs of HaltTest:

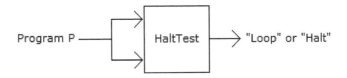

Figure 10.8   HalfTest with _P_ as both its inputs

From this we can construct a simple algorithm called 'StrangeProg' that takes the output of HaltTest and does the following:

1.   If HaltTest outputs 'Loop' then StrangeProg halts.

2.   If HaltTest outputs 'Halt' then StrangeProg goes into an infinite loop.

That is, StrangeProg provides the reverse of HaltTest's output, the equivalent program code of which might look something like:

```
StrangeProg (char * program)
{
   If (HaltTest(program, program) == 'Halt')
   {
          while(true)      /* Infinite loop */
   }
   else
   {
          Return           /* Program halts */
   }
}
```

For those with a dislike of program code, this can also be represented via the schematic shown in Figure 10.9.

Finally we need to feed the function StrangeProg back into itself as input so that it can take a look at itself such as StrangeProg(StrangeProg). And the graphical representation of that is shown in Figure 10.10.

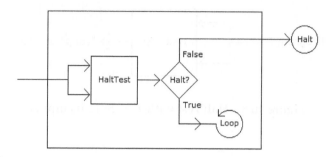

Figure 10.9   A schematic for the schematic for StrangeProg

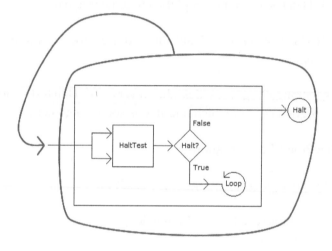

Figure 10.10   StrangeProg inspecting itself

Now let's consider this rather peculiar arrangement given that it produces two possible scenarios depending on the output of HaltTest:

1.   If HaltTest determines that StrangeProg halts when fed itself as input, then StrangeProg goes into an infinite loop.

2.   If HaltTest says that StrangeProg goes into an infinite loop when fed itself as input, then StrangeProg halts.

In either case, HaltTest gives the wrong result for StrangeProg. Therefore, a 'perfect' HaltTest program does not work for all cases. This shows that it is not possible to create a 'halting tester' algorithm which can test for all cases of halting programs.

The halting problem and non-computability in general has serious implications for mathematics. Diophantine equations, for instance, are a group of formulae which demand positive natural integers ($\mathbb{N}$) as the solution to all unknown variables. By far the most famous Diophantine is Fermat's Last Theorem which states that there are no positive integers x, y, and z which satisfy the equation:

$$xn + yn = zn \text{ for } n > 2$$

Puzzles like Fermat's might look simple, but the devil is really in the detail. To solve a Diophantine equation using a conventional computer demands progressively working through every integer until a set of numbers is found which satisfies the equation. However, if, at some point, this fails there is no way of knowing if there still might be a set of suitable larger integers out there waiting to be found. Given this, it is impossible to say for certain if such an equation can ever be solved. Subsequently if we try to use a computer to solve a Diophantine equation we will be unable to say that it cannot be solved for the exactly the same reason that it is impossible to categorically state that a program will never halt. Just like in the halting problem example, we might be tempted to build the equivalent of a 'halting tester' program which could analyse a Diophantine equation and say whether it has any solutions. This would involve writing a program to loop through all possible integers, substituting them into the Diophantine equation. We wouldn't actually run that program, however, we would just pass it to be analysed by our halting tester to determine if the program halts and outputs a solution. If it halts we would know that the Diophantine equation had a solution. However, this approach would be doomed to failure because of the halting problem.

So, does non-computability have relevance in physical reality? This is such an important question because if it could be shown that there were incomputable functions in the universe's mechanics, that could kill stone dead the proposition that the universe behaves like a computer and is also founded on a base fabric of pure data.

If we believe in those like Max Tegmark[18] who propose that the universe is a purely mathematical construct then we would expect to find incomputable functions in the universe as there are certainly incomputable functions in mathematics. If incomputable functions do not appear in physical reality, on the other hand, then there must be some constraints imposed somehow, limiting the subset of mathematics which has relevance to our universe. Those constraints would be responsible for 'filtering-out' any non-computability and would consequently not appear in physical reality.

But if incomputable functions are to be somehow filtered out then how might this be achieved? In trying to address this question the proof of the halting problem comes to the rescue. In our attempt at a proof, it was initially proposed that we could build a 'halting tester' capable of answering any question purely by running through its mechanised process. As a result, the functioning of that halting tester was unhindered by the presence of any incomputable functions which it was incapable of solving. So we can think of the smooth functioning of that halting tester as the smooth functioning of a 'universe computer', if that universe contains no troublesome non-computability. Our proof showed that we were able to construct a peculiar function called StrangeProg that basically broke our halting tester. StrangeProg showed that tests for halting programs do not work in all cases and that begs us to ask what it was about StrangeProg that proved so destructive to the smooth operation of our halting tester. And could a form of StrangeProg exist in physical reality, breaking our 'computer universe' model by proving that incomputable functions existed in our universe?

In answer, StrangeProg works firstly by taking the output of the HaltTest function then inverting it. This inversion is then followed by the creation of a feedback loop which also allows StrangeProg to be fed back into itself. The end result is a form of unstable oscillation which states that when the output of HaltTest is 'Halt' then the input of HaltTest is switched to make its output say 'Loop'. Likewise when the output of HaltTest is 'Loop' its input is switched to make its output say 'Halt'. If such a situation were allowed to exist in physical reality it would lead to a logical inconsistency, a paradox in that the output of HaltTest could not be both 'Loop' and 'Halt'. In physical reality, an object cannot be two things. For example, an orange cannot be both an orange and a carrot at the same time. By such reasoning, if the halting problem is to have relevance in physical reality, as opposed to just being purely a mathematical

---

18 Max Tegmark is a Swedish-American cosmologist. Tegmark is an Associate Professor at the Massachusetts Institute of Technology where he belongs to the scientific directorate of the Foundational Questions Institute.

conceptual model, we should consider if such a paradox could possibly occur the real world.

At first sight there might appear no possibility of such paradoxical circumstances, but, in fact, there are a number of potential candidates for such duality. Take the 'grandfather paradox' as one such example. In this a man is said to travel back in time and kill his paternal grandfather at a time before he has met the women with whom he will conceive the traveller's father. As a result the traveller's father could never have been born. This, of course, further implies that the traveller himself could not have travelled back in time in the first place, which then suggests that the grandfather must remain alive and the traveller must be born, thereby allowing him to travel back in time and kill his grandfather. Thus each possibility seems to imply its own negation and we end up with the same sort of oscillatory paradox found in the halting problem proof.

A Universe within Universes

Note that the grandfather paradox can be considered as a kind of program which treats the universe as a universe computer. By such a token, therefore, the state of the world in which that paradox plays out can be considered in exactly the same way as any abstract input to a theoretic model of the halting problem. This further means that if we could, for example, create a situation where time could be reversed, our universe could not be considered in purely computational terms, being both computable and incomputable.

Some prefer to accept the potential for such situations like the grandfather paradox as being very real, but in fairness there is an equal, if not greater body of evidence against such potentials. As a case in point, the famous physicist Stephen Hawking[19] states one such objection in his chronology protection conjecture.[20] But this does not prevent us from discussing and imagining all mathematical structures, even incomputable ones. As Schmidhuber[21] suggests,

---

19 Stephen Hawking is a British theoretical physicist. Hawking is the Lucasian Professor of Mathematics at the University of Cambridge.

20 The chronology protection conjecture is a conjecture by the physicist Stephen Hawking that the laws of physics are such as to prevent time travel on all but sub-microscopic scales. Mathematically, the permissibility of time travel is represented by the existence of closed time-like curves.

21 Jürgen Schmidhuber is a computer scientist and artist known for his work on machine learning, universal artificial intelligence (AI), artificial neural networks, digital physics, and low-complexity art.

we can talk about time travel and the grandfather paradox even if time travel is not possible in our universe: 'Although we live in a computable universe, we occasionally chat about incomputable things, such as the halting probability of a universal Turing machine. And we sometimes discuss inconsistent worlds in which, say, time travel is possible. Talking about such worlds, however, does not violate the consistency of the processes underlying them.' This is an important point as we are not often prone to think about our universe as being absolute and total. On all but the rarest of occasions we consider the possibility of it having boundaries and there being something 'else', yet undiscovered and totally unknown, beyond and engulfing it. Though, like the innermost skin in an onion with potentially an infinite number of outer skins, it is quite legitimate to think of our universe as being a subset of some grander universal framework. And although our day-to-day reality might appear to be entirely computable and nothing else, there is absolutely nothing stopping any other world further up the hierarchy of such a universal framework from legitimately abiding by physical laws that are both computable and non-computable. In such a world, time might indeed meander to and fro with ease and grandparents might really have to fight for survival with the grandchildren on a daily basis. In fact this actually makes perfect sense. If our universe were inclusive to some other universe, or set of universes, we might genuinely expect our local reality to be different from that of any grander global reality out there, and in many respects it is more likely than not that our reality would be less 'real' than that of our host's. We would simply experience a fraction of the total spectrum of computability possible – all non-computable possibilities also being part of that spectrum. But that would not stop us from determining the full range of computation open to all possible universes.

The Computable Universe Hypothesis

To progress, the idea that there is non-computability in our universe aligns with Max Tegmark's proposal of a mathematical universe which includes a Computable Universe Hypothesis, or CUH for short. The CUH proposes that physical reality can be entirely described by computable functions – in order to avoid all the paradoxes and inconsistencies which would otherwise wreck a mathematical universe. According to the CUH, the mathematical structure that is our universe is computable and hence well defined in the strong sense that all its relations can be evaluated computationally. Accordingly, there are no physical aspects of our universe that are non-computable or undecidable, thereby eliminating the concern that a lack of uncomputability somehow makes the universe incomplete.

Interestingly, Max Tegmark was forced to append the CUH to his mathematical universe model in order to retain the idea that the universe is created by mathematics, in order to avoid destructive paradoxes.

If it could be shown that there were non-computable functions in physical reality it would destroy the idea that the universe behaves like a computer, however. Fortunately so far it would appear that every aspect of the universe's behaviour can be modelled on a computer. We can plot the orbits of the planets around the Sun using a computer, for instance. Nevertheless, if there were no non-computable functions in the universe, why should this be the case?

In order to provide a possible answer to this question, we need to examine a radical approach to mathematics known as constructivism. This states that mathematics should only include statements which can be deduced by a finite sequence of step-by-step constructions, starting from the natural numbers ($\mathbb{N}$), such as 1, 2, 3 and so on. This is a major departure from conventional mathematics because many of the more exotic mathematical structures, such as infinity and irrational numbers, would not have a legitimate claim to be 'mathematical' under constructivism's strict rules. To quote Gregory Chaitin's[22] book *MetaMath!: The Quest for Omega* [49] and its attack on the existence of irrational numbers generated by infinite mathematical series:

> *Some mathematicians have what is called a "constructive" attitude. This means that they only believe in mathematical objects that can be constructed. That, given enough time, in theory one could actually calculate. They think that there ought to be some way to calculate a real number ($\mathbb{R}$) digit by digit, otherwise in what sense can it be said to have some kind of mathematical existence?*

Constructivism is relevant to our discussion because computers construct their results in precisely the same step-by-step method as it prescribes. So if the structure of the universe can really be thought of as the product of some form of computer then mathematical constructivism would appear to be the

---

22 Gregory John Chaitin is an Argentine-American mathematician and computer scientist. Beginning in the late 1960s, he made contributions to algorithmic information theory and metamathematics, in particular a new incompleteness theorem in reaction to Gödel's incompleteness theorem.

perfect type of mathematics to model that universe. Viewed this way, the absence of exotic mathematical structures, such as infinity, from mathematical constructivism appears like a minor omission, given that, for example, if there are no infinities in physical reality then it does not matter if there are no infinities in a mathematics based on constructivism. Hence if the structure of reality[23] is discrete rather than continuous at very small scales, as many physicists now believe, then the natural numbers of constructivism are sufficient to describe our world, rather than requiring the infinite-precision irrational numbers, which are prohibited under constructivism. Under such consideration, constructivism might indeed appear to be a perfect tool for describing the 'real world'. Furthermore CUH suggests that the behaviour of the universe should be reduced to a set of computable functions, and goes on to suggest that mathematical constructivism plays a role in determining this behaviour. According to the Finitist school of mathematicians, which represents the extreme forms of so-called intuitionism[24] and constructivism, a mathematical object cannot not exist unless it can be constructed from natural numbers in a finite number of steps. This leads directly to a computable structure; a computable universe.

To summarise, it appears that there might be no non-computable functions in the universe and that a mathematics based on constructivism might be the best tool to describe such a universe. Given that, let's get a major point out of the way once and for all and state that if the universe does behave like a computer then it must be entirely computable and contain no non-computable functions at all. This might sound obvious but it is important to state it cleanly.

Despite such clarity, several physicists have raised objections, generally focused on examples of how the universe might be seen as having non-computable behaviour. For example, if quantum mechanical behaviour is genuinely random – as opposed to just pseudo-random – then no computer, as we commonly know them today, could possibly produce truly quantum-like behaviour. Even so, many physicists now believe quantum behaviour itself to be fundamentally deterministic in processes which are currently or intrinsically hidden from our analytic methods – through which we can only see the

---

23 Here 'reality' means space-time as defined by Einstein.
24 In the philosophy of mathematics, intuitionism, or neo-intuitionism, is an approach which treats mathematics as the constructive mental activity of humans. That is, mathematics does not consist of analytic activities wherein deep properties of existence are revealed and applied. Instead, logic and mathematics are the application of internally consistent methods to realise more complex mental constructs.

apparently random results of classical quantum activity. As Schmidhuber says in his paper 'A Computer Scientist's View of Life, the Universe, and Everything':

> *Is there true randomness in our universe, in addition to the simple physical laws? True randomness essentially means that there is no short algorithm computing 'the precise collapse of the wave function',[25] and what is perceived as noise by today's physicists. Our fundamental inability to perceive our universe's state does not imply its true randomness, though. For instance, there may be a very short algorithm computing the positions of electrons light-years apart in a way that seems like noise to us but actually is highly regular'. So there might very well not be true randomness[26] in the universe. There might just be the appearance of randomness.*

Being 'Kinky' Might Be Problematic

In his book *New Theories of Everything* ,[50] John Barrow further suggests that if we have a law of physics which depends on some physical property being differentiated – for example, the quantum wave equation – then such laws could be seen as being non-computable if the plot of the curve contains a 'kink' or 'crease'. This would be the case if reality[27] was actually discretely computed and not smooth and continuous:

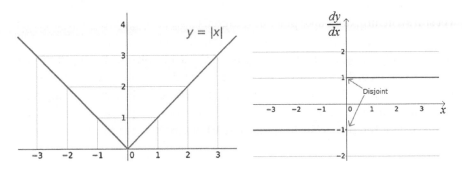

Figures 10.11(a) and 10.11(b)   The plot of the equation $y = |x|$, which contains a 'kink' at $x = 0$ and the plot of its derivative

---

25   Read 'quantum wave function'.
26   Also read 'non-computability'.
27   Again read 'space-time' as defined by Einstein.

Hence, when we consider the derivative of the curve – its rate of change – we find it is not continuous, with a disjoint at the point of the 'kink', or at $x = 0$, in this case. This can be seen in the Figure 10.11(b), which shows the derivative of the wave function as being –1 for negative values of x, and +1 for positive values of x. At $x = 0$ the derivative is not defined, however and can hence be said to be non-computable. Barrow hence argues that this implies that some aspects of the universe are non-computable.

Upon closer inspection, however, Barrow is, in fact, not so much highlighting a potential inconsistency with our universe's computability, but rather an inconsistency with all computability contained within it. For example, we know digital computing to be an absolute reality in our world. There is no debate about that. We have literally millions of digital computers up and running on our planet today, all happily buzzing away their existence founded on the fundamental capabilities of electronic switching. Each of these computers in turn incorporates millions upon millions of such switches, all flicking between one of two discrete states at the command of the program in control at any one time. Yet every single one of these switching events, no matter how fast or slow, takes a finite amount of time to complete. In the simplest case we can think of this as the amount of time it takes for a switch to change from either *on* to *off* or *off* to *on*. Because of this, any switch's activity can never be seen as instantaneous in the purest sense of the word. At the very least, electrons must move from one point to another for the switching act to complete. This therefore means that over an almost infinitesimal period of time the switch is half way through the act of switching, and is neither on nor off. Quite literally its state in indeterminable, yet still switching does take place and digital computing goes on. This therefore does not rule out the possibility of undecidability and hence non-computability from actually being a fundamental part of the act of physical computation, or at least not according to our understanding of the world as physics see it at present. It's more likely, however, that such incompatibility merely highlights the inadequacies or incompleteness of contemporary physical theories and suggests that the physicists have more work to do.

Back to Newton

Before we can really progress further it is necessary to revisit Newton's great work and cover his ideas on gravity, for without a historic perspective it will not be possible to appreciate more contemporary advances relevant to our story on information and computation.

As implied earlier, Newton saw space and time as being quite separate things and formulated his ideas about the world he knew on the accepted science and mathematics of his day, along with his own intellect and some serious measurement – to a level afforded by the accuracy of period instrumentation. Hence Newton gave us an empirical physical law describing the gravitational attraction between bodies with mass. It subsequently became a part of classical mechanics and was first formulated in Newton's work *Philosophiae Naturalis Principia Mathematica*, first published on 5 July 1687. In common parlance it states the following:

> *Every point mass attracts every other point mass by a force pointing along the line intersecting both points. The force is directly proportional to the product of the two masses and inversely proportional to the square of the distance between the point masses.*[51]

This can be stated through the following equation as:

$$F = G \frac{m_1 m_2}{r^2} \ldots, \text{ where}$$

- F is the magnitude of the gravitational force between the two point masses

- G is the gravitational constant and is approximately equal to 6.673 × 10–11 N m2 kg-2

- m_1 is the mass of the first point mass

- m_2 is the mass of the second point mass

- r is the distance between the two point masses

Notice the emphasis on mass and distance in this equation. Distance we have already covered under the guise of space, but mass we have not, and for deliberate reason. Newton's law was superseded by Einstein's work in the early part of the twentieth century and our coverage of this will start in the next chapter, so more about mass and its relationship with information and computation then. For now it is enough to know that although sufficiently accurate for many practical purposes and still widely used today, Newton's gravitational law is best suited to calculations in which the distances involved are small. Small that is on a cosmological scale. Furthermore we now know that it has significant theoretical flaws, such as the in the fact that it requires gravitational force to have instantaneous effect no matter far apart the two bodies involved are. What's more, Newton himself was known to be deeply dissatisfied with a number of implications brought forth by his law. In particular he saw 'action at a distance' as being problematic and 1692, in his third letter to Richard Bentley,[28] he wrote:

> *That one body may act upon another at a distance through a vacuum without the mediation of anything else, by and through which their action and force may be conveyed from one another, is to me so great an absurdity that, I believe, no man who has in philosophic matters a competent faculty of thinking could ever fall into it.*

In his own words, he never 'assigned the cause of this power'. In all other cases, he used the phenomenon of motion to explain the origin of various forces acting on bodies, but in the case of gravity, he was unable to experimentally identify the motion that produces the force of gravity.[29] Likewise, he refused to even offer an idea as to the cause of this force on the grounds that to do so would be contrary to sound science. He grumbled that 'philosophers have hitherto attempted the search of nature in vain' for the source of the gravitational force, as he was convinced 'by many reasons' that there were 'causes hitherto unknown' that were fundamental to all the 'phenomena of nature'. Finally, as if to chastise his great contribution to science further, in the second edition of *Principia*, Newton declared:

> *I have not yet been able to discover the cause of these properties of gravity from phenomena and I feign no hypotheses ... It is enough that gravity does really exist and acts according to the laws I have explained, and that it abundantly serves to account for all the motions of celestial bodies ... .*[51]

Newton was done with gravity, yet still many of its secrets remained hidden.

Today there are still some aspects of gravity that remain elusive, but certainly many less than in Newton's day. This is mostly due to the efforts of a lowly patent clerk from Germany, one Albert Einstein. He worked intensely on the problems that had troubled Newton and came up with a solution that

---

28 Richard Bentley was an English theologian, classical scholar and critic.
29 Although he invented two mechanical hypothesis in 1675 and 1717.

turned large parts of physics on its head. In his theory of general relativity he reframed gravity not as a force propagated between bodies but as an attribute of the curved 'fabric' created when space and time are inseparably bonded together. We now refer this fabric to as 'space-time' and in Einstein's view of the universe, masses distort the space-time surrounding it. This can be mind-bending stuff, but if approached with caution it reveals not only a very strong association with ideas of information and computation already established, but also a number of profound insights into areas and ideas previously unexplored.

Up to this point everything in this book has been preparation for what is to come. Next we will attempt to view the world through Einstein's eyes and truly start to shake down the ideas of information and computation. Through this we will discover a place where the importance of boundaries will start to fade and the possibility of unbounded expression will become a reality. In this place the absolute will be underplayed and the relative will come to the fore. There we will be able to think of information and computation at truly grand scales and appreciate that no one answer to a given problem can ever be seen as the absolute truth. This will take us beyond the familiar, leaving behind the security of computer science's dependence on the small, absolute and precise. In this brave new world we will dare to be different and talk openly of complexity. We will embrace ideas like emergence and evolution while still accepting that they challenge the very limits of humankind's intellect. This will be challenging in the extreme and for such reasons it will be impossible to be totally conclusive. Nevertheless that will not stop us from pushing the envelope in ways that seemed almost unimaginable until all but very recently.

However, it is right that we should approach such new ideas with caution. Just as in both Newton and Einstein's day, any enthusiasm for adventure must be tempered by the relevance and accuracy of the instrumentation and evidence we have available to us, and in such regard, thankfully, we have one up on both. At this moment in history we have a very large elephant in the room, a measure of such scale and power that most would never even consider it as a piece of scientific apparatus. But such worthiness we surely have in the World Wide Web. By pulling away from the cultural confusion that surrounds it, the Web can be seen as the second largest sample set of data we have ever had, the universe itself occupying pole position. And by such a token, if both are indeed deeply rooted in information and computation it is perfectly rational to reason that both might behave in similar ways at similar scales. Today we know lots about the Web at a micro scale but have only just started to understand it at the macro. Likewise there are areas in which we know much about the universe and little in others. Might it be possible to share insights between both to strengthen the weaknesses in each? That is the tantalising question in front of us now as we try to bring together digital physics and Web science, and it is Einstein's unquestionable brilliance that we shall turn to in order to build a bridge between both.

11

Einstein's Torch Bearers

It's not that I'm so smart, it's just that I stay with problems longer.
Albert Einstein

This is where we really start to ramp things up and begin to think about information and computation using a relative, rather than absolute, framework. Ultimately this will lead to Einstein's door, but before we head in that immediate direction it is right to hold back for a while and fully appreciate where his groundbreaking ideas came from.

Turn back the clock and the story of relativity starts with the work of Galileo Galilei in the seventeenth century. Galileo was an Italian physicist, mathematician, astronomer and philosopher who played a major role in the Scientific Revolution of the time. Indeed, even Newton himself followed Galileo's principles of relativity when he formulated his own ideas on space and time as absolute entities.[56] Galileo's achievements were sizable and included improvements to the telescope and consequent astronomical observations, along with a strong support for Copernicanism.[1] Because of such contributions Galileo has since been called the 'father of modern observational astronomy', the 'father of modern physics', the 'father of science', and 'the father of modern science'. Indeed even the likes of Stephen Hawking[2] refer to Galileo as someone who 'perhaps more than any other single person was responsible for the birth of modern science'.[21]

For all of Galileo's great contributions there is one that has special relevance for our purposes. This deals with what are commonly known as 'inertial frames'.

To grossly simplify an inertial frame, it can be thought of as nothing more than a unique point of view attributed to a given observer. This carries

---

1   The doctrine that the Earth moves round the sun, in opposition to the doctrine that the sun moves round the Earth.
2   Stephen William Hawking is an English theoretical physicist and cosmologist.

tremendous significance from an informational perspective as it can be seen as the real world equivalent of the context in which any particular datum or set of data is evaluated. It therefore leads to a reformulation of Conjecture 1, outlined in Chapter 2, as follows:

> Information   ≡   Data   +   Structure   +   Frame of Reference

Conjecture 11   A Reformulation of Conjecture 1

Physics, however, chooses to be more specific when it comes to defining information and places precise constraints on the definition and use of any inertial frame by insisting that it be bound to the motion of the observer. This again carries deep relevance from an informational perspective, as motion can be interpreted as the rate of change of distance over the rate of change of time. Notice the term 'change' twice in this definition and remember that it is just another word for the act of computing. This leads to yet another simple yet profound conjecture:

> Information cannot exist without it being computed

Conjecture 12   Information's reliance on computation

This acts like a double-edged sword, given that we know that computation cannot exist without something on which to compute. This hence also implies a reverse dependency:

> Computation cannot exist without data on which to act

Conjecture 13   Computation's reliance on data

Observe the deliberate play on words here as a precise opposite of Conjecture 12 has not been given. Instead the term 'data' has being used in preference to 'information' and this is because the dependency between Conjecture 1 and Conjecture 12 teases out one further proposition:

> The act of computing forces context and structure on all data, thereby converting it into information

Conjecture 14   Information's reliance on computation

Finally there are a few more implications that appear as a consequence of the concept of inertial frames, only this time they have particular relevance to the physical world. Given that the act of observation requires some form of change to be present,[3] it therefore implies that all observation is computational and that:

> Everything in the universe that can be observed must have an exact and complete information set which is relevant across all possible frames of reference

Conjecture 15   The universe and information

Interpreted literally this can be read as:

> Reality is the computation that converts the universe's data into information

Conjecture 16   Reality as a computation

And that:

---

3   Either directly or indirectly.

> The universe, as we experience it, is informational entity at its most fundamental level

Conjecture 17   Reality and information

or:

> Any physical data in the universe is masked by reality

Conjecture 18   The dataless universe

Galileo applied the concept of reference frames in his *principle of invariance* or *relativity*. This is a theory which states that the fundamental laws of physics are the same across all inertial frames. He first described this principle in 1632 in his 'Dialogue Concerning the Two Chief World Systems' and used the example of a ship travelling at constant speed, without rocking, on a smooth sea. In this he explained that any observer doing experiments below the deck would not be able to tell whether the ship was moving or stationary. The fact that the Earth on which we stand orbits around the sun at approximately 30 kilometres per second offers a somewhat more dramatic example of the same principle.

In Galileo's day the emphasis in science was on the kind of things we might see or experience in everyday life. So, as legend has it, Galileo dropped weights from a leaning tower and watched balls rolling down slopes. His goal in all these investigations was to attune the budding scientist's ear to the harmonics of the universe. To be sure, physical reality was the stuff of experience, but the challenge to Galileo was to go beyond that and hear the rhyme and reason behind the rhythm and regularity.[52]

To continue the timeline forward, most would naturally jump straight to Einstein's work on relativity, but to do that would be a mistake, as the mid part of the nineteenth century saw a series of breakthroughs that, if they had not taken place at the time they did, would have stopped Einstein dead in his tracks.

Carl Friedrich Gauss and Georg Bernhard Riemann were both mathematicians who chose to rebel against one of the mathematical establishment's most cherished theories by challenging Euclid's ideas on geometry. Actually that's not quite fair. They did not so much challenge Euclidean geometry as built upon it to open up a whole new realm of geometric possibilities.

Riemann was a pupil of Gauss and in 1853 he was asked by his teacher to prepare a Habilitationsschrift[4] on the foundations of geometry, and over many months Riemann developed his theory of higher dimensions. When he finally delivered his lecture at Göttingen in 1854, the mathematical public received it with enthusiasm, and it is still today one of the most important works in all of mathematics. It was titled Über *die Hypothesen welche der Geometrie zu Grunde liegen*, which loosely translates as 'On the Foundations of Geometry' and was published in 1868.[53] In plain terms Riemann's and Gauss' work resulted in the synthesis of a number of diverse ideas concerning the geometry of surfaces and the behaviour of geodesics on them. In particular Riemann found the correct way to extend the differential geometry of surfaces into n dimensions, which Gauss himself proved in his *theorema egregium*.

As explained in Chapter 2, in mathematics, a geodesic is a generalisation of the notion of a 'straight line' to 'curved spaces'. In the presence of a metric, or measurement system, geodesics are hence defined to be the shortest local path between points in such spaces. In Riemannian geometry, however, geodesics are not quite the same as 'shortest curves' between two points, though the two concepts are closely related.

Geodesics are commonly seen in the study of Riemannian geometry and more generally metric geometry. In relativistic physics, geodesics describe the motion of point particles under the influence of gravity alone. In particular, the path taken by a falling rock, an orbiting satellite, or the shape of a planetary orbit are all geodesics in curved space-time. More generally, the topic of sub-Riemannian geometry deals with the paths that objects may take when they are not free and their movement is constrained in various ways.[53] But all this aside, for our purposes, Gauss and Riemann did the world one huge favour by

4   Habilitation is the highest academic qualification a person can achieve by their own pursuit in certain European and Asian countries. Earned after obtaining a research doctorate (PhD or equivalent degrees), the habilitation requires the candidate to write a professorial thesis based on independent scholarly accomplishments, reviewed by and defended before an academic committee in a process similar to that for the doctoral dissertation. However, the level of scholarship has to be considerably higher compared to a PhD thesis.

showing how to work with shapes and surfaces that are not flat. They told us how to think about any space, be that real or abstract, and all that goes with it as a curved entity. This is literally the mathematical equivalent of shattering the flat Earth myth,[5] and Einstein was drawn to it with great delight.

Maxwell and his Compensating Current

Next we must pay tribute to James Clerk Maxwell, the nineteenth-century Scottish theoretical physicist and mathematician, as there's a remarkable parallel between Maxwell's development of the field equations of electromagnetism and Einstein's development of the field equations of general relativity. When Maxwell began his work a set of relations were already in place which described the forces of electricity and magnetism, with the earliest calculable theories of electricity and magnetism being presented in terms of forces acting at a distance – similar to Newton's law of gravitation. As an example, in 1750 John Michell[6] showed that the poles of stationary magnets exert a force on each other, directed along the line between them and of a size inversely proportional to the square of their distance apart. 1766 further saw Joseph Priestly[7] discover that the force of attraction or repulsion between stationary electrically charged particles is of this same form – a fact which was verified by Charles Coulomb[8] in 1785. These discoveries, together with the success of the inverse-square law of gravity, as promoted by Newton, led to the belief among most scientists that all the fundamental interactions of nature could be understood in terms of inverse-square forces acting at a distance along a direct line of sight. However, in 1820 Hans Christian Ørsted[9] discovered that a moving charge, such as a current flowing through a wire, produces a magnetic force, and that this force does not act along the direct line in sight. In 1830 Michael Faraday[10] further discovered the reciprocal effect in that a moving magnet induces electric current

---

5   The flat Earth model is an ancient view of the Earth's shape which conceived of it as flat like a piece of paper or an infinite plane.
6   John Michell was an English natural philosopher and geologist whose work spanned a wide range of subjects from astronomy to geology, optics and gravitation.
7   Joseph Priestley was an eighteenth-century British theologian, dissenting clergyman, natural philosopher, educator, and political theorist.
8   Charles-Augustin de Coulomb was a French physicist. He is best known for developing Coulomb's law, the definition of the electrostatic force of attraction and repulsion.
9   Hans Christian Ørsted was a Danish physicist and chemist. He is best known for discovering that electric currents can create magnetic fields.
10 Michael Faraday was an English chemist and physicist who contributed to the fields of electromagnetism and electrochemistry.

in a wire. André-Marie Ampère[11] then interpreted these effects, still within the framework of action at a distance, by formulating a force law that depended not just on the distance but on the velocity of the charged particles. Following this great success, Gauss and Wilhelm Weber[12] devised a fairly successful theory of electro-dynamics by the 1840s.[55]

Beginning in the 1850s, Maxwell elaborated on Faraday's ideas and gave a completely different account of electrodynamics, based on the concept of continuous fields of force. He showed that the inverse-square force laws of Michell and Coulomb can be equally well expressed in terms of such fields. Maxwell also expressed the dynamical relations of Ampère and Faraday in terms of fields associated with moving magnets and electric charges. All told he arrived at a compilation of four partial differential equations which provided equivalence over the laws of Michell, Coulomb, Ampère, and Faraday, with all the information encoded being derived directly from experiment.[55]

Through such work it is evident that Maxwell's main motivation was to formulate electrodynamics in such a way that it did not rely on action at a distance. The essence of his approach, following Faraday, was to treat the fields of force as having consecutive 'parts', and to regard the force as being communicated from one part to adjacent parts over time. In other words, his main allegiance was to the idea of local action, not to the idea of a material mechanism for this action.[55] This is an interesting and compelling difference from the science that had gone before, as Maxwell was one of the first to recognise the value of local symmetry breaking and thereby formatted a set of theories which rely on discrete, rather than continuous dependencies between properties involved. This falls neatly in line with constructivist thinking and therefore ideas on digital computing.

As part of his work Maxwell added a term to Ampère's law, which he called the displacement current. As the magnitude of this term was far too small to have been perceptible in the experiments performed by Ampère and Faraday, its inclusion by Maxwell was inspired purely by theoretical argument. [57] Maxwell's first explanation of displacement current amounted to nothing more than an account of plausibility arising from a rough mechanical analogy. Nonetheless, his explanation matured over time, as his ideas about suitable

---

11 André-Marie Ampère was a French physicist and mathematician who is generally credited as one of the main discoverers of electromagnetism. The SI unit of measurement of electric current, the ampere, is named after him.
12 Wilhelm Eduard Weber was a German physicist.

mechanisms changed, but in essence he argued that the current density at a given location in a field does not actually represent the total current flow at that location – even though that is essentially its definition. According to Maxwell, a non-metal material that does not naturally conduct electricity[13] can be considered to consist of couples of positive and negative charges, and any applied electric field will pull these charges in opposite directions, stretching the links between them until they achieve some kind of equilibrium. If the strength of the applied field is increased, the charges are pulled further apart. Consequently, during periods when the applied electric field is changing there is movement of the electric charge elements in the medium. This movement of charge is Maxwell's displacement current.[55]

Regardless, Maxwell's reasoning is questionable in at least two regards. First, it's reasonable to ask why the displacement current is not already included as part of the total current density at the given point. Second, after introducing the concept of displacement current in non-metallic insulators – where the existence of coupled electric charges is conceivable – Maxwell insisted on applying his extra term to such insulators held in a vacuum, where the presence of coupled electric charges being pulled apart and held in equilibrium by a stationary electric field is questionable. At the time this was a bold step as Maxwell certainly could not point to any evidence of such disembodied charges existing in the vacuum. It's true that some aspects of modern quantum field theory can be expressed in terms of pairs of oppositely charged virtual particles in the vacuum, flashing in and out of existence within the limits of the uncertainty principle, but it is almost certain that such virtual particles were not what Maxwell had in mind when he outlined his thinking. Without the relationships provided under the uncertainty principle such particles would violate conservation of charge, a principle which Maxwell surely accepted.[55] In spite of such matters, Coulomb's law, which describes the electrostatic force between electric charges, came to Maxwell's rescue. This highlights the need for displacement current purely for mathematical consistency.[55]

It is sometimes argued that Maxwell's idea of a displacement current relate to his mechanistic model of the luminiferous aether,[14] a concept deliberately

---

13 The actual text refers to a 'dielectric medium'. Dielectrics are not a narrow class of so-called insulators, but the broad expanse of non-metals considered from the standpoint of their interaction with electric, magnetic, or electromagnetic fields. Thus they are concerned with gases as well as with liquids and solids, and with the storage of electric and magnetic energy as well as its dissipation.
14 In the late nineteenth century, 'luminiferous aether' (or 'ether'), meaning light-bearing aether, was the term used to describe a medium for the propagation of light.

intended to challenge the idea that an absolute vacuum can ever exist. Some further uphold that Maxwell deliberately introduced displacement current to strengthen the case against the concept of 'empty' space, but detailed study of his later publications provides strong confirmation that this was not the case.

In support of displacement current, and in relation to Ampère's Law, three basic justifications can be seen. First, it is sometimes claimed that it arises purely out of a need to obey symmetry. That is to say that since Faraday's law indicates that a changing magnetic field is associated with an electric field, it is right to expect that, by symmetry, a changing electric field should be associated with a magnetic field. Nevertheless, the clear asymmetry arising from the lack of magnets with only one pole tends to undermine the logic of this argument. The second justification, found especially in historical accounts, is Maxwell's heuristic rationale based on the idea of a non-metallic insulator consisting of charge couples that are pulled apart by an electric field. Lastly, the most prevalent justification relates to consistency with Coulomb's law and charge conservation. Under the covers this concerns a discrepancy in Ampère's work with regard to the curvature on any given magnetic field. By adding in Maxwell's displacement current this discrepancy vanishes. This leads to the interesting and important similarity between Maxwell's formulation of this correction and the process by which Einstein arrived at the final field equations of general relativity. Einstein not only noticed that, in the simplest form of the equations, involving only the metric coefficients and their first and second derivatives, the Ricci tensor[15] equals the stress energy tensor, but that the divergence of the energy tensor does not vanish as it should in order to satisfy local conservation of mass-energy. By introducing a corrective term similar to Maxwell's displacement current Einstein managed to bring back harmony to his theory. Don't worry too much about the terms referred to here as general relativity is dealt with in much greater detail later.

Competition from Hilbert

Another stop off on the road to relativity finds us recognising the great influence that David Hilbert had on Einstein's work. Born on 1862, Hilbert was a German

---

15 A tensor is an object which extends the notion of scalar, vector and matrix. The term has slightly different meanings in mathematics and physics. In the mathematical fields of multi-linear algebra and differential geometry, a tensor is a multi-linear function. In physics and engineering, the same term usually means what a mathematician would call a tensor field: an association of a different (mathematical) tensor with each point of a geometric space, varying continuously with position.

mathematician who is recognised as one of the most influential and universal mathematicians of the nineteenth and early twentieth centuries. He discovered or developed a broad range of fundamental ideas in many areas, including the actions of groups on algebra from the perspective of their effect on functions[16] and the characterisation of geometry in terms of its fundamental elements. He also formulated the theory of Hilbert spaces, one of the foundations of functional analysis, the branch of mathematics concerned with the study of vector spaces and operators acting upon them. Furthermore Hilbert approved of Georg Cantor's set theory and its associated implications, which have since proved essential to the field of computer science.

Until 1912, Hilbert almost exclusively occupied his time working in the field of pure mathematics. This was so much so that some years earlier, while on a visit from Bonn, where he was absorbed with his a fascination for physics, his friend and fellow mathematician Hermann Minkowski – of whom we have already spoken highly – quipped openly that he had to spend 10 days in quarantine before he could be granted an audience with Hilbert. This must have been part of an ongoing friendly taunt, as history finds Minkowski alongside Hilbert whenever he publically decides to dabble with physics prior to 1912.

Unfortunately Minkowski died unexpectedly from appendicitis in 1909 which brought an abrupt end to the obviously warm and fruitful relationship with Hilbert. In fact their friendship was so great that Hilbert was moved to write an obituary for Minkowski as follows:

> Since my student years Minkowski was my best, most dependable friend who supported me with all the depth and loyalty that was so characteristic of him. Our science, which we loved above all else, brought us together; it seemed to us a garden full of flowers. In it, we enjoyed looking for hidden pathways and discovered many a new perspective that appealed to our sense of beauty, and when one of us showed it to the other and we marveled over it together, our joy was complete. He was for me a rare gift from heaven and I must be grateful to have possessed that gift for so long. Now death has suddenly torn him from our midst. However, what death cannot take away is his noble image in our hearts and the knowledge that his spirit in us continue to be active.[57]

Three years after his friend's death, Hilbert refocused his attention squarely on physics. He arranged for a tutor and started studying kinetic gas theory,

---

16 More commonly known as invariant theory.

followed by elementary radiation theory and the molecular theory of matter. [56]

By 1907 Einstein had framed the fundamentals of his theory of gravity, but it took him nearly eight further years to work out its final form. By early summer 1915, Hilbert's interest in physics brought him to relativity, and he invited Einstein to Göttingen to deliver a week of lectures on the subject. Einstein accepted and received an enthusiastic reception. Over that summer Einstein learned that Hilbert was also working on the field equations at the centre of general relativity and that spurred him on to work harder. Consequently, in November 1915, Einstein published several papers culminating in 'The Field Equations of Gravitation'. Almost simultaneously Hilbert published 'The Foundations of Physics', an axiomatic derivation of the field equations. Although several historians [58] believe that Hilbert formulated general relativity before Einstein, Hilbert himself fully credited Einstein as the originator of the theory and there was never any public display of ill feeling between the two.[56] Even so, there is strong evidence in Hilbert's favour, for it is well documented that Einstein and Hilbert communicated regularly about their work. So much so that Einstein's personal papers include a correspondence from Hilbert outlining the field equations before Einstein published.[59] Regardless of who completed the work on general relativity first it is almost certain that the pair were caught up in healthy competition and that each had a beneficial effect on the other's endeavours.

Nearly There with Lorentz, Larmor, Wien, Cohn and Poincaré

For centuries the argument had raged in physics about whether the universe is full of an invisible medium often referred to as 'aether'. This was an important debate as many believed it to be essential to explain many of the universe's key properties, such as the ability to allow light to travel from one point to another.

In 1892 the Dutch physicist Hendrik Antoon Lorentz made a significant breakthrough in the aether debate by proposing the existence of electrons which he separated from the aether. This produced a model in which the aether is completely without motion and not effected by the movement of matter through it. An important consequence of this model was that the speed of light is totally independent of the velocity of any source that produces it. Nevertheless, although Lorentz's work was significant, it shed no light on the mechanical nature of the aether or any relationship to electromagnetic processes.

Rather it did the opposite and tried to explain the processes of the aether by electromagnetic mechanics, thereby creating an abstract electromagnetic interpretation. In the framework of his theory, Lorentz also introduced his 'Theorem of Corresponding States'. This states that an observer moving relative to the aether in his 'fictitious' field makes the same observations as a resting observer in his 'real' field. This importantly involved the concept of local time,[17] which paved the way to the Lorentz Transformation, of which we shall hear more later. With the help of this concept, Lorentz could explain the peculiarity of light, the Doppler Effect[18] and the Fizeau experiment as well.[19] However, Lorentz's local time was not the time measured by watches, but only an auxiliary mathematical tool and he freely recognised that his theory violated the principle of action and reaction, since the aether acts on matter, but matter cannot act on the inert aether.[60]

Following on from Lorentz's work, Joseph Larmor[20] later created a model very similar to Lorentz's, but went a step further and described the Lorentz Transformation in greater mathematical detail. So Larmor was the first to put the Lorentz Transformation in the algebraically equivalent form, which is used to this day. Independently of Larmor, Lorentz also extended his transformation and noted, as had Larmor, a mathematical oddity which showed that time could dilate. Furthermore, the amalgamation of the speed-dependence of masses was especially important for his theory. Through this he noticed that mass not only varies due to speed, but is also dependent on the direction of travel. Because of this he introduced what would later become known as 'longitudinal' and 'transverse' mass – transversal may being called 'relativistic mass'.[60]

In 1900 Wilhelm Wien[21] proposed that all mass can be thought of in terms of electromagnetism and produced a formula for the mass-energy-

---

17 Lorenz local time is defined as: $t' = t - \frac{vx}{c^2}$.
18 The Doppler Effect, or Doppler shift, is the change in frequency of a wave for an observer moving relative its source. It is commonly heard when a vehicle sounding a siren approaches, passes and recedes from an observer
19 The Fizeau experiment was carried out by Hippolyte Fizeau in the 1851 to measure the relative speeds of light in moving water. Albert Einstein later pointed out the importance of the experiment for special relativity.
20 Sir Joseph Larmor was a physicist and mathematician who made innovations in the understanding of electricity, dynamics, thermodynamics, and the electron theory of matter. His most influential work was Aether and Matter, a theoretical physics book published in 1900.
21 Wilhelm Carl Werner Otto Fritz Franz Wien (was a German physicist who, in 1893, used theories about heat and electromagnetism to deduce Wien's displacement law, which calculates the emission of a blackbody at any temperature from the emission at any one reference temperature.

relationship which was not unlike Einstein's later work. This also required that all forces of nature be electromagnetic, a perspective now referred to as the Electromagnetic World View. Through his work Wien stated that, if it is assumed that gravitation is an electromagnetic effect too, then there has to be a proportional relationship between electromagnetic energy, inertial mass and gravitational mass. Furthermore, in the same paper Henri Poincaré found another way of combining mass and energy by recognising that electromagnetic energy behaves like a fictitious fluid[22] and defined a fictitious electromagnetic momentum as well. Nevertheless, Poincaré's explanation contained a radiation paradox which was not fully explained until Einstein later published in 1905. [60]

Also in 1900 the German physicist Emil Cohn created an alternative theory of electrodynamics in which he was one of the first to work without the need for the aether. Instead, he used the fixed stars as a reference frame. However, his work lacked clarity in a number of areas, but again it has significant relevance to Einstein's work which would follow.[60]

In 1901 speed picked up again when the German physicist Walter Kaufmann confirmed the velocity dependence of electromagnetic mass by analysing the ratio energy to mass in cathode rays. He found that this ratio decreased with the speed, hence demonstrating that, assuming charge to be constant, the mass of the electron increased with the speed. He also believed that this confirmed the assumption of Wien, that there is no 'real' mechanical mass, but only the 'apparent' electromagnetic mass, or in other words, the mass of all bodies is of electromagnetic origin.[60]

Absolute Space and Time Falls Out of Favour

Towards the end of the nineteenth century many scientists began to disapprove of Newton's definitions of absolute space and time. For example, Carl Neumann[23] introduced a 'Body alpha', which represents some sort of rigid and fixed body for defining inertial motion. Ernst Mach[24] further argued that absolute time and space are meaningless and only relative motion is of real use. He also said that even accelerated motion such as rotation could be related to the fixed stars without using Newtonian principles. Following on from

---

22 With mass density of $m = \dfrac{E}{c^2}$, which is equivalent to $E = mc^2$.
23 Carl Gottfried Neumann was a German mathematician.
24 Ernst Mach was an Austrian physicist and philosopher.

Neumann's research, the Austrian physicist Heinrich Streintz proposed that if gyroscopes don't measure any signs of rotation, then it is possible to speak of inertial motion which is related to a 'fundamental body' and a 'fundamental coordinate system'. Thus, eventually, the German physicist Ludwig Lange was the first to coin the expression 'inertial frame of reference' and 'inertial time scale', in 1885, as operational replacements for absolute space and time.[60]

There were also several attempts to use time as a fourth dimension as early as 1754, and in 1901 a philosophical model was published by the Hungarian philosopher, mathematician and physicist Menyhért Palágyi, in which space and time were both properties of some kind of 'space-time'. Nevertheless, Palagyi's time coordinate system was not connected to the speed of light, unlike Lorentz's theory. He also rejected any connection with the existing constructions of multidimensional spaces and non-Euclidean geometry and consequently rejected the space-time formalism of Einstein and Minkowski – so Palagyi's criticism is considered to be misguided and his model has little in common with special relativity.[60]

The Principle of Relative Motion and Clock Synchronisation

The second half of the nineteenth century saw many attempts to develop a worldwide clock network synchronised by electrical signals. This required the science of the time to be consulted and the finite speed of light taken into consideration. So in his 1898 paper entitled 'The Measure of Time', Henri Poincaré pointed out that in determining the speed of light it is right to simply assume that light has a constant speed, and that this speed is the same in all directions. Poincaré also noted that the propagation speed of light can be used to define simultaneous events which are physically separated.[60]

Poincaré also argued that certain experiments can show the impossibility of detecting the absolute motion of matter or the relative motion of matter in relation to the aether. He called this the 'principle of relative motion'. He further interpreted Lorentz's local time as the result of a synchronisation procedure based on light signals. He assumed that two observers A and B, which are moving in the aether, synchronise their clocks by optical signals. Since both believe they are at rest, they must consider only the transmission time of the signals and then cross-reference their observations to examine whether their clocks are synchronous. However, from the point of view of an observer at rest in the aether, the clocks are not synchronous and indicate only local time as specified by Lorenz's equation. But because the moving observers do not know anything about their movement, they could never possibly recognise this fact. So, contrary to Lorentz, Poincaré-defined local time can be measured and indicated by physical clocks.[60]

Indeed Poincaré admired Lorenz's work so much that he recommended him for the Nobel Prize in 1902 and in the same year he published the philosophical and popular-scientific book *Science and Hypothesis*, which included philosophical assessments on the relativity of space, time and simultaneity, the possible irrelevance of the aether and several comments on non-Euclidean geometry.[60]

1904 Was a Critical Year

Although most would not recognise it, 1904 was an extremely critical year for relativity. First, in his paper of that year, on electromagnetic phenomena in a system moving with any velocity smaller than that of light, Lorentz was led by the suggestion of Poincaré and tried, but unfortunately failed, to equate electrodynamics in such a way which explained the failure of all known aether drift experiments – that is to say the relativity principle. In this he suggested that mass can only ever be considered as an electromagnetic, rather than mechanical, phenomenon, and derived the correct expression for longitudinal and transverse mass. And using the electromagnetic momentum, he explained the negative result of the Trouton–Noble experiment, in which a charged parallel-plate capacitor moving through the aether should orient itself perpendicular to the motion. Another important step was to propose that this transformation has to be valid for non-electrical forces as well.[60]

The year previously Wien also recognised an important consequence of the velocity dependence of mass, in which he argued that speeds greater than that of light were impossible, as they would require an infinite amount of energy to achieve. Furthermore, after he had read Lorentz's 1904 paper, he noticed the same in relation to length contraction, because at speeds greater than that of light the factor …

$$\sqrt{\frac{1-v^2}{c^2}}$$

… becomes mathematically imaginary[25].[60]

---

25 That is, involves the square root of –1.

1904 also saw Max Abraham[26] highlight a defect in Lorentz's theory in that one side the theory obeys the relativity principle, while the other assumes the electromagnetic origin of all forces. Abraham showed that both assumptions were incompatible, because in Lorentz's theory of the contracted electrons, non-electric forces were needed in order to guarantee the stability of matter. Nevertheless, in Abraham's theory of the rigid electron, no such forces were needed. Thus a competition arose between the electromagnetic view of the world and the relativity principle.[60]

In September of 1904 Poincaré was the next to push forward by defining a principle which modified both Galileo's views on relativity and Lorentz's theorem of corresponding states. In this he stated that:

> *The principle of relativity, according to which the laws of physical phenomena must be the same for a stationary observer as for one carried along in a uniform motion of translation, so that we have no means, and can have none, of determining whether or not we are being carried along in such a motion.*

He also specified his clock synchronisation method and explained the possibility of a 'new method' or 'new mechanics', in which no velocity could surpass that of light for all observers. However, he critically noted that the relativity principle, Newton's action and reaction, the conservation of mass and the conservation of energy were not fully established and are were even threatened by some experiments of the time.[60]

1904 also saw Emil Cohn discover some important physical interpretations of the Lorentz transformations. He noted that if rods and clocks are at rest in the Lorentzian aether, they show the true length and time, and if they are moving, they show contracted and dilated values. And like Poincaré, Cohn defined local time as the time, which is based on the assumption of equal propagation of light in all directions. Contrary to Lorentz and Poincaré it was Cohn who noticed that the separation of 'real' and 'apparent' coordinates is artificial, because no experiment can distinguish between them, at least within Lorentz's theory. Therefore, Cohn believed that under the Lorentz transformation quantities were only valid for optical phenomena, but mechanical clocks would capture 'real' time.[60]

---

26 Max Abraham was a German physicist who studied under Max Planck.

Finally in 1904 Friedrich Hasenöhrl[27] suggested that part of the mass of a body – which he chose to call its 'apparent mass' – can be thought of as radiation bouncing around a cavity. This depends on temperature, as every heated body emits radiation, which is proportional to its energy, and from this he concluded that:

$$m = \frac{\frac{8}{3}E}{c^2}$$

Hasenöhrl also stated that this energy-apparent-mass relation only holds as long a body radiates, that is to say, if the temperature of a body is greater than zero degrees Kelvin. However, in 1905 Abraham and Hasenöhrl himself changed the result to be the same value as that for the electromagnetic mass for a body at rest.[60]

1905 Surpasses Even 1904

On 5 June 1905, Henri Poincaré submitted the summary of a work which closed the existing gaps of Lorentz's work. In this he showed that Lorentz's equations of electrodynamics were not varying in accordance with the fixed mathematical relationship he laid out. To correct this flaw he pointed out the group characteristics of the transformation, and he corrected Lorentz's formulae for the transformations of charge density and current. For the first time Poincaré used the term 'Lorentz transformation', and he gave them the symmetrical form which is used to this day. In doing so he introduced a non-electrical binding force – the so called 'Poincaré stresses' – to ensure the stability of the electrons and to explain length contraction. He also sketched a Lorentz-invariant model of gravitation, which included gravitational waves, by extending the validity of Lorentz-invariance to non-electrical forces.[60]

Eventually in 1906, and independently of Einstein's' work, Poincaré finished a substantially extended version of his June paper. In this he spoke explicitly of 'the postulate of relativity'. At the paper's end he wrote that the discovery of magneto-cathode rays by Paul Ulrich Villard in 1904 seemed to threaten the entire theory of Lorentz. Even though this problem was quickly solved, Poincaré continued to refer to the idea of the aether and to distinguish between 'apparent' and 'real' coordinates. Because of this most historians hold

---

27 Friedrich Hasenöhrl was an Austro-Hungarian physicist.

that Poincaré failed to invent what is now commonly referred to as special relativity.[60]

All this points to one overwhelming conclusion, in that Einstein was not alone in his quest for a deeper and relative understanding of the universe. Because of this it would be quite wrong to think of relativity as being a solo effort. Many a great mind visited this terrain before he arrived, but none of that prior art detracts from his undoubted genius. Where others had pointed out individual features of relativity, it was Einstein who had the foresight to stand back and appreciate it in all its glory. It was he who uncluttered the confusion and saw clearly through the brilliance of those who had gone before. And it was he who ultimately led the way to the new and coherent vision of reality which we now look at today. His was a remarkable feat, in fact probably the most remarkable feat that science has seen to this day. Over a period of less than a decade Einstein tore down several centuries of accepted thinking and rebuilt them. True, he knew what most of the building blocks should be and true he may have relied on the assistance of several other 'builders' along the way, but it was he whom history records as the unquestioned architect of relativity and it was he who pushed science on to many of its great breakthroughs in the decades that would follow.

Right up to his death in 1955 Einstein always tried to remain contemporary. The record is clear in that he knew and worked with Alan Turing and that he admired the power of the computing machines he pioneered. Indeed he was even insightful enough to once be quoted as saying that 'computers are incredibly fast, accurate, and stupid. Human beings are incredibly slow, inaccurate, and brilliant. Together they are powerful beyond imagination'. Thus, in essence it is this mantra that powers the new field of Web science and it is interesting to wonder what Einstein might have made of the World Wide Web as we see it today. Might he, for example, have also had the insight to stand back from this system and appraise it with the same clarity he had done before? Unfortunately we will never know, but there are certainly many parallels between the high orders of complexity and data we see on the Web and the informational model of universe only hinted at during Einstein's day.

12

Special Relativity

Data is not information. Information is not knowledge. Knowledge is not understanding. Understanding is not wisdom.

Anonymous

June 1905 saw Einstein submit his famous paper on what is now called Special Relativity. In it he outlined a radical and fundamental reframing of space and time by bringing them together as one. From that point on no longer could they be considered as separate. Together they were renamed 'space-time' and a new and immediate clarity was added to the world of physics. Einstein and relativity had arrived.

Through special relativity Einstein explained that all time and space coordinates in all reference frames are equal, and thereby showed that there is no 'true' or 'apparent' time. He also destroyed the notion of the aether, as previous scientists had tried to describe it, and some even choose to see this as Einstein's announcement that the idea of the aether was dead. Nevertheless this is not strictly true. In his much later 1920 lecture on 'Aether and the Theory of Relativity' Einstein exclaimed that according to relativity[1] space is endowed with physical properties[2] and one could use the word 'aether', if one wished, to refer to such properties in a collective sense, although he acknowledged that this meaning of the word 'differs widely from that of the aether of the mechanical undulatory theory of light'. In particular he explained that this relativistic collective notion of the joined space and time has no mechanical properties at all, not even a state of motion or rest, and so its parts cannot be tracked over time. Although contemporary physicists consider Einstein to have gone too far with his acknowledgement, purely on the ground of lack of apparent mechanics, a concept not dissimilar to Einstein's 1920 statement will come back into play in our story later on.

---

1   Here Einstein is specifically referring to General Relativity, on which he published in 1912.
2   Now commonly referred to as the metric field.

But we digress. Before going further we need to understand special relativity from the perspective of information and computation.

As outlined in the previous chapter, space and time can be considered to be unified by the fact that both can be seen in terms of an ability to hold data. But we have not made clear how the two might be linked, as in Einstein's ideas on relativity. To do this we shall start by considering two examples, one a classical illustration that nicely explains special relativity in physical terms and the other which is much more abstract.

The first is usually told by way of a story involving two duelling gunmen, both of whom are armed with loaded and highly accurate pistols. Both men are also standing apart at, say, twenty paces, are of equal physical proportions and possess exactly the same speed of reaction. As is tradition with duelling, they have only one task on which they must concentrate and that is to shoot their opponent before they themselves are shot. There are two more rules, however, in that both men must fire simultaneously at each other and that two witnesses must be present to confirm that the duel takes place fairly. A clearly described scene, don't you think? Well, not quite yet, or not at least with regard to the requirements of relativity. In order to make things absolutely clear we must next insist that the first of the observers – we shall refer to him as ' $Observer_1$ ' – is placed exactly midway between both the duellers at the exact instant at which both pistols are fired. The reason for being this pedantic rests on yet another constraint placed on the contest. This insists that $Observer_1$ has also to be stationary at the precise time of the shooting, while both gunmen must be travelling at the same high speed and in the same direction parallel to the observer. To achieve this, the story usually places both gunmen on top of a passing train rushing through a railway station at full throttle. It also portrays $Observer_1$ as a motionless spectator on the station's platform. As the train rushes by and at the precise moment that $Observer_1$ is equidistant from both gunmen, they fire their weapons and deadly bullets make their way along perfectly straight trajectories towards their respective targets. To complete the picture there is one final constraint to be added in that the second observer – $Observer_2$ – must also be positioned equidistant from both gunmen at the time of firing, only this time he must also be moving at the same speed and in the same direction as the gunmen. This can be achieved by imagining a second train moving at the same speed and running parallel and in close proximity to the first, with the second observer being perched on top to watch the action unfold. As a result of this positioning, $Observer_2$ will be immediately in front of $Observer_1$ at the time when both trains pass through the station and the shooting takes place.

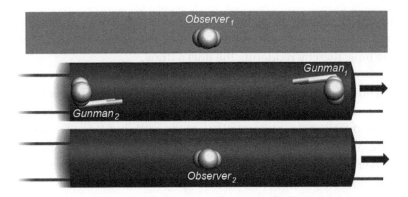

Figure 12.1   The duelling gunmen thought experiment

Now the scene is set and a very simple question is posed, which asks: which one of the gunmen is hit first?

Before attempting to answer this question it's worth mentioning that trains provide a good example of the kind of motion necessary to think about special relativity, and this is for two reasons. Firstly because they tend to move in straight lines, being firmly fixed atop their rails, and secondly because once in motion they generally maintain a consistent speed. Both of these requirements are what make special relativity 'special'. They are highly specific and without them special relativity simply would not work.

Getting back to the question: who gets shot first? Instinctively the answer is that both the gunmen get hit at exactly the same time. But instinct can be misleading. Certainly $Observer_1$ on the platform will see both guns fire at the same time, but $Observer_2$, on the train sees something different. He sees the gun toward the front of the first train go off before the one at the back. This is because the motion of the train is carrying $Observer_2$ closer to the exact position in space where the gunman closest to the front of the first train fired his weapon. Because of this, light has less distance to travel from the point of the front gunman to $Observer_2$ than from the rear gunman. And because light is known to travel at a fixed speed[3] it strikes $Observer_2$'s eyes first and he therefore perceives an order of sequence in the way in which both gunmen go about their task of shooting. This therefore implies to him that the gunman at the rear of the first train loses the duel, though hopefully not his life. $Observer_1$, on the other hand, could, quite legitimately disagree, for he experienced the shooting

_____

3   In any particular medium, such as air in this case.

without observing any order in the firing. For him it was an instantaneous event and, all things being equal, both gunmen should be wounded at precisely the same time, thereby rendering the duel a draw.

But whose perspective is right? This is where the brilliance of special relativity comes in and suggests that both observers are correct. Furthermore there are not only two legitimate interpretations of the truth but there are literately an infinite number of correct interpretations, all dependent on the point of view of the observer and their individual speed of motion. The conclusion that special relativity ultimately draws us to is that space and time are only valid in the eye of the beholder and what one observer might experience as time, another might experience as a mixture of space and time. Each observer and the path he travels carries its own take on observed reality. Each is equally accurate, yet when observers move relative to each other their views on the passage of time begin to disagree. They quite literally drift out of synchronisation, and in a very precise and calculable way. For Einstein, time is a useful measure of things, but nothing at all exceptional. This same peculiarity of perspective de-synchronisation can also be found with distance. Each observer carries his own gauge by which distance may be measured. Again any given gauge is as equally precise and valid as the next, yet the gauges of two observers will never measure the spatial dimensions of the same thing in precisely the same way unless both observers are moving in close proximity to each other and at exactly the same speed. If space and time did not behave like this, the speed of light would not be constant and would depend upon any given observer's state of motion. But relativity tells us that the speed of light is constant and that as a by-product space and time do behave this way. Space and time modify themselves in a precisely compensating ways so that observations of light's speed yield exactly the same result regardless of the observer's speed of motion.[21] In fact, if anyone were to call out the universe's single most constant constant, this would be it. The speed of light is indeed the king of all constants.

Moving on to the second example, let us think purely in terms of information and computation and this time imagine that we are faced with an extremely difficult dilemma; say a member of your immediate family has been taken seriously ill and has fallen unconscious in hospital. You are called to the bedside along with other immediate family members and are asked if consent might be given for an extremely risky operation. The purpose of this example is not so much to canvas your personal opinion on the merits of the operation, but is more to question the very nature of what personal opinion is. So, let's further insist that it is your mother who is ill and that your father and only brother are present at the bedside with you. How likely is it that all three of you will form exactly the same opinion on whether the operation should go ahead? The odds are stacked very strongly against such an outcome unfortunately. All three might easily reach the same conclusion and answer either for or against the operation, but it is almost a forgone conclusion that the degree of certainly will differ widely between all three relatives.

Most will have been in a situation like this, where we are expected to make significant decisions without prior warning. Almost certainly in such circumstance our minds begin to spin. Memories, prejudices, fears, aspirations and ambitions for the future all swirl as we try to make sense of the question we have just been faced with. In the case of our example this will most likely be an intense experience. Both children will most likely flash through strong childhood memories of their mother and contemplate the way that she has ultimately shaped their lives. Likewise the father will retreat to a different place in his past and perhaps remember the first time he met his wife and the impact she has had on him throughout their undoubted happy times together. So now to the point: the flow of information from the doctor to the gathered family, by way of the question, may well be minuscule in comparison with that amount of information they have each stocked up over their lifetimes, but it could easily trigger significant quantities of that stored life-information to be re-evaluated as part of the process of the decision-making taking place. For each family member different types and quantities of information will be retrieved and considered as their various thoughts go into overdrive, and if we were to think of these thought processes as being akin to a kind of map through the brain, it is possible to think of their reasoning process purely in informational and computational terms. So it is theoretically possible not only to calculate the amount of data needed for each individual to reach a decision, but also the amount of energy consumed by the task of reasoning. Almost certainly the results will vary between those present. Maybe, if we consider retrieved data as being analogous to space, we can make a direct comparison with the duelling gunmen example given previously: in simple terms, each of the family members occupies a different observation point and for each, reality is quite different. In computational parlance, they do not possess the same contexts.

Einstein realised this long ago and knew that apparent differences in phenomena may not be intrinsically down to the phenomena but due entirely to the necessity of describing them from the viewpoint of any given observer. Electricity and magnetism, motion and rest, gravity and acceleration were all unified by Einstein in this way. The differences that observers perceive between them are therefore contingent, because they reflect only the viewpoint of the individual.

This all points to Einstein's acute appreciation for, and understanding of, the idea of context, but in the 1960s a further and more fundamental insight was proposed, in that the differences between unified phenomena were contingent but not because of the viewpoint of the observer. Instead the notion of symmetry was introduced to suggest that the various laws that might apply to a given situation may have a symmetry that is not respected by all the features of the world they apply to.

This brings us back to the equation used to describe information in Chapter 2 and emphasises the importance of context.

It has to be said that context is by far the most misunderstood and underplayed concept in the whole of computing, as almost this entire field still treats its subject matter in terms of absolutes. When a procedure is specified or a database designed, it is almost always taken for granted that all those involved will understand both the syntax to be used and the meanings associated with all the items to be used. This is because computer science, and more particularly information technology, is significantly dependent on standards for its various ideas and common practices to hold. Without them the modern information age would simply be a house of cards waiting to fall. We have standards for every widely accepted programming language, communication protocol and data format, and standards for the way that almost all valuable data is stored and shared. Indeed it could be said that we have standards for the way contemporary computing is treated from the cradle to the grave. We even have standards for standards. But has anyone ever bothered to truly question why?

The answer is simple yet profound in that they provide common points of reference and hence make it easier for two individuals to come together and consider the same problem from a shared viewpoint. In essence they provide the origins and axes needed to make both information and computation

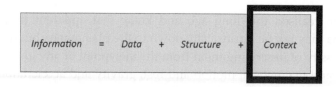

Information = *Data* + *Structure* + *Context*

Figure 12.2   Context makes information and computation relative concepts

absolute. Just like using graph paper to draw a square accurately, the various standards developed in computer science and information technology have captured and tamed the underlying characteristics of the elements they seek to understand. But this in no way implies that these elements are also absolute in nature. No, rather it is quite the opposite in that if they were absolute the need for standards would be much less heightened. In truth, both information and computation are inherently relative.

Not to sound too left field, but from a quantum mechanical perspective, there is a further interesting connection. If the physical theories of quantum mechanics are indeed correct and the quantum mechanical version of the Church–Turing model is indeed valid, then the term 'context' in the above equation is especially relevant. Its inclusion implies that information is a concept which can rarely be treated in absolute terms. In other words context restricts the ability to process or understand information accurately across all observable dimensions and scales. It hence makes the notion of information, and thereby all but the most localised forms of information processing, 'relative'.[61] Besides, there is one further constraint which we must take into account when considering context in relativistic terms. The speed of light is not only an unbeatable absolute but it is also of principal concern in all synthetic computations. This is because its speed is also the absolute upper limit at which information can both flow and be created. It therefore restricts both computational and informational capabilities and introduces exactly the same synchronisation problems as can be found with time and space in real world relativistic problems. Only this time it is more appropriate to trade in terms of abstract memory than the ticking of a clock or the marks on some rule. Thus, according to the theory of special relativity, causality would be violated if information could travel faster than the speed of light in some reference frame, and following this through we find an implication that if the speed of light could be surpassed, for any given computation, the information associated with its output could theoretically be received in some contexts before the information associated with its input. To put it another way, information could be received before it had been created, and the 'effect' of the computation could be observed before that which caused it to occur. This is like something being created from nothing and such a violation of causality has never yet been recorded, nor is it likely to be. The laws of physics are still safe for now.

Light Cones

Information propagates to and from any given point forming a region defined by what is commonly referred to as a 'light cone'. Drawing a line from A to B, as in Figure 12.3 below, can accordingly be thought of as a context, or frame of reference, in which event A and event B occur at the same location in space but are separated only by their occurring at different times. Furthermore, if A proceeds B in that context then A proceeds B in all contexts. Thus, information can hypothetically travel from A to B and demonstrate a causal relationship between both, in that A is the 'cause' and B the 'effect'. Or, to put it another way, A could possibly be seen as the 'input' to a computation which produces B as its 'output'.

Equally, the interval AC is 'space-like' in that there is a frame of reference in which event A and event C occur simultaneously, separated only in space. However, there are also frames in which A precedes C – as shown – or in which C precedes A. Barring some way of travelling faster than light, it is not possible for any mass, or information for that matter, to travel from A to C or from C to A. Thus there is no causal connection between A and C and they are not related in any meaningful informational or computational sense.

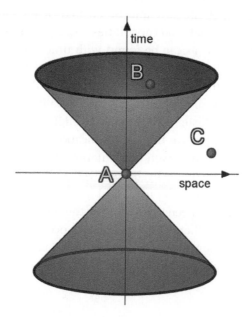

Figure 12.3   A light cone defines locations that are in proper causal, or computable, relation and those that are not, or are incomputable

Space-time Cuts Up Differently as a Consequence of Context

It's easy to glibly pronounce information and computation as being relative concepts, but it does not necessarily follow that they should therefore obey any of laws of relativity. As Brian Green so eloquently points out in his book *The Fabric of the Cosmos*, we are used to the fact that objects can move through space, but there is another kind of motion that is equally important, in that objects also move through time. At this very moment the watch on your wrist or the clock on a nearby wall will be ticking away, demonstrating that you and everything around you are incessantly moving forward from one moment to the next. Newton thought that motion through time was totally apart from motion through space, but Einstein found that they are intimately linked. So when we look at something like a parked car, which from our viewpoint is stationary, all of its motion is through time. The car, its driver, the street, us, our clothes and so on are all moving through time in perfect sychronisation – moment by moment passing by in an identical fashion for all. But if the car speeds away, some of its motion through time is diverted into motion through space. This means that the car's progress through time slows down and as a result time elapses more slowly for the moving car and its driver than it does for us and everything else that remains stationary. This phenomenon is truly amazing in itself, but it is not the only amazing thing about the situation. There is a constant involved, in so much as although the car's speed through space and time may differ, its speed through space-time will not. It stays perfectly regular, always amounting to exactly same value, that being the speed of light. Think about that for one moment, as it is more profound than it may at first appear. Speed, or more precisely velocity, is the rate of change of space over time. Remove the variable involved in this statement and all that remain is 'rate of change', and, as we have laboured many times already, change is merely a pseudonym for computing. The speed of light simply provides an upper limit for this in all cases. Thus although the nature of any computation involved in special relativity may change, regardless of how fast its context moves the *amount* of computation soaked up by the combined processing of space and time together can never change. It is literally like a single computer program balancing its fixed recourses between two microprocessors. But then that's precisely the point that special relativity makes about the universe, or at least as we perceive it, in that it has a finite capability to compute over space-time. In very real terms relativity spells out that our universe is computational and, by implication, an informational 'machine'.

13

General Relativity

Computer science is at a turning point, and it has to go beyond algorithms and understand the social dynamics of issues like trust, responsibility, empathy and privacy in this vast networked space. The technologists and companies that understand those issues will be far more likely to succeed in expanding their markets and enlarging their audiences.

Ben Shneiderman, University of Maryland,

In 1907, two years after proposing the Special Theory of Relativity, Einstein was preparing a review of special relativity when he suddenly wondered how Newtonian gravitation would have to be modified to fit in with special relativity. At this point Einstein had a revelation, an idea that he later described as 'the most fortunate thought of my life'. This made him conscious of the fact that an observer who is falling from the roof of a house experiences no gravity, and led him to propose his famous equivalence principle which declared acceleration to be equivalent to gravity. More precisely he stated the complete physical equivalence of a gravitational field and the corresponding acceleration of the reference frame. This extends the principle of relativity to cover the case of uniformly accelerated motion of the reference frame. In simple terms Einstein told us that it is impossible to distinguish between the effects of acceleration and the effects of gravity and by doing so he succeeded in unifying all kinds of motion. It was already known that uniform motion is indistinguishable from rest, for instance, but Einstein also showed that acceleration is no different to being at rest but under the influence of some gravitational field.[14]

The unification of acceleration with gravity was a marriage with great consequences. For instance we are not accustomed to thinking of space as a thing with properties of its own, but it most certainly is. Space has three dimensions and it also has a particular geometry.[14] This tells us what happens to objects like planets, chairs and raccoons as they move through space and time.

A consequence of Maxwell's theory of electromagnetism is that light rays must move in straight lines. But if we adopt this idea, we see straight away that Einstein's theory has great implications, for light rays are bent by gravitational fields, which in turn respond to the presence of matter. The only conclusion to draw is that the presence of matter affects the geometry of space.[14]

In the flat-plane geometry of Euclid, if two straight lines are initially parallel, they never can and never will meet. But two light rays that are initially parallel can meet in the real world, because if they pass on each side of a star they will be bent towards each other. So Euclidean geometry does not hold in the real world. Furthermore, the geometry of the space-time around us is constantly changing. This geometry is not like a flat infinite plane. It is like the surface of a great ocean – incredibly dynamic with great waves and small ripples in it.[14] In a nutshell these things are what general relativity tells us. It is the current description of gravitation in modern physics. It unifies special relativity and Newton's law of universal gravitation and describes gravity as a geometric property of space and time tied together. In particular, the curvature of space-time is directly related to the generalisation of classical three-dimensional momentum to four-dimensional space-time in relation to whatever matter and radiation are present. The relation is specified by the Einstein field equations, a system of partial differential equations.[63] Today relativity plays a role in many areas such as cosmology, the Big Bang theory and so on, and has now been checked by experiment to an extremely high degree of accuracy.

Whereas special relativity majors of how the universe behaves in relation to an observer at constant speed – and that includes all cases where the observer is at rest and motionless – general relativity steps up a level and concentrates on how acceleration and all its equivalences and implications alter reality. This causes a problem from the perspective of information and computation, however. As special relativity concentrates on velocity, its can easily be described in terms of space and time by virtue of a straightforward equation that relates all three. Substitute space and time for various types of memory and an immediate computational interpretation is formed. It is also true that some further, and simple, mathematics can be applied to the idea of velocity so as to interpret it in terms of acceleration. This can be seen as:

$$a = \frac{\partial v}{\partial t} \qquad\qquad \text{Where: } v = \text{velocity}$$
$$t = \text{time}$$

... which can be interpreted as acceleration corresponding to the rate of change of velocity over time. Acceleration can further be formulated in term of space and time as:

$$a = \frac{\partial^2 s}{\partial t^2}$$

Where: s = distance (space)
t = time

... which can be read as acceleration corresponding to the rate of change of rate of change of distance, or space, over time. In other words the equation for velocity folds back on itself, producing a double emphasis on 'rate of change'. This also implies that acceleration is nothing more than the result of the same computation fed back into itself. This is a subtle yet profound realisation, but it nonetheless adds little value in trying to understand how information and computation might relate to general relativity. For that we need to go in further search or new equivalences.

Meaning

Let's suppose for one moment that you like hamburgers. In fact, let's be wild and suggest that you like hamburgers so much that you consume them to the exclusion of all other food stuffs. Furthermore, let's add a couple more twists and say that you have developed a particular taste for Gregory's burgers and insist that you are a person of means who enjoys travelling extensively. A strange combination of preferences maybe, but one which is not beyond the bounds of reasonable suggestion.

Let's put aside the nutritional value of such an exclusive diet and, for the purpose of illustration, concentrate instead on the benefits of bringing together burgers and you, the global traveller. In many ways this is actually a marriage made in heaven. The Gregory's brand belongs to a well-known international chain of restaurants with branches in most places around the world. Furthermore the company takes great pride in ensuring the consistency of its products, no matter where you sample them. So, a Big Burger in Oslo should be much the same as a Big Burger in Tokyo, Sydney, Los Angeles, Bangalore or wherever. Give or take a few inconsequential variations, the gastronomic experience should be identical.

Now let's also suppose that you have maintained your Gregory fuelled existence for as long as you can practically remember and that you have indeed eaten in their restaurants in just about every location that any human might reasonably every want to visit. Add all this up and we could reasonably assume you to be a real burger expert? Wrong.

You might be able to talk endlessly about how you have enjoyed burgers in the different locations around the world and be able to finely differentiate between the various merits and drawbacks of each eatery in which you have dined, but it is a sure bet that you will not be able to draw from your own experience and describe exactly what a burger 'is'. What the very essence of 'burger' *means*. It is true that you might be able to fake a description, probably having heard various others describe burgers, but you would be stealing from them in the very truest sense. The words you will use would not be your own. You may have devoured tens of thousands, perhaps even hundreds of thousands of burgers in your lifetime, but still the very notion of burger would still be alien to you. The reason for this falls down to exclusivity. Given that all you have ever tasted is a single form of unchanging food, you simply have nothing to compare it against to describe how it really is. In essence, your vocabulary of experience and perception is so limited that it adds no real value at all. You might understand that you find the task of eating pleasurable and you might also understand that burgers are important to you to sustain your existence, but still you will be nowhere near to understanding what it means to taste a burger.

The point about variation is key, as it is only through such change that anything, real or imaginary, can stand out and take its own identity, be that eating burgers, the movement of the stars or the courting dance of two pink elephants. Only by comparison with multiple different things in some coordinated fashion can any of these stand out and find meaning in the eye of the beholder. This illustrates that meaning is not only closely related to the concept of identity, and therefore broken symmetry, but it is also inextricably bound the context of the individual deriving that meaning. It also shows that meaning is dependent on any number of relationships propagating out from that with the meaning to other things or ideas with different meanings. Think of this like the spokes of a wheel spreading out from the centre. This consequently brings structure into the definition of meaning, again making it similar to the equation used to describe information. Only this time a particular subtlety is further highlighted. This states that neither information nor meaning is dependent on time for its existence, but that the consumer of any such information or meaning is dependent on time through the computational act of interpretation. This is because no matter how insignificant, the reliance on structure in both cases demands that every contributing element and every contributing factor involved in the interpretation of any type of information or meaning must be taken into account before the whole can be considered as valid. So, if a piece of information is constituted of a string of three distinct data items, all three must be considered before that information can stand up for itself, so long as all three are relevant to that information. That implies at least three computational *activities* to ingest and do something with the data present. Three steps in a computational process in other words. And each step needs a fixed and precise amount of time to do its business. This leads to a reformulation of the formula for information as follows:

$$\textbf{Information (from the perspective of the observer)} = \frac{\partial(Data + Structure + Context)}{\partial t}$$

Conjecture 19   Information from the perspective of the observer

Following on from this equation it is easy to see a formula for meaning as shown below:

$$\textbf{Meaning (from the perspective of the observer)} = \frac{\partial((\sum Information) + Structure_2 + Context_2)}{\partial t}$$

Conjecture 20   Meaning from the perspective of the observer

In reading this formula it is important to understand that the structure and context elements listed might not the same as those present in the equation for information as they might prove to be supplemental in some way. They have been shown with the subscript '2' for this reason.

For illustration purposes only, it is now possible to think of some piece of information as being made up from a string of integers – say 1, 2 and 3. In this instance the structure if the information can literally be thought of as a string, as if it were a section freshly cut from a wound bobbin. The structure of the meaning associated with that information, however, would be different, fanning out to show linkages to other meaningful pieces of information surrounding it. This would ultimately then go on to form a mesh of understanding as various clusters of meaning come together to completely fill any given meaningful interpretation.

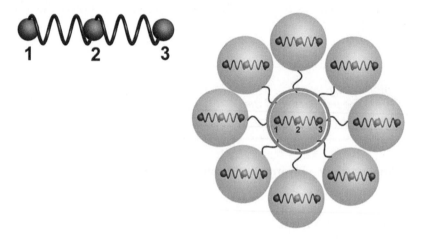

Figures 13.1(a) and 13.1(b)   A conceptualised view of an information 'string' and its participation in localised meaning

Relevance

There is one further addition to both equations before we are done. Concentrate on the structural element of both equations and the data element of the information equation for a moment and, in particular, focus on each of the individual associations and data items making up such composites. Under normal circumstances it will be rare to find a situation where all associations and all data items carry the same weight. Some will obviously have stringer ties than others, so much so in fact that we have a special word to describe that strength. And that word is 'relevance'.

Relevance is the weighting factor that works within the systems of structure and context present in information and meaning. It 'pulls' data together to make information and information together to make meaning and this can be shown by tweaking information and meaning as follows:

$$Information = \frac{\partial((\sum_0^i (Relevance_i * Data_i)) + (\sum_0^j (Relevance_j * Structure_j)) + Context)}{\partial t}$$

Conjecture 21   A reformulation of conjecture 19

Note with this equation that the subscripts i and j are used to indicate that there are two different types of relevance at work; one specific to the data elements involved and one specific to the links between that data. This implies that for any given piece of information there may be more or less links present than data elements, and vice versa, which leaves the way open for an extremely rich collection of structural formations.

Now to stop for a moment and simplify things, as the equations we are trying to discuss are becoming rather verbose. So let's do some abbreviation and shorten things a bit. This allows our equation for information to be read as:

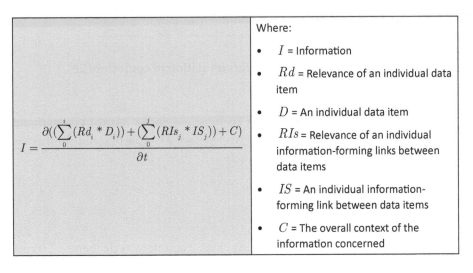

$$I = \frac{\partial((\sum_0^i (Rd_i * D_i)) + (\sum_0^j (RIs_j * IS_j)) + C)}{\partial t}$$

Where:

- I = Information
- Rd = Relevance of an individual data item
- D = An individual data item
- RIs = Relevance of an individual information-forming links between data items
- IS = An individual information-forming link between data items
- C = The overall context of the information concerned

Conjecture 22   Yet more reformulation of conjecture 19

The equation for meaning can also be rewritten as:

$$M = \frac{\partial((\sum_{0}^{k}(RI_{k} * I_{k})) + (\sum_{0}^{l}(RMs_{l} * MS_{l})) + C)}{\partial t}$$	Where: • M = Meaning • I = Information • RI = Relevance of an individual pieces of information • RMs = Relevance of an individual meaning-forming links between pieces of information • MS = An individual meaning-forming link between pieces of information • C = The overall context of the information concerned

Conjecture 23   A reformulation of conjecture 20

Alternatively meaning can be written in terms of data, as:

$$M = \frac{\partial^{2}((\sum_{0}^{i}(Rd_{i} * D_{i})) + (\sum_{0}^{j}(RIs_{j} * IS_{j})) + C)}{\partial t^{2}}$$

Conjecture 24   Yet more reformulation of conjecture 20

That's the algebra out of the way for now, so please reward yourself and relax. In fact take a break and prepare to step back a couple of steps, for there is an alluring comparison about to be made.

Strings and Things

The use of the string analogy in the previous example was deliberate. Strings actually provide just about all the qualities needed to describe the informational and computational model presented in this book. We can spin a string around itself to form a coil of sorts and we can scrunch a whole bunch of them up to form an entangled 'mass' of any required size or shape. Such strings are very 'physical' in such senses. There is another, lesser known, type of string, however, a type that quantum physicists currently cling to with great passion and for much the same reasons as mentioned here.

The strings of the sub-atomic world are the main object of study in String Theory, a branch of theoretical physics. There are different such string theories, many of which are unified by a formulation known as M-theory. A string is a one-dimensional object, unlike an elementary particle which is said to exist in zero-dimensions, or is point-like.[62] Through this one-dimensional structure, many desirable features of a more fundamental theory of physics automatically emerge. Most notably, almost any theory of strings consistent with quantum mechanics must also contain the idea of quantum gravity, which had not been described consistently prior to string theory.

The characteristic length scale of strings is thought to be on the order of the Planck length,[1] the scale at which the effects of quantum gravity are believed to become significant. At much larger length scales, such as the scales visible in physics laboratories, such objects would be indistinguishable from zero-dimensional point particles. However, the styles of vibration and structure of these tiny strings would be observed as different elementary particles in what is known as the standard model of quantum field theory. For instance, one state of the string would be associated with the physical entity we know as a photon,[2] and another state with a quark.[3] This unifying feature of string theory

1 In physics, the Planck length is a unit of length, equal to 1.616252(81)×10–35 metres. It is a base unit in the system of Planck units. The Planck length can be defined from three fundamental physical constants: the speed of light in a vacuum, Planck's constant, and the gravitational constant. Current theory suggests that one Planck length is the smallest distance or size about which anything can be known.

2 In physics, a photon is an elementary particle, the quantum of the electromagnetic field and the basic 'unit' of light and all other forms of electromagnetic radiation. It is also the force carrier for the electromagnetic force. A quantum (plural: quanta) is an indivisible entity of a quantity that has the same units as the Planck constant and is related to both energy and momentum of elementary particles of matter (called fermions) and of photons and other bosons. The word comes from the Latin 'quantus', for 'how much.' The Planck constant, also called 'Planck's constant', is a physical constant used to describe the sizes of quanta in quantum mechanics. It is named after Max Planck, one of the founders of quantum theory. The Planck constant is the proportionality constant between the energy of a photon and the frequency of its associated electromagnetic wave.

3 A quark is an elementary particle and a fundamental constituent of matter. Quarks combine to form composite particles called hadrons, the best-known of which are protons and neutrons.

is amongst its greatest strengths. Nevertheless, no known solution of string theory exactly reproduces the particle content of the standard model of physics.

Propagating in space-time, strings sweep out a two-dimensional surface, called a world-sheet, analogous to the one-dimensional world-line[4] traced out by a point particle.[62] Strings can furthermore be either open or closed. A closed string is a string that has no end-points, and therefore is topologically equivalent to a circle. An open string, on the other hand, has two end-points and is topologically equivalent to a line section. Not all string theories contain open strings, but every theory must contain closed strings, as interactions between open strings can always result in closed strings. Developments in string theory in the 1990s have shown that the open strings should always be thought of as ending on a new type of object called the D-branes, and the spectrum of possibilities for open strings has hence increased greatly.[62]

Open and closed strings are generally associated with characteristic vibrational modes and one of the vibration modes of a closed string can be identified as the graviton.[5] In certain string theories the lowest-energy vibration of an open string is a tachyon[6] and can undergo what is known as tachyon condensation. Other vibrational modes of open strings exhibit the properties of photons and gluons.[7] Strings can also possess an orientation, which can be thought of as an internal 'arrow' which distinguishes the string from one with the opposite orientation. By contrast, an unoriented string is one with no such arrow on it.

---

4   In physics, the world-line of an object is the unique path of that object as it travels through four-dimensional space-time. The concept of 'world line' is distinguished from the concept of 'orbit' or 'trajectory' – such as an orbit in space or a trajectory of a truck on a road map – by the time dimension, and typically encompasses a large area of space-time wherein perceptually straight paths are recalculated to show their (relatively) more absolute position states – to reveal the nature of special relativity or gravitational interactions. The idea of world-lines originates in physics and was pioneered by Einstein.

However, world-lines are a general way of representing the course of events. The use of it is not bound to any specific theory. Thus in general usage, a world-line is the sequential path of personal human events, with time and place as dimensions, that marks the history of a person – perhaps starting at the time and place of one's birth until their death. The log book of a ship is a description of the ship's world-line, as long as it contains a time tag attached to every position. The world line allows one to calculate the speed of the ship, given a measure of distance – a so-called metric – appropriate for the curved surface of the Earth

5   In physics, the graviton is a hypothetical elementary particle that mediates the force of gravity in the framework of quantum field theory. If it exists, the graviton must be massless because the gravitational force has unlimited range.

6   A tachyon is a hypothetical sub atomic particle that travels faster than the speed of light.

7   Gluons are elementary expressions of quark interaction, and are indirectly involved with the binding of protons and neutrons together in atomic nuclei.

From Strings to Gravity

Strings are a useful model from informational and computational perspectives, not least because they afford the opportunity to conceptualise across multiple dimensions in a very 'physical' sense. It has long been appreciated that information especially is a multidimensional concept. The idea of an orange, for example, carries many dimensions, such as its colour, weight and taste. Furthermore such dimensions are continuous across scales of appropriate size. Thus it is possible to talk about an orange being particularly juicy or heavier than your average orange, as opposed to simply being big and juicy. Nevertheless such dimensions carry no physical relevance in that they merely help to locate the precise qualities of a particular thing or idea with in a theoretical space of all its possible descriptions. They are a kind of pointer that locates an exact position within a space of potentially infinite dimensions and scales. In fact, mathematicians have a name for such pointers, preferring to refer to them as vectors.

Not surprisingly such a concept also exists in quantum mechanics to help understand the mind bending abstractness of that field. Such pointers are known as Eigen vectors and they are used to both qualify and quantify the characteristics of some extremely complex and non-intuitive ideas. But even with such expressive tools, physicists still need another type of model in support of their Eigen descriptions, one that reaches out to conjure up explanations in terms of how the parts of any given thing connect to make the whole 'real'. This model is provided by the Feynman diagrams favoured in.quantum mechanics These are a type of schematic similar to that first introduced in Chapter 5 via the ' X '-shaped pattern and, as we have seen, such diagrams can also be used when thinking about information and computation. In such a way, as strings increase the expressivity of fundamental particles from zero-dimensional points to higher dimensional geometric objects, the abstract notion of a 'string' can do the same for the fundamental concepts involved in both information and computation. Thus it is possible to conceptualise information and computation across any number of dimensions as if they were physically 'real', through the use of strings. Hence using two dimensions it is possible to think in terms of lines, vectors and ultimately shapes. Adding more dimensions then allows us to think in terms of 'objects' and ultimately the passage of these objects through still higher dimensions. This leads to the realisation that both information and computation might be viewed in equivalent terms to physical properties such as velocity, given that mandatory dimensions for computation and information to exist are space and time. Furthermore as both information and meaning have derivative relationships with time, it is possible to play with the idea of the following equivalences:

> *Information = distance*

Conjecture 25   Information and distance

And:

> *Meaning = velocity*

Conjecture 26   Meaning and velocity

If you can make that leap of faith, it is not much further to a huge revelation.

> *The Rate of Change of Meaning = Acceleration = Gravity*

Conjecture 27   Meaning, acceleration and gravity

As Einstein realised way back at the start of the twentieth century, science had been missing a staringly obvious equivalence in that acceleration and gravity are the same thing. Once that was established a crucial doorway was opened and a whole new interpretation of the world around us was made available. Even so, Einstein and his ideas were very much still caught up in the old fashioned ways of thinking. For him, no matter how radical his theories, he still wanted all matter to behave in predictable ways just as Newton had taught centuries before. When his peers pushed forward in parallel with the revolution that would become quantum mechanics Einstein struggled.

Quantum mechanics' dependence on the absolute uncertainty of the universe at small scales caused him massive conflict. It was a battle the Einstein eventually took to the grave as he tried to reconcile the minute with the massive and still today no one has been able to glue quantum mechanics and relativity together successfully. Regardless, is it not profound that as the twentieth century closed and the twenty-first century opened, two remarkable ideas started to emerge? On the one hand Tim Berners-Lee and his colleagues at the CERN laboratories in Geneva began to understand how to bring together the largest synthetic information construct mankind has ever seen, while at the same location, yet more of his colleagues were probing the very essence of physical reality and beginning to understand that at its most fundamental it demands to be describe purely in terms of information. Berners-Lee's efforts resulted in the birth of the World Wide Web, while those of his physicist friends resulted in the largest and most powerful particle acceleration on Earth today – the Large Hadron Collider, or LHC for short. While the LHC is proving an essential tool in penetrating the smallest reaches of the universe, would it not be amazing if the Web could do the same at the other end of the spectrum and shed further light on relativity and gravity?

14

Beyond the Fourth Dimension

*It is a curious fact about the human mind that people will work harder
to do something which captures their imagination than they will for any
practical purpose.*

Ian Richards

Unfortunately we can't quite move on and leave physics behind quite just yet. Before we do, for a short while, we need to take a further look at the detail of relativity and try to marry it up with the theories laid out in previous chapters.

Information, Computation and Einstein's Field Equations

Chapter 8 introduced a framework through which it might be possible to think of both information and computation in terms of fields. These are formed from connected meshes of either singular data instances or singular transformations on such data, be that at the singular data instances level or on higher order concepts formed from the aggregation of such instances. In a similar way Einstein formalised space-time through a set of ten equations which describe the fundamental interaction of gravitation as a result of space-time being curved by matter and energy. First published by Einstein in 1915, they use a form of mathematics which employs multidimensional arrays, commonly referred to as tensors or tensor fields. These can be thought of as simple 'containers' for all the relevant energy and momentum data relating to every point instance within a given a region of space-time. They are also, in very simple terms, mathematical tools used to describe complex motion in uneven space. Similar to the way in which electromagnetic fields are determined using charges and currents via Maxwell's equations, the field equations hence equate space-time's curvature with the energy and linear momentum, or stress-energy, within a space-time region.[64] Accordingly in local coordinates, the stress-energy tensor may be regarded as a four-by-four array, or matrix, of properties specific to each point in a space-time region. This collection of data is the thing that appears on the right side of Einstein's equation for general relativity:[65]

$$G_{ij} = \frac{8\pi K}{c^4} T_{ij}$$

where K is Newton's gravitational constant and c is the speed of light.

The four-by-four matrix on the left of this equation is the Einstein tensor, which summarises the relevant information about space-time curvature. The right side stress-energy tensor hence tells us everything we need to know about what energy and momentum are doing at a given point of space-time, in that T_{ab} is the flow of momentum in the b direction.[65]

To understand this we must understand that the various rows and columns of the matrix correspond to time plus the three spatial dimensions. We must also be aware that 'energy' is the same as 'momentum in the time direction', and that 'density' is the same as 'flow in the time direction'. Thus the top row of the stress-energy tensor keeps track of the density of energy, via the data at T_{00}, and the density of momentum in the x, y and z directions respectively. The first column of the matrix consequently also accounts for the flow of energy in the x, y and z directions, respectively. The other entries keep track of the flow of spatial momentum in various spatial directions. So, for example, if we look at the entry one row down and two columns in we will find a value for the flow in the x direction of momentum in the y direction.[65]

The stress-energy tensor is an important tool throughout most of physics, since most of its branches are interested in where energy and momentum are going and how much there is at any particular place and point in time. But it's only in general relativity where the stress-energy tensor takes a truly dominant role and dictates how another set of physical properties should behave – in this case demanding that space-time warp and curve at its behest. As a result the stress-energy tensor plays an integral part in Einstein's field equations for it provides the function which tells how to compute the distance between any two points in a given region of space-time, the left-hand solutions of the field equations being the components of the 'distance' tensor array produced. The inertial geodesic paths of particles and radiation in the resulting geometry are then calculated as part of a geodesic landscape.

Matter, Force and Relevance

Now let's develop things a little and think about Einstein's field equations in terms of information and data, and particularly in terms of the equivalences we have proposed so far. Given that nothing more than energy and momentum lie at the heart of the magic of relativity, we might suspect it possible to immediately go straight to an interpretation purely in terms of data and time. But that would be wholly inaccurate, given that, and as explained in the previous chapter, relevance plays a key part in a deep understanding of information.

To find relevance's true place in an informational interpretation of the field equations we need to go right back to the start and think about space again. Originally we described space as a type of memory, or more precisely a capability to hold data. What was not explained, however, was how we might think about that data and its placement within any given space. To do that simply imagine a region of space – any space – to be like a giant chess board, with each square representing a discrete location within that region. At this point there is no need to worry about the scale or size of each location, so it's perfectly all right for us to think in terms of planet-sized squares or even sub-Planck length units; here our squares are just abstract containers which may or may not contain 'something'. In the case of general relativity that 'something' is mass and the more of that that is present the more bearing or value that location has in terms of space-time's curvature. Massless or empty spatial 'squares' also contribute to the geometry of any given space-time region, but they obviously carry less influence on the curvature present.

Figure 14.1   Space as a chess board

Significance, weight, influence and so on, these are all just other names for one thing and that is relevance. In plain terms the more mass present at any location and point in time, the more it is relevant to the curvature or the space-time around it. That gives rise to the following final equivalence proposition, in that:

> *Relevance = Matter*

Conjecture 28   Relevance and matter

Given that matter is anything that has mass and mass is the measure of the amount of matter, this can also be read as:

> *Relevance = Mass*

Conjecture 29   Relevance and mass

If these propositions were to hold true it would be a relatively simple task to reformulate Einstein's thinking purely in terms of information and computation. Unfortunately, however, matters are not that simple and more has to be considered.

The Sum Has to Be the Whole of its Parts

Think of good old-fashioned atomic physics for one moment and put aside all the craziness that quantum mechanics has to offer. But don't get too comfortable. We have spent a long time introducing such craziness and we are not about to abandon it now yet. This digression into the classical is merely to support a point that will be of value later.

In 'traditional' definitions of an atom it can be seen as being made up of a collection of extremely small particles, like tiny billiard balls clustered together as if having found sanctuary. The names of these particles should be familiar to most, with protons, neutrons and electrons being the most common labels used for them. Push a bit harder and these particles can be seen to further fall apart, perhaps even several times over, to provide the fundamental particles of subatomic physics. Here classical interpretations of physics begin to fail and once again we have to call in the nonsensical help of quantum mechanics. But there is one belief that remains constant across both classical and quantum viewpoints, in that both ultimately rest of the bedrock of there being some set of fundamental particles out there somewhere. Keep smashing at atoms to grind out their innards and there will come some definable point where it is physically impossible to produce fragments of any smaller size. That is still the most fundamental of all scientific fundamentals. Whether it is ultimately right only time will tell, but, for now it's the best science has. At the very finest of fine levels, the physical world is still material in some very real sense.

The same type of reductionist approach crosses over to form a central concept in information theory as we currently know it, but this normally implies the use of language, and especially natural language to formulate core ideas. Much of this work is rather flowery – literally – with the floral analogy forming a wide range of frameworks through which collections of 'information' can be dissected and understood in terms of the fundamental 'ideas' they attempt to convey. In such a way information theorists can be heard to talk about language in terms of 'leaves', 'branches', 'stems' and 'roots'. So, if, for example, the phrase 'the catty woman thought there was something fishy about the situation' where analysed, the word 'catty' might be traced back to its most fundamental morphological form, or root, of 'cat'. The process by which this done is known as stemming and, likewise a stemming algorithm might trace the words 'fishing', 'fished', 'fish', and 'fisher' back to the root word, 'fish'. [72] More generally, categories of 'information' can be seen to branch out and form trees of more specific terms. Hence we could theoretically follow the term 'doctor' back along its tree to the more general description of 'health professional', so long as the relevant 'information' tree were restricted purely to describing health professionals. Similarly the term 'health professional' could be traced back to a root of 'professional 'or even 'person' if the subject matter of the tree were broadened.

Adding tree structure to 'information' in this way brings several distinct advantages, not least of which involves the treatment of informational derivation in geometric terms. More specifically, the application of geographic techniques allows the introduction of distance into the consideration of relationships between words and their underlying concepts or ideas. Particularly, through 'straight line' geometry, it is possible to obtain a numeric value which describes the similarity of any two ideas or concepts, no matter how abstract they might be. This is a proven and powerful idea. Indeed it is so powerful that it is now not only important to the theory of information, but is essential to the modern-day practice of information retrieval. Google, for instance, would not function nearly as well if it were not for its heavy reliance on geometric proximity between search terms and the various types of Web content its search engine indexes.

By way of an example, consider the term 'Doctor' in the information tree presented in Figure 14.2. Now ask how similar that term is in relation to the terms 'Nurse' and 'Chieftain'? To answer this question we simply need to follow the shortest path through the tree from 'Doctor' to both 'Nurse' and 'Chieftain', then analyse the respective distances found. So, in the first instance, it is easy to see that to get from 'Doctor' to 'Nurse' takes two steps – stopping off at 'Health Professional' midway. Similarly it takes five steps to get from 'Doctor' to 'Chieftain', taking in 'Health Professional', 'Professional', 'Person' and 'Leader' on route. From such journeys we can therefore deduce that the Doctor–Nurse relationship has a similarity rating of two and the Doctor–Chieftain relationship has a similarity rating of five. Obviously the lower such a rating the more similar the terms or concepts involved, so we can now convincingly rationalise the statement that Doctors are more similar to Nurses than they are to Chieftains, or at least according-to the information contained in Figure 14.2.

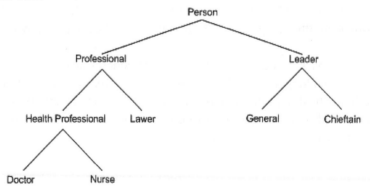

Figure 14.2   The 'information' tree for Person [73]

Now, returning to the chessboard analogy of space, a further type of questions arises. If mass equates to relevance, then if any given 'square' in space contained the term 'Doctor', would that have more mass than the term 'Chieftain' and might it, hence, create more curvature in the space around it? To answer this question we must first ask another question and probe what all relevances in the question are actually relevant to? In the case of our person tree example, part of the answer is easy, as all relevances must ultimately tie back to, and be solely of concern to, the root of the tree. In such a way we can use a similarity score to quantify any 'difference' or 'distance' between a given branch or leaf term from its root. This gives 'Doctor' a score of three as opposed to a score of just two for 'Chieftain'. From this is clear that more work needs to be done to interpret the term 'Doctor' within the specific context of the Person tree. That implies that the term 'Doctor' carries more information or, in simple terms, when viewed through the context of the Person tree, the term 'Doctor' carries more informational weight than the term 'Chieftain'. Hence, from now on we shall refer to such weight as 'branch weight' or b_w for short and use it as a multiplier of relevance to refine our mass equivalence as follows:

$$\sum (\text{Branch Weight} * \text{Relevance}) = \text{Mass}$$

Conjecture 30   A reformulation of conjecture 29

On Light and the Range of Elementary Particles

Relativity tells us a number of seemingly diverse things, not least of which are the facts that, firstly, space-time is sensitive to the condition of the observer and, secondly, that gravity and acceleration are the same. Regardless, despite their apparent diversity, at their core both special and general relativity have a common theme running through them and that theme is light. General relativity in particular tackles light head-on and shatters one of the science's longest-held beliefs by demonstrating that it does not always travel in a straight line. This is not because of any particular property of light itself, for it does indeed try to maintain the straightest path possible. Rather, general relativity explains that light bends in accordance with the curvature of space-time through which it travels and that that curvature is the direct consequence of gravity, or rather the matter generating that gravity. Indeed, so strong is this emphasis on geometric curvature that Einstein's work resulted in a complete redefinition of gravity, changing it from something that was considered to be a force in Newton's mind, to nothing more than a consequence of space-time's geometry bending.

With this revelation in mind, let us propose one further revelation. In fact let's be truly heretical and suggest that there might be no such thing as light! Or more exactly let's propose that our commonly accepted understandings of light are wrong. Rather than battling with convention and establishing a case as to why conventional thinking might be wrong, let us instead propose another model which will hopefully serve to reinterpret the things we already know about light and possibly some things we that don't.

There are some properties of light that we understand well. We know, for example, that it exhibits a duality and so can be legitimately thought of as both a particle and a wave depending upon how it is observed. We also know that light is made up of discrete packets of 'energy' known as photons. These are elementary particles, the quantum[1] of the electromagnetic field and the basic 'unit' of light and all other forms of electromagnetic radiation. Photons are also the force carrier for the electromagnetic force and like all elementary particles, photons are governed by quantum mechanics and hence exhibit wave-particle like behaviour. A single photon, for example, may be refracted by a lens or exhibit wave interference, but also acts as a particle giving a definite result when its location is measured.[66]

The contemporary idea of the photon was developed gradually by Albert Einstein to explain experimental observations that did not fit the classical wave model of light. Even so, initially Einstein's light quanta were nearly universally rejected by all physicists, including Max Planck and Niels Bohr. They only became universally accepted in 1919, with Robert Millikan's[2] detailed experiments on the photoelectric effect, and his measurement of an increase in wavelength of an X-ray or gamma ray photon, when it interacts with matter. Regardless, it was Einstein's influence in this area that helped kick-start the quantum revolution and theories it brought forth on how the universe

---

1   In physics, a quantum is an indivisible entity of a quantity that has the same units as the Planck constant and is related to both energy and momentum of elementary particles of matter (called fermions) and of photons and other bosons. The word comes from the Latin 'quantus', for 'how much.'

2   Robert Andrews Millikan was an American experimental physicist, and Nobel laureate in physics for his measurement of the charge on the electron and for his work on the photoelectric effect.

works at its most fundamental level. At first such theories concentrated on matter and how it might be composed at scales smaller than the nucleus of an atom. Soon it moved on to think in less restricted terms until eventually matter was replaced by information as the most fundamental building block. This leads to a computational view of the world that automatically subsumes all universal laws, including those centred on light. Hence, by implication, we must be able to explain light fundamentally in terms of information and computation. And that suggests that the partial-wave duality of light must have some computational basis, or at least a reasonable explanation in either informational or computational terms. So that's where we shall head next, to try and look for characteristics in the ideas conveyed thus far that might explain some of the properties of light. In short we shall seek to understand if light, or rather its outcome through observability's fundamental role in the way we understand the universe. We will try and reformulate light's behaviour as if it were a natural consequence of some deeper computational pattern, as if it were simply a computational pattern itself.

Quantum Field Theory and Uncertainty

In Chapter 8 the Minkowski configuration was introduced as a fundamental model for both information and computation, but there is one particular property of this configuration that has not yet been discussed.

The model is based on the idea of a field, which is familiar to us by way of magnetic fields with their influence spreading out through space from some source. Because modern field theory incorporates ideas from quantum physics it is now called quantum field theory. In particular, the specific piece of quantum physics that is now integrated into the theory of electromagnetic interaction is that of light, or more specifically any form of electromagnetic radiation, which comes in the form of quantised photons.

Quantum field theory provides a theoretical framework for constructing quantum mechanical models of arrangements classically described as fields or many-body systems. It is widely used in particle physics and condensed matter physics. In quantum field theory the forces between particles are mediated by other particles. So, for instance, the electromagnetic force between two electrons is caused by an exchange of photons. There is currently no complete quantum theory which includes gravity, however, but many of the proposed theories suggest the existence of a graviton particle which mediates it. These force-carrying particles are virtual particles and, by definition, cannot be detected while carrying the force, because such detection will imply that the force is not being carried. Quantum field theory also does not treat photons as discrete units, or like 'little billiard balls' if you will. Rather it thinks of them as field quanta, necessarily partitioned ripples in a field that 'look like' particles. This makes quantum field theory somewhat circular in that the classical conceptualisation of 'everything as particles and fields', resolves into 'everything as particles', which then resolves into 'everything as fields'. In the end, particles are regarded as excited states of a field, thus giving rise to the field quanta central to the theory. Follow this to its conclusion and it implies that point, or individual, instances of information and computation may similarly be considered as excited states in some broader field.

In the 1930s physicists developed the idea that electromagnetic interaction could be described in terms of the exchange of photons between charged particles. The first version of this model made predictions about the behaviour of charged particles which were close to the properties observed in the laboratory, but didn't quite match up to measurements of what was happening between charged particles. Nevertheless, a decade later these differences were resolved and the modern theory of quantum electrodynamics was formed by encompassing the strangest aspect of the quantum world, that of absolute uncertainty.

Quantum uncertainty is actually a very precise notion. It was first developed by Werner Heisenberg, a German physicist in the late 1920s and was first formulated in the familiar terms of particle position and momentum. In the everyday world we are used to the idea that we can, in theory, measure both the position and momentum of an object at the same time. Take, for example, an infamous billiard ball moving across a normal billiard table. In such a case it is relatively easy to measure its speed and precise direction of motion. Well understood laws of dynamics tell us exactly where the ball will be in a second's time, so long as we know exactly where it is now and how fast it is travelling. Heisenberg realised, however, that quantum components, such as electrons and photons, don't behave like that – something that is obvious with hindsight if particle wave duality is considered. Position is definitely a typical property, but waves do not have a precise position in space. If a quantum entity has, or behaves as if it has, aspects of both particle and wave in its composition, it is no surprise to find that it can never be located precisely at a point.[67] Heisenberg hence found that the amount of uncertainty in the position of a quantum entity is related to the amount of uncertainty in its motion in such a way that the more precisely the position is confined, the less certainty there is about its momentum and vice versa. The two uncertainties are linked mathematically by a now-famous equation known as Heisenberg's uncertainty relation. And the crucial thing to understand is that this uncertainty is not a result of the inaccuracy of experiment or human error. Rather it is it is intrinsic to the way the quantum world works. An electron literally does not have a precise position or a precise momentum. It is simply and normally trapped within an atom and it thus can be found within the 'proximity' of that atom, but its momentum is constantly changing as it 'moves' within that atomic 'space' as if partaking in a 'cloud'.

As peculiar as this is, it's not the end of the story. The same uncertainty carries over into other pairs of properties in the quantum world and one such pair is energy and time. Heisenberg's uncertainty relation combined with special relativity tells us that if we take a seemingly empty space and watch it for a certain time we cannot be sure how much energy it contains. It's not just personal either, as any given arbitrary observer cannot be sure. This is because when it comes down to position and momentum, the universe itself does not know. Over a long enough period of time we can be sure the space is empty. But the shorter the period of time involved, the less certain we can be about the amount of energy present. For a short enough period, energy can fill the volume, provided it disappears again within the time limit set by the uncertainty equation.[67]

This energy could be in the form of photons, which appear out of nothing at all and quickly disappear again. Or it might even be in the form of familiar particles like electrons, provided that they exist only for the tiniest amount of time allowed by the uncertainty principle. Such sort-lived phenomena are known as 'virtual' particles, and the entire process is called the 'fluctuation of the vacuum'. In this model, the void, or 'vacuum' is seen as seething with caldron of activity at the Planck scale. In particular, a charged particle, such as an electron, is embedded in a sea of virtual particles and photons, and even in their short lifetimes the particles interact with the electron. When quantum electrodynamics was adapted to take into account the presence of this morass of virtual particles, it gave predictions that precisely matched the properties of charged particles measured in experiments. In fact, the experiments and the model match to an accuracy of one part in ten billion. Furthermore, the only reason this accuracy is not even more precise is that experiments have not yet been devised that can measure at finer scales. This level of accuracy should not be underestimated, however, as it represents the most accurate agreement between theory and experimentation ever seen for any model tested on Earth thus far; even Newton's law of gravity has not been tested with such accuracy. By that yard stick, quantum electrodynamics is the most successful model the entire scientific world, and the agreement is only that good if the effects of quantum mechanics in creating this boiling vacuum of virtual particles are included. Indeed the whole model depends upon it.[67]

For us, the fluctuation of the vacuum is extremely important as it implies that there may indeed be no such thing as empty space. Through this fluctuation it is possible to see all of space as being occupied at the Planck scale and that, for any given point in space, its content can be seen as participating in reality simply by way of its relevance over any given period of time, so long as that period is greater than that also specified by Plank's equations. In fact, it is even possible to think of relevance as a sort of 'reality switch'. We currently believe that at the subatomic level, elementary particles come in only two types – those concerned with the composition, or the creation of matter, and those whose purpose is to mediate force as to influence that matter. But that does not mean to say that there are no other valid particle types, whether they be classified as mass-creating, force-carrying or whatever. It is perfectly legitimate to propose that other types might exist outside the currently accepted catalogue of subatomic particles. This leads to an extension of our relevance proposal, in that:

> Relevance = The capability to contribute towards matter or to mediate force of a specific type

Conjecture 31   Relevance and matter

Consequently a particle might legitimately exist, but we would have no way of detecting it if it could not be classified as being 'relevant' to our reality as we perceive it. It may well even be that there are many, many different types of the sub-atomic particles and that the characteristics needed to include such variants in quantum models are extremely subtle and, as yet, unknown. We know this to be partially true already, as virtual particles cannot be described in terms of real particles and, by definition, cannot be detected while carrying. Furthermore, by a similar inference we might consider the possibility of our universe having more than the four dimensions of space and time, and by doing so it indeed becomes plausible for types of subatomic particle to be oriented in such a way that they preserve perfect symmetry with respect to our familiar space-time dimensions and hence avoid detection by all means known to us at this present time. This does not, however, imply though that such particles could not be anchored at a point in whatever our n-dimensional universe ultimately is. Think of it this way. Image you have three good friends all of similar height, weight, build, hair colour and so on. Also imagine that all come from large families in which all members are of similar height, weight hair colour and so on. Now suppose that all three families decide to invite you to a picnic, but that you know that at least one of your friends is extremely busy that day and may not be able to attend. You decide to go along anyway and show up at the appropriate time and place. There you see a hub of activity, with all three families merrily enjoying themselves. Because of their physical similarities, most individuals seem familiar to you, but you know that you must specifically find your three friends. Still you find the task of recognising your friends almost impossible, firstly because they could be hidden behind other individuals in the crowd or secondly, and most importantly, because if any of your friends have their back to you they will be indistinguishable from those surrounding them. This literally makes it impossible to determine if all three friends are present or not unless they are all aligned to face in your direct line of sight. In simple terms, it is only when a person faces you that they are open to recognition in the circumstance we have just described. Or more precisely, it is their orientation in relation to you that breaks the surrounding symmetry and gives up their identity. Without such symmetry breaking it is impossible to say for certain where any of your friends might be. It's purely a matter of guess work.

Including the potential for 'hidden' elementary particle types therefore implies an expansion of the Standard Model of physics.[3] But this presents a problem as there are already a bewildering number of elementary particles in this model. String theory, however, addresses this by proposing that strings vibrate below the subatomic level that and each mode of vibration has a distinct resonance which corresponds to a particular elementary particle. Thus, if we could magnify a quantum particle we would see a tiny vibrating string or loop wiggling away below Planck length. And, given that there are an endless number of vibrations possible that implies an endless number of possible resonances and the possibility to legitimately extend the Standard Model.

---

3   Or more specifically the Standard Model of quantum mechanics.

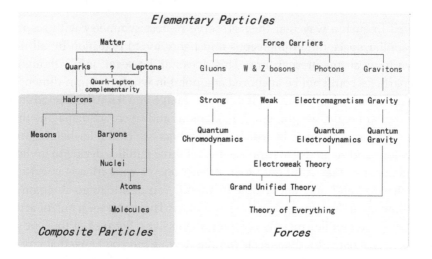

Figure 14.3   How the major particle types in the standard model of quantum mechanics fit together to create matter and carry force

The fantastic thing about string theory is that it not only explains the nature of quantum particles but it also explains space-time as well. Strings can be broken into smaller strings or combined to form larger strings. This complicated set of motions must obey self-consistent rules and results in the same relations described by relativity. Furthermore, for our purposes, another aspect of string theory that appeals is its aesthetic beauty. For string theory is a geometric theory, one that, like general relativity and the framework outlined in this book, describes entities and interactions through the use of geometry. And here's the thing: strings can be considered as vibrating entities in one dimension, but vibration is nothing more than spin with some of the dimensions thrown out. Furthermore strings are known to consist of nothing more than energy, so if data can be seen an energy equivalence, from a computational and informational perspective, strings are nothing more than data and their vibration are nothing more than the dimensionally deficient paths that such data traverses through whatever expanse exists below Planck length. In such ways the concept of string theory is consistent with the informational and computational framework set up in earlier chapters. Furthermore, this framework may well be more advanced than current ideas on string theory, for as it is subsumes logic it offers up a method for prescribing the entire list of valid string types.

String theory also, and almost too conveniently, solves a particular and disconcerting problem with the framework. Back in Chapter 8 we jumped from thinking about information and computation in terms of circular paths to paths based on spirals and cones. This provided a convenient vehicle to extend the framework out into additional dimensions and ultimately arrive at the idea of fields and Minkowski cones. Nevertheless the argument for moving from circular to spiral paths was rather rash in some respects. It is true that such a shift can be argued persuasively if computational efficiency is majored and closely compared with the energy efficiencies we might expect from circular and spiral trajectories in the real world. It is also true that computational efficiency is at the heart of the argument that ultimately toppled the Turing model of computation in favour of one based on quantum mechanics [68][6],[69] but even in the face of such arguments it's a close call as to whether spiral paths hold the edge over circular variants. String theory neatly gets around this problem, however, by proposing that strings can be either open or closed. A closed string is a string that has no end-points, and therefore is topologically equivalent to a circle. An open string, on the other hand, has two end-points and is topologically equivalent to a line interval. That line interval could also conceivably be part of a spiral in higher dimensions … .[62]

The oldest superstring theory containing open strings was type 'one' string theory. However, developments during the 1990s showed that the open strings should always be thought of as ending on a new type of objects called a D-brane. Since then the spectrum of possibilities for open strings has increased greatly.[62]

Strings can also possess an orientation, again in agreement with the ideas presented in earlier chapters. Such orientation can be thought of as an internal 'arrow' which distinguishes the string from one with the opposite orientation. By contrast, an unoriented string is one with no such arrow on it.

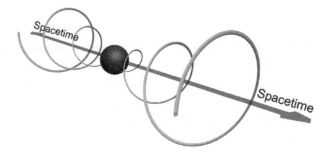

Figure 14.4   A spiralling (or open) informational or computational string with its space-time orientation shown. Note: The central dot indicates the point at which symmetry can break

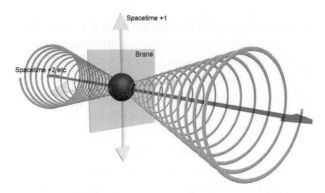

Figure 14.5   A spiralling (or open) informational or computational string with its space-time orientation shown as well as its connection to a brane

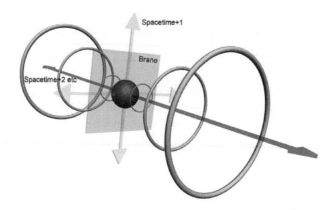

Figure 14.6   A circular (or closed) informational or computational string(s) with its space-time orientation shown as well as its connection to a brane

In theoretical physics, a membrane, brane, or p-brane is a spatially extended mathematical concept that appears in string theory and has a fixed number of dimensions. The variable p refers to the number of spatial dimensions of the brane. That is a 0-brane is a zero-dimensional point-like particle, a 1-brane is a string, a 2-brane is a 'membrane', and so on. Every p-brane sweeps out a $(p+1)$-dimensional world volume as it propagates through space-time.[70]

Originally string theory was a theory of 1-branes called strings, but this was later extended to also include higher dimensional objects. Besides the fundamental one dimensional string of string theory, the most important type of branes contained in string theory are D-branes. These are a class of extended objects upon which open strings can end under specific boundary conditions. The equations of motion of string theory consequently require that the end-points of an open string satisfy one of two types of boundary condition: The Neumann boundary condition, corresponding to free end-points moving through space-time at the speed of light, or the Dirichlet boundary condition, which 'pins' a strings end-point. Each coordinate of the string must satisfy one or the other of these conditions. So, if p spatial dimensions satisfy the Neumann boundary condition, then the string end-point is, by definition, confined to 'flap about' within a p-dimensional hyperplane[4] – much like a flag tied to a flagpole on a windy day. This hyperplane consequently provides one description of a Dp-brane. But it would be wrong to think of branes as being static or fixed objects. Just like the flagpole in our analogy, close up the pole might appear to be stationary, but it is actually moving in accordance with the Earth's daily rotation, its orbit around the sun, our solar system's movement in our galaxy and so on. It's all simply a matter of how and from where it is being observed. Furthermore the spectrum of open strings ending on a D-brane contains modes associated with its fluctuations, implying that D-branes are dynamical objects, and when a number of D-branes are nearly synchronized, the spectrum of strings stretching between them becomes very rich. Again this supports the potential for 'hidden' elementary particles to exist in accordance with the ideas presented earlier.

Framing the concept of branes in an informational or computational context it is possible to think of an informational field fixed on a plane – the brane – that anchors its mesh of data points in space-time for example. As such a brane provides the field's origin in reality as it were, or the point from which all relevance arises and all symmetries originally started to break. It is quite literally the field's birthplace. At the same time it is also possible to think of such a plane moving through higher space-time dimensions. In such a scenario it is easier just to think of all dimensions as being informational and consider the four dimensions or space-time simply as being orientations with relevance to reality as we experience it. This is a concept commonly referred to as Eigenspace with the branes and strings contained also being referred to as Eigenplanes and Eigenfunctions. Such spaces allow all space-time, and consequently all reality, to be considered as a purely informational concept, subject to computation only when the time dimension is included as part of an

---

4   A hyperplane is a concept in geometry. It is a generalization of the concept of a plane into a different number of dimensions.

observation within such spaces. This is a great leap as it seamlessly merges the real with the synthetic and makes everything, literally everything, a matter of information and how it is interpreted.

The concept of Eigenspaces will either be obvious or will twist your mind to the point of acute pain. Either way, and whatever your disposition, our universe's inclusion as part of much broader universe of informational possibilities is a truly profound possibility. It immediately opens up the potential for valid informational and computational permutations that, by definition, are completely unimaginable to us. But that does not mean to say that such unimaginability cannot 'exist' or be any less 'real' than the reality we commonly perceive. Furthermore Eigenspaces imply the possibility that there are inner workings of the universe that, again by definition, are completely out of our reach other than through purely theoretic means. For some this will be an emancipating thought as it opens up probable routes to justify all manner of unexplained phenomena. Nevertheless the trick to true enlightenment is to incrementally build on prior advances based on what has been proven before or has been justified from multiple independent standpoints. So it is always best to be cautious about beyond what is observably credible.

World Views, Informational Views and Meaning

If we continue the theme of informational or computational fields, or cones, meandering their way through some highly dimensional Eigenspace, and concentrate on only those fields of relevance to our four worldly dimensions, we can intuitively consider their resultant output, or state, as being some form of real world observable, via symmetry breaking. Such observables can hence be considered as events over time, if the cones involved are of a computational nature, and when several such events are linked together through some common trait, what results is often referred to as a world line. These represent unique paths through space-time as records of reality, and are also a kind of Eigenfunction. Thus in general practice, a world line is the sequential path of events, with time and place as the markers that point out the history of an activity or computation. For instance the log book of a ship can be seen as a world line of sorts as it contains a time tag attached to every port the ship has visited. This world line so allows a means to calculate the speed of the ship, given a measure of distance appropriate for the curved surface of the Earth.

In physics, the world line of an object is the sequence of space-time events corresponding to the history of that object and can be viewed as is a special type of curve in space-time. For example, the orbit of the Earth in space is approximately a circle, a three-dimensional closed curve in space. As a consequence the Earth returns every year to the same point in space. However, it arrives there at a different, later, time. As a result, the world line of the Earth is helical in space-time and does not return to the same point.

Space-time is awash with world lines as it is nothing more than as collection of points which we call events, together with a continuous and smooth coordinate system separating and identifying them. So, obviously, each event can be referenced by four numbers: a time coordinate and three spatial coordinates, which, in the lingo of mathematics, makes it a four-dimensional manifold. The concept may be applied to higher-dimensional spaces as well in that a world line can trace out the path of a single point in such spaces. A world sheet is an extension to the world line concept and is an analogous two-dimensional surface traced out by a one-dimensional line, like a string, travelling through space-time. The world sheet of an open string with loose ends is a strip; that of a closed string, or a loop, is a volume.

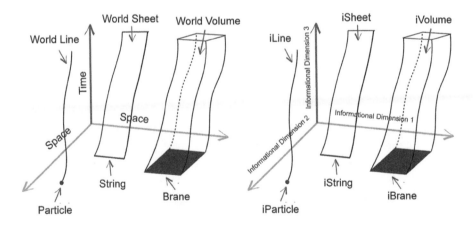

Figures 14.7(a) and 14.7(b)   World lines, sheets and volumes and their more generic informational counterparts

Obviously it is possible to extend the world geometry concept to take into account generic, highly dimensional Eigen spaces, and, in fact, this is that foundation behind Eigen-based mathematics. As such, Eigenspaces may or may not contain the dimensions need to construct a classical world-view, or Eigen graph, and can be arbitrary and open to classification using generic informational dimensions: all that matters if that one of the informational properties being represented changes with respect others present over the course of the graph. Thus we get a more generalised 'world-view' that can be wholly abstract in its composition and content, and with this comes a more generic interpretation of world lines, sheets and volumes, which, for the sake of clarity we shall refer to iLines, iSheets and iVolumes, as seen in Figure 14.7(b). This hence gives us an extremely expressive way to represent informational change.

15

Time to Reformulate with a Little Help from Information Retrieval Research

Physicists analyse systems. Web scientists, however, can create the systems.

Tim Berners-Lee

Up to this point there has been much discussion about information, computation and experimentation with various physical frameworks that might be used to formulate new interpretations of both. What's more, much of this discussion has been almost entirely theoretical and has typically only given credit to proven works coming out of the physical sciences communities. This wrongly implies that the use of 'classically physical' frameworks in the study of information and computation is a new thing. To believe that would be entirely wrong. A number of computing related disciplines have already found strong and practical synergies with some very well know physical frameworks, not least of which is the field of information retrieval which underwent a huge rise in prominence with the arrival of the World Wide Web and its overwhelming need to sift out specific details from the biggest corpus of synthetic information humankind has ever encountered.

Information retrieval, or IR as it is commonly abbreviated, is the science of searching for documents, for information within documents, and for metadata about documents, as well as that of searching relational databases and the World Wide Web. This imposes an overlap in the usage of the terms data retrieval, document retrieval, information retrieval and text retrieval, but each also has its own body of literature, theory, praxis and technologies. IR is hence interdisciplinary, being based on computer science, mathematics, library science, information science, information architecture, cognitive psychology, linguistics, statistics and physics.[74]

Surprisingly many of the geometric techniques applied in recent years to information technology, and especially information retrieval, are centuries old and have been deployed through contact with mechanics, electronics, acoustics, biology, relativity and, particularly, quantum mechanics.[73] This is not because of any driving ambition to incorporate new models into IR, and more generally computer science, but is because quantum mechanics comes 'pre-packed' with a number central concepts that are also core to information retrieval. Specifically quantum mechanics shares common ground with its interest in probability, logic and vector spaces. This in itself would provide compelling reason for information retrieval aficionados to sit up and take notice, but quantum mechanics adds one further killer advantage in that unlike traditional methods for information retrieval quantum mechanics can bring together probability, logic and vector spaces into a single unified framework. Make no mistake, for this is not just a clever trick, quantum mechanical approaches to information retrieval have demonstrated their worth many times over with many of the Web's successful search engines now using algorithms founded on quantum theory under the hood as one of their key differentiators. But before we can understand how IR interpretations of quantum mechanics can add value to our story, we must first explain a few of the fundamentals. Thankfully this will not take too long as much of the preparatory work has been already done.

Sets and Boolean Logic

First we must cover the concept of sets and how it is entwined with 'classical' variants of logic.

Sets are one of the most fundamental and flexible notions in all of modern mathematics, probably only being of lesser importance to the very concept of numbers themselves. Broadly speaking a set is any collection of distinct objects, be they real or imaginary. A collection of passengers on a train forms a set, the collection of trains in the world forms a set and the points on the earth's surface over which all these trains run forms a further set. Consequently we are all a member of a set which comprises all the humans alive on this planet at today, and if, for whatever reason, your name were ' N ', then mathematically it would be accurate to state that $N \in A$ – which translates from the mathematical gibberish into 'you (N) are a member of all living humans', so long as A represents the set of everyone alive at this moment. Obviously the ' $\in$ ' symbol acts to specify the act of inclusion in such a club, and by doing so it provides and entry point into a whole branch of formal mathematics known as set theory, which has its own vocabulary of terms and rules.

Exploring this branch starts to become interesting when multiple sets are allowed to interact. This not only provides a way of describing relationships between sets and the things they contain, but also provides several important ways of getting new sets from old.

Consider another example: let's suppose we have two sets, say M and F, representing perhaps all the men alive today and all the women alive today respectively. With these two sets it would be a relatively easy task to also list all the members found in A without having to itemise A separately. This is obviously because A is made up from the collection of all the members of M plus all the members of F. To put it another way, we would be guaranteed to pick the name of a living human if we selected any member from either set M or set F. This is because the unified whole formed by bringing M and F together is absolutely equivalent to A, give or take a few difficult arguments around gender with a specialised medical professional. Now, if we were to try and find the name of anyone deceased in either M, F or N, our labours would go unrewarded. This is because M, F and A are not concerned with those who have passed on. Likewise, try to pull out a desk, a koala or a pineapple from these sets and again we would be disappointed, as no set mentioned allows for such things to be a member of their gathering.

So where is all this leading? The answer lies not in the definition of any of the sets in our example, but rather in what happens when such sets are considered in a combinatorial way. This is because when sets are combined, the underlying dependencies come from a branch of mathematics, often considered separately, known as discrete or Boolean logic.[1] Thus terms like 'and', 'or' and 'not', in the above illustration, actually form strong and formal logic in a mathematical sense. To help understand this point, sets are often conceptualised using a form of representation known as a Venn diagram and the three examples below show just how the common Boolean operators of AND, OR and NOT can be seen as playing a part in set theory. To read these diagrams all you need to know is that the ellipses represent individual sets and the shaded areas show the various forms of logic connecting them.

---

1   Named after George Bool who was English mathematician and philosopher. As the inventor of Boolean logic, which is the basis of modern digital computer logic, Boole is regarded in hindsight as one of the founders of the field of computer science.

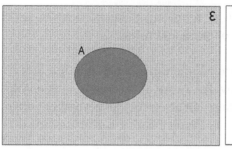 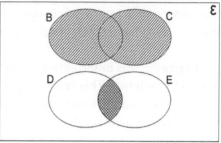

Mathematical Description	Logic Description	Plain English
ε : read as the *universal* set, or set of all relevant sets		Everything of interest to a given Venn diagram
A : read as set A	A	Everything in set A
A' : read as the compliment of set A	NOT A	Everything not in set A , but still of interest to the Venn diagram
$B \cup C$: read as the *union* of set B and set C	B OR C	All the contents of set B combined with those of set C
$B \cap C$: read as the *intersection* of set B and set C	B AND C	The contents shared by sets B and C . That's is those members found in both sets

Figures 15.1(a) and 15.1(b)   Two Venn diagram examples

Vectors and Vector Spaces

To consider vectors and vector spaces, let's do so through yet another example, and this time think of teddy bears. Say there was a sale at the local toy shop and it was close to Christmas. Suppose also that we have a number of friends who are just crazy about teddy bears and we decided to buy them all a bear as a present. When we purchase the bears we buy several of the same type at once so that our friends don't fight over whose bear is best, yet when we get home we each notice several subtle differences between them. For the sake of argument let's say that the fur of some bears is browner than others and that some bears are softer to the touch than others – both extremely important matters to bear connoisseurs. Now, to be specific, let's imagine we bought five bears and we were able to measure their respective brownness and softness accurately, both being given a score out of ten. If this were so then we would be able to plot a graph of brownness against softness for all bears, just like the one overleaf:

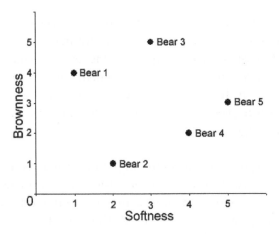

Figure 15.2   A point graph of teddy bear brownness against softness

In this graph the various points can be seen as showing the individual combinations of brownness and softness on a bear by bear basis. Even so, this is not the only way to represent such a relationship on a diagram of this type. Rather than using points as the comparison method, lines can be used in their place, so long as one end of each line is tied to a fixed point within the graph. This point is commonly known as the graph's 'origin' and is usually located at the point where any axis involved in the graph meet with the least value point – $(0,0)$, in our Cartesian bear graph example. In such a way Figure 15.2 can be redrawn as:

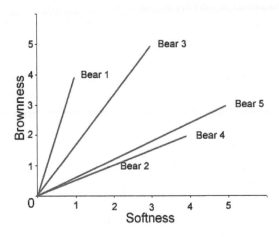

Figure 15.3   A line graph, or vector model, of teddy bear brownness against softness

In this form, the lines used to represent the respective combinations of brownness and softness can be mathematically named as vectors and the overall range of possible values covered by the graph becomes known as the vector space in which these vectors are contained. This is a valuable transition, as unlike points, which can only convey the magnitude of any particular property against examples of that property, vectors can be seen as also depicting direction of that property.

What's really special about comparing things using geometric techniques such as point, and especially vector, analysis is that we need not limit the number of properties being compared. In the case of our teddy bear example for instance, only two properties are involved. This leads to a graph being drawn in two dimensions – these obviously corresponding to brownness and softness. This therefore translates into the vector space needed for such a representation also being two dimensional. But we could further add the weight of the bears if we so desired, which would mean pushing the graph out into a three dimensional vector space. Add height, and the number of dimensions goes up to four and so on. In fact we could go on adding dimensions forever if we so wished, which opens the way to an extremely powerful and expressive means of comparing properties.

Given that vectors are nothing more than straight lines stretching out over some space supported by a collection of dimensions, this implies that such lines have length and thus some form of measurable magnitude or metric. Not surprisingly, since we are dealing with straight lines, the mathematics used to manipulate and constrain such lines, and any associated metric, is provided from Euclidean geometry. This contains three rules explicitly aimed at measuring straight lines, and these state:

- The distance between any two points or places within any given space can only be considered as a positive number – that is to say, that magnitude of any line is independent from the direction in which it is measured.

- It will always be possible to measure a line along its length in either direction.

- If we have two lines spanning out from any common point (a), the distance between their end points (b and c) can't be made any less by taking a shortcut through either b or c. This is sometimes known as the *triangle inequality* – for every triangle with points a, b and c, the length of the longest side is never greater than the sum of the length of the two shorter sides.[73]

By applying these three rules while, at the same time, deliberately applying some form of gauge or measurement system over a vector, space changes that space into what is known as a 'metric space' – a term introduced by Felix Hausdorff[2] in 1914. Such metric spaces require common measurement practices, or functions, to be applied to any vectors they contain and the single most widely used metric function remains the Euclidean distance function derived from Pythagoras' theorem. This states that, in the case of right angle triangles, the square on the side opposite the right angle equals the sum of the squares on the sides containing the right angle.

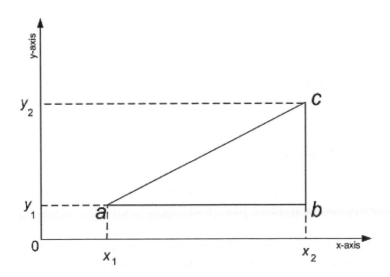

Figure 15.4   Pythagoras' theorem

Thus it is possible to calculate the length of the diagonal edge, or hypotenuse, of the triangle in Figure 15.4 as follows:

2   Felix Hausdorff was a German mathematician who is considered to be one of the founders of modern topology and who contributed significantly to set theory, descriptive set theory, measure theory, function theory, and functional analysis.

Suppose $d(a,b)$ represented the distance between points a and b, and $d(b,c)$ the distance between points b and c, then Pythagoras' theorem gives us the distance $d(a,c)$ as $(d(a,b))^2 + (d(b,c))^2 = (d(a,c))^2$. Furthermore, suppose we know the x and y coordinates of the points $a = (x_1, y_1)$, $b = (x_2, y_1)$ and $c = (x_2, y_2)$. Then a and b only differ in their x coordinates, so we can easily measure $d(a,b)$ as $x_2 - x_1$, and similarly $d(b,c)$ is easily measured as $y_2 - y_1$. From this, Pythagoras' theorem can be used to deduce that:

$$(d(a,b))^2 + (d(b,c))^2 = (d(a,c))^2 = (x_2 - x_1)^2 + (y_2 - y_1)^2$$

or just

$$d(a,c) = \sqrt{(x_2 - x_1)^2 + (y_2 - y_1)^2}$$

Given that all but those vectors which are perfectly perpendicular to the axes[3] of any vector space can be viewed as the hypotenuse of some form of right angle triangle, Pythagoras' theorem consequently provides a convenient method of calculating the scale, of such vectors. This provides a very convenient tool indeed, as will be demonstrated very shortly.

Vectors and Relevance

A relevance or similarity measure, as it is often referred to in IR, can be thought of as the opposite of distance when thinking of information and computation in geometric terms. Accordingly the generally accepted convention specifies that for any given set A, its similarity function may be denoted by ' $sim()$", a function which needs two parameters as input to work, and which produces a positive measure of similarity as its output. In such a way the similarity measure for any two members of A can be written as $sim(a,b)$ so long as a and b do indeed belong to set A. Furthermore convention prescribes that the more similar a is to b, the greater the value returned by $sim(a,b)$. Likewise the more different a is to b, the smaller the value returned by $sim(a,b)$.

In the parlance of geometry, similarity obviously corresponds to proximity and dissimilarity corresponds to distance. So, if two points are somewhat distant from one another they will be regarded as dissimilar, and if they are close together, they will be considered as being similar. For this reason a

---

3   Such axes are normally referred to as 'base' vectors in vector theory.

similarity measure is, in a very clear sense, the opposite of a distance measure such as that calculated by Pythagoras' theorem above.

In its most basic form similarity can mathematically be seen as the inverse of distance, as in:

$$sim(a,b) = \frac{1}{d(a,b)}$$

This type of inversion is used, for instance, to transform a resistance into a conductance in physics. But such a simplistic formulation can cause problems in special cases. For example it is perfectly plausible to think of the distance $d(a,a)$, which reads as the distance between point a and itself. Given that both the points in this calculation are identical, this inadvertently leads to there being no distance between them. Feed such a distance into the similarity function listed above and conventional mathematics fails. This is because the value produced would be infinitely large and our current understandings of infinity simply cause mathematics to explode. So, to get around this problem, we can reformulate our equation as:

$$sim(a,b) = \frac{1}{1 + d(a,b)}$$

This version of the equation thereby limits the maximum value of $sim(a,b)$ to be one and ensures that it can never fall below zero.

Bringing Probability, Vectors and Sets Together

Recall that at the start of this chapter there was a great deal of fuss over the idea of applying a quantum mechanical framework to information retrieval. This was because such a framework could provide a unified approach to bring together sets, vectors and probability, yet up to this point it has not been clearly explained how this might be so. Now we can start to offer an explanation.

Looking back at the previous explanation of similarity, it is possible to see that for it to work any two things being compared must come from the same set. This is identical to saying that any two points being considered must be present in the same metric space. This thereby unifies sets and vectors in one easy step. Furthermore you will remember that in the last equation for similarity above, the range of values allowed was deliberately restricted to fall between zero and one. This is of particular interest to the field of probability as that field also limits itself to only producing outputs in the range of zero to one. That is why, for example, if it is absolutely impossible for something to happen, mathematically we say that it has a probability of zero. Equally, if it is an absolute certainty that something will happen, it is said to have a probability of one. This hence allows us to interpret $sim(a,b)$ as being the exact same thing as the probability of a and b being entirely interchangeable.[73] In this way, vectors and probability are brought together seamlessly and thereby complete the hat-trick required to become analogous with a quantum mechanical framework. Through such mathematical alliance, and although we may not be dealing with the bits and pieces that make up the innards of atoms, the various tools of quantum mechanics also conveniently become a framework of choice for IR.

Back to Vectors and Similarity with a Sprinkling of Trigonometry

The fact that such an abstract concept as similarity can be calculated accurately using simple mathematics is indeed miraculous, but with a little more assistance the results are truly amazing. At the moment our function for calculating similarity only works when two dimensions are under consideration. This is essentially the same as saying that the function will only work with triangles drawn on a flat sheet of paper. All the same we will need more than two dimensions if we are ultimately to push our way into an arena where such a method can be seen as compatible with the equations of relativity or string theory. Hence we need an enhanced formula for similarity that generalises easily across any number of dimensions. This will enable us to calculate similarities between points comprising any number of dimensions, so long as sufficient dimensions are available within the metric space in which they exist. That's a big ask, as we are fundamentally trying to find a simple solution to potentially complex problems, which themselves could be contained in what might potentially be infinitely dimensional problem spaces. For such reasons it is best to first caveat the broad brush approach that will follow by stating that if something is complex, then by definition it is complex and any attempt to simplify it must, at the very least, throw away some of the essence of that complexity. In other words, it is not possible to simplify something that is complex without changing the original understanding of that thing. That then applies here in that no simple means for measuring similarity can be expected to perform well in all situations.[73] Unfortunately, however, information and, by implication, information retrieval are complex areas that carry many special cases. For such reason there will always be circumstances where a specialised similarity method will outperform a more generalised approach. Even so this should not stop us from generalising for illustrative purposes, as one such method for assessing similarity across multiple dimensions is well tried and tested. This is cosine similarity and it has proved a remarkably versatile and popular measure in many situations.[73]

Cosine Similarity

For now we will only consider points on a unit circle. That is to say a circle whose edge's distance is one unit from the origin $(0,0)$.

Dealing only with points on a unit circle provides a way of concentrating on the directions of any two vectors, a and b, rather than on their respective magnitudes as well – the direct distances of their end points from the origin $(0,0)$. So, let $a = (x_1, y_1)$ and $b = (x_2, y_2)$ be points on a unit circle, as shown in Figure 15.5. In such circumstances the angle θ between the lines joining both points and the origin provides a good measure of the distance between them and inverting this measure hence provides the generic measure of similarity we are after.[73] Thus if the two points lie close together, the angle between them will be small, and we might say that they are fairly similar to one another: if they are exactly the same point, then the cosine sought would equal 1 and this is seen as the convention for cosine point equivalence. Similarly, suppose the points a and b are at right angles, or $90°$, to one and other, then we might be tempted to say that they have nothing in common at all. In this case their similarity, in accordance with the cosine of their angle, would be equal to 0. If

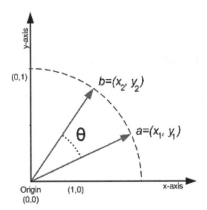

Figure 15.5   If two points are in similar parts of a circle, the angle between them will be small[73]

a and *b* were completely opposite, at $180°$ to each other, then we might reason their similarity to be –1, and if we go any further around the circle than $180°$ we start going back to our initial point.

Two pieces of good fortune enter at this point. Firstly, the cosine function, from the field of mathematics knows as trigonometry,[4] provides an ideal transformation from any angle θ to a similarity measure. Secondly we don't even have to work out the angle itself to calculate its cosine. For two points *a* and *b* on a unit circle, all we have to do is multiply each of the coordinates of point *a* with the corresponding coordinate of point *b*, add the results together and we get the same answer.[73] This leads to the following definition for cosine similarity based on a unit circle model: if two points $a = (x_1, y_1)$ and $b = (x_2, y_2)$ lie on the perimeter of a unit circle, their cosine similarity will be written as $\cos(a, b)$ and is given by the formula :[73]

$$\cos(a, b) = x_1 x_2 + y_1 y_2$$

So cosine similarity gives a very efficient, convenient and general purpose method for taking the coordinates of two points on a circle, multiplying them, and adding the answers together to give a single number between one and minus one, which tells us whether these points are similar, opposite or perpendicular.[73] This follows through into general informational terms by providing a means by which the similarity of concepts can be rigorously compared and measured so long as their characteristics can be mapped within some metric space. It gives a numeric range whose values swing from absolute concordance through complete disagreement and on to total opposition.

Pushing Out into Multiple Dimensions

We have already seen how Pythagoras' theorem can be used to calculate the size of any vector in a two-dimensional, or Cartesian-like, metric space and this technique corresponds exactly to the well-known practice taught in elementary geometry classes. It is less well known, however, that the same theorem can be used in three dimensions to calculate the length of the diagonal through a solid

---

4   Trigonometry is a branch of mathematics that studies triangles, particularly right triangles. Trigonometry deals with relationships between the sides and the angles of triangles and with the trigonometric functions, which describe those relationships.

cuboid.[5] For instance, if the three perpendicular sides of a box have lengths p, q and r, then the diagonal of the box will have the length $\sqrt{p^2 + q^2 + r^2}$.

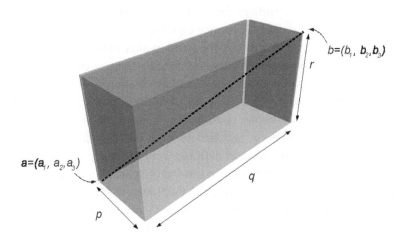

Figure 15.6   Measuring the diagonal from a to b in a cuboid

If any two opposite corners of the cuboid are the points a and b, with coordinates (a_1, a_2, a_3) and (b_1, b_2, b_3) respectively, then the lengths of the sides needed for calculating the diagonal directly between them are $p = b_1 - a_1$, $q = b_2 - a_2$ and $r = b_3 - a_3$. Thus the length of the diagonal, which is the distance $d(a, b)$ between a and b, is given by the formula:[73]

$$d(a,b) = \sqrt{(b_1 - a_1)^2 + (b_2 - a_2)^2 (b_3 - a_3)^2}$$

This is fundamentally the same as the two-dimensional distance formula given earlier, with a slight twist to the notation. Furthermore it can be condensed using still further different notation, as follows:

$$d(a,b) = \sqrt{\sum_{i=1}^{3} (b_i - a_i)^2}$$

In this form, the subscript, i, stands for each of the indices in turn, ranging from 1 up to 3 in this case, but it is possible to use any range or indices, thereby generalising the equation to:

5   The three-dimensional version of a rectangle.

$$d(a,b) = \sqrt{\sum (b_i - a_i)^2}$$

The capability to use indices for coordinates and summation in this way leads to being able to define a distance equation for a vector space with any number of dimensions and without any need to alter the equation in any way. So far we have only considered vectors needing up to three dimensions in their surrounding metric space – often referred to as $\mathbb{R}^3$ spaces – where each vector has three coordinates of the type (a_1, a_2, a_3), but the above equation works just as well for longer sets of vector coordinates of the form $(a_1, a_2, ..., a_n)$, where the number of coordinates, n, needed to map out any singular point in a vector space can be as big as we like. In this way Pythagoras' theorem can be adapted to give a distance measure on the vector space $\mathbb{R}^n$, for any number of dimensions n. This measure is called the Euclidean Distance measure on $\mathbb{R}^n$, as it obeys the three basic rules for measuring a straight line. Because of this it is sometimes referred to as the Euclidean Metric.[73]

Normalisation and Unit Vectors

Now that we have worked out how to calculate the size of any given vector without needing to worry about the number of dimensions across which it holds relevance, we need to take what at first might seem a backward step. The ability of vectors to possess varying scale can actually be counterproductive in a number of circumstances – for example in cases were only the directions of a given collection of vectors needs to be considered. To get around this problem a technique similar to the percentage scheme commonly used in arithmetic is applied. This provides a way of comparing any two or more vectors by precisely the same metric, or measurement scheme, regardless of their respective sizes or individual scalar measurement systems. So, whereas, say, the comparisons '5 is to 20' and '3 is to 12' can be seen as equivalent by stating that both 5 and 3 represent exactly 25 per cent of the other figure in both cases, so a similar scheme can be applied to vector magnitudes. This is done by measuring the length of any given vector from a pre-specified origin – usually $(0,0,...,0)$ then finding the square root of the sum of the squares for each component making up a vector. This can be formulated as:

$$d(0,a) = \sqrt{\sum (a_i)^2} = \|a\|$$

Such a distance is referred to as a vector's 'norm' and is often written as $\|a\|$, for a given vector a.

The norm is exactly the amount we need to divide by to provide the unit vector needed when comparing vectors for the purpose of similarity measurement, and convention dictates that the length of this vector must always be equal to 1. Thus the unit vector, traditionally denoted by $\hat{a}$ for any vector can be derived from:

$$\hat{a} = \frac{a}{\|a\|}$$

As an example we can take vector $v = (2,4,0)$ and note that $\|v\|$ is the same as $\sqrt{2^2 + 4^2 + 0^2}$ or $\sqrt{20}$. This gives $\hat{v} = (\frac{2}{\sqrt{20}}, \frac{4}{\sqrt{20}}, \frac{0}{\sqrt{20}})$ or $\hat{v} = (0.447, 0.894, 0)$, to three decimal places for each dimensional element.

Latent Analysis

We now need to move on to consider the problems of informational or computational spaces with many, many dimensions. In such spaces each dimension will be associated with a particular characteristic of that space; say, height, breadth and depth of material objects in the real word for instance. Now, again for the sake of argument, let's suppose we have a collection of relevant vectors, say v_1 ... v_n, contained within some information space of interest and perhaps they relate to the size of the different wooden building blocks in a child's play set. With that in mind some will have more width than depth, or perhaps more height than width, and so on. Let's further suppose that each individual vector not only holds the physical size of a particular block, but lots of other information too, like its weight, colour, density, opacity, luminosity, age, country of manufacture and so on. Now ask yourself what if we are only interested in the singular idea of physical size and not the specifics any of the other details contained in the overall metric space specified?

To do this we essentially have to 'squash' the dimensional components together by drawing some form of straight-edged best fit 'surface' between the vector components of interest. This is a process commonly known as latent (semantic)[6] analysis and, as can be seen in the sample illustrations in Figure 15.7. It effectively crushes several measurement dimensions into a lower

---

6   The term 'semantic' is included here as the concept was first used in the fields of natural language processing and information retrieval by Scott Deerwester in 1990.

order dimensional entity[7] known as a latent axis, plane or object. Hence three dimensions can be combined into a single vector, as in Figure 15.7(a) or a two-dimensional plane, as in Figure 15.7(b) and by using such latent objects, the relevant properties of individual vectors within a space can be replaced by a smaller subset by dropping a perpendicular from their original end-point[8] onto a new compressed latent object. This is sometimes referred to as *projecting* the original vector instance onto the latent object.

Interestingly it has been shown that, in certain circumstances, latent semantic analysis can help search engines trawl vastly complex information spaces like the Web with surprising effectiveness. This is because it can match queries with documents[9] which share underlying themes even if they don't contain exactly the same keywords. Thus we might, for instance, enter the terms 'car', 'destination', 'steering wheel' and 'speed' into a search engine and get out information relating to driving, even if the term 'driving' does not directly appear in the content of any of the returned Web pages – it is

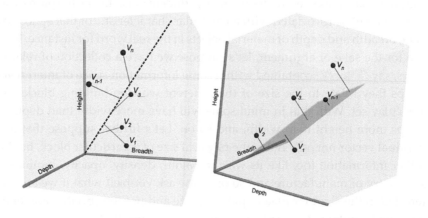

Figures 15.7(a) and 15.7(b)   An example of 'squashing' information space dimensions using latent semantic analysis. Figure 15.7(a) shows the space's three base vectors (axes) collapsed into a single-base vector. Figure 15.7(b) shows the space's three base vectors (axes) collapsed into a two-dimensional vector plane

---

7   So long as the number of dimensions is greater than 0. Note also that a surface can be considered as an object in this context.
8   Shown as points in the above diagrams.
9   Web resources like web pages and XML files.

simply implied. By association, the idea that we might combine information from different sources and contexts by recognising underlying dependencies between superficially different variables has been suggested as an answer to the psychological question 'how do humans manage to learn so much about language and the world in such a short lifetime?'.[73]

The Quantum Twist on Information Retrieval

As stated already, quantum mechanical frameworks are popular in information retrieval circles because they provide a method for bringing together particularly important mathematical tools. This is extremely advantageous, but it is not the only benefit involved, as they can also help with a common frustration in 'classical' approaches to information and computation; that of discreet logic.

When George Boole unleashed his thoughts on logic to the world in 1854 he changed the course of science and, more importantly, technology forever. Boolean algebra, for instance, is used in every computer, digital watch and microchip found today. But rather than being technology-centric, Boole was actually a passionate mathematician and his – most famous – work was centred on algebra. So he showed how to replace concepts and ideas with symbols and then manipulate them as if they were numbers caught up in equations.[73] By way of an illustration, if the symbol t represents the collection of all the towns in the world and the symbol u represents the collection of all towns residing in the United Kingdom, the mnemonic tu can be used to signify the collection of all towns located in the United Kingdom. Writing this the other way around as ut, or United Kingdom towns, gives the same collection, so logically $tu = ut$.

Equations with these symbols can hence be understood as propositions, so:

$t = 0$ means that, in the case of our example, there are no towns in the world. An unlikely prospect in the real world, but, nevertheless, a proposition we can easily play with algebraically.

Given that if we multiply zero by anything, the answer is still zero, multiplying both sides of this equation by the symbol u gives the result:

$tu = 0$ means that, in the case of our example, there are no towns in the United Kingdom.

In this way Boole's binary algebra of collections, or sets, can be used to draw conclusions about a problem or information space. Consequently, in our example, we can conclude that there are no UK towns based on the premise that there are no towns in the world.

Boolean-based arithmetic lies at the heart of modern digital computing, but it has its limitations. By restricting the potential outputs of any Boolean reasoning activity to zero or one – or $TRUE$ or $FALSE$, depending on how we might wish to interpret the logic – we close off all routes to measuring relevance on a sliding scale. So any question asked either proves to be entirely relevant – completely $TRUE$ - or wholly irrelevant – completely $FALSE$. No uncertainty, no ambiguity or any vagueness of truth is allowed; it's all very black and white. However, as well we know from common experience, sometimes the world is not clear cut and black and white simply will not do. What we really need is the ability to describe things with continuous and infinite precision without having to sacrifice any degree of accuracy in the description process. Such measurement problems have troubled science for millennia, but it was not until the early part of the last century that this particular conundrum almost stopped the scientific community in its tracks.

Until all but relatively recently up to that time physical science had come on in leaps and bounds, having successfully formulated many new theories to describe physical phenomena both at grand and minute scales. Most notably, at the bottom end, the idea of the atom as the most basic unit of matter had become the de facto standard.[10] At the same time Einstein had started to flex his muscles and special and general relativity were both experiencing their first flushes of success. Yet still there was an inescapable problem. All the theories offered at that time relied upon the universe being made up of discrete parts at all scales. That caused a problem as it did not tie up with the evidence being generated from most of the experiments of the time, all aimed at probing the universe at scales smaller than the size of a single atom. At such subatomic scale all the known laws of physics apparently broke down and the world could not be measured with certainty. This was the fuzzy problematic nature

---

10 The term 'element' was defined by the French nobleman and scientific researcher Antoine Lavoisier to mean basic substances that could not be further broken down by the methods of chemistry.

 In 1803, English instructor and natural philosopher John Dalton used the concept of atoms to explain why elements always react in a ratio of small whole numbers—the law of multiple proportions—and why certain gases dissolve better in water than others. He proposed that each element consists of atoms of a single, unique type, and that these atoms can join together to form chemical compounds [75]

of science at that precise moment in time and it needed a radical change in thinking to let science carry on its way. In truth the resulting change was more a revolution than an adjustment, more a realisation that science needed a completely different perspective. And the name of that new perspective was quantum mechanics.

Quantum mechanics sidesteps the problem of discreteness by considering fundamental particles as being composed from different states of pure energy, which can be superimposed on one another to make combined states. In fact the 'quantum' in quantum mechanics can literally be interpreted to mean the ability by which something is divisible into two or more constituent parts, each of which, by its own nature, is 'one' and is 'this'. In this view of the world, elementary particles are represented by basic continuous wave patterns and because these basic building blocks are waves they are, by definition, perfectly continuous and lead to the representation of a particle being spread out 'evenly' over a whole region of space. This also leads to the conclusion that quantum particles can interact over vast distances. By contrast, interactions in classical physics are limited to a local area which is firmly fixed by the distance a light beam can travel in a given time.

In actuality there are a number of strong similarities between the description of elementary physical particles as composite wave functions and the concept of using a metric (vector) space as a framework for modelling information and computation. For instance, the space in which a quantum wave function resides can be seen as being closely if not completely analogous to a purely mathematical metric space. Furthermore the blurring of pure waves as they combine to form elementary partials can be seen as analogous to the notion of ambiguity when thinking purely in informational terms. Furthermore, as well as being appealing on a general intuitive level, the exact same operations in vector spaces can be used to model both processes.[11][73]

Young's Twin-Slit Experiment

In the simplest of terms, quantum mechanics is literally built on the concept of vagueness and many well tried experiments provide testament to this fact. Take, for example, the famous double-split experiment – often referred to as

---

11 Although due to some remarkable matrix symmetries, we have reason to expect these operations to be more accurate models in physics than they are in linguistics.[73]

Young's[12] experiment – which demonstrates the inseparability of the wave and particle natures of light and other quantum particles. In such an experiment a coherent light source is used to illuminate a thin plate containing two parallel slits (*A* and *B*), and the light passing through them is then observed as it strikes a screen behind.

When this experiment is undertaken it soon becomes apparent that it is impossible to foresee with certainty whether a particle will pass through the slit *A* or the slit *B*. What's more, it is impossible to account for a particle's behaviour without assuming that it can travel through both slits at precisely the same time. More exactly a particle is represented by the sum of different waves, some of which can be seen as going through slit *A* and some through *B*. This leads to naturally thinking of light as a wave form, as waves can quite naturally travel through two or more points in space at the same time. Strangely enough though, if we place a detector across each of the slits and use it to watch which path a particle takes, then the complete particle will be observed as if it where whole once more and has passed through one or other of the two slits, not both as if were a wave. In such circumstances the wave-like behaviours of light are not evident.[73]

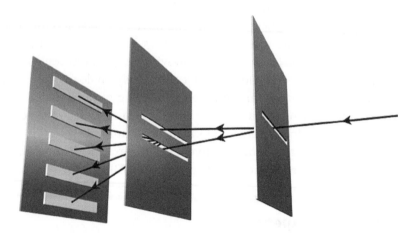

Figure 15.8   Young's twin-split experiment

---

12 Thomas Young was an English genius and polymath. He made notable scientific contributions to the fields of vision, light, solid mechanics, energy, physiology, language, musical harmony and Egyptology.

Dirac Notation

To model the strange state of affairs in Young's experiment a mathematical model was developed by Paul Dirac[13] in 1939.[14] In this Dirac presented a formal axiomatic approach to quantum mechanics in which the state of any system can be represented by a state vector. For instance, if a particle in a double-split experiment is know to have passed through slit A, this would be represented by the using the monoculture $|A\rangle$, and if it passed through slit B, that would be written as $|B\rangle$. Each of these possibilities is known as a pure state. But these are not the only possibilities as there are also a number of hybrid possibilities where part of a particle (or wave) goes through A and part goes through B, and these two parts then interfere with each other. The state of such a hybrid particle can hence be written as:[73]

$$\alpha_1|A\rangle + \alpha_2|B\rangle$$

where α_1 and α_2 are numbers.[15] Consequently, if we think of the pure states $|A\rangle$ and $|B\rangle$ as vectors and the numbers α_1 and α_2 as coordinates, then the combined state represented in the equation above is also a vector. We assume that $|A\rangle$ and $|B\rangle$ each have unit length, by default, and that $|A\rangle$ and $|B\rangle$ are orthogonal to each other,[16] which in Dirac notation is written as:

$$\langle A|A\rangle = \langle B|B\rangle = 1, \langle A|B\rangle = 0$$

This vector approach allows multiples of the wave function for the states $|A\rangle$ and $|B\rangle$ to be superimposed on one and another to yield another new wave. In this way, the vector approach enables us to model interference patterns like those seen in Young's double-split experiment.

---

13 Paul Dirac, OM, FRS was a British theoretical physicist. Dirac made fundamental contributions to the early development of both quantum mechanics and quantum electrodynamics.

14 In the 6th edition of his book *Principles of Quantum Mechanics*, originally published in 1930.

15 In quantum mechanics the coordinates α_1 and α_2 are complex numbers, though the most significant property of these coordinated is their magnitude, or length, which is a real number. The adaptation of vector spaces to use complex numbers as coordinates is standard and complex numbers make matters easier, given that they enable more equations to be uniquely solved.

16 That is to say, vectors that are perpendicular to each other.

Young's Experiment and the 'X'-Shaped Pattern

As just mentioned, if the state of a particle is observed by placing detectors over slits A and B, only the pure states $|A\rangle$ and $|B\rangle$ will be encountered. Somehow, the combined hybrid state $\alpha_1|A\rangle + \alpha_2|B\rangle$ becomes 'quantized' into one of the pure states $|A\rangle$ or $|B\rangle$ and this interestingly fits with the idea of the ' X '-shaped pattern introduced in Chapter 5. To see this, first realise that Young's experiment requires two slits to work; no more, no less. Next realise that the detector in question must be positioned so as to simultaneously monitor both slits. Now consider the following version of the ' X '-shaped pattern:

Think about the input to this this pattern – $\alpha_1|A\rangle + \alpha_2|B\rangle$ in this case – and its potential to yield a collection of outputs once it has undergone the transformation imposed by the pattern. At first inspection it might appear that there are only two possible output combinations, namely $|A\rangle$ and $|B\rangle$. That is to say either of $|A\rangle$ or $|B\rangle$, but not both at the same time. This corresponds to what is known in Boolean logic as in an XOR operation.[17] Nevertheless there is no rule to stop both $|A\rangle$ and $|B\rangle$ being output at the same time – which corresponds to the Boolean AND operation, or neither for that matter – which essentially corresponds to the same thing with a twist, producing a halting operation. This is also essentially the same as both $|A\rangle$ and $|B\rangle$ being completely symmetrical and hence being totally unobservable to a detector.

In fact the XOR operation is just a logical OR operation in disguise. This is because the pattern does not restrict the use of the coordinate parameter, α, on

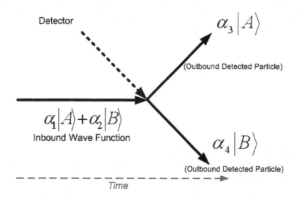

Figure 15.9   The ' X '–shaped in relation to Young's twin-split experiment

---

17   Also known as an exclusive disjunction. Also called exclusive or (XOR).

either side of the ' X '. So although $|A\rangle$ may well be scaled by a non-zero factor of α_1 on the left hand side of the X , it could well be scaled by a factor of zero on the right-hand side. This essentially provides one of a number of possible cases which nullify $|A\rangle$'s presence in the pattern's output, hence making it invisible to any observer. $|A\rangle$ is still present, it is just that it has been scaled (or looped) back to the point where it has no apparent relevance to the outside world, and this is exactly the same as saying that $|A\rangle$ is symmetrical to any given observer's point of view. In a similar way $|B\rangle$ can be nullified simply by setting its scaling parameter to zero. This obviously means that the ' X '-shaped pattern is not dependent on input scaling factors being the same as those affecting output legs, and for this reason four different α_1 values are included in the diagram above.

Interestingly, the freedom given by allowing scaling values to flex on both sides of the pattern leads to some interesting consequences. For instance, the pattern can effectively act as:

- **A switch**: by only allowing $\alpha_1|A\rangle + \alpha_2|B\rangle$ through or nothing through, without the use of the detector to actuate the switch.[18]

- **An actuator**: by only allowing $\alpha_1|A\rangle + \alpha_2|B\rangle$ through or nothing through, using of the detector to actuate the switch.

- **An unassisted amplifier or limiter**: by allowing $\alpha_3|A\rangle + \alpha_4|B\rangle$ through, where $\alpha_1 \neq \alpha_3$ and $\alpha_2 \neq \alpha_4$, without being triggered by the detector's presence.

- **A switched amplifier or limiter**: by allowing $\alpha_3|A\rangle + \alpha_4|B\rangle$ through, where $\alpha_1 \neq \alpha_3$ and $\alpha_2 \neq \alpha_4$, depending upon being triggered by the detector's presence.

- **A terminator**: A switch or actuator that has no, null or entirely symmetrical outputs.

There is an important point to note here in that the detector in Young's experiment plays a critical role, acting as the triggering signal for decoherence[19]

---

18 The equivalent of setting $\alpha = 0$ for the detector leg.
19 In quantum mechanics, quantum decoherence is the mechanism by which quantum systems interact with their environments to exhibit probabilistically additive behavior. Quantum decoherence gives the appearance of wave function collapse and justifies the framework and

to take place. What is also interesting is that unlike Young's experiment the pattern does allow $\langle A|B \rangle$ as a possible outcome. This is because, unlike the standard convention for Young's experiment, the ' X '-shaped pattern does not assume $|A\rangle$ and $|B\rangle$ to be orthogonal to each other. In geometric terms this means that the twin slit experiment predicates the related mathematics by stating:

$$a \cdot b = |a||b|\cos\phi = 0$$

where $|a| = \sqrt{a \cdot a}$

whereas the pattern does not impose this restriction. By not insisting on this constraint the pattern not only allows wave inputs to be transformed into discrete 'pure' outputs, but it also allows composite wave forms to be transformed into differently composed wave forms. This provides a range of possible outputs open to the pattern, often referred to as a quantum disjunctions of the states $|A\rangle$ or $|B\rangle$. Such a disjunction is more general than the Boolean disjunction, or OR, as it contains not only the pure states $|A\rangle$ and $|B\rangle$ but also all combined states of relevance between them. This smooths out the discrete Boolean set into a perfectly continuous and complete vector space which shows the ' X '-shaped pattern as nothing more than a tool for transforming from one localised vector sub-space into another. In essence that simply makes it a vector space transformer:

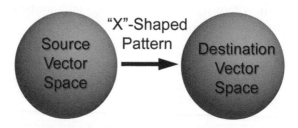

Figure 15.10   The ' X '-shaped pattern as a vector transformation

intuition of classical physics as an acceptable approximation. In simple terms it is the process by which a wave function changes into some other entity the exhibits particle-like behaviour.

The Reformulation

Time for a refresh. All the material presented in this chapter so far has been a brief lead in to explain how contemporary information retrieval techniques exploit thinking from the field of quantum mechanics. Little if anything has been of relevance to the ideas laid out in earlier chapters, other than the fact that we have proposed that the 'X'-shaped pattern might be intimately linked. We have not, for instance, made particular reference to the notion of relativity in either information or computation. Now, hopefully, all of that can be corrected, but there is a warning associated. Many of ideas involved need to come together quickly and all demand mathematical representation. This brings a significant number of variables into play and each one needs a name. Mathematical convention suggests that such names should correspond to a single letter from either a modern-day alphabet, such as that often referred to as the Latin alphabet,[78] or the alphabet used by the ancient Greeks. However, many of these letters have commonly recognised meanings already as a hangover from other prior mathematical uses. For instance, e, m and c are often associated with the concepts of energy, mass and the speed of light, because of their use in Einstein's famous equation $e = mc^2$. Furthermore the specific use of sub and superscripting in relation to such letters also comes with the same hangover. For such reasons it is important to understand that no particular naming convention has been adopted in the mathematics to follow. Hence algebraic formulations involving vectors should look like vector algebra and so on, but the variable names involved are, for all intents and purposes, arbitrary. Where appropriate and explanation of any variable names is due, such is provided on a case by case basis.

Reading instructions over. Now, to reformulate we must first conjure up an informational or computational semantic space with a fixed set of dimensions, n. This will be the theoretical space in which all our possible combinations of information or computation can be found, so it will quite literally represent a universal arena in which we can experiment using the power of mathematics. It will be our sandpit in which we can play. More precisely this space should be referred to as a manifold in mathematical parlance. Such manifolds are mathematical spaces that, on a small enough scale, resemble the Euclidean space of a specific dimension, called the dimension of the manifold. Thus a line and a circle are two-dimensional manifolds, a plane and sphere are three-dimensional manifolds and so on up to any number of dimensions, n. Henceforth we shall refer to the manifold we shall use as ε and given that, in principle, n can be infinite, this space is inherently impossible to visualise in the mind's eye. For this reason, and for ease of understanding only, we shall also restrict this space to having no more than three dimensions – clearly for the purpose of illustration only. With $n = 3$ this space can, in effect, be thought of as a flat sided space, or 'box', with 'height', 'width' and 'depth' dimensions; although in actuality the names and meanings of the constraining dimensions and their associated metrics are arbitrary. Lastly, as we are going to let some vectors free inside ε, we need to consider it as a vector space whose dimensions relate to some form of measurable scale, which, in turn, will more formally make ε a metric space.

Next we need to think of a lower dimensional object to represent all the dimensions within our universal space that are relevant to our immediate interests. In our three-dimensional example that means creating a flat two-dimensional plane captured within the space. We shall refer to this as the *Latent Relevance Hyperplane* (LRH), and loosely think of it as being like a flat piece of paper dangling in a rectangular fish tank of known size – our universal space ε in this instance. Both of these fixed dimensional objects now give us the framework necessary to bring together all the really important ideas introduced in earlier chapters. To do this within the framework – our fish tank (ε) – we must accordingly allow a sequence of linked information or computation to flow within its bounds and hence let it potentially 'interact' with or 'intercept' the LRH. The path of this sequence – hereafter referred to as ICP, for *Information or Computation Path* – will be created by an arbitrary, and possibly infinite, succession of transformations stamped out by the 'X'-shaped pattern. This results in an ICP conceptualisation comprising of a helical or conical band 'spinning' through ε, as in Figures 15.12(a) and 15.12b):

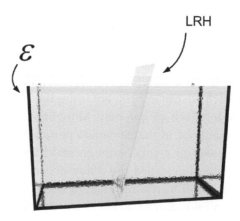

Figure 15.11   The fish tank analogy

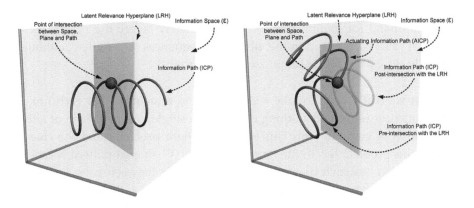

Figure 15.12 (a) and 15.12(b)   A curved information or computation path though a space of all possibilities as in Figure 15.12(a), and with an accompanying actuation path as in Figure 15.12(b)

Superimposed on this diagram you will see a small sphere, or dot, to represent the point at which ε, the LRH and the ICP 'meet' and this will be the location about which we shall obviously concentrate.

To formulate further we need to magnify the area around this dot to expose the various links that make up the local ICP sequence. This gives us a perspective as roughly drawn out in Figure 15.13. However, please note that this diagram is deliberately distorted and simplified so as to exaggerate the necessary points of importance. Because of this the size of each contiguous link is purposely scaled up. Furthermore, given that each link is created as an output of an ' X '-shaped pattern instance, only one of the four legs associated with each pattern occurrence is shown for every link that does not immediately touch the dot and hence intersect with the LRH. Such single-legged links represent an individual asymmetric output from a pattern instance and this purposefully simplifies the diagram to show the characteristic underlying 'spin' path of an ICP with its history of undeviating behaviour – that is to say a path produced by patterns that gave the exact same type of output over and over again. Hence the occurrence of the ' X '-shaped pattern which intersects the LRP can be seen as being fed by I_n and A_n. These are shorthand for the n th link in the ICP positioned immediately before the LRH and one further link from another information or computation path which may act as an actuator in the pattern instance intersecting with the LRH. We shall refer to this additional path as an AICP, for *Actuating Information or Computation Path*, and associate

A_n as shorthand for its link positioned immediately before the LRH. Clearly I_n and A_n also correspond to the nth link in sequences on length n, although naturally n may not be the same size in both cases.

Next we really need to take a step back and remember that each link of both sequences represents nothing more than a single unit in a chain or either information of computation. This leads to a slight problem, and the clue to solving this problem lies in the term 'unit'. The 'X'-shaped pattern is exactly that, a pattern. As such its application cannot vary between uses. So, at the highest level it expects to be supplied with two inputs, with acceptable types of characteristic, and it can only ever produce two outputs with, perhaps, two other sets of acceptable characteristics. Such inputs and outputs can indeed be vectors, but because of a need for pattern reuse, the implication is that the size of all four vectors involved in an instance of the pattern must be the same for it to work properly. That implies normalising any vectors associated with a given instance and leads to a need for the input legs I_n and A_n to be more appropriately referenced as $\hat{I}_n$ and $\hat{A}_n$. In their raw, de-normalised, or non-unit states I_n and A_n obviously need not be of unit magnitude. By using $\hat{I}_n$ and $\hat{A}_n$ it is also necessary to associate two norm divisors, $\|I_n\|$ and $\|A_n\|$, with $\hat{I}_n$ and $\hat{A}_n$ respectively. In addition, and to follow the normal mathematical convention of vector algebra, we should also use lower case notion when referring to such vectors. That gives the correct vector nomenclature for inbound legs and their norms as:

Information or Computation Path (ICP): unit vector = $\hat{i}_n$, norm = $\|\hat{i}_n\|$

Actuating Information or Computation Path (AICP): unit vector = $\hat{a}_n$, norm = $\|a_n\|$

Now that we have the inputs pinned down into our 'X'-shaped pattern about the LRH, we need to think about the relationship between these inputs and the LRH itself. To do this we must establish how similar the inputs are to the LRH. This can be done firstly by finding the cosine similarity value between $\hat{i}_n$ and a unitised subsection of the LRP – which we shall refer to as $\hat{l}$. This gives a cosine similarity of $\cos(\hat{i}_n, \hat{l})$ and we shall refer to the angle associated with this similarity function as being φ. Two further cosine similarities are also relevant to the input legs, the first of which relates to the similarity between $\hat{i}_n$ and $\hat{a}_n$ and is the same as the cosine of the angle shown below as θ or the cosine similarity of $\cos(\hat{a}_n, \hat{i}_n)$. The remaining angle, γ, can be deduced from $180° - \theta - \varphi$ and likewise has a cosine similarity of $\cos(\hat{a}_n, \hat{l})$.

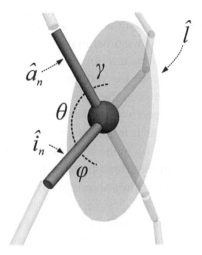

**Figure 15.13   A vector representation of the inputs to an ' X '-shaped
pattern about a localised unit LRH**

An identical scheme can be applied to the outputs of the ' X '-Shaped
pattern about the LRH.

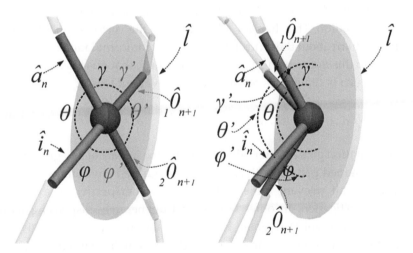

**Figures 15.14(a) and 15.14(b)   Two different versions of a vector
representation of the inputs to and outputs from an ' X '-shaped pattern about
a localised unit LRH. In Figure 15.14(a) the outputs of the pattern occur on the
opposite side of the LRH to the inputs. In Figure 15.14(b), inputs and outputs
occur on the same side of the LRH**

Next we need to apply the same treatment we have given to a pattern's inputs to its outputs. To do this we must first provide suitable nomenclature to name each output in vector form, and obvious candidates for this are $_1\hat{o}_{n+1}$ and $_2\hat{o}_{n+1}$. The 'o' here simply stands for 'output' and the subscripts, firstly before the 'o' act to distinguish between the first and second output, and secondly the subscript after the 'o', specify the position of both leg in the sequence of information or computation as it interacts with the LRH – that is to say they immediately follow any input leg in the nth position in the sequence. Given that the nth elements in the sequence correspond to the pattern's inputs, it should hopefully be obvious that its outputs should be the $n+1^{th}$ elements.

So, at last to the point. The most fundamental tenant of both classically defined information and computation is that symmetry will be broken between any two contiguous elements in any given sequence. In layman's terms that basically translates into 'under normal circumstances any piece of information that naturally follows another will be different from the first' or 'under normal circumstances the outputs from any computational step will differ from its inputs'. In terms of the 'X'-shaped pattern that means that we should look for differences between input and output vector pairs once their relevance to the LRH has been taken into account. This leads us to seek differences in terms of the scale and direction of their respective sums and can be done using the following equation. This, happily, also provides the vector gradient of the 'X'-shaped pattern about the central dot. And so if, for formulations purposes, we now refer to this dot as being at a point p within ε, that gives a vector gradient of ∇X_p, which is sometimes referred to as a covariant tensor:

$$\nabla X_p = \left[\left({_1\hat{o}_{n+1}} + {_2\hat{o}_{n+1}} \right) \cdot \left(\left\| {_1o_{n+1}} \right\| \cdot \cos(\gamma') \cdot \left\| {_2o_{n+1}} \right\| \cdot \cos(\varphi') \right) \right] - \left[\left(\hat{a}_n + \hat{i}_n \right) \cdot \left(\left\| a_n \right\| \cdot \cos(\gamma) \cdot \left\| i_n \right\| \cdot \cos(\varphi) \right) \right]$$

This equation give a vector which qualifies the impact of any given instance of an 'X'-shaped pattern with respect to its localised environment and takes into account all relevant dimensions from the perspective of a particular point of investigation. In other words, and deliberately dispensing with all the mathematical gobbledygook, it describes the influence of any given 'X'-shaped pattern as seen by an observer. Or, in even simpler terms, it tells us how a particular pattern instance might 'appear', or what it 'looks like', in other words.

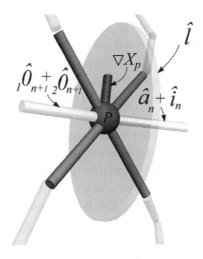

**Figure 15.15   A graphical representation of how input and output vectors
contribute to ∇X_p (shown in dark grey at the top of the image)**

It should be noted that although this equation produces a differential as
its results – in the form of ∇X_p – it cannot be considered as a differential
equation in the strictest sense of the term. This is because differential calculus is
generally constructed so as to work over functions that are predictable in nature
and which do not vary wildly over each step. No such guarantees are present
here, however, with every single instance of the 'X'-shaped pattern having
to be evaluated both on its own merits and its impact on any encompassing
ε evaluated without needing prior knowledge of other patterns instances in
the vicinity. At its core differential calculus does exactly that but, when the
mathematical mechanics are abstracted for general use, such attention to detail
is scarified in favour of simplicity of working.

When considering ∇X_p it is important to understand that it is not a
normalised unit vector although it is produced from a function which takes
in four unit vectors. It is not normalised in the strictest sense because the
norms of the vectors involved are multiplied by their cosine similarity with
the LRH so as to take the pattern's relevance into consideration. This adds a re-
scaling element to ∇X_p, thereby de-normalising its scalar element against its
normalised inputs. The result is an indirect measure of the change produced by
an 'X'-shaped pattern instance and so long as all values of ∇X_p are calculated
in exactly the same manner, this measure of change is perfectly adequate.

All this is fine, but how does it fit with quantum mechanics, you might ask? Well, to answer that question first we need to notice that neither of the angles θ or θ' were used in the equation to formulate ∇X_p. That is because both actually specify the range of inputs and outputs relevant to a particular occurrence of an 'X'-shaped pattern. Or in quantum terms, they dictate the continuous range of values a pattern can consume and produce, rather than the actual discrete inputs and outputs used to form the pattern. Thus the outputs $_1O_{n+1}$ and $_2O_{n+1}$ can both be seen as being analogous to the two collapsed waveform outputs produced by a pattern – similar to 'particles' being seen coming out of the two slits in Young's experiment – or the limits of all the possible outputs that a pattern instance can produce. Similarly a_n and i_n also correspond to two collapsed waveform inputs into a pattern. In such a way the regions marked out by θ and θ' represent the source and destination vector subspaces actually covered by a pattern instance. If such subspaces were stretched over three dimensions, they would form the same geometry as also seen in a Minkowski, or light cone as can be seen in Figure 15.16 below.

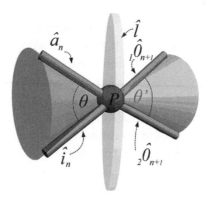

Figure 15.16   The three-dimensional vector spaces contributing to ∇X_p

Tensors

More generally, we have now created a framework that allows us to formally think of ε as a sort of filing cabinet – properly referred to as matrix in mathematical terms – where every one of the points it contains corresponds to a 'draw' containing information on an overarching subject. In fact it's smarter than that, as ε comes with its own indexing system for free. If we know the coordinates of any given point P in ε, that automatically shows us the way to the information contained in the 'draw' at that location. In such a way it is possible to think of each instance of the ' X '-shaped pattern as being a referenceable function, e , applied to its input – namely the transformation of its two inbound vectors, $a_n + i_n$. And if we consider these inputs as being made up of multiple constituent parts representing the various dimensions over ε , then an ' X '-Shaped pattern instance can be represented as a function, thus:

$$e_p = f(d_1, d_2, ...d_n)$$

Where d_n is a given dimension over ε .

$$\nabla X_p = \frac{\partial e}{\partial h} = \left[\frac{\partial e}{\partial h_1}, \frac{\partial e}{\partial h_2}, ..., \frac{\partial e}{\partial h_n} \right]$$

where h represent each of the respective dimensional components contributing to the function e and $\partial e / \partial h_n$ represents the partial derivative of e with respect to h .

∇X_p is, in fact, a type of geometric object, which we have already named as a covariant tensor. Consequently it can be thought of as a filing cabinet containing partial derivatives, or 'gradient parts', contributing to the overall informational gradient generated by an ' X '-shaped pattern at point p . Not only that, but given that p can be thought of as but one point in an higher dimensional matrix of points within ε . This makes ∇X_p a kind of a filing cabinet within a filing cabinet, similar to that shown in the mathematical conceptualisation below:

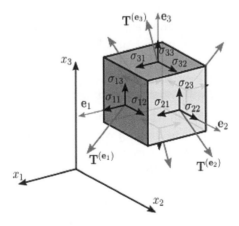

Figure 15.17   Components of stress. An example of a second-order tensor, in three dimensions[77]

Unfortunately, understanding ∇X_p as a covariant tensor is not the end of the story as there is a further tensor associated with an ' X '-shaped pattern at point p. This is known as a contravariant tensor, which we shall refer to as dX. Whereas ∇X_p purely focuses on the rate of informational or computational chance about point p, dX focuses on the actual difference between its inputs and outputs produced by that change rate. This is equivalent to:

$$dX_p = \left({}_1 o_{n+1} + {}_2 o_{n+1}\right) - \left(a_n + i_n\right)$$

or

$$dX_p = \left[dh_{1}, dh_{2}, ...dh_{n}\right]$$

There is an important relationship between covariant and contravariant functions involving continuous functions of multiple continuous variables – as is the case here with the ' X '-shaped pattern. This is generally referred to as the *total differential*, and is given by:

$$de_p = \frac{\partial e}{\partial h_1} dh_1 + \frac{\partial e}{\partial h_2} dh_2 + ... + \frac{\partial e}{\partial h_n} dh_n$$

Or, if we were to consider ∇X_p and dX_p to be compound vectors with arbitrary names v and w respectively, that would give the total differential as:

$$v \cdot w$$

By using the dot product operator, the total differentiation reduces the representation of the transformation at point p in to a single scalar value. This adds particular value, as the impact of all ' X '–shaped patterns applicable across all of ε can now be modelled as if it were an extra dimension of ε. Thus if we think about ε as being uniformly made up as a n-dimensional manifold of points – much like the fish tank in our analogy, and being filled with a perfect pool of 'water' in which all molecules are evenly spaced and of exact size – it is now possible to think of each point in this lattice as having a value of de associated with it. This essentially gives us a map of de across all relevant dimensions of ε. Indeed this is much like considering a contour map – which, by way of example, is physically a two-dimensional object flat, yet can still conveys all the required details to think of the world in three dimensions. For such reasons de can be referred to a scalar field over the manifold ε. Likewise, as ∇X and dX contain a directional element, they can be referred to as a vector fields over ε.

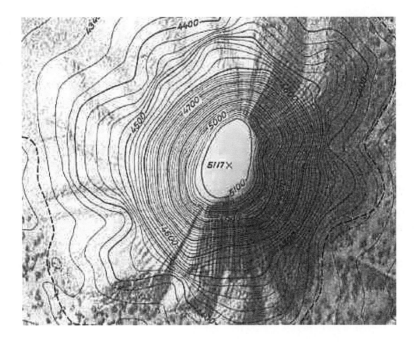

Figure 15.18   An example of an Ordinance Survey map

Putting Relativity Back into the Picture

Physicists particularly like tensors and put them to good use in a number of areas, including extensive application in the idea of relativity.[76] This is because they can successfully bring together the four ingredients needed to make gravity work. These obviously start with distance, time and mass, which require only scalar[20] representation. But when mixed up with the final ingredient, that being direction, relativity's formulation takes us out into the realm of vectors. Tensors are hence geometrical entities introduced to extend the notion of scalars, geometric vectors and matrices.

Many physical quantities are naturally regarded not as vectors themselves but as transformations from one set of vectors into another. One example is the stress, which takes a vector as input and produces another vector as output, consequently expressing a relationship between the input and output vectors.

In general relativity, the tensor and its associated measurement system, or metric, is the fundamental object of study. It may loosely be thought of as a

20   That is to say a denominate number – a magnitude with associated units, such as 3 km.

generalisation of the gravitational field familiar from Newtonian gravitation. The metric captures all the geometric and causal structure of space-time, being used to define notions such as distance, volume, curvature, angle, future and past and can be seen in the following formulation of Einstein's field equations:

$$R_{\mu\nu} - \frac{1}{2}g_{\mu\nu}R + g_{\mu\nu}\Lambda = \frac{8\pi K}{c^4}T_{\mu\nu}$$

Where $R_{\alpha\nu}$ is the Ricci curvature tensor,[21] R the scalar curvature,[22] $g_{\alpha\nu}$ the metric tensor, Λ is the cosmological constant, K is Newton's gravitational constant,[23] c is the speed of light and $T_{\alpha\nu}$ is the stress energy tensor.

This can be reformulated relatively painlessly into the following form:

$$G_{\mu\nu} = \frac{8\pi K}{c^4}T_{\mu\nu}$$

where $G_{\alpha\nu}$ is an Einstein tensor, K is Newton's gravitational constant and c is the speed of light.

Although it might appear that some extreme feats of mathematical contortion have taken place here, the underlying principle is very simple. The above equations basically state that the inherent geometric curvature of any point in space-time can be calculated from the inherent stress – in terms of energy and momentum – also found at that point multiplied by some constant. In the case of Einstein's equations that constant is $\frac{8\pi K}{c^4}$, but it is easy to simplify that by just thinking of that bunch of stuff as a single variable name – and indeed physicists regularly do something similar to get it out of the way through a

---

21 In differential geometry, the Ricci curvature tensor, named after Gregorio Ricci-Curbastro, represents the amount by which the volume element of a geodesic ball in a curved Riemannian manifold deviates from that of the standard ball in Euclidean space. As such, it provides one way of measuring the degree to which the geometry determined by a given Riemannian metric might differ from that of ordinary Euclidean n-space.

22 In Riemannian geometry, the scalar curvature (or Ricci scalar) is the simplest curvature invariant of a Riemannian manifold. To each point on a Riemannian manifold, it assigns a single real number determined by the intrinsic geometry of the manifold near that point. Specifically, the scalar curvature represents the amount by which the volume of a geodesic ball in a curved Riemannian manifold deviates from that of the standard ball in Euclidean space.

23 The gravitational constant is an empirical physical constant involved in the calculation of the gravitational attraction between objects with mass.

system known as the a geometrised units.[24] So let's indeed simplify the above equation by using a much more restricted group of variables:

$$_pC_{1..n} = T\partial e_p$$

In this formulation C represents curvature of a given point, p, in any given information or computation space, ε, and its subscript, $1..n$, denotes that such curvature is restricted to the relevant dimensions or characteristics within ε. Likewise the right-hand side of the equation relates to the total differential associated with an 'X'-shaped pattern at point p in ε, multiplied by some scalar constant T.

Note that T is scalar, which implies that it changes the size of one side of the equation in relation to the other. This is a common theme that runs through most of physics. In a certain way it tells us that the way we observe the curvature of an information or computation space is not necessarily the way it actually is, and to think in terms of 'perfect' reality we have to compensate. Similar examples of such compensation form the very fabric from which science is built, with some of the most widely recognised compensators being the speed of light in vacuum c, the gravitational constant K (in our equations), Planck's constant h, the electric constant ε_o and the elementary charge e. Physical constants can take many dimensional forms: the speed of light signifies a maximum speed limit of the universe and is expressed dimensionally as length divided by time, while the fine-structure constant α, which characterises the strength of the electromagnetic interaction, is dimensionless.

Viewing such compensation analogously brings us back to our example of an information space, ε, being represented by a fish tank of sorts. In this tank we can think of information or computation 'swimming' about under the influences of everything else in the tank and, to a certain extent, the tank itself. Framed in such a way it is easy to visualise such information or computation as if it were indeed a fish merrily going about its business and occasionally bumping into or passing through the odd LRH along the way. In fact, why not, let's go the whole distance with the analogy and think of such LRH's as being similar to long weeds growing from the floor of the tank and stretching all the way up to the surface of the water it contains – the tank obviously being full to the brim. Think about such a tank for a second and consider our fish and the

---

24 A geometrized unit system or geometric unit system is a system of natural units in which, in this specific case, the base physical units are chosen so that the speed of light and the gravitational constant are set to a value of 1.

**Figure 15.19   The fish tank analogy as a means of understanding
multiplication by a constant**

journey it takes as it glugs its way peacefully through its life. Got that picture firmly in your mind? Good. But there is a problem. What we are actually seeing is a fallacy, a trick, a lie almost! The actual size of the fish and the weeds in the tank are not what they might appear to you. They may actually be larger or they may be smaller, but the chances that they are precisely the same size as that which you, hypothetically of course, see, are close to nil. This is because the glass in the tank walls and the water it holds back are playing tricks with process of observation and are acting like a magnifying class. In other words they are altering reality by their very participation in reality. And to correct this we need to compensate by a fixed factor.

But let's just pause for a quick moment, as before going further there is an interesting digression that really should be made. Notice carefully the key word in the last sentence but one in the paragraph above. The term 'alter' has been used for deliberate reason again to indicate that something has changed. Equally any of the verbs 'transform', 'modify', 'adjust' or, and here's the clue once again, 'compute', could have been used, for the same purpose, as, essentially, constants play a fixed computational role on the act of observation. That in effect tells us that T in Einstein's field equations corresponds to an 'X'-shaped pattern that remains the same over time, so long as none of its key characteristics are changed. This is a powerful realisation for it not only tells us that if we are interested in any 'X'-shaped patterns within a designated ε, then ε itself must be taken into account in order to fully understand any outputs from those patterns. To put that another way, no output from any 'X'-shaped pattern can be viewed with absolute credibility on its own. Take a step back here and if you quiet your mind you will hear special relativity singing out with a pure pitch. What we are really saying is that reality is absolutely and completely in the eye of the beholder and that the interpretation of any piece of information or act of computing is intimately bound with the perspective, or point, from which it is being observed or consumed.

The Big Punch Line: Synthetic Gravity

So, to the point: to put bluntly in analogous terms, you should hopefully realise by now that when we look at a fish in a tank, that the fish is actually different in at least one regard to what we see. However, just because such a fish might be misrepresented across one or even many of its characteristics when it is observed, that does not mean in any way that the fish is anything other than a fish! The act observation does not add or take away any of the 'fishiness' to be found in the fish. It does not magically change it into a cat or a walnut or anything else for that matter. And believe it or not, that is the magic the lies at the heart of Einstein's field equations. Not the fact that fish remain fish if we place them under a magnifying glass or watch them swimming in a tank, but rather the fact that equivalence may be disguised but cannot be hidden.

Remember that Einstein's field equations tell us that the curvature of any given region in space-time is proportionally equivalent to the stress energy also present in that region. Now, in one step, think of energy as being analogous to information or computation and the following proposition jumps out:

> The curvature of any definable informational or computational space is proportionally equivalent to the sum of total differentials arising from the 'X'-shaped patterns present within that space

Conjecture 32   The curvature of any definable informational or computational space

This presents a conclusion of unforgettable significance and is essentially the whole point of this entire book. Why? Because, according to Einstein's definition, gravity is not a force but rather results from the curvature of space-time. And for us that means we can infer one of two things:

> If there is such a thing as informational or computational (synthetic) gravity, it is proportionally equivalent to the sum of total differentials arising from the ' X '-shaped patterns present within any given space

Conjecture 33   Synthetic gravity and the ' X '-Shaped pattern

Or, and more profoundly:

> If, at its most fundamental level, the universe is an informational entity, gravity itself might be formulated purely using informational or computational principles

Conjecture 34   Gravity from the ground up

There we have it, gravity in information and computation! But there is one thing about gravity that we should not forget. Take any small number of atoms and try to measure the gravitational attraction between them. It will be there but it will be miniscule. In fact the attraction present will be so small that for all intents and purposes it will be unnoticeable and irrelevant to any immediate context. So, we might suggest, it must also be with synthetic gravity. Take any small amount of information – say from a paragraph in this book – and there will most likely be little attraction to the ideas it contains. Ramp things up, however, and consider millions, if not billions, of such paragraphs, and things might be quite different. But where might we find such a source of information? Why, the World Wide Web of course. So it is there that we shall partially head next to see if we can find any corroborating evidence of the radical and far reaching ideas we have just covered.

16

Supporting Evidence

... a variety of evidence suggests that underlying Riemann's Zeta function is some unknown classical, mechanical system whose trajectories are chaotic and without [time-reversal] symmetry, with the property that, when quantised, its allowed energies are the Riemann zeros. These connections between the seemingly disparate worlds of quantum mechanics and number theory are tantalising.

Michael Berry

So, at last we may have found it: synthetic gravity! But wait one minute, that's not enough. At this point we should really be shouting out 'big wow, so what?' This is because just claiming such a thing is insufficient. Science does not work like that. Science needs proof.

Scientific discovery usually comes in one of three forms. The first is the stuff of legend and is very rare indeed. In this form it is instantaneous, like a bolt of lightning from the blue. This is inspirational discovery, where ideas just happen. The Greek mathematician and astronomer Archimedes made such a discovery style famous when in his bath one day. While in the process of lowering himself into the water he realised that the volume of water he was displacing was exactly equivalent to the volume of the submerged portion of his body at the time. When he realised this, or so the story goes, he jumped out of the bath and ran naked down the street screaming 'eureka!' It was quite literally his eureka moment and, in fact, that's exactly where the saying comes from. The second form of discover is the most common, and unfortunately the most bland. In this a diligent scientist, often backed up by an equally diligent group of helpers or peers, spots an existing problem in science and commits to solving it. This is done slowly, laboriously and carefully, by delving into every nook and cranny of the problem and fastidiously pouring over the findings of numerous experiments. If all works well a pattern eventually emerges and the problem slowly reveals its secrets. In plain terms the problem is literally overpowered by the tenacity and brilliance of the individual, or individuals, working on it. The third is somewhat more exquisite than the other two. In this form discovery is not instantaneous, nor is it hard won. Rather it grows in an organic manner, almost as if dancing around those who show interest. Slowly it reveals itself as if in some kind of courtship, dropping little hints in sometimes unexpected ways. So it is with synthetic gravity and the courtship is not over yet. There are only those tantalising hints of more to come. Some may relate to false hope while some may prove genuine pointers to a greater understanding. What is important for now, however, is that they all appear to relate to a common theme and that theme can be articulated via the language of geometry.

Let the Web Lead the Way with Its Apparent Reluctance to Be Normal

The thing about gravity, real gravity that is, is that so far it has only chosen to reveal itself at scale, as we alluded to at the end of the last chapter. In other words it needs lots of matter to be present in a relatively small volume of space-time for it to become obvious. One or two atoms simply will not do. Scale needs to be increased considerably until we reach the point where trillions upon trillions of such atoms are all crammed together. In a similar way it is simply might not be good enough to expect synthetic gravity to make a substantive appearance if we link a couple of dozen data items together. No, to get synthetic gravity motivated we need lots and lots of data, all bound up via a multitude of connections too great to count by any sensibly human.

In the past the Web has been criticised as being a just a jumbled up mess of nonsense with no structure and no particular place to go. But now the new field of Web science is providing valuable information to argue the contrary. It is showing, for example, that the Web is actually about lots of very structured data; too structured in fact for us to naturally take in without help. And it's confirming what we knew already in that the Web is complex – oh boy, is it complex! But it's not complex in any run of the mill way. No, rather it is complex in ways we understand already and have studied many times over in other systems – such as the weather, the migration of species or the ebb and flow of the world's economy. Now we're beginning to see that these too are complex webs of interaction and data, and that our Web is just one fine example mingled in with a set of wonderfully complex and equally fine examples. With each step back we are seeing new beauty. The Web has pattern, for instance, and that pattern is highly regular, no matter at what level we choose to view it.

It also has direction, as some areas show up as more active than others, again with surprising regularity. Indeed, it's the Web's consistency that overpowers and it is this consistency that drives out the belief that synthetic gravity might just exist at Web scale.[79]

In particular, at scale, the Web does not behave how we might instinctively expect and to demonstrate this peculiarity we need to reintroduce our fish tank analogy. This time around let's imagine that our tank is not occupied by just one fish, but rather a whole shoal of fish. In fact let's image that the tank is so large that it can hold a shoal of unimaginable size and yet still have just enough room left over for each fish to swim freely. Fish being fish, nonetheless, they will always follow their natural instinct and choose to swim together, occasionally bumping into one and other as they do. Finally let's add a rather special scientific detector into the tank and propose that it can precisely measure the force involved in each and every collision between fishes as they go about their business.

Accordingly, if the record of such collisions were examined, we might reasonably expect that there would be an average force with which the fish collide. We might also reason that this average would nicely fall midway between the lightest of bump measurements and the most extreme of crashes. It might further be reasonable to expect the range of bump forces to be arranged around the average in some mathematically predicable way. That would be normal, would it not? That would fall within our normal expectations of how the world works?

Figure 16.1   The extended fish tank analogy

In fact, such data distributions, like that of the spread of force values in the fish's collisions, are often 'normal' at scale and mathematicians actually refer to such phenomena by that very name, by calling them 'normal distributions'. Continuous random variables that can take any value within a given range are common place and many naturally occurring variable distributions approximate to 'normal' representation. The heights of females and the weights of Russian ballet dancers, for instance, both show normal distribution characteristics. In such cases much of the data is centred on the average or 'mean' value of the data involved. Such distributions are also organised so as to form a, commonly, symmetrical shape which is not dissimilar to that of a bell, and for that reason you may often hear normal distributions being also referred to as a form of 'bell' curve. Other names include the Gaussian distribution after the famous mathematician Carl Friedrich Gauss who used such models to analyse astronomical data.

Normal distributions are actually a family of distributions with a symmetrical bell shape. In this family the height and width of the bell crest can vary, but the important thing is that the overall bell shape is always prominent. In essence we get one central hump of data that usually tails off in equal measure on both sides of the peak in a 'child's slide-like' way.

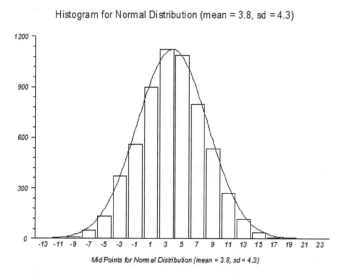

Figure 16.2   An example of a normal distribution. This shows the characteristic bell-shaped curve of a normal (Gaussian) distribution superimposed on a histogram of a sample from a normal distribution

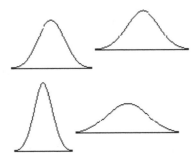

Figure 16.3   Various forms of the normal, or 'bell'-shaped distribution

It is difficult to over emphasise the importance of the term 'normal' in this naming convention. It is there for precisely the reason that such distributions are exactly that, normal. That is in the sense of being common place. Look at any random variable that has the capacity to change across any measurable characteristic and the chances are that its variation will be exhibited in a statistically normal way. And here's the thing. Notice that the term 'change' is again deliberately used. Replace that with the term 'compute' and things starts to become interesting. Essentially we are saying is that any computation capable of generating a wide range of values, if left to its own devises and not deliberately constructed so as to not to show statistically normal behaviour, might reasonably be expected to be statically normal in its output. Got that? It's important. To rephrase, what we are saying is that non-contrived computations capable of producing a range of outputs will tend to produce such outputs in accordance with a normal pattern of distribution.

So now back to the Web. It is a computational entity, so it computes. It is not contrived, or at least not in the sense that any single authority has any control over it. It produces a wide range of outputs. Ok … So, all things considered its dominant statistical behaviour should be normal, right? Wrong! It's not normal at all! Actually that's strictly not true. Look at certain isolated areas of the Web and normal behaviour can indeed be found, but abstract above the everyday chatter of the Web and inspect it in any meaningful macro-like way and the statistics that are prevalent do not follow the convention of normal distribution. If that were the case, for example, we would find that a significant number of the Web's search engines would be relatively similar in popularity. A significant number would also experience approximately the same number of hits each day, and that number could plausibly be accepted as the average. Lesser search engines would similarly experience fewer hits and more popular search engines more, but such hit rates could reasonably be predicted simply by studying the average hit rate amongst search engines and the respective variances in the hit rates between such sites – just as the theory behind the normal distribution prescribes. But the Web is not like that. Google, Yahoo and Bing's hit rates do not hover around some average and we cannot predict the daily number of visitors to AltaVista simply by studying the pack leaders and then extrapolating along some bell-shaped curve. In reality Google dominates by a significant margin and is followed by the second-place search engine, which again leads the third by a lesser, but still significant, edge. In statistical terms these sights stand out as significant outliers. This is not statistically normal by any stretch of the imagination; it is more like a power struggle with only a very few of the players winning, and again this is a deliberate play on words.

About the Web

What a strange construction we have made for ourselves: we have built the Web, but we cannot easily tell exactly what we have built. Rather, we must investigate its form as though we were blind, feeling out its contours little by little, as it's simply too big for us to take in in one go.[2] In 1999 Réka Albert, Hawoong Jeong and Albert-László Barabási of the University of Notre Dame in Indiana did exactly this, by sending a robot out into the maze of the Web and directing it to map out its virtual pathways.[7] The robot was a computer program which was instructed to enter a website and follow all its hyperlinks. These took the robot to an assortment of other websites, at each of which it would repeat the same process. On each outing the robot kept a record of the number of outgoing hyperlinks it encountered from each page. To conduct this search for all 1 billion or so of the pages on the Web would have been far too much for the robot to accomplish. Instead, the researchers told their program simply to stay within the bounds of their university's many web pages. This alone comprised a fine sample of some 325,729 HTML documents, interconnected by nearly 1.5 million hypertext links, and the researchers hoped that it would be a sufficiently large and representative sample to act as a model of the Web as a whole.[7]

As a result of this study Albert and his fellow workers found that the probability distributions of both incoming and outgoing links in the graph their studies produced were dependant on a statistical phenomenon known as a power law.[2] Most pages had few links, a few had many, and each time the number of links was doubled, the number of pages with that many links decreased by a constant factor. This finding is not intuitive. Although we might expect fewer pages with many links, a power law is by no means the only mathematical formulation that might produce such data spread. In fact we could plausibly reach out to a bell-curve distribution for an explanation, which would duly also imply that significant number of page pages should cluster around an average of perhaps three or four links. But the power law relationship says that there is no such preference – no scale to the connectivity of the network. A power law is scale free.[7]

A power law relationship between two scalar quantities x and y is such that it can be generally written as:

$$y = ax^k$$

where a – the constant of proportionality – and a – the exponent of the power law – are constants.

Power laws can be seen as a straight line on a log-log graph since, taking logs of both sides, the above equation is equal to that shown in the reformulation below:

$$\log(y) = k \log(x) + \log(a)$$

Such straight-line plots are the most commonly way in which power laws are visually portrayed, but take away the mathematical assistance provided by logs to iron out such distributions and the following shape of graph can be seen:

Look at such plots carefully and a very sharp decline in slope can be seen followed by a very slow decline as the plot tails off to the right. Power law distributions are often also referred to as being long, heavy or flat-tailed because of this very reason. In such distributions a high-frequency, low-amplitude population is followed by a low-frequency, high-amplitude population in a manner that 'tails off' asymptotically, the events or items at the far end of the tail having a very low probability of occurrence.

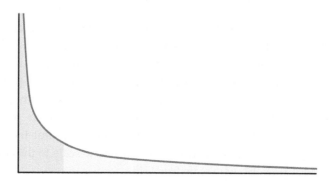

Figure 16.4   A non-log example of a power law graph showing popularity ranking. To the left is the long tail containing the few that dominate. Notice that the areas of both regions match[8]

As a rule of thumb, for such population distributions the majority of occurrences – more than half – are accounted for by the first 20 per cent of item types in the distribution. And what is unusual about a long-tailed distribution is that the most frequently-occurring 20 per cent of item types represent less than 50 per cent of occurrences; or in other words, the least-frequently-occurring 80 per cent of item types are more important as a proportion of the total population.[86]

Because of their general, almost right angular shape and the fact that they as asymptotically constrained by axis which, of course, intersect at right angles, power law are sometimes referred to as being hyperbolic in nature. Nevertheless this is potentially misleading as we shall see shortly.

Power laws tell us that the Web is a special kind of network, one in which small average path lengths between two randomly selected nodes, coupled with a high degree of node clustering combine to give a compelling criterion for connectivity: as the number of nodes in the network grows, the average path length increases very slowly. Essentially it is relatively easy to get from one point in the network to another, no matter how large the network is.

The researchers at Notre Dame also found that a graph constructed to have the same power law distribution of connectivity, as they had observed for their section of the Web, does indeed show such characteristics.

So the Web is a network in which its organisation is very specifically characterised by a power law: by scale-free connectivity – in that a scale-free network is a network whose degree distribution follows a power law, at least asymptotically.[1] Albert and his colleagues estimate that if the entire Web has the same structure as the Notre Dame University domain, than any two of its Web pages are separated by just an average of just 19 links. This is a somewhat larger span than in the six degrees common in certain famous types of social networks, such as that often associated with the actor Kevin Bacon,[2] but it is still a remarkably small number. This means that anyone can get from one extreme of the Web to another in fewer steps than it takes a normal man to run a hundred yards! From hand care to hacking, Homer Simpson to homeopathy, it's all just around the corner on the Web.

In fact power laws seem to be a recurring pattern on the Web. Lada Adamic, while at the Xerox Research Centre, has uncovered this kind of probability distribution in the number of pages per Web site, for instance. Furthermore, in 1998 she and her collaborators discovered that users who surf the Web also obey power law statistics. Surfing is the common alternative to using search engines such as Google directly. You find a Web site that looks as though it might contain the information you want and then follow its hyperlinks to other pages until either you find what you are looking for or you conclude that it is not out there at all. Most users will happily surf not just from one page to another but from site to site. But Adamic and her colleagues considered only the surfing pathways that surfers take within single sites. They were interested in how 'deep' people go, how many clicks they follow, on average, before quitting the site. By looking at various data sets – the behaviour of over 23,000 users registered with the service provider AOL, and visitors to the Xerox Web site, for example – they found that the probability distribution function of the number of clicks on a site obeyed a power law, or something very close.[7]

But what does a scale-free network actually look like? In a random graph most nodes have roughly the same number of connections and the structure looks relatively uniform throughout – as exemplified in the graph shown in Figure 9.8(a). In a scale-free network, however, most nodes have only one or two links, yet a small but significant proportion are highly connected as

---

1   Approaching a given value or condition, as a variable or an expression containing a variable approaches a limit, usually infinity.
2   'Six Degrees of Kevin Bacon' is a trivia game based on the concept of the small world phenomenon and rests on the assumption that any actor can be linked through his or her film roles to actor Kevin Bacon within six steps. The name of the game is a pun on the philosophical 'six degrees of separation' concept.

if clustering in a 'bursty' fashion – as illustrated in Figure 9.8(b). Thus the structure is very uneven, almost 'lumpy', seemingly dense or pinched in some places but sparse in others.[7] It is these highly linked nodes that provide the short cuts, the backbones that make the Web such a small world.

From an organisational perspective it is interesting to note that such structures also appear to be emerging spontaneously at many levels on the Web. Recent studies [80] into the overall associative geometry of the Web have statistically analysed tens of millions of Web sites and the hyperlinks between them. Through this research it has been empirically demonstrated that the Web is emerging as the outcome of a number of essentially independent and random processes that evolve at various scales. A striking consequence of this scale difference is that the structure of the Web is a pervasive and robust self-similar pattern, closely approximating to well understood mathematical phenomena such as Zipf's Power Law [80] – an order coincidentally also known to be present the structure of natural language, the population ranks of cities in various countries, corporation sizes, income rankings and many other types of aggregated data.

Pressure of an Ideal Gas

So we now know that the Web does not generally behave in a statistically normal manner, but let's put that to one side for a moment and return to our fish. Picture them in your mind's eye once again as they gracefully glide about within the limits of their tank, occasionally grazing off one and other as previously described. Now picture the fish being fed with a particularly magical kind of fish food. This excites the fish, thereby allowing them to swim faster and faster. Up and up goes their individual speeds until eventually the tank froths in a golden blur of motion so fast that it is impossible to make out any particular fish, or even determine if the blur results from the shoal's movement. At this point the idea of fish becomes superfluous to the concept we need to explore. We might as well be talking of turnips, hippopotami or even atoms bouncing around in the tank. In fact, hold that though and let's swap our fish for atoms, lots of atoms, all free to leap around within the confines of some fixed container and all under the influence of some energy source such as the heat from a Bunsen burner. Think in these terms and we have actually reformulated our fish tank analogy into a very well-known thought experiment – that of the pressure of an ideal gas at fixed volume.

As might be expected, having now swapped fish for atoms, we have also swapped our fish shoal for a dynamic body and implicitly replaced the water in the tank with, well, nothing, essentially allowing the atoms to move in a theoretical vacuum. Now, if we remember our basic chemistry, atoms can only coalesce in four basic physical forms, those being solids, liquids, gases and plasmas. For our purposes we need to remember that solids cannot be compressed without significant and purposeful persuasion, that liquids resist compression entirely and that plasmas can only exist under very special conditions. That only leaves us with gases to play with. We hence refer to such gasses as being 'ideal' because, in this instance, they are being dealt with in purely theoretical terms and with physical perfection in every regard – they must be 'ideal' for us to use in our thought experiment in other words. An ideal gas is thus a theoretical gas composed of a set of randomly-moving, non-interacting point particles. This is useful because such a gas obeys the ideal gas law, a simplified equation of state, and is thereby amenable to analysis using statistical mechanics.

Under normal ambient conditions such as standard temperature and pressure,[3] most real gases behave qualitatively like an ideal gas. Generally, deviation from an ideal gas tends to decrease with higher temperature and lower density, as the work performed by intermolecular forces becomes less significant compared with the particles' kinetic energy, and the size of the molecules becomes less significant compared to the empty space between them.

Now to the point: if the detail behind the ideal gas experiment is studied carefully, the mathematics describes what is known as the Maxwell–Boltsmann distribution. This is a probability distribution with applications in physics and chemistry. The most common application is in the field of statistical mechanics. The temperature of any (massive) physical system is the result of the motions of the molecules and atoms which make up the system. These particles have a range of different velocities, and the velocity of any single particle constantly changes due to collisions with other particles. However, the fraction of a large number of particles within a particular velocity range is nearly constant. The Maxwell–Boltsmann distribution of velocities specifies this fraction, for any velocity range, as a function of the temperature of the system. It is named after the scientists James Clerk Maxwell and Ludwig Boltsmann.[81]

---

3   In chemistry, standard conditions for temperature and pressure (informally abbreviated as STP) are standard sets of conditions for experimental measurements, to allow comparisons to be made between different sets of data. The most used standards are those of the International Union of Pure and Applied Chemistry (IUPAC) and the National Institute of Standards and Technology (NIST), although these are not universally accepted standards.

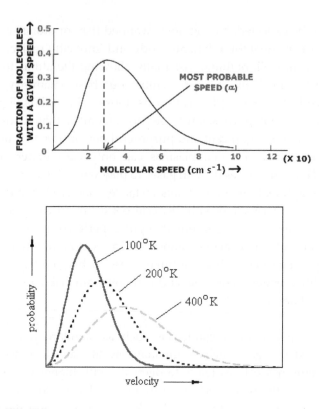

Figures 16.5(a) and 16.5(b)   Example plots of the Maxwell–Boltsmann distribution

The important features of such a distribution are:

- The fraction of molecules with very low or very high speeds is very small.

- The fraction of molecules possessing higher and higher speeds goes on increasing till it reaches a peak and then starts decreasing.

- The greatest group of molecules possesses a speed corresponding to the peak in the curve and this is hence referred to as most probable speed.

By implication the Maxwell–Boltsmann distribution can also be seen to hold true for the momentum of the particles in an ideal gas, as momentum can simply be calculated by multiplying any given particle's mass by its velocity. Hence the distribution can be thought of as a magnitude function whose components are independent and normally distributed, and that's critical. Look into the heart of the Maxwell–Boltsmann distribution and a normal distribution will be found tucked away all safe and secure. Or is it?

On Containment

There is one critical condition involved in the ideal gas experiment, as normally described, which is typically underplayed. In essence the experiment is simple and only requires four constituent parts to work perfectly: the gas under consideration, a heat source to supply energy to the gas, some theoretical measuring device to gauge the gas's resultant pressure from the influx of energy, and, critically, a container to enclose the gas while the experiment takes place. As commonly formulated, the mathematics involved relies heavily on the presence of the container to work and the Maxwell–Boltsmann distribution to form. More precisely the mathematics relies on the container to act as a reference point and allow the calculations involved to be absolute. In other words the relevant equations come from Newtonian mechanics in that they need measurement systems built off a fixed frame of reference, and the container provides that frame admirably. But ask yourself one question: might the experiment work without the use of any container?

In the 1980s the renowned Danish statistician Ole Barndorff-Nielsen asked that very question and in essence set to work to reformulate the mathematics involved minus the container in the experiment's apparatus. In doing so he noted that the Newtonian equations for kinetic energy and the relationship between momentum and velocity differ from those worked out by Einstein in his theory of relativity.[82] By swapping out Newton for Einstein, Barndorff-Nielsen noticed something remarkable. He found that the normal distribution which typically lies beneath the Maxwell–Boltsmann distribution changes and in its place can be found a different type of statistical distribution. This distribution type had been discovered by Barndorff-Nielsen some years earlier in his work on modelling of the size distribution of sand grains. Take the mathematical log of such a distribution and a hyperbola is formed, and for such reason it is generally referred to as a hyperbolic distribution.

Classical (Newtonian) Physics

$$K(p) = \tfrac{1}{2}\, p.p \,/\, m = \tfrac{1}{2}(p_x^2 + p_y^2 + p_z^2)\,/\,m$$

$$p = mv$$

Contemporary (Einsteinian) Physics

$$K(p) = mc^2\,/\,\sqrt{1 - v.v\,/\,c^2}\, - mc^2$$

$$p = mv\,/\,\sqrt{1 - v.v\,/\,c^2}$$

The hyperbolic distribution is a continuous probability distribution that is characterised by the fact that the logarithm of the relative likelihood for any random variable or event appearing is a hyperbola – unlike the log density of a normal distribution which presents as a parabolic plot. Thus the distribution's drop-off, or slop, is exponentially constrained, which provides a slower decay than found in normal distributions. It is therefore suitable to model phenomena where numerically large values are more probable than is the case for normally distributed data.[83] The slope's decay is not as severe as that found in power law distribution, however, and we shall hear more of power laws very shortly. Because of the midway position of its slope the hyperbolic distribution is often referred to as a 'semi-heavy tailed' distribution.[84]

Hyperbolic distributions form a subclass of the generalised hyperbolic distributions. As the name suggests this is of a very general form of distribution, being the superclass of, among others, the Student's t-distribution, the Laplace distribution, the normal-inverse Gaussian distribution and the variance-gamma distribution.

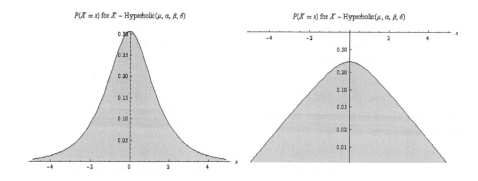

Figures 16.6(a) and 16.6(b)   Density and log-density plots of a hyperbolic distribution

The Web and Zipf's Law

Next we need to discuss a phenomenon commonly known as Zipf's Law, named after the Harvard linguistic professor George Kingsley Zipf. This models the occurrence of distinct objects or events in particular sorts of collections and is most famous for describing a number of patterns in the distributions of linguistic units, such as words and phonemes in texts. So, suppose we consider a natural language corpus, such as a book or collection of magazines written in English. Suppose also that we decide to go about counting of the frequency of the words in the book or magazines and list them. That is to say we count the number of occurrences of words like 'the', 'and', 'of' and so on. Finally consider that we arrange the words we find in decreasing order of the frequency of their occurrence, so that the most frequent work has rank 1, the next most frequent rank 2, and so on. Zipf's Law now tells us the approximate constraining relationship between the frequency of a word in a corpus and its rank in our list. Accordingly this relationship can be written down as:

$$rf = c$$

where r is the rank of a word-type, f is the frequency of occurrence of the word-type and c is some constant dependant on the corpus. When quoted algebraically Zipf's Law is often reformulated into log form as:

$$\log r + \log f = \log c$$

Formulating using logs is convenient as it produces a straight line plot. Because of this twist Zipf's Law is therefore often referred to as log-log relationship or, more generally, a power or exponentiation law.

More generally again, analytic geometry tells us that the equation for an arbitrary line whose slop is $-S$ can be written as:

$$S(\log r) + \log f = \log c$$

Note that if S takes on the value of 1, then the previous two equations above become equivalent. For this reason the latter of these is sometimes referred to as a generalisation of Zipf's Law.

Given that the Web is predominantly text-based, it should, perhaps, come as no surprise to hear that Zipf's Law is dominant in the Web's content. It should further come as no surprise that Zipf's Law is actually a very specific type of power law. Nevertheless what is surprising is that Zipf's Law and other similar power laws are written all over the Web, relating to many features that we might not expect to be linked in such a way.[95] In such a way the number of Web pages amongst Web sites, the distribution of users amongst Web sites and the various links pouring in and out of such sites can all be seen as being under the influence of the law in some way.

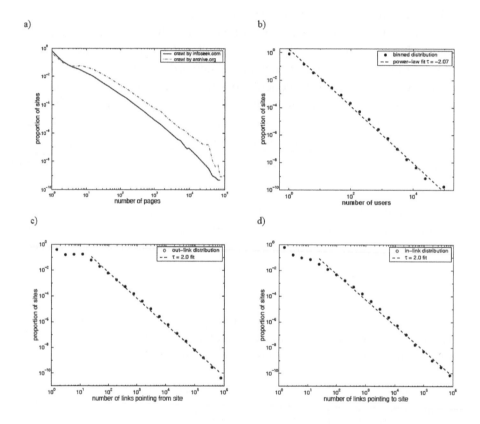

Figures 16.7(a), 16.7(b), 16.7(c) and 16.7(d)   Fitted power law distributions of the number of site a) pages, b) visitors, c) out links, and d) in links, measured in 1997

Note: Although the distributions plotted above are given in terms of the probability density function, they can also be easily recast in terms of Zipf's ranked distribution. In fact, any purely power law probability density function will yield a Zipf-ranked distribution [95]

A Tail of Tails

Power-law distributions occur in many situations of scientific interest, not just those specifically related to the Web, and have significant consequences for our understanding of both natural and man-made phenomena. Unfortunately, however, the detection and characterisation of power laws behaviour is complicated by the large fluctuations that occur in the tail of the distribution – the part of the distribution representing large rare events or item types such as popular websites – and by the difficulty of identifying the range over which such power law behaviour holds. Commonly used methods for analysing power law data can produce substantially inaccurate estimates of parameters for power law distributions, and even in cases where such methods return accurate answers they are still unsatisfactory because they give no indication of whether the data involved obeys a power law at all.[85] Even so, look at the key geometric characteristic of a power law plot and something very interesting will be seen. In fact, reach out to the various names used to describe such plots and one name in particular cries out for attention. The closer you get to power law behaviour, the 'heavier' the tail of the related plot becomes. Look at any run-of-the-mill normal distribution plot and two relatively 'light' tails will be seen. Power laws only have one tail and that makes them geometrically very different. Try as we might, but no one will ever be able to persuade a normal distribution to give up one of its tails no matter how skewed a distribution it might be. Study your run of the mill hyperbolic distribution, however, and more weight will be found added to the tails present. Furthermore such distributions are not as precious about their symmetry as their normal cousins. If a hyperbolic distribution is pushed hard enough it is possible to just about delete one of its tails and produce a surprisingly power law-like plot. Get to a power law, however and the weightiest tail of all will be found and we break free of the need for it to be part of any pair of slopes at all.

Bring mathematical logarithms to bear and an even clearer story is revealed. Take the log-plot of a normal distribution and a parabola will be seen. Take the log-plot of a hyperbolic distribution and we get its namesake. Take the log plot of a power law and out falls a straight line. This hence raises the question as to the possibility of a log-based relationship between all three types of distribution and indeed such a relationship can be found.

Back to Conic Sections, with a Heavy Sprinkling of Causality and Quantum Entanglement this Time

As discussed previously, parabolas and hyperbolas are both forms of conic section. Nevertheless the geometric relationship between both is often confusing. Both are actually linked by a mathematical property known as eccentricity and this can be thought of as a measure of how much any given conic section deviates from being a precisely circular intersection. Thus a circle has an eccentricity of zero, an ellipse has an eccentricity greater than zero but less than one, a parabola forms when eccentricity hits a value of one and hyperbolas form at most eccentric values above one. Take eccentricity up to a value of infinity and the capability to form of hyperbola, or any conic section for that matter, is overpowered and instead is replaced by a straight line. Anecdotally, therefore, it is almost as if as the log of any statistical distribution is telling us that something about the very nature that of distribution itself, in that the greater the eccentricity of the distribution's log plot, the more the inclination for attraction between the underlying members of the distribution, perhaps? So, in essence, log function eccentricity could be an indicator of the potential for gravity-like properties to be present within a distribution. Or if not gravity, perhaps something equally as caught up in relativity like, maybe, causality.

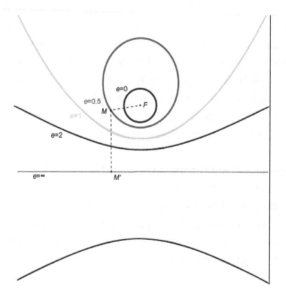

Figure 16.8   All types of conic sections, arranged with increasing eccentricity. Note that curvature decreases as eccentricity rises, and that none of these curves intersect

Indeed there is strong evidence to suggest that 'some other property' might be causality. When studying relativity it soon becomes apparent that causality plays a central role, but what exactly might that be?

To most, the concept of cause and effect is obvious: if someone accidentally knocks a cup off a table onto a hard surface it smashes. If someone pierces the skin of an inflated balloon with a pin it pops. In both cases we can attribute the end effect – the smashed cup and the popped balloon – to two events, the accidental knock and the pin prick. These are events that cause the eventual outcome and as such both can be represented by the following 'X'-shaped diagrams:

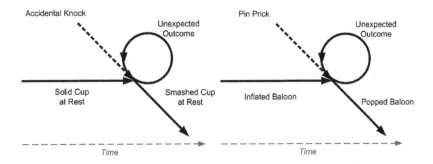

Figures 16.9(a) and 16.9(b)   Cause and effect illustrated via two 'X'-shaped patterns. Note the symmetrical legs for outputs that are not observed

In the simplest mechanical sense the idea of cause and effect states that for any given event to occur it must be triggered and thus preceded by some action. *Given that in computational terms the notion of an event is completely interchangeable with that of a* transformation, then cause and effect can literally be interpreted as stating that for any given transformation to occur it must be triggered and thus preceded by another specific transformation. This, in many ways, is the quintessential definition of the 'X'-shaped pattern, but when articulated in this way, a particular point of importance becomes apparent. The triggering, and thus causal, action can never happen after the resultant effect. For instance, the smashed cup can never exists before the accident that causes it to fall onto the floor. Likewise the balloon will never pop before it is pierced by the pin. This may appear overly obvious, but to a physicist this is absolutely not the case. Cause and effect states that sequence must be maintained in a forward direction for reality to be maintained, forward that is with respect to that passage of time. From our everyday human perspective this appears very natural and very real, yet it conceals one of the most puzzling problems in all of physics. In contrast to the macroscopic universe, the microscopic laws of physics that allegedly underlie its behaviour are perfectly reversible. The puzzle is to reconcile microscopic reversibility with macroscopic irreversibility. Below atomic scale, physics simply does not need cause and effect to be maintained in a forward direction. All its equations have no need for time to travel along a single bearing. All are equally happy and will work just as well if time were allowed to reverse. Yet time still relentlessly insists on tick-tocking forward.[4] Scientists refer to this as time's 'arrow'.

Although everything we observe in the real world tells us that the direction of time is constant, relativity tells us that the rate at which it passes is not. According to Einstein, time can slow down or quicken up depending on the relative motion of that being observed to the observer. Likewise distances shrink and expand as a consequence of relative motion. It is only when space and time are viewed in unison as space-time that we find invariance with regard to any type of motion. Space-time hence provides the only way to get all observers from all observation points to agree on how reality is presented and this can be best seen through a simple example: suppose you are standing by a wall and you walk from your current position at constant speed until you have travelled a distance of 10 metres after 10 seconds, ending up at the position of a nearby chair. In doing so, your journey through space-time can be shown as the following graph:

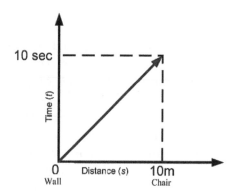

Figure 16.10   An example of a simple journey in space-time

---

4   Although Richard Feynman did find cases where reverse time was permissible.

More correctly it would be better to construct this graph using similar units on both axes. From Newton's laws of motion we know that distance can be calculated as velocity multiplied by time, and in the special case of space-time we can state velocity to be the speed of light c. This gives us the following corrected representation of our journey:

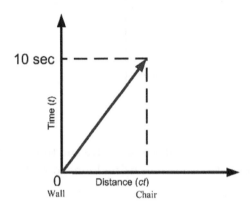

Figure 16.11   A corrected example of a simple journey in space-time

To find the invariant space-time distance travelled we could now apply good old Pythagoras' theorem and take the square root of the sum of the squares taken from the lengths travelled along both axes. This would give us an accurate and unchanging measurement in all cases, but unfortunately not all of values returned would be of use when trying to describe the version space-time we commonly understand as being real in the world around us. This is because when the nagging complication of causality is mixed in with relativity it tells us that that Pythagoras cannot come to the rescue in all situations. To understand why, we need to think about all possible values that distance and time can take when calculating a certain fixed space-time distance. When these are overlaid on our graph, all equidistant space-time points from the wall can be seen and these correspond to the various distance and time values that will make Pythagoras' theorem work for our journey to the chair. This is exactly the same imagining a piece of string of the same length as our trip and fixing it to our start point. Keeping the string taught and moving it around in a circle will obviously produce a trace like the one shown overleaf:

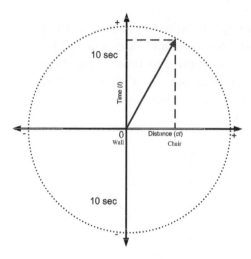

**Figure 16.12   All possible values of distance and time feeding a calculation
of space-time distance using Pythagoras' theorem**

Look closely and a problem is revealed: some of the distance and
time values permissible are negative and this is like saying that we can get
to our chair by travelling into the wall, rather than away from it and/or by
travelling backwards in time rather than forwards. Instinctively this is crazy
and obviously does not correspond to the everyday reality we experience, so
something must be wrong. Applying Pythagoras' theorem in a literal manner
allows the laws of causality to be broken. In fact 75 per cent of the distance and
time values permissible under the strict application Pythagoras' theorem lead
to acausal outcomes. This is because they lie outside the region cast by a light,
or Minkowski, cone facing forward in time as can be seen in Figure 6.13

So only space-time distances found in the uppermost, and unshaded,
quadrant of the diagram above are allowable if we are to maintain causality
and depict reality as we naturally perceive it. To do this Pythagoras' Theorem
needs to be reworked and a surprisingly simple method for doing so was
discovered by Hermann Minkowski in 1907 – hence the prominence of his
name in the field of relativity.

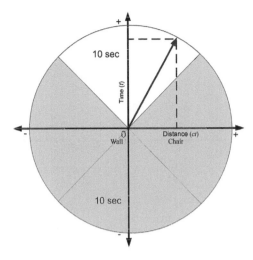

Figure 16.13   The values of distance and time feeding a calculation of space-time distance using Pythagoras' theorem which produce acausal outcomes. Grey areas represent the regions producing error

To maintain causality Minkowski simply reversed the sign in Pythagoras' famous equation from positive to negative:

Suppose $x(a,b)$ represented the distance between points a and b in space, and $t(a,b)$ the time interval taken to travel between points a and b, then Minkowski gives us the space-time distance $s(a,b)$ as:

$$\left(s(a,b)\right)^2 = \left(t(a,b)c\right)^2 - \left(x(a,b)\right)^2.$$

Or just

$$s(a,b) = \sqrt{\left(t(a,b)c\right)^2 - \left(x(a,b)\right)^2}$$ where c is the speed of light.

This leads to the following formulation of space-time and the above equation is exactly the same as that used to produce a hyperbola:

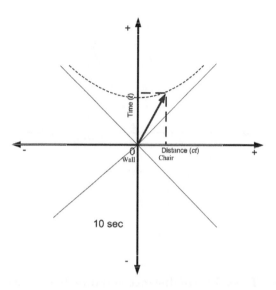

10 sec

**Figure 16.14   The Minkowski geometry of space-time, often quoted as
'Minkowski space-time'**

In this formulation the dashed line marking out a hyperbola gives all the points where causal behaviour can be encountered in space-time and it is exactly this structure that Einstein adopted for his latter works on relativity. This should come as no shock when it is realised that Minkowski was one of Einstein's teachers at the Eidgenössische Polytechnikum in Zurich. It was he who accordingly best understood that special relativity could be formulated in a four dimensional space, since known as 'Minkowski space-time', in which time and space are not separated entities but intertwined in a four dimensional space-time, and in which the geometry of special relativity can be elegantly represented. As such, the beginning part of his address delivered at the 80th Assembly of German Natural Scientists and Physicians in 1908 is now famous:

> *The views of space and time which I wish to lay before you have sprung from the soil of experimental physics, and therein lies their strength. They are radical. Henceforth space by itself, and time by itself, are doomed to fade away into mere shadows, and only a kind of union of the two will preserve an independent reality.*

This is important for us, for if we think about the various types of statistical distribution we have previously considered, they can in fact be seen to be linked through the notion of causality. Normal distributions, for example, depend on the random selection of the same type of data element they cover. Because of this randomness we might legitimately expect some of the elements in any given sample set of normal data to be connected in some way and others not. If time is involved in the data's distribution it is therefore valid to assert that one possible form of such connectedness might be causal. We also know that the log function of a normal distribution's 'bell' curve, gives us an approximate parabola, which has an eccentricity close to one. Lower eccentricity values drive out ellipses and circles which we have seen can be associated with the full range of causal and acausal space-time relationships, as shown in Figure 16.13. So, more circular log function plots could be associated with underlying phenomena less likely to behave in any recognisably real world way. In other words the data underlying the distribution might have a story to tell, but that story would most probably not correlate with our everyday experience of physical reality. Information associated with time travel might be one good example, as such practice is known to break causality and defy the laws of physics as we commonly understand them. Parabolic log plots have a much closer eccentricity value to that of the hyperbola necessary for Minkowski's causal space-time's structure, so it is therefore plausible to suggest that associated phenomenon and their respective distribution data might be partially causal in a close to real world sense. This indeed matches our everyday intuition about things and events that are normally distributed, in that some can be causally related while some quite legitimately not. Things or events that are distributed according to a hyperbolic distribution, such as Barndorff-Nielsen's ideal gas interpretation, must therefore be entirely causal in their nature and indeed that is exactly the basis on which the equation for the pressure of an ideal gas is based. That now only leaves power law distributions for us to think about.

To consider what the log function of a power law might be telling us in relativistic terms, we need to remember that such a plot appears as an approximate straight line and that such geometry only occur when there is the underlying relationship between the things being plotted is of the form $y = zx$, in two dimensions and so on – z being an arbitrary constant in all cases. Next we also need to need to ask if this type of relationship corresponds to any form of conic section and might hence be associated with Minkowski's space-time geometry. By doing so we find that indeed it does and the type of conic section to be considered is a particularly special case, as shown overleaf:

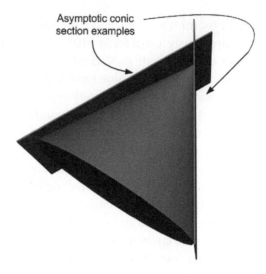

Asymptotic conic
section examples

Figure 16.15   Two examples of asymptotic conic section

Conic sections like this are actually the asymptotes, or bounding lines, of a cone. In other words they mark the edge of such objects. The diagram above shows these as flat planes, but this is only to emphasis their existence. Asymptotes actually only represent the group of points lying along the intersection of such planes with a cone and that makes them nothing more than a straight line of infinitesimal width, height and depth. Only their length and direction has relevance Thus, if we can think of a Minkowski cone as a four-dimensional object in space-time with its own direction,[5] its asymptotes can be thought of as the very most outer limits of that four-dimensional space and hence mark out the boundary between what is permissible in a causal sense and what is not. In a very real sense they mark out the boundary between what we perceive as being 'allowable' in our understanding of the universe and what is not. This is a strange place to be as it literally challenges our understanding of how everything around us behaves and its intimate relationship with the speed of light and its role in observability. It is a twilight zone that physicists find fascinating and one that we might expect not to be inhabited by any physical phenomena. But that is not quite true. Physics knows of at least one phenomenon that appears to sit right at the edge of causality apparently being independent of the passage of time.

---

5   That is to say that it is a vector quantity.

Quantum entanglement, also known as the quantum non-local connection, is a property of the quantum mechanical state of a system containing two or more elements, where those elements are linked in a way such that we cannot adequately describe the quantum state of a constituent of the system without full mention of its counterparts, even if the individual elements are spatially separated. This interconnection leads to non-classical correlations between observable physical properties of remote systems, often referred to as nonlocal correlations. During the formation of quantum theory, this property of entanglement was recognised as a direct consequence.[94]

Quantum entanglement is a controversial subject because of its ramifications. Normally, under the Copenhagen interpretation[6] of quantum mechanics, the state a particle occupies is determined at the moment the state is measured. However, in an entangled pair when the first particle is measured, the state of the other is known at the same time without measurement, regardless of the separation of the two particles. This knowledge of the second particle's state is at the heart of the debate. If the distance between particles is large enough, information or influence might be travelling faster than the speed of light which violates the principle of special relativity. One experiment that is in agreement with the effect of entanglement 'travelling faster than light' was performed in 2008. This experiment found that the 'speed' of quantum entanglement has a minimum lower bound of 10,000 times the speed of light. However, because the method involves uncontrollable observation rather than controllable changing of state, no actual information is transmitted in this process. Therefore, the speed of light remains the communication speed limit.[94]

Think about this very carefully. Replace quantum particles with information on the Web and does not this description fit the Web perfectly? If we change the information contained in a particular Web page and that Web page is linked to and from other Web pages, then they too instantaneously and implicitly contain that information as well. That's the way the Web works. Each Web page is like a Russian doll with the hyperlinks it contains acting as the means to reveal the various layers of dolls contained within. Indeed, intuitively the Web has to be entangled as its very most fundamental principles rely on the intimacy of connections between information items. Because of this we could

---

6   The Copenhagen interpretation is an interpretation of quantum mechanics. A key feature of
     quantum mechanics is that the state of every particle can be described by a wave function,
     which is a mathematical representation used to calculate the probability for it to be found in a
     location or a state of motion. According to this interpretation, the act of measurement causes
     the calculated set of probabilities to 'collapse' to the value defined by the measurement. This
     feature of the mathematical representations is known as wave-function collapse.

never characterise any Web page containing hyperlinks just by looking at that single page. The only way to fully understand it is to also follow all the hyperlinks it contains and read the content on those pages as well. In fact, even that would be a pointless task, for to understand those pages fully we must further follow the links they contain and so on. This would ultimately involve consuming a vast portion of the Web, if not all if it! This is exactly the signature of entanglement.

But what about relativity and the cosmic speed limit set by light's movement? How come the Web might be breaking such limitations? To answer this question we need to be very careful with the words we use. Change any simple piece of linked data or information on the Web and it will have an instantaneous effect on every piece of information to which it is connected. However, for us to read and interpret such detail some interaction with at least one electronic computer somewhere in the world is needed. Such a device must read the particulars of the information involved from memory or disk somewhere and transmit them over the Internet back to us. Such interaction – the act of retrieving the information that is – is constrained by the speed of light because of the various physical interactions involved in this process. Disks cannot spin faster than the speed of light, for instance, computers, no matter how powerful and fast are also limited in such a way and information cannot travel down any of the Internet's wires at warp speed. This limits the very act of retrieving and viewing information on the Web and corrects the problem with relativity. This is why we can interact with the Web in such a 'natural' way and yet, under the hood, it can be still theoretically work according to the weird and wonderful guidelines of quantum mechanics. It can be instantaneously entangled yet worldly consistent with our expectations of relativity at exactly the same time.

So, to summarise and to specifically reiterate two startling propositions: firstly, the log function of a statistical distribution type might give us some insight into the causal nature of the information or data that underlies it and, secondly, information might be a construct that negates the laws of relativity via the notion of entanglement.

Table 16.1   The possible relationship between information and causality

Distribution Log Function Conic Section Type	Type of Causality in Underlying Data Set
Circle	Acausal
Ellipse	Acausal
Parabola	Partially causal
Hyperbola	Causal
Straight Line	Entangled

What Does Barabási Have to Say?

You may remember that we introduced the work of Albert-László Barabási earlier in this chapter and his particular focus on the power law characteristic of the Web. In fact Barabási has a broader interest in power laws and has written widely on the subject. In his 2011 book *Bursts*, he specifically tackles such phenomena in relation to the nature of human activity and attempts to define the properties of such laws than make such activity different to, say, that of the random motion reported by Robert Brown in 1828. Brown was a British botanist who had noticed that pollen that fell in dew drops underwent jittery, irregular motion. What is particularly strange about Brown's observation is that the pollen never stops moving,[98] a phenomenon that was later explained by the continual movement of water atoms surrounding the pollen grains. The motion that Barabási studies does not behave like the grains, however. True, his studies do find periods of apparently localised random motion but these are interspersed with rare periods where such motion is not so randomly characteristic. During these period, or 'bursts' as Barabási chooses to call them, atypical journeys of much longer distance than normal are encountered, hence moving the more commonly localised activity away from its last setting. Such burstyness, according to Barabási, is a key hallmark of power law behaviour and he has spent a significant amount of time trying to understand its causes.

One such explanation that Barabási offers relates to prioritisation, in that he has been able to show that power law behaviour can be generated when activities on a list are assigned a level of importance at random and then dealt with in accordance with that importance. If the procedure for doing this is tuned right then lower level priorities items or tasks mount up as the occasional high priority items hit the list and are attended to first. This hence explains the prominence of low value data instances in any data set governed by a power law. It is interesting that Barabási should pick on priority a key differentiator in his power law studies, however, as this leads to a question that asks what drives such prioritisation? Although not make explicit in his book, he infers that the some form of deliberate choice is made by those involved and that prioritisation is somehow the outcome of an act of human will and hence requires intelligence. This might indeed be the case with power laws solely associated with human activity, but it does not account for occurrences in cases where human activity is not involved, such as in the case of the sizes of earthquakes, craters on the moon and of solar flares, the foraging pattern of various species or the sizes of activity patterns of neuronal populations. Indeed a great many power law distributions have been conjectured in recent years but much debate remains as to which of these tails are actually power law distributed and which are not. Regardless, obviously prioritisation is something that cannot exist in isolation and this could be significant. There must be something to be prioritised and something to create the need for priority, so, at the very least, two entities or concepts must be involved. It is like one thing attracting another as if connected by rubber bands. The stronger the band and the tension between the two entities, the stronger the desire to act, the stronger the priority to change from one current state and move to another.

The Validity of Physical Comparison

This is all clearly heading to a conclusion, a conclusion that synthetic gravity might exist in large connected collections of information such as that found on the Web. But one question still remains. Gravity in the real world is overly obvious, or at least to us as humans. It sticks out feet to the floor and stops everything dear to us from floating off into space for instance. So why is gravity not as obvious on the Web?

Actually it is, or rather it might be if we were comparing apples with apples. Think about the physical world in terms of the constituents from which it is made. At the subatomic level each atom is composed from a relatively small range of particle types. Decrease the magnification and focus on the atoms themselves and again we find that there to be a rather small number of atom types – specifically from the periodic table which currently only lists one hundred and eighteen elements in total. Furthermore, each of these elements can only mix and react with all other elements in a relatively small number of ways. That gives us the various molecules and compounds that make up the world around us. These can only interact in accordance with the known laws of physics in a finite number of ways – or so we believe- and such interactions ultimately dictate the ways in which our world is observed to be 'real'. Now, follow the same thought process with the Web. True, the Web is only constructed from a small number of technologies; the IP protocol of its underlying Internet, HTML for Web pages and so on. Also true that there are few fundamental rules that dictate how the Web fits together – that's ultimately what makes it so flexible. But think about the end result of combining just those few technologies and protocols with what essentially amounts to naked human imagination and the combinatorial effect results in and almost infinite number of possible outputs. But why add human imagination at this point and what does it actually mean? Well, the Web allows us to mix up thoughts in the form of written language, images, audio and alike, does it not? And each of these essentially amounts to a mechanism for capturing human experience and expression, right? Hence the Web's embodiment is also built from a set of richly expressive syntaxes that have evolved over many millions of years' worth or human interaction and communication. They are as complex as they are comprehensive and as expressive as they are exquisite. This is the predominant reason why the Web is poorly understood. Most who think they understand the Web do not. They will tell you that it is made up of a morass of 'unstructured' data that manifests itself as a massive yet simple blob of human outpouring. An outpouring it may well be, but simple it is not. What such 'experts' are really doing is comparing the Web to the type of data structures common in contemporary computer science. Such structures are often known as relational data and they conform to a small and well-understood set of structuring rules based on set theory and Boolean logic. In such structures all data is given its specific place to live and is provided with specific and simple relationships to all other data within the structure – hence the name 'relational'. Navigation through such data is strictly by the relationships defined between the data types present and by no other means. Build a large collection of such data and store it in a 'single location' and we get what computer scientists affectionately refer to as a relational database. Such databases can indeed be large and can become complex, but the level of complexity involved is many times less than that found on even the most simple of Web pages. Tell your average computer scientists this and the chances are that they will laugh at you, but confidence can soon be displaced when one simple fact is explained. Even the most lacking of students can learn the basics behind building a relational database in a couple of months. Give them a couple of years and the chances are that they will even be earning a good living from it. Even so, take someone who is illiterate and ask them to learn a modern language from scratch and we are talking about many months' worth of hard effort, of not years to get to grip with the grammars, vocabularies, abbreviations and so on involved. Furthermore get involved in the underlying subtleties of natural language and it is easy to soak up a lifetime and still not succeed. Try writing a sonnet or a couplet, for example.

The point is that natural language on its own is complex, but add it to other means of communicating information, such as image and sound, and phenomenal complexity is produced. But this is not some kind of random complexity. Natural language embodies many thousands upon thousands of rules and every one adds to creating structure. Thus every word, every sentence and every paragraph contain lots of structure, very precise and specific structure designed to interact precisely with the immediate context of the reader. Put such text on the Web and not only can it create a very intimate and personal relationship with the user, but it also makes the Web a specifically complex and well-structured entity. It is so structured in fact that we cannot take it all in without considerable help. The algorithms underlying search engines like Google, for instance, are amongst the most algorithmically complicated to be found anywhere.

There is a still further twist in the Web's complexity which adds yet another multiplier to the equation. But to understand this and use it to compare the Web with physical reality requires a reasonable dose of philosophy. The anthropomorphic view of the universe states that it could not exist at all without humankind's involvement. The argument goes that for the universe to be present it needs some mechanism by which it can be described, and that implies some form of human involvement in the description process. Furthermore, even if the universe were not described by human hand – as if charted automatically by some intelligent machine for example – human involvement would still be needed for that machine, or the machine that created that machine to be crafted in the first place. Get the idea it's rather serf-serving and circular? Even more surreal, take us out of the picture altogether and replace humankind with some form of alien life doing the describing and still the universe would not exist because although the aliens might do a fine job of describing the universe; whatever they produce would solely be their interpretation, constructed solely for their purposes. It would be their view of the universe and not ours. Therefore there would be no guarantee that such a description would have any relevance to the concept of human sensation – sight, touch, hearing and so on – as aliens might experience their surroundings in totally different ways to us. Thus, for all intents and purposes it would be useless and the anthropomorphic interpretation of physics is hardwired to have humans at the centre. It is purpose-built for our use and in that regard it is context specific at the level of the human race. The Web is also context specific, but at a much finer granularity and in much more dynamic ways. The laws of physics are static and locked, but the Web is much more organic. It evolves and oozes, ebbs and flows, creaks and groans as the demands of public attention pull on it in an ever increasing number of ways. Consequently Web pages can change to reflect the needs of the individual at any point instance and that takes us beyond any strict anthropomorphic interpretation: the Web is not humankind-centric, it is individual-centric in many ways, right down to every last man, woman and child. This gives not one plausible interpretation of the Web, but many millions, if not billions upon billions. Think about that a moment: one anthropomorphic interpretation of the world based on a relatively small set of rules and structures, as opposed to a billions of different views of the Web based on an extremely complex set of rules, structures and contexts.

If indeed such a comparison between the Web and the physical world were relevant, might there not at least be room in the many Web interpretations for at least one to fit with something close to the anthropomorphic interpretation of physics? Some might agree, while others might think this to be a proposition too far. But who? Certainly not the physicists. Contemporary physics is full of ideas in which a single view of the universe plays off against many other interpretations. Indeed some have even been empirically proven. Take the concept of antimatter, for example. The physics community was treated to many revelations in the early part of the twentieth century, not least of which was Paul Dirac's discovery of antimatter. In 1928 he Paul Dirac realised that his relativistic version of the Schrödinger wave equation for electrons could be seen as predicting two types of matter – the classical atoms from which our normal experiences are built and their exact opposites in terms of electrical charge. Such opposites were coined 'antimatter' and were duly discovered by Carl D. Anderson in 1932. Because of its opposite charge to standard matter, antimatter composes positrons – a contraction of 'positive electrons' and antielectrons. Although Dirac did not himself use the term antimatter, its use follows on naturally enough from antielectrons, antiprotons and so on.

On its own the concept of antimatter might plausibly seem anecdotally supportive of comparing the Web with the real world, but there is still more convincing support from the world of physics. The 'multiverse' hypothesis is a theory taken very seriously in contemporary research. This proposes a hypothetical set of multiple possible universes – of which our universe is only one – that come together to comprise everything that physically exists: the entirety of space and time, all forms of matter, energy and momentum, and the physical laws and constants that govern them. The term was coined in 1895 by the American philosopher and psychologist William James, the various universes within the multiverse being sometimes referred to as parallel universes.

The structure of the multiverse, the nature of each universe within it and the relationship between the various constituent universes depend on the specific multiverse hypothesis considered. Multiverses have been hypothesised in cosmology, physics, astronomy, philosophy, transpersonal psychology and fiction, particularly in science fiction and fantasy. In these contexts, parallel universes are also called 'alternative universes', 'quantum universes', 'interpenetrating dimensions', 'parallel dimensions', 'parallel worlds', 'alternative realities' and 'alternative timelines', among others.

One Last Helping Hand from the Fish: Spin Glass, Eccentricity and Curie's Law

But wait one moment. All this theorising may be great fun but it really gets us nowhere without a framework within which it can be meaningfully discussed. So let us create such a framework and to do that we shall visit our fish tank analogy one last time.

Recall that when we last visited our fish we had done them a great injustice, first by taking away their tank and then, rather rudely, replacing them by atoms moving at speed. This time unfortunately we have an equally unjust to trick to play, for we still have to keep the tank at a safe distance and this time replace the fish not with atoms, but with Minkowski cones, as last discussed in Chapter 14, to represent our information and computation in geometric terms. By doing so we get a representation like that shown in Figure 16.16.

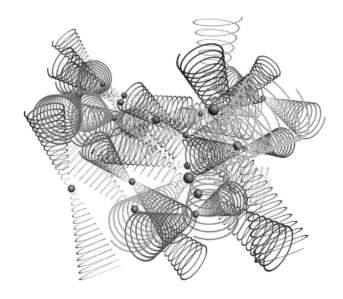

Figure 16.16   Multiple Minkowski cones providing a 'random'
interference pattern

Cast any object – such as a plane – through such a collection of cones, so as to capture any relevancies of the collective and the pattern produced through such an object's intersection is bound to appear jumbled, if not completely random. Essentially, with the various cones being independent of one and other, their overlap will be intensely complex, thereby giving the impression of randomness.

This is the type of formation we might expect to find in any random collection of Web pages. Each will have its own subject matter, intent and target audience. In essence each is shouting out its own message independently and offering its own set of potentials for interpretation. Collect a number of such messages together and it will be like a crowd of focused salesmen all intent on selling their own wares. Add them together and their individual stories will be drowned in a sea of noise. No individual message will get through. But that does not mean to say that the capability to create a coherent message is not present. Such 'noise' is not unlike the physical characteristic present in a range of materials typically known as spin glasses. These are highly disordered magnetic systems with competing ferromagnetic and anti-ferromagnetic interactions as found in some alloys, like copper/magnesium. When a typically ferromagnetic[7] material,

---

7   Read 'normal' magnet here.

like iron, is magnetised by an external magnetic field, electron spins are aligned with the direction of that field. When a spin glass is magnetised, however, the internal forces appear quite random, a state physicists call 'glassy'.[40] This glassy quality is not really random at all but is merely complex to the point where easily recognisable patterns are obscured. So, in much the same way as the Web, spin glasses are a maelstrom of interactions that accumulate and cross over to create many higher orders of observable complexity. To the uneducated observer this complexity might just appear as random magnetic noise, when, in fact, something far richer and far more interesting is going on. The atomic scale disorder in spin glasses means that such materials are a complex mixture of positive and negative feedbacks as their atoms try to align their spins in parallel with some neighbours but opposite to others.

Interestingly it is time dependence that really distinguishes spin glasses from other magnetic systems. In particular if a spin glass is heated to above its transition temperature (Tc) – where it exhibits more typical magnetic behaviour, and if an external magnetic field is applied, the resultant plot of magnetisation against temperature follows the typical curve found with more normal magnetic substances. This follows a phenomenon discovered by the French physicist Pierre Curie, which states that magnetisation in glassy materials is inversely proportional to temperature until Tc is reached, at which point the magnetisation becomes virtually constant – a property referred to as 'field cooled magnetisation'. When the external field is removed, the spin glass has a rapid decrease of magnetisation to a value referred to as its remnant magnetisation. This is followed by a slow decay as the magnetisation approaches zero or some small fraction of the original value – a complex phenomenon that is particular to spin glass. If a similar procedure were followed for a standard ferromagnetic substance, when the external field is removed, there would be a rapid change to a remnant value, but this value is a constant in time. For a material like a paramagnet,[8] when the external field is removed, the magnetisation rapidly goes to zero. In each case, the change is very rapid and if carefully examined it has exponential decay with a very small time constant.

If instead, the spin glass is cooled below Tc in the absence of an external field, and then a field is applied, there is a rapid increase to a the level of magnetisation, which is less than the field-cooled magnetisation, followed by a slow upward drift toward the field-cooled value.

---

8   A magnet made of a substance whose magnetisation is proportional to the strength of the magnetic field applied to it.

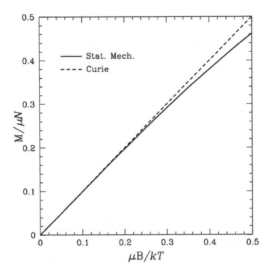

Figure 16.17   Magnetisation of a paramagnet as a function of inverse temperature

Interestingly a great deal of early theoretical work on spin-glasses has been used in a form of 'mean field theory', a particular branch of science aimed at describing many-body or multi-agent systems involving complex interactions. The goal of mean field theory is therefore to resolve combinatorial problems in such systems.[2]

The main idea of mean field theory is to replace all the interactions with any given entity in a system with an average of effective interaction. This effectively reduces multi-body issues into a single-entity problem. The ease of solving complex problems using mean field theory means that some insight into the behaviour of complex systems can be achieved at a relatively low cost.[2]

An influential exactly-solvable model of a spin-glass has been produced which has led to considerable theoretical extensions of mean field theory to model the slow dynamics of the magnetisation, and the complex non-ergodic[9] equilibrium state systems. The same variant of mean field theory has also been

---

9   Attribute of a behaviour that is in certain crucial respects incomprehensible through observation either for lack of repetition, for example, by involving only transient states which are unique, or for lack of stabilities, for example, when transition probabilities (see probabilities) are so variable that there are not enough observations available to ascertain them. . Evolution and social processes involving structural changes are inherently non-ergodic.

applied in the study of neural networks,[10] where it has enabled calculations of properties such as the storage capacity of simple neural network architectures without requiring implementation of a training algorithm. Such practices have also now been directly applied to the Web and have proved useful in the producing new methods for extracting information and predicting such properties as growth dynamics, connectivity distribution and the scaling exponents.[2]

Now imagine the Web as if it were a spin glass without any assistance from an external heat source or magnetic field. In this state it would be just as a spin glass in similar circumstances, all complex and mixed up with differing alignments all working at cross purposes. To most it would quite simply appear as a jumbled up mess. Next consider placing the Web under the equivalent of heat and magnetism. This would not actually be hard to do. Think of human motivation as the replacement for heat – the drive to achieve or retain something, for example – and think of some common cause as the magnetic field producing such drive. Indeed, both of these are together are akin to Barabási's prioritisation theory focused at human group level. To assist with this take an extreme example, purely for illustrative purposes. Take the fight for personal survival as the motivation and some world crisis as the cause behind this motivation. Think of a world war, a significant famine, drought or the global spread of some significant disease. All will do just so long as they are substantive enough to drive a reaction from a significant proportion of the world's population. Now ask yourself what might happen and how might the Web behave?

The answer is both overly obvious and strikingly insightful. Those affected with access to the Web will reach out to for advice and those with the technical knowhow to advise will do so for personal gain or for the betterment of society as a whole. In essence the Web will line up and the individuals and sites involved will behave as if part of a magnet. The Web will prioritise significantly and power laws behaviour will dominate to actively assist this process. Indeed we see this today in less extreme forms such as on social networking sites and the blogosphere. Here authority appears to be the attractor, with studies showing that it has influence over the numbers of readers received and inbound links created. Social networks, or at least those on the Web, do not overt classical

---

10 Artificial neural networks are made up of interconnecting artificial neurons (programming constructs that mimic the properties of biological neurons). Artificial neural networks may either be used to gain an understanding of biological neural networks, or for solving artificial intelligence problems without necessarily creating a model of a real biological system.

randomness. Furthermore, research has shown that there are lots of blogs with few inbound links and not very many blogs with lots of inbound links – a classical power law trait, and the numbers change by some exponential power. With more inbound links, traffic to more authoritative blogs grows faster, the blogs rank higher in search results and the whole cycle becomes self-reinforcing. The Web is also 'sticky', in that it likes to preserve links once created, and thus naturally supports this self-reinforcement. Link to any given blog or social network and the chances are that the ongoing affiliation created will be non-negotiable. Even if mechanisms are available by which you can disassociate yourself, your details will have been captured and your association noted, even perhaps by some Web resource external to the site itself. This outlines a golden rule on the Web in that once data is 'out there' it might as well be consider as being out there forever! This is the equivalent of not being able to resist the 'pull' of the Web once interest is shown. It is literally like being caught in a gravitational field were the effort to overcome the attraction is simply too great once under its influence.

There is, of cause, a practical limit to this self-reinforcement, as the number of blogs, sites or whatever, though very large, is ultimately finite. Thus the Web cannot swallow up 'all' information and thus overpower the informational content of the very universe itself! But its capability to 'attract' is indeed significant and certainly enough to form the basis for some very serious study. Furthermore this type of behaviour should not be dismissed out of hand. We know the Web to exhibit power law behaviour and similar behaviours are almost universal across physics. Power-law relations characterise a staggering number of naturally occurring phenomena, and this is one of the principal reasons why they have attracted such wide interest. For instance, inverse-square laws, such as gravitation[11] and the Coulomb force,[12] are power laws

Schrödinger's Cat, the 'X'-Shaped Pattern and Many-Worlds Interpretation of Quantum Mechanics

If you have read this book from the start it should hopefully be clear that a story has unfolded. First a discussion was had on various mathematical axioms

---

11 As formulated by Newton.
12 The Coulomb force between two or more charged bodies is the force between them due to Coulomb's law. If the particles are both positively or negatively charged, the force is repulsive; if they are of opposite charge, it is attractive.

and a range of associated schools of representation. This ultimately led to the decision to use geometry as the most appropriate means to describe the concepts that would follow. Through the use of geometry the ' X '-shaped pattern was introduced and from there various patterns were overlaid until eventually we came to the idea of using Minkowski cones and conic sections for discussing relativity and ultimately the meta-properties of large scale informational and computational constructs like the World Wide Web. As part of this journey we laboured on the importance of symmetry in information and computation and the fact that a generalised axiomatic pattern, such as the ' X '-shaped pattern, can be seen as having great descriptive potential. Integral to this discussion was the inclusion of a fourth leg in the pattern to work as an actuator; the external triggering element or impetus that can effect change beyond that encapsulated in any informational or computational entity. If this forth leg is considered hard enough it should become apparent that it is, in fact, similar to a rather famous irritant that has been troubling physicists, and especially quantum physicists, for years.

The 'observation problem' has had the scientific community in turmoil ever since quantum mechanics was first proposed in the early twentieth century. In essence the problem describes a paradox that goes something like this: for the mathematics of quantum mechanics to work there is a need to assume that subatomic particles are instantaneously distributed across all space at any given point in time. In simple terms that means that any one subatomic particle is everywhere all at once and in all possible states. Theoretically this is fine and the mathematics backs up this strange proposition perfectly. Furthermore such mathematics is elegant in that to achieve this bizarre feet it simply considers each subatomic entity to behave like a wave rather than a particle. Even so, when such mathematics is tested through experimentation the wave argument collapses, literally. When someone or something tries to 'see' such waveforms, they instantaneously reject their waveform behaviour and 'appear' as particles in only ever one place at one given time. This still leaves us asking just what subatomic particles actually are: particles, or waveforms or both?

This conundrum was immortalised in the famous thought experiment proposed by the Austrian physicist Erwin Schrödinger in 1935. In this Schrödinger suggested that a cat,[13] along with a flask containing a poison, a

---

13 Nearly everyone who refers to this thought experiment emphasises that the cat is purely theoretical and that no actual felines come to harm during as a result of the experiment being carried out.

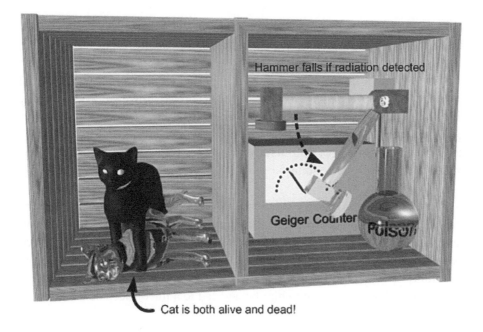

Hammer falls if radiation detected

Geiger Counter

Poison

Cat is both alive and dead!

Figure 16.18   Schrödinger's famous thought experiment

small radioactive source and a Geiger counter are placed in a sealed box shielded against environmentally induced quantum effects. If the Geiger counter detects radiation over whatever period of time that the experiment runs, the flask is shattered, thereby releasing the poison which hence kills the cat. Now, because the box is completely sealed and has no windows, it is impossible to see if, or precisely when, the cat dies. At least, that is, until the box is opened, and herein can be found the paradox. According to the Copenhagen interpretation of quantum mechanics and the concept of superposition, subatomic particles can exist in all their possible states at once. So it is quite legitimate to consider any given radioactive particle as being both having decayed and not decayed at the same time. This obviously follows through to imply that the Geiger counter has both triggered and not triggered at the same time and that Schrödinger's cat is both alive and dead while in the box.

The important point to note here is that until the box is opened and someone actually looks inside, everything in the box can be thought of as being both a waveform and a particle. When that someone interacts with the box's contents through the act of observation, quantum decoherence kicks in and only particles in fixed positions and states can be found. In essence the act of observation behaves so as to actuate change in the system. It is quite literally the fourth leg of the system's ' X '-shaped pattern.

Schrödinger's interpretation of this experiment is significantly different from the ' X '-shaped pattern, as classically interpreted, however. Taken literally there can only ever be one observable outcome in that the cat will either be alive or dead when the box is opened. This is the equivalent to an exclusive OR[14] condition in the tongue of traditional computer science, or in simple terms 'one or the other but not both' states or mortality will be allowed.

But Schrödinger's interpretation is not the only legitimate way to look at the cat's fate. At the age of twenty four the young quantum physicist Hugh Everett first proposed the many-worlds interpretation of quantum physics, which he called his 'relative state' formulation. This flew in the face of conventional quantum mechanics and initially led to great scorn from his contemporaries[15] – something that those close to him believe led to a life of deep self-doubt and depression.

Although several versions of the many-worlds interpretation have been proposed since Hugh Everett's original work, they all contain one key idea in that the equations of physics which model the time evolution of systems without embedded observers are sufficient for modelling systems which do contain observers. In essence they play down the role of 'switching' in a computation

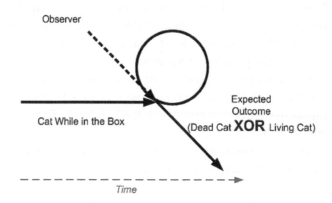

Figure 16.19   A strict Schrödinger interpretation of his famous thought experiment

---

14 Read XOR.
15 Including Niels Bohr, whom he met in the spring of 1959.

view of the universe and play up the potential for multiple output types. In particular the many-worlds view removes the need to respect observation-triggered wave function collapse, as the Copenhagen interpretation of quantum mechanics proposes. Or more precisely, an observation trigger may be present but it has no material impact on the capability of a waveform to continue its existence of holding all possible states at any given time. This means that once the lid is lifted from Schrödinger's box, his cat is allowed to continue on as being both alive and dead without any negative effect on the 'reality' of the universe. This might sound absolutely crazy, but apart from being extremely abstract, Everett's thinking is remarkably sound. To allow Schrödinger's cat both life and death simultaneously, Everett suggested that reality is not made up from just one universe, but rather many, so many in fact that an almost infinite number of universes are allowed to exist in parallel. Each time a computation occurs in the universe and multiple options exist for how that computation might change things, the universe, or Everett's imagination of the universe at least, actually splits off into several parallel universes to accommodate all possible outcomes. Thus when the cat's box is opened the universe splits in two according to Everett. In one of these universes the cat lives on quite happily while in the other it is destined never to purr again.

In this interpretation every event is a branch point; the cat is both alive and dead, even before the box is opened, but the 'alive' and 'dead' cats are in different branches of the universe, both of which are equally real, but which cannot interact with each other.[87]

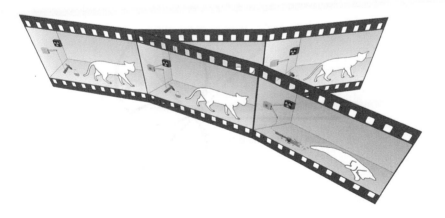

Figure 16.20   Schrödinger's cat' paradox according to the many-worlds interpretation

Thus the many-worlds interpretation is supremely accommodating by allowing all valid computational states of the universe to coexist at once. In such a view our existence merely becomes built from a series of steps through what followers of Everett's ideas call the 'multiverse' of all possible states and positions. This inherently turns our interpretation of reality into a single lens on a much greater reality created from the interaction of a huge collection of wave functions rather than their collapsed quantum states as particles. The majority of the multiverse is simply not visible to us as a consequence of its constant splitting, although it is as theoretically real as anything we care to think of as real in 'our world'. No one has yet provided a definitive answer as to why anything other than our one reality in the multiverse is evident, but there is plenty of reasoning to suggest that such a multiverse is out there. One possible reason for such a singular view of reality could be that all other parallel universes are completely symmetrical, both computationally and informationally, with respect to all our various observation points. This would be entirely complimentary to the notion of the ' X '-shaped pattern and the metapatterns that arise from it.

Indeed the many-worlds interpretation is highly complementary to the ' X '-shaped, itself being a metatheory. It is hence independent of any physical models that underlie it or might be associated with it. Given that the theory is linear with respect to the wave functions over which it is concerned, the exact form of the quantum dynamics modelled, be it the non-relativistic Schrödinger equation, relativistic quantum field theory or some form of quantum gravity or string theory, does not alter the validity of the many-worlds interpretation.

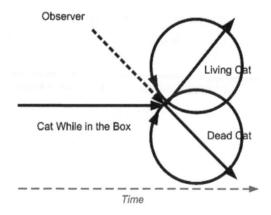

Figure 16.21   An ' X '-shaped representation of the many-worlds'
interpretation of Schrödinger's cat paradox

It is hence applicable to all linear quantum theories,[87] and given that there is no experimental evidence for any non-linearity of the wave function in physics yet, this makes the many-worlds interpretation particularly interesting and valid for now.

Saving Possibly the Most Tantalising Evidence until Last

At this point we need to take one final pause and remind ourselves again about the core idea of this book; the idea that the synthetic nature of the Web might somehow be linked to some of the most fundamental ideas underpinning the physical universe . To test this conjecture we have visited many of the most mysterious and impenetrable ideas in physics today. But still there are more mysteries left, mysteries that the world's best minds believe to be important but have yet to fathom their significance and precise relevance. One such mystery has held the attention of both physicists and mathematicians for many years and dates back to Leonhard Euler's[16] work in the eighteenth century on number theory and a critical mathematical function[17] of his discovery. This was later followed up by Bernhard Riemann's, again a famous mathematician, who, in a memoir in 1859, established a relation between the points at which Euler's function equates to zero and the distribution of prime numbers. Over time Riemann's paper grew in importance and for that reason the underlying mathematical theory has adopted his name and has attracted almost unprecedented interest. Despite this, a proof for the hypothesis associated with Riemann's relation still remains tantalisingly out of reach.

What the Riemann hypothesis says is that the non-trivial zeros of the Riemann Zeta function – his linkage to prime number distribution – all have a real part equal to 1/2. Broadly speaking, this suggests that there is an underlying order, akin to musical harmonics, in the way prime numbers are distributed. So, it is known that for any given number n there are approximately $n / \log n$ prime numbers that are less than its value. The formula is not exact, however, but it is close enough to get mathematicians excited, and because of this Riemann looked at the errors in prediction this relationship produces and found that they contain periodicities. His hypothesis quantifies and formalises this discovery, concluding that the points at which his equation equates to zero can be regarded as the harmonic frequencies in the distribution of primes.[88]

---

16 Leonhard Euler was a pioneering Swiss mathematician and physicist.
17 Generally referred to as the Euler product formula.

Notice, however, something very important about Riemann's hypothesis in that it only works for non-trivial zeros, and an explanation of 'non-trivial' is due in this context. In crude terms, numbers can be split into types or groups, typically referred to as number systems. These are arranged in a precise hierarchy, much like the arrangement of skins in an onion or figures inside a Russian doll, and this arrangement can be shown as follows:

Table 16.2   The arrangement of the number systems

Number System	Examples
Naturals ($\mathbb{N}$)	0, 1, 2, 3, 4, 5, 6, 7, ..., n
Integers ($\mathbb{Z}$)	$-n$, ..., -5, -4, -3, -2, -1, 0, 1, 2, 3, 4, 5, ..., n
Positive Integers	1, 2, 3, 4, 5, ..., n
Rationals ($\mathbb{Q}$)	a/b where a and b are integers and b is not zero
Reals ($\mathbb{R}$)	A rational number or the limit of a convergent sequence of rational numbers
Complex Numbers ($\mathbb{C}$)	$a + bi$ where a and b are real numbers and i is the square root of –1

In set terms this hierarchy can be written as $\mathbb{N} \subset \mathbb{Z} \subset \mathbb{Q} \subset \mathbb{R} \subset \mathbb{C}$. That is to say that each number system is a proper subset of the next system.

For our immediate purposes the most important number system to focus on is the complex number system ($\mathbb{C}$) at the bottom of the stack. We need concentrate on this system because it introduces a very special number indeed, namely $- i$, which is mathematically equivalent to $\sqrt{-1}$.

i is special for a very good reason in that mathematically it breaks all the rules. Quite literally, there is no square route of -1, and thus i has no proper place in the realm of quantities that can be calculated accorded to all the known and trusted axioms of common or garden number crunching. For precisely that reason it is most often referred to as being the 'imaginary' unit. But imaginary or not it is still very much needed for more advanced mathematics to break free of the limits of 'normal' numbers and for this reason i is tolerated without objection under most circumstances. In effect i gives mathematicians another degree of freedom within which to work. It adds another dimension, almost for the sake of it, just as we did with the ' X '-shaped pattern in Chapter 8. Add this dimension and the Russian doll of number systems extends beyond the triviality of mere calculation, thereby allowing mathematical imagination to be formally included in the workings of contemporary theories. Constraining such imagination and putting it to good use is a non-trivial task, however, and for this reason complex numbers ($\mathbb{C}$), or those numbers containing a certain amount of $\sqrt{-1}$, or i, are sometimes referred to as being 'non-trivial'. Such non-trivial numbers are essential to the workings of both Riemann's zeta equation and its notoriously illusive and accompanying hypothesis. This is important for us as Riemann fundamentally had to do the same thing we did to get a full theory in place. He added an extra dimension, which in his case was an imaginary dimension in the strictest mathematical sense. But once that dimension was in place Riemann's work was transformed from something particularly clever into something so mystical and profound that many of the world's geniuses still marvel at it today.

The Zeta function is not just some mathematical puzzle though, as it is proving to be of fascinating and frustrating value to science as well. Frustrating that is because scientists now know that it can tell them many things about the way that the real world works, but as yet they have no real idea why. Science is used to such frustration, however, and has almost always known that there are deep and intricate relationships between the truths it seeks and the cold innards of mathematics. But there are very few examples that illustrate this maddening relationship better than Riemann's Zeta function. It is both beautiful and beguiling to the trained eye, be that the eye of a scientist or a mathematician, it makes very little difference. One remarkable example of such beauty can be found in the studies of the physicist Michael Berry and his colleagues. They have found that there is a deep connection between the harmonics[18] of Riemann's zeros and the allowable energy states of physical systems that are on the border between the quantum world and the everyday atomic world. This suggests that Riemann's equation behaves exactly like the energy levels[19] in quantum systems that would classically be considered as being chaotic. This deep connection between number theory and the physics of the real universe, if upheld, is utterly astonishing. If the Riemann hypothesis is proved to be true it could open an entirely new window on the nature of reality and the relationship between the abstract worlds of mathematics, information and the behaviour of matter and energy.[88]

---

18 The frequency of a particular property or event.
19 A stationary state of a physical system characterised by its having or being able to have a fixed quantity of energy. Quantum mechanics assumes that physical systems can only exist in a well-defined set of energy levels. The emission of electromagnetic radiation is associated with transitions of electronic and molecular systems between energy levels.

Information and indeed the World Wide Web fit into this new insight for two very clear reasons. Firstly it goes without saying that information, computation and mathematics are intimately linked – large parts of this book have been dedicated to articulating that very point. Secondly there is a strong and well understood relationship between Riemann's Zeta function and Zipf's Law, the undisputed king of mathematical laws on the Web. Originally Zipf's Law related to the observation of Harvard linguist George Kingsley Zipf which stated that the frequency of use of the nth-most-frequently-used word in any natural language text is inversely proportional to n. However, this relationship is based on the assumption that the natural language vocabulary in use is bounded and finite. Try and allow for a vocabulary of infinite size and the mathematics simply breaks down. This is because the sum of all values produced by such and infinite series of words itself equates to an infinite value; dictated by a famous mathematical equation knows as the harmonic thus:

$$\sum_{n=1}^{\infty} \frac{1}{n} = \infty$$

All the same there is a mathematical way to approximate Zipf's Law for infinite vocabularies and that involves substituting Riemann's Zeta function for the harmonic series.

$$\sum_{n=1}^{\infty} \frac{1}{n^s} = \infty$$

Notice that the difference between the two equations is subtle, with the Zeta only having the addition of an exponent - s - about the denominator n. Set $s = 1$ and we find that the Zeta function and the harmonic series are identical. Set s to a value very close to one and we produce a series that will converge to a finite value. This gets over the killer problem of infinity when dealing with unbounded vocabularies and intimately weds the findings of Riemann's work with those of Zipf's. In fact, in many ways, Riemann's Zeta function and Zipf's Law are synonymous. And by immediate implication and hard empirical evidence, the Web is bonded to that relationship as well.

Notice also the twist that brought the Zeta function into play with Zipf's law. Restrict the vocabulary involved and Zipf's Law works just fine, but remove any such restriction and Riemann's perspective needs to take over: constrained to unconstrained, absolute to relative, random distribution to power law, do you see the theme flowing through? The melding of pure Zipf with pure Riemann leads to a relativistic model with trusted empirical evidence taken directly from the Web.

All the hard maths aside, there is one final similarity that shines through. Easily the most significant hypothesis in this book proposes that unconstrained information and computation can be seen to spin out into a metapattern not dissimilar to that of a Minkowski cone. This is further followed up by the suggestion that various types of conic section through such a cone might reveal interesting, and possibly emergent, metabehaviours arising from the individual informational and computational units involved. Because of this we have danced around the rather large conjecture by trying to find ways to suggest that gravity might be one of these metabehaviours. But wait, we now know that the Web can be linked to the Zeta function with relative ease and we know that there is some very good reasoning is in place to suggests that the Zeta function can indeed be used to describe borderline conditions between quantum descriptions of reality and classically atomic equivalents, so what might be the similarities between the Zeta function and the ideas laid out in this book?

Remember the favoured branch of mathematics we adopted early on to describe our ideas? That branch was geometry so, of course, it is correct to wonder if the Zeta function itself can also be described in geometric terms. As it turns out, this is precisely the case and the outputs from such a description have undeniably added great value as mathematicians have tried to listen in to what the Zeta function is trying to say. Given that the Zeta is a complicated beast, when we interrogate it properly it should come as no surprise it can throw up different many geometric graphs, all of which tell us something different. Looking across this catalogue of geometric descriptions turns up a number of particularly interesting coincidences. Before discussing such coincidences it is important to note one thing, however, in that most mathematical functions can be represented geometrically; that's general knowledge and is commonly referred as a function's 'plot'. Essentially, therefore, each plot acts like a kind of geometric fingerprint of its algebraic master, thereby translating the abstract nature its mathematics into something very visual. Some mathematicians hate this approach, believing that it detracts from the very essence of what they are trying to describe and unnecessarily promotes intuition. But, on the whole, their numbers are small and such intuition is considered to be an essential tool of the trade.[20] Of course, if we work hard enough, we will most

---

20 For instance the brilliant but eccentric mathematician Theodor Estermann wrote a book entitled *Complex Numbers and Functions* which contains just two diagrams because of his disdain for

likely find a family of functions that share the same geometric fingerprint or something very similar, but the important thing to note is that each function in this family will be different. Furthermore, if a particular function can be interpreted in several ways that obviously increases the chances of the family of equations with similar plots being smaller. Thus the Zeta function is rather special. There are mathematical functions that can produce similar plots to those of the Zeta's many mathematical characteristics, but the likelihood of a another function getting close across a range of different plots is close to nil.[21] Hence, working on the principle that a geometric similarity on one plot associated with the Zeta function is a coincidence, two is fluke and three or more points towards some form of connection, then it might be possible to make a valid comparison can be made between various Zeta plots and the ideas presented earlier in this book.

First let's look at a particularly well-known plot of the Zeta function's argument plane. This is shown below and is used to highlight all the function's complex argument values that produce results that are either wholly real or wholly imaginary. To understand this properly consider that the general form of a complex number is $n + mi$ where n is the real part or the number and m is the multiplier of the imaginary unit – that is to say the imaginary part of the number. Now consider setting n or m to zero. That essentially removes one of the two number types making up a complex number. Thus the plot below shows the argument values that drive out zero values of n or m in the function's output. Also notice a curious thing in that there is a repeating geometric pattern as we traverse vertically up or down the imaginary vertical axis away from the horizontal real axis. This is most acute around the line $real = \frac{1}{2}$[22] and looks strikingly similar to the ' X '-shaped pattern. Granted this may be pure coincidence, but for the doubters ask a simple question: why four spokes fanning out from a single point? It could just as easily be two of 1 million.

Next let's look at probably the most famous plot of the Zeta function. This is presented below and shows the outputs of the Zeta function that come from taking all the possible arguments that fall on the vertical line $real = \frac{1}{2}$. In other words this is the plot that is produced by following the straight line on the

---

mathematical 'intuition.'
21 This excludes that fact that Euler's product formula is equivalent to Riemann's Zeta function.
22 To those familiar with Cartesian geometry it might be easier to think of this as $x = \frac{1}{2}$, although this is purely an analogy in this case.

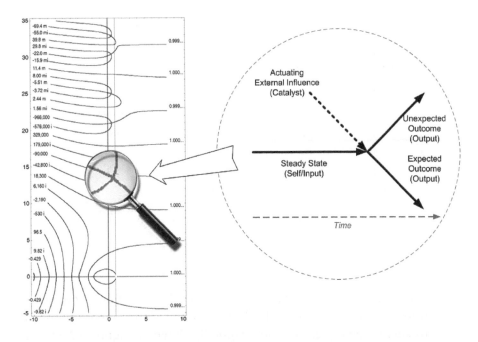

Figure 16.22   The argument plane of Riemann's Zeta function, showing points that it 'sends to' the real and imaginary axes.[89] This frequently shows a remarkable resemblance to the ' X '-Shaped pattern, first described in Figure 5.3, around what mathematicians refer to as the critical line of the function

argument plot on which all our ' X '-like patterns lie. Look at this carefully and consider the likeness to a swirling hand carefully drawing out a figure eight-shaped pattern much like the $_8X_0$ pattern introduced in Chapter 8. Furthermore imagine this as if an extra dimension had been added and does it not look like a Minkowski cone viewed almost as if from below or above? Again for the doubters, ask why a spiralling pattern and why centred on one, and only one, particular point?

Lastly let's visit a particular plot relating to the proof of Riemann's hypothesis – namely that the above plot will pass through zero an infinite number of times and that all the arguments producing this intersection have $real = \frac{1}{2}$. Interestingly in 1901 the mathematician Helge Von Koch showed that if this the hypothesis were true then the number of prime numbers below a certain figure must equal $Li(x) + O(\sqrt{x} \log x)$. This is a particularly hard mathematical equation to explain to anyone with anything less than an all-

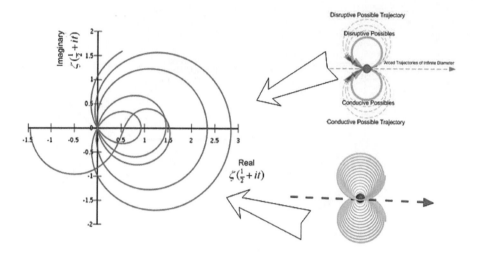

**Figure 16.23   The value plane of Riemann's Zeta function, showing
points that come from the critical line.[89] This shows and uncanny
resemblance to the representations originally shown in Figures 8.3 and 8.4**

consuming interest in higher mathematics, but fortunately for us we do not
need to understand the specifics. The only important thing is to understand
that it is an equation of two very distinct parts, one of which is obviously
$O(\sqrt{x}\log x)$. This is commonly known as the Derbyshire function and can be
seen as the horizontal parabola[23] in Figure 16.24.

Now, one last time for the doubters, why should a function that is so
obviously mathematically eccentric play a critical role in proving or disproving
the worth of Riemann's Zeta function? Why not a straight line or a sine wave, a
squiggle or any other formation from an inordinate number of possible plots?

Admittedly, and at the end of the day, all we have here is conjecture,
coincidence and intuition, but the similarities are tantalising at the very least.
Furthermore it would be foolish to play down the significance of Riemann's
Zeta function. Not only is it proving to be one of the hardest objects in all
contemporary mathematics to crack, but its subtleties are starting to light up

---

23 The other squiggly line on the diagram is $\sqrt{x}\log x$. Hence O is the mathematical function that
bounds $\sqrt{x}\log x$ – think of it like a prison cell in which the equation is doomed to play out its
existence for eternity.

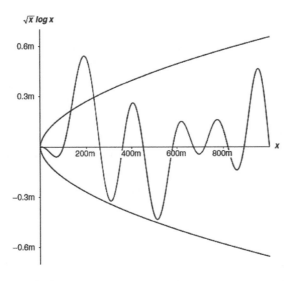

Figure 16.24 The Derbyshire function, which algebraically is $O(\sqrt{x}\log x)$ and was used in Von Koch's 1901 theorem. This is a key tool in the proof that the non-trivial zeros of Riemann's Zeta function go on forever[89]

many, often unexpected, fields of modern science. Because of this, those gifted enough to gaze at the Zeta's full power also appreciate that it may well be pivotal to the way in which reality works at some fundamental and profound level; a level that has hitherto evaded description and is perhaps even beyond the reach of physical detection. By this fundamental involvement, there also follows the implication of the overwhelming pervasiveness of the function, and that, therefore, makes it a perfectly legitimate target for association with all naturally occurring phenomena. Most might consider the Web as a being synthetic and man-made, and therefore a contrived object, but it is not. No single man, group, nation or enterprise controls the Web in its totality. This makes it holistically natural to the point where discussions about engineering influence become pointless and hollow. The Web waxes and wanes, it evolves and mutates, it is natural in all relevant respects and hence it may itself by under the hypnotic spell of the Zeta function.

Interestingly, such pervasiveness has now been demonstrated beyond all reasonable doubt with regard to another key player in our story. Referring back to the work of Albert-László Barabási who, in the late 1990s, first introduced the world to the idea that the Web was not linked in some ideally random or statistically normal way. It was he who banished the bell curve forever and proved that power laws reign. For a while that was enough for Barabási, but he soon saw the same pattern in other networks, as we have already mentioned. Somehow, the collective actions of individual agents – be they Websites, proteins or dating teenagers – generate network architectures that conform to a single well-defined mathematical scheme. This then leads to the question as to how Riemann's Zeta function might corroborate with such a scheme other than through its well-known relationship with Zipf's law. One of Barabási colleagues, Ginestra Biaconi, made an extraordinary leap when she started thinking of nodes in a scale-free network as being analogous to quantum energy levels and the links in such networks as being similarly analogous to electrons that can roam free between such levels. By further thinking about competition between nodes she established the idea of 'fitness' within such networks and, thereby, established a way to vary the level of attraction between nodes and links. This created a model that allowed scale-free networks to evolve under their own control and when she ran such a model she discovered a most remarkable thing. Most of the links gravitated towards the fittest node, the equivalent to the lowest energy level in quantum terms. This, to a physicist, is precisely what happens during the formation of a Bose–Einstein condensate, a bizarre quantum state of matter that forms when atoms are cooled very close to absolute zero. At the time this discovery was both novel and ironic, in that by correcting the scale-free model to make it agree with the everyday competition we see in the world around us we should also reveal the rarest of quantum phenomenon. However, today, scale-free networks, and in particular the Web, have been studied in far greater detail. We now suspect, for example, that phenomena such as Curie's Law might regulate how attraction varies in scale-free environments – almost as if it where heat regulating the jump in and out of some quasi Bose–Einstein state. And we also know that the Web does not just randomly flail around in terms or attraction. Rather it 'clumps' according to a particular ratio of attractiveness as dictated by the mechanics of power laws. What is compelling to the point of striking coincidence, however, is that the Zeta function also predicts such clumping.

At a chance meeting in 1972 between the number theorist Hugh Montgomery and the famous physicist Freeman Dyson a remarkable coincidence was unearthed. Montgomery's work at that time had been into the distribution of the non-trivial zeros in the Zeta, not because of any desire to try and prove or disprove the Riemann Hypothesis, but simply because the distribution was closely aligned with his interest in a particularly deep branch of number theory. At this chance encounter Montgomery, who had never met Dyson before, happened to mention that he had developed a conjecture that the distribution function of zero's distribution had the integral of $1 - (\sin \pi u / \pi u)^2$. Upon hearing this Dyson became very excited and is quoted as saying 'That's the form factor for the pair correlation of eigenvalues of random Hermitian matrices!' To those not versed in higher mathematics or quantum mechanics, such a sentence should strike fear into your heart and rightly so. For our purposes, however, none of the meaning of its content is particularly relevant. What is relevant though is that a particularly eminent quantum physicist should immediately pick up on a property of the Zeta function and its similarity to his own work of the configuration of energy levels in quantum mechanics. To see the real value of this we actually need to roll forward a couple of years and visit the conclusion of some work carried out by Andrew Odlyzko, a young researcher working for AT&T at the time. Based on papers published by Montgomery after his chance meeting with Dyson, Odlyzko poured over the specifics of the coincidence Dyson had spotted. From this came a conjecture that became known as the Mongomery–Odlyzko Law, which can be stated as:

> The distribution of the spacings between successive non-trivial zeros of the Riemann Zeta function (suitably normalised) is statistically identical to the distribution of eigenspacings in the GUE operator.

GUE here is an acronym for the Gaussian Unitary Ensemble, a particular mathematical model that proved to be of pivotal importance in modelling work aimed at understanding the energy levels observed in quantum mechanical experiments in the 1960s. The Mongomery–Odlyzko Law and Freeman Dyson's insight, which ultimately spawned it, are of paramount importance for one very simple reason: Riemann's Zeta function is entirely abstract in nature, coming from nothing more than a fertile mind and a keen curiosity into how certain sequences of numbers hang together. It has nothing to do with anything we encounter in the real world. The study of quantum energy levels, however, is the exact opposite in that its findings are forged from hard empirical evidence gathered directly from real world observation. It has nothing to do with abstract mathematics or any correlation between interesting series of numbers. This therefore tells us one of two overpoweringly profound things: either quantum mechanics is telling us something very deep about the way that abstract number systems work or, more likely, Riemann's Zeta is telling us something very fundamental about the way our very universe hangs together. This is the exact reason why the Zeta is treated with such reverence today. It shows that where, at first inspection, there should be no links between the truly abstract and the truly real, in some cases that is clearly not true. Thus, although most if not all of the world's top scientists have an ingrained mistrust of instinct and gut feel in the absence of hard evidence to back them up, whenever the Zeta rears its head in a new field of enquiry, their eyes start to glint. The study of the Web is one such new field and relatively little data has been gathered thus far to support any related Riemannian theories. But what evidence we do have clearly states that the Zeta, or at least one particular sub-class of it, is alive and well on the Web, and given the function's pedigree for gluing physics to apparently disconnected phenomena, at the very least an interesting bet is on the cards.

17

Where Does This Get Us?

It is not unreasonable to imagine that information sits at the core of physics, just as it sits at the core of a computer.

John Archibald Wheeler

This book was intended to be entirely about information and computation. More precisely it was intended to focus on large scale synthetic collections of such things in one particular system, that being the World Wide Web. The reason for this was exclusively to investigate the nature of the Web and to speculate on the underlying causes behind its various macro-level behaviours. This led us straight to the door of modern mathematics and physics to provide a comparison between the behaviours we see and understand in the everyday world and those now apparent on the man-made creation we have come to know as 'the Web'. By doing this we actually had to be ambitious and reach beyond the Web to think about the possibility of there being fundamental laws which underlie the very notions of information and computation, perhaps even to enquire about the very stuff of digital physics itself. So the core themes of this book might appear straightforward, as being information, computing, mathematics and physics, nothing more, nothing less. But a further and unavoidable theme has been implicit throughout the text and this is all to do with language. The very notion of digital physics, the idea that the universe and everything within it might be forged from nothing more than raw information, is intrinsically dependent upon the notion of language. We are not talking about any natural language spoken by the human tongue, however. Rather we are referring to the type of language that can accurately capture the intricacies of the universe in such a way that it affords rigorous testing and absolute proof wherever possible. This may appear to be a contradiction, as we have already just stated that mathematics is a core theme of this book. But a contradiction it is not. Mathematics is both a tool with which we can probe the problems that interest us and the crucial mechanism needed to describe our findings once such probing is over. This book has primarily focused on mathematics as a tool and not as a language, but as a language its properties are particularly special. It is, literally, the binding that holds information and computation together, thereby turning the sum of their parts into something greater than their whole. It allows us to turn the raw units and connections we discern through observation and experience – the gibbering abstract nonsense of individual bits, bytes, quarks or whatever other fundamental 'dust' the universe might, or might not, be made from – and turn them into communicable concepts that we can understand and trust. It is the glue that holds together the very essence of the reality we perceive and believe to be true. It is the bridge that can lead humankind from absolute nothingness to high enlightenment. And the only thing that will stop us from reaching such enlightenment will ultimately come entirely from within. The limits of our talents and the capabilities of the, no doubt, awesome computing devices we will produce in the future will be the only things holding us back. Such limits will be frustratingly finite whereas the limits of mathematics and the computational capabilities it describes may indeed flex close to infinity. For such reasons we should treat the concepts of information, computation and the very nature of universe itself with equal reverence, for in many ways they are one and the same thing.

To all but those who choose to rest upon religious faith as the ultimate truth, the idea of the universe as a massive computer can be mind-bendingly disturbing, but a computer it is nonetheless. As we first suggested many pages ago, the universe takes in information in the form of matter and processes it over time. At the dawn of the universe, just milliseconds after the point when physicists tell us the Big Bang occurred, all that information came in the form of ultra-hot plasma, but the universe happily sucked that in, processed it and computed unstable chemical compounds as a result. These were then re-entered and out came the chemicals we recognise around us today, gases first then heavier elements later. Again the universe got to work and planets and solar systems were delivered through further cycles of computation. Then, most recently, and within relatively recent times, the universe brought forth life. We enter just after this point as the universal computer's evolutionary algorithm dials in humankind, computers in our own right, ourselves capable of creating yet more computers. But that's not the end of the story. The universe is not yet finished with its upward cycle of computational achievement. Predicting what it will output next is a game best played by gamblers and not those of a scientific inclination, but there are some signs that might help stack the odds in our favour. Take the example of life, or at least life on planet Earth as we know it. We know that life first emerged as single-celled organisms swimming in the primordial soup billions of years ago. We also know that they were followed by more advanced life forms made up from multiple cells. We, for instance, are multi-cellular organisms. So what's next? The obvious answer is the arrival of multi-multi-cellular organisms, life forms made up of a mass of lower life-forms like ourselves. This might appear strange, but when it is considered that the very cells from which we are all made are themselves autonomous in many ways, this starts to become a less than crazy concept. Such cells are born from other cells, undergo their daily lives with a certain level of inbuilt 'intelligence' and then they die, as we all eventually will. This is the common pattern that multi-multi-cellular beings will also most likely follow. But what will such meta-creatures look like? We may not need to wonder, as a growing number of scientists believe they are here, engulfing us already. Cities, for example, have been upheld many times as higher-level life-forms, for instance, and if you think about it long enough it makes perfect sense. Cities are usually formed out of smaller settlements, they are manned and maintained by smart, multi-cellular units in the form of us humans and the many other forms of animal that inhabit them, then eventually they die as time moves on. This is not fiction, given that much evidence has been produced to support the proposition at many levels.

Cities are not the only form of meta-being currently trumpeted by contemporary science, because – surprise, surprise – the Web is also showing many of the characteristics that make it a prime contender. It too appeared from a much smaller version of itself, first being hand-crafted by Sir Tim Berners-Lee in the late 1980s[1] while he was working for the research teams at CERN. It also operates in an arguably intelligent way under the cumulative influence of its many users and technologies. Likewise it will no doubt wither and die at some point in the future[2] when a more worthy successor is found. This unwittingly makes Berners-Lee something of a modern-day Frankenstein, a title from which he shies away for all the right reasons. A very humble man, Berners-Lee deserves credit for far more than is apparent to the everyday Web user.

But we digress. This is all great, but where does physics fit in and in particular relativity, gravity or quantum behaviour? That's still a complex question to answer, and in a very literal sense of the word as well. Today modern science is starting to understand that many of the rules that underlie the complex systems we see around us, like life itself, are themselves complex, and whole new branches of science are beginning to appear as a result. Those who have seen the movie *Jurassic Park* will already be familiar with the signs

---

1   Berners-Lee also produced a software solution similar in concept to the Web in the early 1980s which he called ENQUIRE.
2   This is a topic of intense interest amongst the Web Science community as of September 2010.

of this change. In that movie Jeff Goldblum's[3] character talks a lot about chaos theory, the new branch of science that studies how dynamic systems can undergo huge and apparently random changes through relatively tiny variations in their initial condition. Thus, or so chaos theory tells us, the action of a butterfly fluttering its wings in China can bring on a thunderstorm in New York. Interestingly though, the 'chaos' described in chaos theory is not the random disorder that instinctively comes to mind. Its chaos is far from random and unpredictable in that its underlying structure is relatively easy to explain and model mathematically. This makes it interesting to note that although the amount of information contained in such 'chaotic' systems may well be massive, the amount of information needed to describe the mathematical equations to create that information is surprisingly small, minute, in fact in some cases. Indeed one of the best modern scientific descriptions of complexity rests on the amount of information needed to describe the behaviour of any system in question. In such a way most chaotic systems are informationally simple. Carry this description forward and it raises a question which asks if there might be a type of system that contains lots of information and which itself needs a lot of information to describe that information? The answer is obviously yes, and this has taken science beyond the idea of chaos and into the domain that is now formally referred to as 'complexity'. Hence formally complex systems are both large and assorted in terms of the information they hold and produce and the computations at their heart, but also take large amounts of information to describe.

With such complexity comes a number of particularly interesting characteristics. Many complex systems are known to emerge as a result of the myriad of interactions taking place between their various component parts. Weather, for instance, is a complex system that is manifested from the billions of atoms in our atmosphere. Likewise the group intelligence of a swarm of bees is emergent. Just as with the atoms in a weather front, each bee can tell us little or nothing about the capabilities of its parent group. On its own a bee is a relatively 'simple' and inert creature, but combine it with many similar bees and magic happens when a new, higher, order is brought forth. Emergence is one of the most powerful phenomena in the universe, accounting for large parts of the hierarchy that shapes the very structure of reality. Take, for instance, the properties of both the humble hydrogen and oxygen atom. We might know every single trait of both of these elements individually, yet all this

---

3   Jeff Goldblum is an American actor. His career began in the mid 1970s and since then he
     has appeared in major box-office successes including *Jurassic Park*, *Independence Day* and *The Fly*.

knowledge would tell us little about the molecule they create when they react together to give us water.[4] Emergence sees to that. Similarly we could claim to know everything there is to know about water molecules but that would tell us almost nothing about how a tsunami behaves.

So, might gravity itself be an emergent property of large scale quantum behaviour? In 1971, physicist Martin Gutzwiller found a way to relate complex, chaotic systems on the classical scale with analogous systems down in the quantum world. He did this by allowing the quantum factor, Planck's constant, in the quantum-mechanical equations to tend towards zero, and then taking limits. Through this he discovered that the periodic orbits that underlie a classical-chaotic system correspond to the eigenvalues of the vector mapping that defines this 'semi-classical' system. Later, the physicist Michael Berry argued that if there is indeed such a thing as a Riemann mapping, then it models one of these semi-classical chaotic systems itself, and its eigenvalues, the imaginary parts of the Zeta zeros, are then the energy levels of that system. Thus the periodic orbits in the analogous classical-chaotic system would correspond to the prime numbers. Or, more precisely, to their log values. Berry further argued that this semi-classical system would not have the quality of 'time reversal symmetry' – that is, if all the velocities of all the particles in the system were to be instantly and simultaneously reversed, the system would not return to its initial state. Complexly chaotic systems can be time-reversible or not.[89]

Through the work of scientists like Berry and Gutzwiller ways have been found to relate the micro-quantum world to that of the macro-atomic simply by varying one or more key parameters. This work is today proving particularly important as it is helping to shed light on the difficult physical scale where the fuzzy quantum world gives way to the solid and regular arena of classical physics. What is interesting is that Riemann's Zeta function appears to be one of the critical instruments in this investigation. Until all but recently this quantum-atomic border was impenetrable to science, but now evidence is being produced to indicate that the cross-over between quantum and atomic worlds might be much broader than first expected. For example, a remarkable piece of evidence which shows how quantum effects can be seen in some macroscopic objects was demonstrated by Syantani Ghosh and her colleagues in 2003. Ghosh showed that quantum superposition between many atoms exists in a piece of salt containing billions of atoms and at remarkably high temperatures for phenomena of that kind. This proved a massive shock to the

---

4   Chemically described, of course, as H_2O.

scientific establishment as it showed that quantum effects, whose power was thought only to be confined to the infinitesimal world of subatomic particles, can produce characteristics that remain measurable at macroscopic scales.[90] Because of such work we are now realising that advanced quantum effects are much more ubiquitous in macroscopic systems than previously thought. Indeed the picture that seems to be emerging is that larger and larger systems may be capable of exhibiting quantum effects under the right conditions. We are not quite sure if and how we can generalise this yet, but the arguments and evidence in favour grow steadily. Perhaps everything might exhibit quantum effects if only we knew how to look at it in the right way. [90]

So we now know that the quantum world can push out far into the domain of the macroscopic and classically physical. We also know that, at the macroscopic level at least, things can get very chaotic and complex, and that that can lead to emergent characteristics. For such reasons it is not unreasonable at all to propose that gravity itself might be an emergent property arising from quantum phenomena either at micro or macroscopic scales. If this is so, then the world around us is more intricate and exquisitely beautiful than we could ever have imagined. It would be a jumble of micro and macroscopic interference, a creation of relative certainty crafted from the absolute uncertainty of its quantum underpinnings. It would, surely, simply be the most stunningly attractive paradox that could ever exist!

But that's all to do with the physical world, what about the sociotechnical, synthetic environment of the Web? Several studies, such as those undertaken by IBM, AltaVista and Compaq, [91][2] have already shown that the Web is chaotically complex but in rather uniform ways. Furthermore such uniform complexity is known to be similar to that found in traditionally emergent systems. Perhaps this is all just grasping at straws, but a few things are certain. There is, for instance, a relatively easy route to get from Riemann's Zeta function straight into the mathematics that describes the Web at large scale, as we have already discussed. Also, there is acknowledged evidence to suggest that the Zeta is important in our understanding of how reality behaves at the borderline between quantum and classically atomic interpretations of particle physics. The Web has a remarkable ability to behave as if it were both quantum-like and Einsteinian at the same time. To prove this, simply ask yourself how many Web pages there are out there at this very second. The answer is, of course, a very large number, but that number is finite. Now ask yourself how many hyperlinks there are out there at this very second. The answer is, obviously, considerably larger than the number of Web pages, but it is still a finite number. Keep going and now ask yourself how many possible interpretations there might be of each hyperlink on each Web page. To answer that consider that there are over six billion people alive on our planet today and that, of that number, statisticians estimate that about 1.9 billion of us, or about 28 per cent of the world's population,[5] accesses the Web on a regular basis. Remember also that the interpretation of information is wholly dependent on context, so think about the endless number of contexts in which each of those 1.9 billion users might find themselves and within those, which they might, theoretically, use to try to understand every single hyperlink on the Web. The resulting multiplier is massive, so massive in fact that, although in the strictest mathematical sense the result produced will still be a finite number, it is so vast that it would be computationally out of the reach of all calculation techniques known. For all intents and purposes that makes the number infinite and, by direct implication, that makes the Web equivalent to an infinite space of interpretational or 'meaningful' possibilities. Conversely, think about how the mechanics of the Web work at an everyday level. Most people interact with the Web via a search engine – typically Google these days. Through such software they 'ask' the Web the questions they want answering and the Web, hopefully, 'replies'. Accordingly the search engine does its work and returns not an infinite list of potential answers, but rather a remarkably small and well-focused list of alternative suggestions in the form of web pages comprising search results. The user then ultimately clicks on one, and only ever one of the hyperlinks within the search results returned. That's the way that hyperlinks work: you only get one Web page[6] at the end of each hyperlink. Now think about what has just been described. An infinite space of possibilities has been reduced to one, and only one, actual opportunity for interpretation. Tell such a tale to a physicist and he or she will immediately recognise a precise and compelling comparison. Under any other name what we have just described is quantum decoherence, the collapse of an infinite space of possible states into just one actual observed state. This is probably the most well-known and frustrating characteristic of quantum mechanics. It is the very stuff that drives mad scientists mad!

It is important to stress, however, that decoherence in quantum systems with many interacting quantum variables is still only partially understood. How decoherence actually happens is recognised by modern science as being deeply important, but it is most definitely on the cutting edge of physics. It

---

5   By August 2010.

6   This is strictly not true as the Web is not solely restricted to Web 'pages'. It is more correct to state that one, and only one, Universal Resource Indicator (URI) is returned.

is known that if the quantum environment is made up of a 'bath' of what are called quantum oscillations, the quantum analogy of many frictionless pendulums, decoherence approaches classicality for all practical purposes. But if the environment is what is called a quantum spin bath, then it has been shown that the entire system does not decohere to classicality and so quantum decoherence still remains.[25] In short, everything depends on how decoherence occurs, which depends on the actual system decohering, its quantum or quantum plus environment and all its details. We are only just beginning to understand how decoherence happens. Furthermore, some theorists even believe that decoherence may not require a quantum system to interact with the environment at all. It may be intrinsic, and due to the relativistic curvature of space-time or to events on the Planck length scale.[25]

There is further insight. Notice again that our average Web user normally uses just one search engine to question the Web, not several. This is all about the power law characteristic of the Web and the fact that it naturally promotes front runners as part of its evolutionary processes. Several studies have looked at this and have spotted the predominant factors concerned. For instance, authority appears to be a key relevance to readership growth amongst blog sites. If a blogger has many subscribers or receives comments from many bloggers, he or she may attract further bloggers to visit, make comments and subscribe to their blog. Such a blogger then becomes an authority in the network. Accordingly, their beliefs can influence more people faster than before. Conversely, a blogger who subscribes to many blogs can serve as a 'hub' that points to many blogs of those central, influential leaders.[92] So, in essence, studies support the idea that the more authoritative a blog appears, the more readers it is likely to attract. This, it turns out, drives up its authority, which again drives up readership in a self-supporting loop. In the similar way Google attracts users because of the accuracy of its search results. This supports the underlying theme which states that the more of something there is in a particular place on the Web the more likely it is to pull in more of that something. Think of this in physical terms and it is clearly analogous to gravity. The more massive a planet, the more mass it concentrates about a particular point in space-time and the more likely it is to attract additional mass towards it. A common interpretation of this phenomenon is that the greater the mass of the planet, the greater the gravitational force it exerts upon its surroundings. Einstein, however, taught us that gravitation is, in fact, not a force in the truest sense of the word, but is rather the result of space-time's curvature resulting from the mass within it. Likewise, it is acceptable to consider the attraction of, say, Google, to be a direct result of the curvature it creates in the informational and computational spaces connecting to it on the Web.

Before accepting such 'gravity' as a fait accompli on the Web, however, it is worth mentioning that there is another similar phenomenon at play in the Web's world. Complex chaotic behaviour is well known to create centres of attention, or attraction, and describing such attraction has been one of the greatest achievements of chaos theory. Such attraction concentrates about specific locations, or attraction basins, which correspond to sets of characteristics towards which a dynamic system evolves over time. That is, points that get close enough to an attractor remain close even if slightly disturbed. Geometrically, an attractor can be thought of as a point, a curve, a surface,[7] or even a complex set with a fractal structure known as a strange attractor, but, at its heart, the analogy with space-time curvature is a close fit. Put something close to a chaotic attractor that is similar to the attractor itself and it will be dragged toward it in much the same way that very small masses are attracted to very large masses under the effects of gravity. But there the major similarities end. Chaotic attractors are distinctly time-dependent, whereas gravity is not in the strictest sense. It takes time for a chaotic attractor to build up its influence and that influence is tightly bound to the initial conditions of the system in which it lives. To the best of our knowledge, gravity does not work like that. If, for instance, we could instantaneously magic-up another planet the size of our Sun and place it somewhere in our solar system, we would also see an instantaneous gravitational effect: instantaneous, that is, in that its gravitational pull would radiate out at the speed of light and very quickly influence everything with a mass around it. Likewise we might expect something similar on the Web if gravity were to exist there too. So, if, for example, the famous Elvis Presley conspiracy were true and the king of rock and roll were indeed alive and well and living somewhere like Lost Springs, Wyoming, and if he were to launch a Website tomorrow, chances are that word would spread like wildfire and it would become an overnight sensation; an immediate sensation of the contemporary Web. That is so long as it carried enough authority instantaneously and irrefutably to establish that the site was indeed produced by Elvis himself.

We must also remember that the Web appears as a rough and seething mass simply because we are viewing it close up. Gravity is not like that. It typically presents itself as being smooth and continuous simply because we are naturally forced to view it from a distance. This tells us something important, reminding us that irregularity is often only due to the point of view from which observations are made. As a consequence it is wrong to think of gravity merely in terms of smooth space-time curves. To get an accurate picture we need to

---

7   For the more mathematically inclined, read 'manifold' here.

recall that it is dependent on the amount of mass present in any given region of space-time. Add to this the fact that the earth's body mass is in a constant state flux, as the hot metal at its core moves in a highly complex manner, and a close proximity picture of the gravitational field is thus decidedly lumpy.

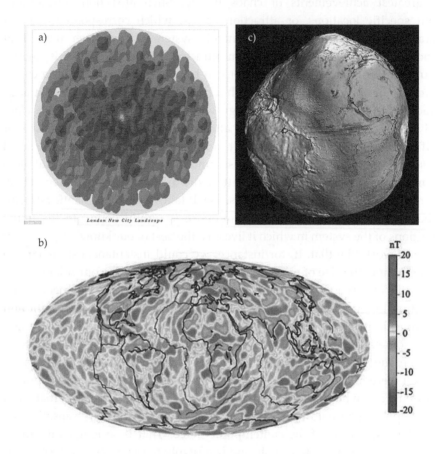

Figures 17.1(a), 17.1(b) and 17.1(c)   Figure 17.1(a) shows the density of Twitter[8] users in central London. Figure 17.1(b) shows the various densities of the Earth's magnetic field resulting from movements of molten iron in its core. Figure 17.1(c) shows a map of gravitational strength across the Earth as calculated using data from the European Space Agency's GOCE satellite

All this leads to a simple and significant conclusion about the fundamental laws of the physical world crossing over into the synthetic world of the Web.

---

8   www.twitter.com

To add credence to this perspective it is clear that several of these laws are dependent on the use of constants. We have already discussed Planck's constant in Michael Berry's work, for example, and it is common knowledge that other constants, such as the speed of light, play important roles in our understanding of relativity. We know too that the concept of authority plays a significant role when the Web coalesces and that human behaviour when sending electronic and paper mails is controlled by power laws with different and calculable coefficients, so might there be underlying constants at work there too? For now all we can do is speculate and pull evidence from a very small spectrum of research, but the point to be made is not about the stability of such constants, but rather the role that they play in our workings. Constants are merely variables upon which we depend to stay the same in all possible circumstances. Similarly, the equations in which they are used are merely lenses we use to see things for what they are, rather than the way in which they appear at face value. Thus, constants are nothing more than fixed compensators, values that provide an unchanging shift in perception purely to accommodate a lack of insight or capability on our part. Under normal circumstances such constants are treated with reverence in science and are almost never tweaked. Almost never, that is, but not always. Some of the bravest, most challenging scientists, like Michael Berry, have dared to confront their stability head-on and have deliberately degraded the status of certain constants to that of lowly changelings. Open such constants up to variability and weird things can happen. The quantum world can feel remarkably like the macroscopic for instance. Fiddle with constants and you can create an overlap between quantum interpretations of reality and those that Einstein might tolerate.[9] What's more, by varying some well-known constants it is quite easy to create the type of behaviour we might be seeing on the Web today!

So in one easy step we might be able to draw an immediate and compelling comparison between the Web and physical reality. If we imagine the Web to be a world lacking constants in the rules that govern its behaviour, it becomes quite sensible to reason with ideas borrowed from the classical sciences. Sensible, that is, based on the very strong principle of modern science which states that good science can only be based on proof, which itself must be based on hard evidence gained through well controlled experimentation. Here traditional science has the advantage over Web science however, as it has a significant back catalogue of experimental data, whereas web science has little to offer as yet. Nevertheless web science is pushing hard to find such evidence and that

---

9   Einstein had an in-built dislike for quantum mechanics and to his dying day he worked tirelessly to find ideas that might replace it.

which has been gathered so far appears to support strong synergies between the physical world and the Web. This is indeed important, for if true it literally adds another dimension to science. Until all but very recently when scientists have talked about a universal law or property, such universality has been wholly restricted to observations related to the real world. Would it not be exiting, would it not be utterly exhilarating, if such a restriction were proved to be too limiting? What if a universal law could be shown to hold true in a place not thrown up by nature? What if a universal law could be shown to transcend the real and encompass the synthetic as well? Would that not be truly astounding? Would not that challenge the very meaning of 'universal' itself and bring into question the very definition of the universe itself? That marvellous and grand proposition has been the first of the two primary targets in this book: to challenge the real by offering up ideas and comparisons from the man-made. At present the ideas offered are nothing more than that, they are just ideas, and this book denotes nothing more than a story that attempts to string them together on a path towards such a proposition. But the importance of ideas and stories should never be underplayed. Without human imagination, science would not exist at all and we would still be cracking nuts with stones in the shadows of some cold dark cave. It is imagination that pushes us forward. It is imagination that makes us human.

Now onto the second objective of this book. This was to probe the very nature of information and computation themselves. So what have we found that may be new? Again that's a tricky question to answer as science is particularly precious about both notions. Nevertheless, and regardless of the endless posturing found in these pages, two strong ideas have emerged and it is particularly interesting that the various threads leading to them appear to entwine without much resistance. The first of these is the idea that information is simply the concept of computation with its time dimension removed. This is a simple and powerful notion that may prove heretical to some. In particular, computer science has an engrained belief that all it must account for should be dynamic, and that includes information. But then computer science would believe that, for if we consider the inverse of our proposition, we might state that computation is simply information with time added. This makes computer science a discipline with a need to concentrate on time for its very existence. So for those who would doubt the validity of our proposition, ask yourself two simple questions: if the universe were to stop in an instant, if it were to be frozen in time in a heartbeat, how much information would be lost as a result? The answer would be none. Every single ounce of information would remain intact as the universe faltered in a state of suspended animation. Now ask yourself how much computation would continue while the universe was in this state. The answer has to be none. Not one single instruction would compute or one single cycle of one single computer execute. Existence would be devoid of any computation and the universe would be computationally dead. This agrees with the idea of information as devised by the mathematician Andrei Kolmogorove, who proposed that the information in a symbolic string is equal to the shortest path that will produce it on a universal computer. In other words, the information content of a sequence of symbols is defined by the specification of the algorithm needed to produce it.[25] But 'production' needs time for it to take place. That therefore implies that information is indebted to computation to come into existence, but is wholly happy to exist without it once created.

We have also played with ideas of how information and computation might be tied up with supposedly fundamental physical concepts such as space, time and energy, and it is valuable to note that others have also found such sport to be of value. In particular, Stuart Kauffman[10] has worked tirelessly to marry information and computation with broader ideas in science. Through this he has thereby tried to anchor both in the complex and emergent worlds of physics, chemistry and biology. He chiefly sees information as being central to some of the very deepest understandings in science and suspects that we might need a concept of information as a constraint on the release of energy that then constitutes work. Through this he hopes to show that natural selection maximises the diversity of work that is performed in cells, organisms, ecosystems and biospheres.[25] Kauffman goes even further to propose that information could play a pivotal role in overthrowing one of the most secure tenets of all science, that being the second law of thermodynamics. This essentially states that the amount of disorder, or entropy, in any closed system left to its own devices, will stay the same or increase over time. Or to paraphrase, that the universe has a propensity to tend towards a state of chaos.

Kauffman sees things differently, however, and for good reason. He points out that if the universe entirely obeyed the second law, the amount of disorder in it would have continued to increase since the very first instant after the Big Bang. This is plainly not true, as modern science has it that the boiling mass of plasma that formed immediately after the Big Bang was highly irregular. So, projecting forward, the second law wrongly predicts that the universe

---

10 Stuart Kauffman is an American theoretical biologist and complex systems researcher concerning the origin of life on Earth. He is best known for arguing that the complexity of biological systems and organisms might result as much from self-organisation and far-from-equilibrium dynamics as from Darwinian natural selection, as well as for applying models of Boolean networks to simplified genetic circuits.

should be an absolute mess by now. Quite clearly it is not, as galaxies and planets have formed from this plasma as it cooled and, on at least one of these planets, life itself has come into existence. Considering that alone gives instant insight into the fact that the second law is flawed in some serious regard that we simply do not yet understand. This is why Kauffman talks of his fourth law of thermodynamics; a law that is a reverse of the second and that actively promotes order over disorder. Through this he proposes that thermodynamics can also be conducive to the increase of regularity in an open system like that of the biosphere and states that through such a law in certain open systems might actually be critically self-organising. He also suggests that the biosphere might evolve so that the product of the total work done – organised computations involving the contained release of energy – is maximised. What's more he even overtly proposes that, if his fourth law is true, it might apply more generally to all kinds of co-constructing, co-evolving systems such as the economy and common law. In his mind at least, such systems may well be self-organisingly critical and tend toward maximisation through some generalisation of what the physicists might refer to as 'work', but more broadly might be considered as 'activity'. And, although he does not extend such generalisation to the Web in any of his published works, in closed conversation Kauffman readily accepts the Web as being inclusive to his club of critically self-organising systems.

But why all the fuss, as many authors and quasi-scientists have talked endlessly about self-organising systems? In Kauffman's case the answer is easy, as he is one of the most thorough and meticulous scientists we have in our presence today. Not only has he supported his thinking on countless occasions with hard empirical evidence, but he is insistent on chasing his theories through the use of precise mathematical tools. Kauffman is hence recognised as one of the pioneers of complexity theory and has applied his ideas many times with clear and unparalleled success. This on its own should be enough for us to pay attention, but the mere fact he has chosen to pick on the second law of thermodynamics as the crescendo of his revered career is utterly breathtaking. This is not only because the second law is so highly respected by modern science, but because it runs so deep into the very core of many things fundamental. As Sir Arthur Stanley Eddington was famously quoted as saying in 1927:

> The law that entropy always increases holds, I think, the supreme position among the laws of Nature. If someone points out to you that your pet theory of the universe is in disagreement with Maxwell's equations – then so much the worse for Maxwell's equations. If it is

> *found to be contradicted by observation — well, these experimentalists do bungle things sometimes. But if your theory is found to be against the second law of thermodynamics I can give you no hope; there is nothing for it but to collapse in deepest humiliation.*

But Kauffman is not new to challenging the scientific establishment and perhaps that explains the absence of his arguably much-deserved Nobel medal. Regardless, he has never been troubled when pushing the envelope and openly proclaims his concerns over science's false security in the stability of its laws. He recognises that the status of commandments such as the second law of thermodynamics has been much debated, but goes on to comment that, in some metaphysical way, such laws may seem 'real' in the sense of prescriptively 'governing' how things 'must' unfold, but he is unsure of the degree to which such laws can truly be descriptive. Thus he agrees with the physicist Murray Gell-Man in his opinion that a law is a short, or compressed, description of the regularities of the phenomena it covers. But if that law cannot pre-state, let alone predict, the outcome of any given situation, it must be called into question. So it is with the second law and the situations in which it fails are not insignificant either. Kauffman does, however, agree that the quantum effect and information are closely linked and often reaches out to make comparison between quantum and classically macro-worlds, using information as the carrier of his arguments in his more recent works. In one example he discusses the possibility that vast webs of quantum coherent or partially coherent degrees of freedom might span large volumes of a biological cell. He then goes on to discuss how the injection of information can protect or return decoherent quantum variables to a coherent state and proposes that such behaviour might promote quantum systems at body temperature. This allows him to advocate that information injection implies quantum systems might, perhaps, be thermodynamically open to the transfer of matter and energy and thereby be resistant to the second law of thermodynamics. Think about this, what Kauffman is saying is that quantum-like systems at noticeably macro-scales might have a propensity to reject disorder and embrace order. Follow this back through his most successful work on complexity and what he is actually telling us is that, under the right circumstances, macro-scale quantum systems might have the capability to coalesce and emerge, just as singular celled organisms emerged from the primordial soup on our planet. What he is hinting at suggests that from macro-level quantum systems something can appear that is not naturally associated with the base phenomena present. Might such a preference for order ultimately translate into a propensity to 'attract' and thus emerge from the quantum into the atomic? Might Kauffman actually be playing with the borderline laws that bring forth atoms, molecules, planets and galaxies? Might he have successfully navigated the elusive river of science and found one of its sources, hidden from us for so long. Could Kauffman's fourth law actually be gravity? If so, that not only makes the atomic world an emergent phenomenon based on complex quantum interaction at borderline macro-scales, but it also makes gravity an emergent property that has recognisable and pervasive presence across both physically real and synthetically man-made systems. It would not only be a universally present property but could just be the one thing that holds all we know in state of equilibrium between the fundamental randomness of the quantum and the fundamental order of the familiarly macro. Perhaps this is a proposition too far and perhaps it is ridiculous in the extreme. But then science has never moved forward by choosing to play safe. That route leads to stagnation, negativity and ultimate demise. Besides, in the face of such a rapid advance of the Web, surely the mood must be to be brave, if for no other reason than just to try to keep up.

But such brave talk does need regulation and constraint, for it ultimately points towards the biggest prize in of all science, a general Theory of Everything in which all the fundamental laws of physics will become unified under the banner of one grand idea or set of coherent rules. Science is replete with the skeletons of many failed attempts at such a grandly unifying theory, but that has never stopped the boldest or the most well-equipped from continuing the search. Of late there have been one or two attempts at unification worthy of note including that from Garrett Lisi.[11] In his Exceptionally Simple Theory of Everything, he proposes a unified field theory which combines a grand unification theory of particle physics with the general relativistic description of gravitation, using the largest simple exceptional Lie algebra,[12] E8. In a paper posted to the physics arXiv in 2007, he describes how gravity, the standard model, bosons and fermions can be unified as parts of an E8 'superconnection'. This, according to Lisi, describes all fundamental interactions observed in nature, and stands as a possible way to unify general relativity with the standard model of particle physics.[96] His theory also predicts the existence of many new fundamental particles and this is key to us, as Lisi uses multidimensional geometries and hidden symmetries to make his point. But then that's the idea behind the mathematics he uses. It deliberately encourages the introduction of new dimensions and geometric transformation to unveil new and interesting

---

11 Antony Garrett Lisi is an American theoretical physicist and adventure sports enthusiast.
12 In mathematics, a Lie group is a group which is also a type of manifold that is locally similar enough to Euclidean space to allow calculus upon it, with the property that the group operations are compatible with the smooth structure. E_8 is, hence, any of several closely-related exceptional simple Lie groups, linear algebraic groups or Lie algebras of dimension 248.

properties of the problem spaces over which it sits. In that regard, Lisi's approach to his work is identical to that we have used in this book. He treats the universe as if it were a highly dimensional information space in which fundamental patterns and symmetries must be preserved. What Lisi does not do, though, is play with the word 'universal' as we have here. For us, 'universal' has meant more than just everything physical, but, for now at least, Lisi is happy to stay within the bounds of classical reality. This merely serves to emphasise just how controversial our journey through information and computation has been. Lisi himself is highly controversial in the scientific community, but, regardless, his ideas do appear to be on the verge of acceptance, most likely because of their compellingly simple and elegant beauty. He further chooses not to put his work through rigorous academic review, which is predominantly the same approach as that taken with regard to the ideas contained in this book. But then Lisi appears to be the type of free-minded individual who prefers to let his ideas run free, rather than hold them down while his contemporaries fight over them. So it is with the ideas contained here. Maybe they are right, maybe they are wrong, but at least they are now running free and, hopefully, a compelling story has been told. Regardless of such rhetoric, there is one thing that cannot be denied. The Web is the largest single source of man-made information we have ever seen, and we should not let the opportunities that present pass us by. Not only does it contain vast amounts of information but it naturally generates lots of information about that information, and such properties help to make it beguilingly complex. But the essence of complexity itself does not quite capture the true nature of the Web, for it is the emergent properties produced by such complexity that truly make it stand apart. Not only do we know that the Web is emergent in its structure, but we also know that it is capable of bringing forth many new and exciting phenomena from within. Social networks, the blogosphere and e-commerce are all good examples. None can be characterised properly by just a single Web site, or even a small group of such sites with similar content. No, it is the combined effect of all such sites under any one given category that gives that category its ultimate essence and style. And here too can be found a very strong link with contemporary physics.

In his book 'A Different Universe', the Nobel laureate Robert Laughlin[13] tells of how modern physics is learning to embrace the concept of emergence and is starting to reformulate some of its most fundamental ideas in the wake of this new understanding. In particular he highlights the research of another

---

13 Laughlin was awarded a share of the 1998 Nobel Prize in physics for their explanation of the fractional quantum Hall effect.

Nobel laureate, Klaus von Klitzing,[14] as both worked respectively on quantum interpretations of a physical phenomenon known as the Hall Effect. First discovered in 1870 by Edwin Hall, this concerns the production of a voltage difference across an electrical conductor, transverse to an electric current in the conductor and a magnetic field perpendicular to the current. In his studies von Klitzing found something quite remarkable that should not have been there, when in 1980 he was performing some interesting experiments on state-of-the-art electronic components built to tolerances more accurate than those common even today. When these were cooled to ultralow temperatures he began to consider the effect in these samples which appeared abnormally steady over a range of magnetic field strengths.[97]

The usual explanation of the Hall Effect involves a magnet being brought close to a wire carrying an electric current. This causes a voltage to develop at right angles to the current flow because of the electrons moving in the wire due to the influence of the magnet. This is because the electrons moving in the wire are deflected by the magnet, just as they would be in free space, and thus pile up on one side of the wire until the resultant voltage they produce exactly compensates the deflection due to the magnet. As a result it is ordinarily accounted for as a resistance, calculated by dividing the resultant voltage by the current present. At normal temperatures the Hall Resistance shows the density of electrons in the wire and is therefore important in the design of semiconductor technology. At very low temperatures, however, quantum mechanics interferes and the normally straight line plot of the Hall Resistance verses electron density is taken over by a somewhat meandering replacement. In the case of the components von Klitzing was studying, nonetheless, such meanderings evolve into a staircase with rather flat steps as the temperature is lowered. The heights of these steps are hence understood as universal quantized values of the Hall Resistance.[97]

After convincing himself of its universality, von Klitzing soon realised that the quantum Hall Resistance could be understood through a combination of fundamental physical constants, these being the supposedly indivisible quantum of electric charge (e) Planck's constant (h) and the speed of light (c). This fact has the obvious implication that you can measure these constants with unbelievable accuracy without dealing with any of them directly. This is deeply important and deeply unsettling to most physicists.[97]

---

14 Klitzing was awarded the Nobel Prize in Physics in 1985 for his work on the integer quantum Hall Effect

The impact that this discovery had on physics is hard to overstate. Those who poured over von Klitzing's results knew that the electronic components on which he performed his tests had to have imperfections and thus were expected to detract from the experimental accuracy he reported. Yet repeated tests since von Klitzing's first findings have demonstrated over and over again that his results were sound. Even so, worries about the imperfections present are sound, as in the manufacture of semiconductors there are always flaws that cannot be controlled, such as structural defects in the crystal lattice, randomly incorporated dopants, amorphous oxides at the surface, ragged edges left over from photolithography and so on. These are known to impact other electrical measurements, for the matter is important for micro-circuitry and has thus been studied heavily. But this expectation turned out to be wrong. As a result of recent and significant theoretical work, we now know that imperfection has exactly the opposite effect and causes perfection of the measurement in this context. The Quantum Hall Effect is, in fact, a magnificent example of perfection emerging out of imperfection and it is magnificent not least for two reasons. Firstly, although emergence in the natural world is relatively common, to see it at such a micro, and close to fundamental, scale is extraordinary. Add to this the extreme accuracy that it produces and something very special indeed becomes clear. This makes von Klitzing's contribution to physics a watershed event, as Laughlin so rightly points out. It is the moment at which physical science stepped firmly out of the age of reductionism and into the light of emergence. It is the point at which physics joined the family of sciences who now appreciate that the aim of understanding the world around us by breaking it down into ever smaller parts is surpassed by the need to understand how this world organises itself.[97] This again is of fundamental importance to our story as both physicists and web scientists alike now share something significant in common in their appreciation that emergence plays a crucial role in the mechanics of that which they seek to understand.

So deep is the infiltration of emergence in physics these days that it is now even bringing into doubt the fundamentality of at least one fundamental physical constant. Laughlin's follow-on work on a version of the Quantum Hall Effect, commonly known as the Fractional Quantum Hall Effect, is telling us that the ostensibly indivisible quanta of the electron charge (e) can be broken down through the self-organisation of phases. In essence it proves the existence of new phases of matter in which the elementary excitations – the particles – carry an exact fraction of e. This again questions the role of matter as a grounding notion in our understandings of reality. So, could it be that the Fractional Quantum Hall Effect is revealing the first glimmer of a staircase of dissection that will lead us through the quantum realm and on to somewhere less familiar yet so familiar at the same time. Might this land-beyond-land actually be the true home of information and computation?

In his book Laughlin also takes time out to consider Einstein's work in light of physics' new fondness for emergence and self-organisation, and to do this he picks on a nagging problem with relativity. We know today, for example, that special relativity's insistence on doing away with the notion of the luminiferous aether is flawed. Close to the time of Einstein's publication on special relativity, work on radioactivity was beginning to show that the empty vacuum of space had spectroscopic structure similar to that of ordinary quantum solids or fluids. More recent studies with large particle accelerators now lead us to believe that the emptiness of space is not actually empty at all but is rather filled with some kind of something that we do not yet fully understand. Most of the time this something is invisible, but if we hit it hard enough, as in the experiments for which particle accelerators are famous, it can be made to reveal itself. Today, the contemporary idea of the vacuum of space, confirmed every day by experiment, is a relativistic aether for all intents and purposes. This serves to highlight a contradiction in Einstein's work on relativity, as general relativity holds a propensity to treat space-time as if it were a material thing. We know this because there are clear similarities between Einsteinian gravity and the dynamic warping of real surfaces, leading us to describe space-time as a fabric.

The view of space-time as a non-substance with substance-like properties is neither logical or consistent with the facts. At its core is the belief that the invariance, or unbreakable symmetry, of motion in space-time is sacrosanct, and is therefore different to all other symmetries in being absolute under all conditions. This view may well be correct, but it is an enormous speculative leap as the idea of absolute symmetry makes little or no sense. Symmetries are caused by things and are not the cause of things. If relativity is always true, then there has to be an underlying reason, a deeper set of mechanisms that come together to lock tight the symmetry on which it depends. This has to be the way and attempts to evade this inevitably lead to contradiction. Thus, if we try to write down relativistic equations describing the spectroscopy of the vacuum, we discover that the equations are mathematically nonsense unless either relativity or gauge invariance, an equally important symmetry, is postulated to fail at extremely short distances. No workable fix to this problem has yet been discovered.[97]

If Einstein had been alive today he would have been mortified at this state of affairs. He would condemn today's scientists for allowing such a discrepancy to linger and would most likely despair that his works had been allowed to fuel the proliferation of logical inconsistencies we now see. Einstein was an artist, a scholar and, above all, a revolutionary. His approach to physics might be summed up as theorising minimally, never arguing with experiment, demanding total logical consistency and mistrusting unfounded beliefs. The unfounded belief of his day was the aether, or more precisely the naïve version of the aether that went before relativity. The unsubstantiated belief of our day is relativity itself. It would hence be perfectly in Einstein's character to re-examine the facts, mull things over, and conclude that his beloved principle of relativity was not fundamental at all but emergent – a collective property of whatever constitutes space-time becoming increasingly exact at long length scales but which fails at short ones. This is a different idea from his original, but one that is fully compatible with it logically, and even more exciting and potentially important.[97] It would mean that the fabric of space-time was not simply the stage on which reality plays out, but is rather an organisational phenomenon, and that there might be something beyond in a very real, informational and computational sense. If we dare consider such beyondness as being the very stuff of information itself then again little or no logical inconsistency will be found and, at the very least, two amazing realisations become apparent. Firstly we see a reaffirmation that the universe is a computational entity at its most fundamental level and secondly we are offered the tantalising idea that both relativity and the Web are emergent spectacles born out of a sea of information. By such a token, if we continue to monitor the ways in which the informational fabric of the Web grows and changes we are bound to learn new and amazing things about it, about us and perhaps about much more besides. In simple terms, the Web is just one big 'datastore' with a huge volcano of human capability behind it. It spews forth a new and rich aether in which we can amble and enrich, advance and entertain. At the same time it is a source from which evil can arise and carnage can consume. It is in many ways like a mirror, reflecting back all that we are as individuals and as collective units. It shows us what we show it and thereby illuminates and enhances our lives. But then science is a simply a mirror also, in that it shows what physical reality has chosen to show it. Thus, by the very virtue of the wondrous beauty of the world around us, science must surely be the most wondrously beautiful thing humankind has ever had the good fortune to create.

It will be interesting to see if the experimental results that will follow do indeed confirm the propositions contained in these pages. If such propositions are indeed true, it will further be fascinating to see if we might even, perhaps, use the Web itself as a scientific instrument to probe the reality around us and help explain some of the most challenging problems faced by science today. Might this make the science of the Web a real science? Might this legitimise the position of the Web as one of the most powerful and insightful inventions of our age? Who knows, but one thing is certain in that exciting times lie ahead for both the Web and the new discipline of Web science. If you don't believe that then there is one simple way to find out – ask Google!

A Very Brief After-Note

In September 2010 a small gathering of the eminent, interested and well informed met at the Royal Society in London. They were there not only to help celebrate the 350th anniversary of that illustrious organisation, but also to attend its first gathering to discuss Web Science. Over a period of three days many eclectic and interesting presentations were given, but one caused a particular stir. Late on the first day Jonathan Zittrain, a professor at the Berkman Center for Internet and Society at Harvard University, crystallised a concern that had been nagging at the back of the minds of many of those present. His slot was entitled 'Will the Web Break?' and in it he listed a number of potential threats to the Web's future existence. Not least of these was the fact that the Web has not evolved in ways originally envisaged. Through his acknowledgement of characteristics like power laws he openly reached out to gravity as a suitable analogy for the clumping behaviour now prominent on the Web, further suggesting that this might offer great potential to harm to the its independence. In particular he laboured on the fact that that those in control of the Web's major centres of attraction hold the ability to regulate the data within their grasp. This unavoidably generates bias and hence threatens to undermine the most central principle of the Web.

Zittrain further used general themes from physics to paint a picture of an idealised Web that appears to be vanishing. He hence proposed that the Web should be isotropic, in that it should be 'evenly lain out' no matter what direction you look, time symmetric, in that once information is placed on the Web it should remain there without undue cause for removal, and entropic in that it should be random in all discernible features of relevance. Alas, we now know the Web to be none of these things, while at the same time we know it to be growing at a phenomenal rate. Such characteristics point to one final physical comparison. Cosmology tells us that a body will collapse under its own weight past a certain point, so might we be seeing the warning signs of something similar on the Web? That would be a shame as the Web is indeed a wondrous thing, but perhaps physics is lurking out there somewhere, just out of sight, waiting to demonstrate that it too is a wondrous thing.

References

1. Grady Booch, 'Handbook of SoftwareArchitecture', retrieved 1 October 2007 from http://www.booch.com/architecture/index.jsp.
2. Philip Tetlow, *The Web's Awake*, 2007, IEEE Press, ISBN 0470137940.
3. Jeannette M. Wing, 'FAQ on ϖ Calculus', retrieved and checked 5 March 2012 from http://www.eecs.harvard.edu/~nr/cs257/archive/jeannette-wing/pi.pdf.
4. 'Semantic Web', in Wikipedia, the free encyclopedia, retrieved and checked 27 July 2011 from http://en.wikipedia.org/wiki/Semantic_Web.
5. Stephen Pinker, *How the Mind Works*, 1998, Penguin, ISBN 0713991305.
6. Michael A. Nielsen and Isaac L. Chuang, *Quantum Computation and Quantum Information*, 2000, Cambridge University Press, ISBN 9780521635035.
7. Philip Ball, *Critical Mass: How One Thing Leads to Another*, 2004, Arrow Books, ISBN 0099457865.
8. 'History of Physics' (20 January 2006), in Wikipedia, the free encyclopedia, retrieved and checked 1 October 2007 from http://en.wikipedia.org/wiki/History_of_Physics.
9. Gary W. Flake, *The Computational Beauty of Nature*, 1998, MIT Press, ISBN 0262561271.
10. Ralph Edney, Nigel Lesmoir-Gordon and Will Rood, 2000, *Introducing Fractal Geometry*, Totem Books, ISBN 1840467134.
11. Bruce Bassett and Ralph Edney, *Introducing Relativity*, 2002, Icon Books, ISBN 97801840467, p. 77.
12. Kenneth W. Ford, *The Quantum World: Quantum Physics for Everyone*, 2004, Harvard University Press, ISBN 0674013425.
13. M. How, 'The Industry of Life', *Physics World*, 20(11), pp. 25–7.
14. Lee Somlin, *The Trouble with Physics*, Penguin, 2007, ISBN 9780713997996.
15. Cristian S. Calude, Elena. Calude, M.J. Dinneen, 'Developments in Language Theory: 8th International Conference', retrieved and checked 4 September 2007 from http://books.google.com/books?id=j_tM-g68VOMC&pg=PA109&ots=QH73zixLse&dq=context+free+grammar+theory&sig=vDwIGemUaaFTkrOWmefG2LJmQCQ.
16. Toby Ord, 'Hypercomputation: Computing More Than the Turing Machine', University of Melbourne, retrieved and checked 4 September 2007 from http://arxiv.org/ftp/math/papers/0209/0209332.pdf.
17. Claude E. Shannon, *A Mathematical Theory of Communication*, 1998, University of Illinois Press, ISBN 9780252725463.
18. Michael S. Schneider, *A Beginner's Guide to Constructing the Universe*, 2003, HarperPerennial, ISBN 9780060926717.
19. Timothy Berners-Lee, *Weaving the Web*, Texere Publishing, ISBN 9781587990182.
20. 'History Topic: Newton's Bucket', retrieved and checked 5 May 2008 from http://www-groups.dcs.st-and.ac.uk/~history/PrintHT/Newton_bucket.html.
21. Brian Green, *The Fabric of the Cosmos*, 2005, ISBN 9780141011110.
22. Evelyn Fox Keller, *Making Sense of Life: Explaining Biological Development with Models, Metaphors, and Machines*, 2003, Harvard University Press, ISBN 067401250X.

23.   'Euclidian Geometry', in Wikipedia, the free encyclopedia, retrieved and checked 27 July 2011 from http://en.wikipedia.org/wiki/Euclidian_geometry.

24.   'Alan Turing', in Wikipedia, the free encyclopedia, retrieved and checked July 27 2010 from http://en.wikipedia.org/wiki/Alan_turing.

25.   Stuart Kauffman, *Reinventing the Sacred: Finding God in Complexity*, 2010, Basic Books, ISBN 9780465003006.

26.   Lawrence Edward, *The Vortex of Life: Nature's Patterns in Space and Time*, 1993, Floris Books, ISBN 9780863155512, p. 206.

27.   'Solovay-Strassen Primality Test', in Wikipedia, the free encyclopedia, retrieved and checked 4 September 2007 from http://en.wikipedia.org/wiki/Solovay-Strassen_primality_test.

28.   'Spiral', in Wikipedia, the free encyclopedia, retrieved and checked 23 December 2008 from http://en.wikipedia.org/wiki/Spiral.

29.   'Complex Plane', in Wikipedia, the free encyclopedia, retrieved and checked 23 December 2008 from htp://en.wikipedia.org/wiki/Complex_plane.

30.   Ian Stewart, *Why Beauty is Truth*, 2008, Basic Books, ISBN 978046508236.

31.   'The Early History of Mathematics', in Wikipedia, the free encyclopedia, retrieved and checked 9 January 2009 from http://en.wikipedia.org/wiki/History_of_mathematics#Early_mathematics.

32.   'Number Types', in Wikipedia, the free encyclopedia, retrieved and checked 9 January 2009 from http://www.purplemath.com/modules/numtypes.htm.

33.   'Greek Mathematics', in Wikipedia, the free encyclopedia, retrieved and checked 12 January 2009 from http://en.wikipedia.org/wiki/Greek_mathematics.

34.   'Euclid', in Wikipedia, the free encyclopedia, retrieved and checked 12 January 2009 from http://en.wikipedia.org/wiki/Euclid.

35.   'Georg Cantor', in Wikipedia, the free encyclopedia, retrieved and checked 12 January 2009 from http://en.wikipedia.org/wiki/Georg_Cantor.

36.   'Hermann Minkowski', in Wikipedia, the free encyclopedia, retrieved and checked 12 January 2009 from http://en.wikipedia.org/wiki/Hermann_Minkowski.

37.   'Linearity', in Wikipedia, the free encyclopedia, retrieved and checked 16 January 2009 from http://www.numberwatch.co.uk/linearity.htm.

38.   'Nonlinear System', in Wikipedia, the free encyclopedia, retrieved and checked 16 January 2009 from http://en.wikipedia.org/wiki/Nonlinearity.

39.   'Conic Section', in Wikipedia, the free encyclopedia, retrieved and checked 16 January 2009 from http://en.wikipedia.org/wiki/Conic_section.

40.   Mitchell Waldrop, *Complexity: The Emerging Science at the Edge of Order and Chaos*, 1994, Simon and Schuster, ISBN 0671872346.

41.   'Newton's Three Laws of Motion', in Wikipedia, the free encyclopedia, retrieved and checked 23 March 2009 from http://csep10.phys.utk.edu/astr161/lect/history/newton3laws.html.

42.   'Equations of Motion', in Wikipedia, the free encyclopedia, retrieved and checked 23 March 2009 from http://en.wikipedia.org/wiki/Equation_of_motion.

43.   'Differential Calculus', in Wikipedia, the free encyclopedia, retrieved and checked 23 March 2009 from http://en.wikipedia.org/wiki/Differential_calculus.

44.   'Dark Matter', in Wikipedia, the free encyclopedia, retrieved and checked 31 March 2009 from http://en.wikipedia.org/wiki/Dark_matter.

45.   Stephen Worlfram, *A New Kind of Science*, 2002, Wolfram Media, ISBN 9781579550080.

46.   Klaus Mainzer, *Symmetry and Complexity*, World Scientific, ISBN 9789812561923.

47. 'Living in the Matrix', in Wikipedia, the free encyclopedia, retrieved and checked 15 April 2009 from http://www.ipod.org.uk/reality/reality_big_brother.asp.

48. Seth Lloyd, *Programming the Universe*, 2007, Vintage, ISBN 9781400033867.

49. Gregory Chaitin, *Meta Math!: The Quest for Omega*, 2005, Vintage, ISBN 9781400077977.

50. John D. Barrow, *New Theories of Everything*, 2008, ISBN 9780199548170.

51. 'Newton's Law of Universal Gravitation', in Wikipedia, the free encyclopedia, retrieved and checked 29 April 2009 from http://en.wikipedia.org/wiki/Newton's_law_of_universal_gravitation.

52. 'Galileo Galilei', in Wikipedia, the free encyclopedia, retrieved and checked 5 May 2009 from http://en.wikipedia.org/wiki/Galileo.

53. 'Bernhard Riemann', in Wikipedia, the free encyclopedia, retrieved and checked 6 May 2009 from http://en.wikipedia.org/wiki/Riemann.

54. 'Geodesic', in Wikipedia, the free encyclopedia, retrieved and checked 6 May 2009 from http://en.wikipedia.org/wiki/Geodesic.

55. 'Maxwell's Displacement and Einstein's Trace', in Wikipedia, the free encyclopedia, retrieved and checked 6 May 2009 from http://www.mathpages.com/home/kmath103/kmath103.htm.

56. 'David Hilbert', in Wikipedia, the free encyclopedia, retrieved and checked 7 May 2009 fromhttp://en.wikipedia.org/wiki/David_hilbert.

57. 'Hermann Minkowski', in Wikipedia, the free encyclopedia, retrieved and checked 7 May 2009 from http://en.wikipedia.org/wiki/Hermann_Minkowski.

58. Christopher J. Bjerknes, *Albert Einstein: The Incorrigible Plagiarist*, 2002, XTX, ISBN 9780971962989.

59. Robert Schulmann et al. (eds), *The Collected Papers of Albert Einstein. Vol. 8. The Berlin Years: Correspondence, 1914–1918*, 1998, Princeton University Press.

60. 'History of Special Relativity', in Wikipedia, the free encyclopedia, retrieved and checked 7 May 2009 from http://en.wikipedia.org/wiki/History_of_special_relativity.

61. Philip Tetlow, PhD commentary, 31 January 2009.

62. 'String (physics)', in Wikipedia, the free encyclopedia, retrieved and checked 18 June 2009 from http://en.wikipedia.org/wiki/String_(physics).

63. 'General Relativity', in Wikipedia, the free encyclopedia, retrieved and checked 23 June 2009 from http://en.wikipedia.org/wiki/General_relativity.

64. 'Einstein Field Equations', in Wikipedia, the free encyclopedia, retrieved and checked 23 June 2009 from http://en.wikipedia.org/wiki/Einstein's_field_equation.

65. 'General Relativity Tutorial: The Stress-Energy Tensor', retrieved and checked 23 June 2009 from http://math.ucr.edu/home/baez/gr/stress.energy.html.

66. 'Photon', in Wikipedia, the free encyclopedia, retrieved and checked 23 June 2009 from http://en.wikipedia.org/wiki/Photon.

67. John Gribbin, *The Universe: A Biography*, 2007, Penguin, ISBN 9780141021478.

68. 'Solovay-Strassen Primality Test' (24 September 2004), in Wikipedia, the free encyclopedia, retrieved and checked 4 September 2007 from http://en.wikipedia.org/wiki/Solovay-Strassen_primality_test.

69. David Deutsch, in Wikipedia, the free encyclopedia, retrieved and checked 4 September 2007 from http://en.wikipedia.org/wiki/David_Deutsch.

70. 'Membrane (M-Theory)', in Wikipedia, the free encyclopedia, retrieved and checked 28 July 2009 from http://en.wikipedia.org/wiki/Brane.

71. Kieth van Rijsbergen, *The Geometry of Information Retrieval*, 2004, Cambridge University Press, ISBN 9708521838054.

72.   'Stemming', in Wikipedia, the free encyclopedia, retrieved and checked 23 June 2009 from http://en.wikipedia.org/wiki/Stemming.

73.   Dominic Widdows, *Geometry and Meaning*, 2004, CSLI Publications, ISBN 1575864487.

74.   'Information Retrieval', in Wikipedia, the free encyclopedia, retrieved and checked 6 November 2009 from http://en.wikipedia.org/wiki/Information_retrieval.

75.   'Atom', in Wikipedia, the free encyclopedia, retrieved and checked 8 December 2009 from http://en.wikipedia.org/wiki/Atom.

76.   'An Introduction to Tensors', retrieved and checked 18 January 2010 from http://www.mta.ca/faculty/Courses/Physics/4701/EText/TensorIntroduction.html.

77.   'Tensor', in Wikipedia, the free encyclopedia, retrieved and checked 19 January 2010 from http://en.wikipedia.org/wiki/Tensor.

78.   'Latin Alphabet', in Wikipedia, the free encyclopedia, retrieved and checked 20 January 2101 from http://en.wikipedia.org/wiki/Latin_alphabet.

79.   Philip Tetlow, 'Welcome to Web Science', *Net Magazine*, December 2009.

80.   Stephen Dill, Ravi Kumar, Kevin S. McCurley, Sridhar Rajagop, Alan D. Sivakumar and Andrew Tomkins, 'Self-Similarity in the Web', IBM Almaden Research Center, Jose, http://www.almaden.ibm.com/cs/people/mccurley/pdfs/fractal.pdf.

81.   'Maxwell–Boltzmann Distribution', retrieved and checked 7 June 2010 from http://en.academic.ru/dic.nsf/enwiki/11995.

82.   Ole Barndorff-Nielsen, 'The Hyperbolic Distribution in Statistical Physics', *Scandinavian Journal of Statistics*, 1982.

83.   'Hyperbolic Distribution', in Wikipedia, the free encyclopedia, retrieved and checked 1 June 2010 from http://en.wikipedia.org/wiki/Hyperbolic_distribution.

84.   'Hyperbolic Distribution', retrieved and checked 14 June 2010 from http://demonstrations.wolfram.com/HyperbolicDistribution/.

85.   'Power-Law Distributions in Empirical Data', retrieved and checked from 16 June 2010 from http://arxiv.org/PS_cache/arxiv/pdf/0706/0706.1062v2.pdf.

86.   'Long Tail', in Wikipedia, the free encyclopedia, retrieved and checked 16 June 2010 from http://en.wikipedia.org/wiki/Long_Tail.

87.   'Many-Worlds Interpretation', in Wikipedia, the free encyclopedia, retrieved and checked 25 June 2010 from http://en.wikipedia.org/wiki/Many-worlds_interpretation.

88.   'Riemann Hypothesis', retrieved and checked 30 June 2010 from http://www.daviddarling.info/encyclopedia/R/Riemann_hypothesis.html.

89.   John Derbyshire, *Prime Obsession: Bernhard Riemann and the Greatest Unsolved Problem in Mathematics*, 2004, First Plume Printing, ISBN 0452285259.

90.   Vlatko Vedral, *Decoding Reality*, 2010, Oxford University Press, ISBN 9780199237692.

91.   Andrei Broder, Ravi Kumar, Farzin Maghoul, Parbhakar Raghavan, Sridhar Rajagopalan, Raymie Stata, Andrew Tomkins and Janet Wiener, 'Graph Structure in the Web', retrieved and checked 2 August 2010 from http://www9.org/w9cdrom/160/160.html.

92.   Jennifer. Xu, 'Analyzing Networks of Hate Groups in the Blogosphere: Subscription, Comment, and Co-membership Relationships', retrieved and checked 3 August 2010 from http://citeseerx.ist.psu.edu/viewdoc/download?doi=10.1.1.86.9306&rep=rep1&type=pdf.

93.   'Einstein was Right – Again!', retrieved and checked 13 August 2010 from http://science.nasa.gov/science-news/science-at-nasa/1997/ast06nov97_1/.

94.   'Quantum Entanglement', in Wikipedia, the free encyclopedia, retrieved and checked 3 September 2010 from http://en.wikipedia.org/wiki/Quantum_entanglement.

95. Lada Adamic and Bernado A. Huberman, 'Zipf's Law and the Internet', *Glottometrics* 3, 2002, 143–50.

96. 'Antony Garrett Lisi', in Wikipedia, the free encyclopedia, retrieved and checked 10 November 2010 from http://en.wikipedia.org/wiki/Antony_Garrett_Lisi.

97. Robert .B. Laughlin, *A Different Universe (Reinventing Physics from the Bottom Up)*, 2005, Basic Books, ISBN 13978046503828.

98. Albert Barabási, *Bursts*, 2011, First Plume Printing, ISBN 9780525951650.

99. Einstein Archives Online. Retrieved and Checked, September 06, 2007, from http://www.alberteinstein.info/

100. Albert Einstein. Relativity: the Special and General Theory. Retrieved and Checked, September 06, 2007, from http://www.gutenberg.org/etext/5001

101. Shape of the Universe, In Wikipedia, The Free Encyclopedia. Retrieved and Checked, September 06, 2007, from http://en.wikipedia.org/wiki/Shape_of_the_universe

102. Paul Benacerraf, In Wikipedia, The Free Encyclopedia. Retrieved and Checked, March 08, 2012, from http://en.wikipedia.org/wiki/Paul_Benacerraf

Index